Erotic Preference, Gender Identity, and Aggression in Men:
New Research Studies

Erotic Preference, Gender Identity, and Aggression in Men:
New Research Studies

edited by

Ron Langevin
Clarke Institute of Psychiatry, Toronto

LAWRENCE ERLBAUM ASSOCIATES, PUBLISHERS

1985   Hillsdale, New Jersey   London

616.8583
E71

Lawrence Erlbaum Associates, Inc., Publishers
365 Broadway
Hillsdale, New Jersey 07642

Library of Congress Cataloging in Publication Data
Main entry under title:

Erotic preference, gender identity, and aggression in men.

  Bibliography: p.
  Includes indexes.
  1. Psychosexual disorders. 2. Violence—Psychological
aspects. 3. Men—Mental health. 4. Men—Sexual behavior.
I. Langevin, Ron.
RC556.E76 **1985**   616.85′83   84-18645
ISBN 0-89859-445-6

Printed in the United States of America
10 9 8 7 6 5 4 3 2 1

One sin, I know, another doth provoke;
Murder's as near to lust as flame to smoke.

From W. Shakespeare's Pericles, Act 1, Scene 1

Contents

Introduction

The studies in this volume have been collected for two reasons. First, there is a surprising dearth of controlled research on sexual anomalies, even on those of great social concern such as rape and pedophilia. We have been forced in our practices to rely on problematic case studies and worse, on speculations from outdated theories. Too often sexual anomalies have been viewed as distortions of conventional heterosexuality rather than as behaviors in their own right. The studies herein attempt to change our perspective and provide some new answers to fundamental questions that clinicians, therapists, sex researchers, practitioners, and forensic workers face in their every day dealing with sex offenders and patients. For example, we ask: "Are rapists sexually abnormal?" and "Are pedophiles aggressive?" The answers have been assumed or are obviated by the nature of the anomaly but the studies collected here indicate that our assumptions are suspect and in some cases blatantly incorrect.

Throughout we attempt to define the erotic profile, gender identity, and aggressiveness for a range of men with unusual sexual behaviors, namely, sadists, rapists, pedophiles, voyeurs, incest offenders, homosexuals, transvestites, and transsexuals. This is a first step in understanding the anomalies and in some cases, determining treatment goals. However, this book is not concerned with social policy. Our goal is to understand erotic behavior through an examination of sexual anomalies. We have included consenting victimless relations as well as brutal murders. This is not meant to imply that we believe all sexually anomalous men shoud be treated the same way. We do believe that further knowledge will help to improve conditions for both the sexually anomalous men and the community at large. All of the studies in this volume are original research projects that have not been previously published. In some cases there are no existing studies

on the questions raised in this collection. We hope our results will stimulate the research efforts and clinical practices of our readers.

The second purpose of this book is to examine the interrelation of the three factors contained in its title. The terms, erotic preference, gender identity, and aggression, will have specific meanings for all the studies in this volume, so they will be defined now. We will discuss males throughout because the majority of sexual anomalies apparently occur only in men.

DEFINITIONS

Erotic Preference

The average person engages in a variety of sexual *behaviors,* some out of curiosity, others from circumstance or deprivation, for example, homosexual acts in prison. However, most men appear to *prefer* certain types of sexual outlets with a specific class of person. The heterosexual pedophile prefers to fondle or have intercourse with female minors, the homosexual androphile desires mutual masturbation with adult men, and so on. It is important, wherever possible to define an *erotic preference* such as pedophilia, because it indicates the most desired stimuli and responses leading to sexual climax or orgasm. It is likely that whenever pedophiles are spontaneously sexually aroused, they will be having fantasies or thoughts of children and they will be tempted to act out their sexual impulses. They may engage in other less desired or *surrogate* sexual activities but the preferred one is most satisfying.

The concept of erotic preference brings order to sexual behaviors that at times can appear hopelessly confusing. According to Kinsey, Pomeroy, and Martin (1948) 37% of American men have had orgasmic homosexual experience at some time in their lives. However, only 4% were exclusively homosexual and had an erotic preference for men. The rest were probably curious or deprived heterosexuals. Similarly if one examines the use of pornographic books and movies, burlesque or strip shows, or even fortuitous peeping in windows, a substantial number of men would qualify as voyeurs. Nevertheless, the clincian is concerned only with the rare men who seek out situations for peeping, climax in so doing, and prefer this over other sexual outlets.

Many sexual behaviors present the same difficulties in sorting out the unusual and the conventional. It is the men who prefer the atypical sexual behavior that we call *sexually anomalous*. This term is used rather than sexual deviant or pervert because the latter has perjorative and moral connotations that are inappropriate in scientific investigations. A more detailed discussion of erotic preference is presented elsewhere for the interested reader (cf. Freund, 1974; Langevin, 1983).

Gender Identity

Gender identity is a hypothetical variable like erotic preference. It is the subjective *feeling and conviction* of belonging to one sex or the other. Most men feel like they are men and report masculine gender identification but some, in spite of anatomical evidence to the contrary, feel like they are women and claim they are feminine gender identified. The gender identity is reflected in large part, in *gender role* behavior. Males and females within cultures dress, act, and have certain attitudes, beliefs, and expectations that are more or less sterotypic for their sex and which define gender role. In contrast, gender dysphoric men often dress in female clothes and attempt to copy the gender role of females. Through an examination of their overt gender behaviors we infer the disturbances in gender identity.

Erotic preference and gender identity interact in complex ways which are not fully understood at present. Usually the two are congruous in that the average man who is masculine identified and adopts male role behaviors, prefers to interact sexually with adult females. However,it is not always so straightforward. We will return to this later.

Aggression

Aggression is a nebulous concept with a variety of meanings that have been used to characterize men from the persistent salesman to the sadistic murderer. We cannot always be sure that researchers mean the same thing when they use the term. There are many measurement problems in aggression research too, which makes our task even more difficult. To some extent, we are forced at present to keep an open mind until better measures are available. However, in our studies we have looked specifically for *violence* in the form of physical contact or assault in which an attempt was made to injure another person. This is our *marker behavior* around which we have organized the less exact aggressive behaviors such as verbal threats, anger, property damage, familial bickering, and the like. Our focus of attention will be the sex offender's behaviors that involve criminal charges and the physical injury of his victim. Nevertheless, for lack of better and more comprehensive measures, other less exact indices have also been examined.

THE INTERRELATION OF EROTIC PREFERENCE, GENDER IDENTITY, AND AGGRESSION

Table 1 presents currently held beliefs about erotic preference, gender identity, and aggression in the groups that will be examined throughout this book. There are question marks in the table to indicate our ignorance and unfortunately some of the questions will be unresolved at the end of this volume.

TABLE 1
Current Theoretical Relationships of Erotic Preference, Gender
Identity & Aggression in Sex Anomalies

| Sex Anomaly | Erotic Preference | | Gender Identity | Aggression |
	Stimulus	Response		
Transsexual	Adult Male "Hetero- sexuals"	"Normal" hetero- sexual mutual pleasuring	Ultra Feminine	Passive
Homosexual	Adult Male	Mutual pleasuring	Feminine	Passive
Transvestite	Female/Self?	Automasturbation Crossdressed?	?	Passive
Pedophiles	Children	Exhibiting, touch- ing, other?	?	Passive
Incest Offenders	Child/Adult?	?	?	Aggressive?
Voyeurs	?	?	Ultra Mas- culine?	Aggressive?
Sexual Aggressives & Rapists	Adult Female	Mutual pleasur- ing, sadism, other?	Ultra Mas- culine	Very Aggressive

Certain assumptions are inherent in the table. First, there is a positive correlation between an erotic stimulus preference for men and feminine gender identity.
Thus the transsexual is *ultra* feminine and prefers "heterosexual" male partners.
The homosexual who is less feminine identified is satisfied with other gay men.
At the other extreme, the rapist is *ultra* masculine identified and prefers adult
females whom he takes by force. Linking feminine gender identity to "passivity" and masculine gender identity to aggressiveness are also noteworthy. Not
all research investigators accept the information in Table 1 but many do and it
has influenced the course of research studies, theories and treatment programs.
For example, some psychoanalytic theorists assume that the homosexual male is
the victim of a domineering close binding mother and a weak father so he comes
to identify with the mother (Bieber,I., Bieber, T., Dain, Dince, Drellick, Grand,
Gundlack, Kremer, Refkin, Wilbur, 1962). He ends up feminine identified,
preferring male sex partners and is passive ("feminine") in his sexual behaviors.
Thus the erotic preference is bound inextricably to gender role and identity.

Similar assumptions have been made by behavior modifiers working with
effeminate boys, although as a rule, behavior therapists deny theoretical orientation. They have attempted to change the effeminacy of some boys and, in so
doing, prevent later homosexuality, transvestism, or transsexualism (Green,
Newman, & Stoller, 1972; Rekers, Lovaas, & Low, 1974). Thus, change gender
identity or gender role early in life and a sexually anomalous preference will not
develop at puberty. Zuger (1978) and Green (1979) presented evidence that some
effeminate boys do later become homosexuals but Freund, Langevin, Nagler,

Steiner and Zajac (1974) presented retrospective evidence from adult homosexuals that many, in fact, never experienced feminine gender identification.

It is interesting how our theoretical assumptions can direct research and therapy efforts. A few years ago I worked with Kurt Freund and others (Freund et al. 1974), in developing a Feminine Gender Identity (FGI) Scale based on differences in heterosexual, homosexual, and transsexual men. To our dismay, about a third of the scores for homosexuals overlapped with those of hetersexuals although the discrimination of transsexuals from the other two groups was almost perfect. Predisposed by the theoretical expectation that homosexual men *are* more feminine, we naturally assumed that the scale was at fault. We unsuccessfully attempted to improve the discrimination of the FGI scale (Freund, Langevin, Satterberg and Steiner 1977). In the present volume we are asking a different question: How important is feminine gender identity in a homoerotic preference?

Another assumption noted in Table 1 is the correlation of masculinity, "ultra" masculinity and aggression with sexual acts such as voyeurism and rape. Stoller (1975) has described "perversions" as "erotic forms of hatred." Abel (1977) has coined the term "sexual aggression" for rape and other indecent assaults. Groth and Birnbaum (1979) believe that rape is an aggressive *rather than* a sexual act. "Rapists hate women especially their mothers" so their sexual acts become a means of humiliating or hurting women (cf. Rada, 1978). Aggression toward women is also a means of "asserting masculinity." In some cases, violence does appear to be an integral part of the sexual act but in others it seems only a means to a goal, namely, intercourse. Barbaree, Marshall, and Lanthier (1979) argue that rapists are aroused *in spite of* their victim's distress, not because of it. The relationship of aggression to rapists' gender role/identity and erotic preference remains a debated issue.

A further assumption noted in Table 1 is the passivity of offenders against children. Traditionally pedophiles have been considered passive, unassertive, and childlike. Their overall profile suggests they might align more with the homosexuals in the stereotypic picture presented in Table 1. However, aggression in conjunction with sexual anomalies such as pedophilia and incest has been an increasing concern to research investigators. Christie, Marshall, and Lanthier (1978) suggested that pedophiles may be more aggressive than commonly believed.

Incest has often, and perhaps incorrectly, been considered a variation of pedophilia. One distinction between them has been the degree of alcoholism and the history of violence, both believed to be prominent features of incest but not necessarily of pedophilia. One might expect from current beliefs that incest offenders should be placed between pedophiles and sexual aggressives in Table 1. Voyeurs too, are believed to be aggressive and even dangerous. The association of voyeurism with sadism and even murder suggests that it be subjected to investigation.

The simple theoretical framework relating erotic preference, gender identity, and aggression has many gaps in the empirical foundation on which it is based. The main assumptions have been that: (a) gender identity causes erotic preference; (b) they are one and the same thing or are inseparable; or (c) both are caused by a third factor. We are particularly puzzled by cases of rapists seeking sex reassignment surgery; by men who claim to erotically prefer women and yet say they want sex reassignment surgery; and by homosexual men who are clearly masculine gender identified. I have suggested elsewhere (Langevin, 1983) that erotic preference and gender identity may be independent factors. It was our belief in doing the studies which follow that, at the very least, the relationship of erotic preference, gender identity, and aggression needs serious reconsideration.

MEASURES USED IN THIS BOOK

Erotic Preference

Table 2 shows the measures used in our studies. Foremost in the measure of erotic preference is the Clarke Sex History Questionnaire (SHQ). It is a comprehensive self reporting SHQ sampling a range of sexually anomalous behavior as well as conventional heterosexual behavior. It has been developed over a 15 year period (Paitich, Langevin, Freeman, Mann, & Handy, 1977). An updated shorter version of the SHQ is validated in Appendix A for the interested reader. The actual questionnaire and its scoring are presented in Appendix B. Each of the SHQ scales is reliable and discriminates pertinent sexually anomalous groups from controls. It offers a more or less comprehensive sex history of the research subjects in our studies and, along with a clinical interview, helps greatly in defining erotic preferences in each case.

The Derogatis Sexual Functioning Inventory (DSFI, Derogatis, 1978) is a relatively new instrument designed to assess sexual dysfunction. Because of its limited validation, it is only examined in Chapter 2.

Complimentary to the SHQ is phallometric testing in which penile tumescence is measured in reference to visual and auditory erotica. The penile volume plythysmograph was described by Zuckerman (1971) as one of the most reliable and valid indices of erotic arousal, and that claim remains true today. Nevertheless, the measure is not infallible and faking of results is possible. Therefore cooperative subjects must be used and the results of phallometry must be considered in conjunction with sexual history and self reports.

Our device, the volumetry plethysmograph, originally invented by Freund, Sedlacek, and Knob (1965), is extremely sensitive. It even measures volume changes that are subliminal and that reliably discriminate homerotic and pedophilic erotic preferences. Unfortunately, penile tumescence is being recorded only by a few sex research investigators, who in greater numbers use a less

TABLE 2
Direct and Contributing Measures of Erotic Preference,
Gender Identity and Aggression Used in this Volume

Erotic Preference:	Clarke Sex History Questionnaire
	Derogatis Sexual Functioning Inventory (DSFI)
	Phallometric Tests
	Sex Hormones
	Brain Abnormalities
	(EEG, CT Scan, Reitan, Luria, IQ)
Gender Identity/Role:	Freund Feminine Gender Identity Scale
	MMPI Mf Scale
	16PF I Factor
	Bem Androgyny Scale
	Sex Hormones
	Brain Abnormalities (as above)
Aggression:	Criminal Record
	Fighting
	Clarke Parent Child Relations Questionnaire
	Personality Diagnosis
	MMPI
	16 PF
	Buss Durkee Hostility Inventory
	Clarke Violence Scale
	Sex Hormones
	Substance Abuse (esp. Alcoholism; eg. The MAST)
	Drug Survey
	Brain Abnormalities (as above)

precise, if more convenient, circumference strain gauge. In the present book, phallometry was used in some cases to define erotic preference and in others to explore theories of erotic anomalies.

This book also examines indirect but major factors thought to play a role in erotic, gender, and aggressive behaviors, namely sex hormones, brain states, and alcohol. Sex hormones are believed to be indices of sex "drive" and aggressiveness but they also define male-female differences. Essentially, males have more androgens in their makeup and females have more estrogens. A number of investigations have attempted, with mixed results, to relate an excess of estrogens to male homosexuality. Similarly, excess androgens, in particular, testosterone, have been related to general aggressiveness. Measurements of sex hormones have improved dramatically over the last 40 years and now very accurate radioimmuno assay procedures are available. The latter have been used in some of our studies.

Brain pathology, especially temporal lobe abnormalities, may be essential to a wide range of sexually anomalous behavior. In some cases with surgery, the unusual sexual behavior disappears (Blumer, 1970). More subtle abnormalities in electrical activity may also be important and will be noted. In some studies,

neuropsychological tests have been used, for example, the Reitan Neurop-sychological Test Battery (Reitan, 1979), to seek correlations between brain states and erotic behavior. In Chapter 2, the CT scan was used, which offers a qualitative advance in the technology available to examine the brain.

Gender Identity and Role

By far the most commonly available scales measure gender roles or masculinity–femininity. In this volume the MMPI MF scale and in some instances, the Cattell 16PF I Factor were used because they provide not only an index of gender role but also of personality pathology in general. Both indices are acceptable but the Freund Feminine Gender Identity (FGI) (Freund et al, 1974, 1977) is more pertinent because it focuses on gender *identity*. Freund et al. (1974, 1977) found the FGI scale reliable and valid with a sizable single factor defining the scale. The MMPI and 16PF scales have been well documented in the literature. In some cases the more controversial Bem (1974) Sex Role Inventory was examined.

Sex hormones provide an index of gender identity as well as of erotic prefer-ence. Similarly brain pathology, mainly in the temporal lobe, has been found in gender disturbed men (Hoenig & Kenna, 1979). Results indicate that brain functioning should be measured in reference to gender identity as well as to erotic preference.

Aggression

Violence may be subtle or pronounced and it can occur in many contexts or only in a few, perhaps specifically in sexual behavior. It therefore seems unlikely that a single measure will prove itself comprehensive in the study of aggression. We are forced at this time to examine a range of measures in order to understand this complex phenomenon. A criminal record for assaultiveness is one sign of ag-gressiveness and it was used. Fighting in which the research participant was involved but for which he was not necessarily arrested is a more inclusive measure of violence; not without its problems, but we asked it routinely.

Modelling theory would suggest that parents who are aggressive to each other and to their child will produce in some cases, a violent or aggressive child. In others, there may be emotional disturbance without evident violent behavior. Nevertheless, aggression in the family background of patients is one predictor of adult violence and it was examined using the self rating and retrospective Clarke Parent Child Relations (PCR) Questionnaire (Paitich et al., 1976). There are 16 scales, the first eight of which measure aggressive exchanges between mother, father, and son. The scales are:

Mother Aggression to Respondent (her son)
Father Aggression to Respondent

Respondent Aggression to Mother
Respondent Aggression to Father
Mother Aggression to Father
Father Aggression to Mother
Mother Strictness
Father Strictness

Mother Competence
Father Competence
Mother Affection
Father Affection
Mother Identification
Father Identification
Mother Indulgence
Father Indulgence.

The PCR is a reliable instrument with some discriminant validity.

Personality tests and diagnosis also provide a clue to aggressiveness over time as long lasting traits or behavioral predispositions. The antisocial or explosive personalities for example, would be of great concern. Psychotic states such as paranoid schizophrenia would also be noteworthy in the presence of a sexual anomaly although this is atypical. The MMPI (Dahlstrom & Welsh, 1975) 4-8 profile (Psychopathic Deviate - Schizophrenia) has been considered an important index of aggressiveness although it is controversial. Similarly the 16PF has measures of assertiveness, shyness, masculinity-femininity, and introversion that are important factors in several theories of sexual anomalies. The Buss Durkee Hostility Inventory (Buss & Durkee, 1957) was used in one study along with the Clarke Violence Scale developed in Chapter 2. The latter was constructed because there are few adequate aggression measures. Its validation is currently under investigation.

A range of brain abnormalities also may reflect violent behavior. Temporal lobe epilepsy sometimes has been associated with violent behavior but so have other brain abnormalities. Temporal lobe abnormalities are of particular interest because they may reflect both sexual anomalies and aggressive behavior (Blumer, 1970; Epstein, 1961; Hoenig & Kenna, 1979; Kolarsky, Freund, Machek & Polak, 1967).

Alcohol has been consistently associated with violence including sexual aggression. Alcoholism and alcohol abuse have been examined in diagnosis, clinical report, and patient self report. In Chapter 2, the Michigan Alcoholism Screening Test (MAST) was used (Selzer, 1971). It is a valid and reliable instrument which is short and self administering.

Other substances may be important in the release of aggression. Amphetamines especially are associated with paranoid states. However, in general, we

do not know what role they play in sexual anomalies. An unpublished Drug Survey is routinely administered to all forensic patients in our hospital. The questionnaire examines the major families of illicit drugs for the frequency of use, maximum frequency of use ever, and the affect experienced from each drug during its use and while its effects are wearing off.

Unfortunately not all patients were administered the tests we now wish they had been. Time, cost, and an evolving field of information have precluded this. Nevertheless many questions have been addressed to provide some direction for future investigation.

THE RESEARCH PARTICIPANTS

Most of the foregoing measures depend on honest report from the research participant. This is a worry for researchers because sex is a difficult topic to discuss openly, especially when it is one's own sexuality in question and the discussant, one's therapist, is a relative stranger. Moreover, most participants are facing criminal charges which also make them less open. In an attempt to cope with these problems, we did not include in our studies (unless specifically indicated) any man who did not admit his sexually anomalous behavior. We have found from experience that "nonadmittors" lie and provide worthless information. Thus, we are forced to deal with selected cases. "Admittors" may be shy but we encourage them to be open and help us understand their problem. The fact that we are "ignorant researchers" who want to know "what makes them tick" often provides a spirit of cooperation and openness that we find helpful. Many men are not shy and tell us our theories are wrong. The therapy environment is also important in promoting honesty in our participants. The Forensic Service of the Clarke Institute is known locally among criminals as the "Clarke Hilton" because of its comfortable accommodations and easy going atmosphere. A milieu therapy environment is in constant operation to help the offenders cope with the multiple problems they often face. The service psychiatrists are seen as defence psychiatrists. Many are researchers who try to help offenders keep their problem in check without offering false hope of change. The atmosphere is honest and defensiveness is confronted by staff and other patients. In spite of all this, one must still keep in mind that both self report questionnaires and phallometric testing can be faked.

A NOTE ON STATISTICAL ANALYSIS

Data presentation in each paper has been made as simple as possible although appropriate parametric statistical analyses have been done. Relevant facts about these analyses, with a few necessary exceptions, are contained in notes at the end

of each chapter. An attempt has been made to avoid presentation of complex statistical analyses although at the same time, presenting pertinent results. The present section is for the reader with a statistical interest.

Standard package SPSS, BMD, and SAS analyses have been used throughout. When discriminant analyses have been used, prior probabilities have been weighted by group size and the stepwise procedure has been used with Wilks Lambda. Percent of groups correctly identified are presented in notes throughout.

Multivariate analyses of variance (MANOVA) were invariably followed by univariate analyses of variance (ANOVA). When inhomogeneity of variance was a problem, data transformations were tried, usually logarithm or square root, although, for penile volume changes, Z scores have been used most successfully. Dichotomization of multiple choice sex behavior items into *yes* and *no* or "ever did it" versus "never did it" also has been used to overcome the problem of great variation of behavior patterns within groups.

Principal axes factor analysis has been used with iteration for communalities. Squared multiple correlation of each variable with all others was used as an initial communality estimate. Factors with eigenvalues greater than one (Kaiser Rule) were retained for Varimax rotation.

Chi Square tests have been used throughout *without* Yates Corrections for Continuity. Low cell frequencies have been handled by collapsing cells or using the Fisher Exact Test which is free of the Chi Square assumptions and distribution difficulties.

Values of F, t, r, or Chi Square usually have not been presented in order to simplify tables of results. Statistical significance has been indicated using the following convention:

P less than	Designation
0.10	+
0.05	*
0.01	**
0.001	***
0.0001	****

Arithmetic means have been used to compare groups but percentages have been presented in many cases to afford the nonstatistician a simpler overview of results. Means differing significantly have letters superscripted beside them. For example:

	Group			
	1	*2*	*3*	*4*
Mean	5.9[a]	8.3[b]	9.1[b]	12.2[c]

The letters a, b, and c show that Group 1 scored significantly lower than the other three groups and that Groups 2 and 3 did not differ from each other but both scored significantly lower than Group 4. If two letters appear beside a mean (e.g., 16.9[ab]), it indicates an overlap of that score with two other means. No superscripting but a significant overall effect indicates a range effect of the mean scores. In some tables of results, numbers of cases may vary slightly because of missing data. When percentages have been used, rounding may result in totals equalling slightly more or less than 100%.

ACKNOWLEDGMENTS

Many people helped to make this volume possible. We wish to thank the administrative and frontline workers for their support: B. Trudell and Z. Medwid and their forensic nursing staff; Ms. P. Cook, Ms. J. Brentnall, Ms. G. Mantini, and Mr. W. Curnoe for assistance in data collection; Mr. J. Mourant for technical advice; Drs. E. Stasiak and R. Reynolds and their staff at O.C.I. Brampton; Ms. Carmella Schoenberg, Mt. Sinai Hospital; Ms. W. Michelson and J. Hurst of Computer Services, C.I.P.; Dr. M. D'Costa and his staff, Mt. Sinai Hospital; and Dr. R. Holgate and his staff at Toronto General Hospital. We thank Mrs. Lori Panzarella and Merle Jaggernauth who carefully typed the manuscripts. We wish to thank Dr. R. Blanchard, Dr. K. Zucker, Clarke Institute of Psychiatry, Dr. V. Quinsey, Penetanguishene Mental Health Centre, Dr. W. Marshall, Queens University, Ms. S. Curnoe-Langevin and Ms. J. Chambers for their helpful comments on the book. We also wish to thank the granting agencies who funded our research: The Clarke Foundation, The Psychiatry Research Fund, Clarke Institute of Psychiatry, The Dean's Fund, University of Toronto, and the National Institute of Mental Health, U.S.A. Most of all we thank the research participants who offered their time and interest and helped to cast light on a much neglected area of research.

REFERENCES

Abel, G. G. Conference on sexual aggressives. Memphis, Tennessee, 1977, *TSA Newsletter*, 1977, *1*.

Barbaree, H. E., Marshall, W. L. & Lanthier, R. D. Deviant sexual arousal in rapists. *Behavior Research & Therapy*, 1979, *17*, 215–222.

Bem, S. The measurement of psychological androgyny. *Journal of Consulting and Clinical Psychology*, 1974, *42*, 155–162.

Bieber, I., Dain, H., Dince, P., Drellick, M., Grand, H., Gundlack, R., Kremer, M., Refkin, A., Wilbur, C., & Bieber, T. *Homosexuality: A psychoanalytic study of male homosexuals.* New York: Basic Books, 1962.

Blumer, D. Changes in sexual behavior related to temporal lobe disorders in man. *Journal of Sex Research*, 1970, *6*, 173–180.

Buss, A. H., & Durkee, A. An inventory for assessing different kinds of hostility. *Journal of Consulting Psychology*, 1957, *21*, 343–349.

Christie, M., Marshall, W. R., & Lanthier, R. *A descriptive study of incarcerated rapists and pedophiles.* Unpublished manuscript, 1978, Canadian Penetentiary Services, Kingston, Ontario.

Dahlstrom, W., & Welsh, G. *An MMPI handbook,* Vol. 2. Minneapolis, MN: University of Minnesota Press, 1975.

Derogatis, L. *The DSFI (Derogatis Sexual Functioning Inventory).* Leonard R. Derogatis, 1228 Wine Spring Road, Baltimore, Md. 21204, 1978.

Epstein, A. W. Relationship of fetishism and transvestism to brain and particularly to temporal lobe dysfunction. *Journal of Nervous and Mental Disease,* 1961, *133,* 247–253.

Freund, K. Male homosexuality: An analysis of the pattern. In J. A. Loraine (Ed.), *Understanding homosexuality: Its biological and psychological Bases.* Lancaster, England: Medical & Technical Publishing Co., 1974.

Freund K., Langevin, R., Satterberg, J., & Steiner, B. Extension of the Gender Identity Scale for Males. *Archives of Sexual Behavior,* 1977, *6,* 507–519.

Freund, K., Nagler, E., Langevin, R., Zajac, A., & Steiner, B. Measuring feminine gender identity in homosexual males. *Archives of Sexual Behavior,* 1974, *3,* 249–260.

Freund, K., Sedlacek, F., & Knob, K. A simple transducer for mechanical plethysmography of the male genital. *Journal of Experimental Analysis of Behavior,* 1965, *8,* 169–170.

Green, R. Childhood gender behavior and subsequent sexual preference. *American Journal of Psychiatry,* 1979, *136,* 106–108.

Green, R., Newman, L. E., & Stoller, R. J. Treatment of boyhood "transsexualism." *Archives of General Psychiatry,* 1972, *26,* 213–217.

Groth, A. N., & Birnbaum, H. J. *Men who rape.* New York: Plenum Press, 1979.

Hoenig, J., & Kenna, J. EEG abnormalities and transsexualism. *British Journal of Psychiatry,* 1979, *134,* 293–300.

Kinsey, A. C., Pomeroy, W. B., & Martin, C. E. *Sexual behavior in the human male.* Philadelphia: Saunders Co., 1948.

Kolarsky, A., Freund, K., Machek, J., & Polak, O. Male sexual deviation: Association with early temporal lobe damage. *Archives of General Psychiatry,* 1967, *17,* 735–743.

Langevin, R. *Sexual strands: Understanding and treating sexual anomalies in men.* Hillsdale, N.J.: Lawrence Erlbaum Associates, 1983.

Paitich, D., Langevin, R. The Clarke parent-child relations questionnaire: A clinically useful test for adults. *Journal of Consulting & Clinical Psychology,* 1976, *44,* 428–436.

Paitich, D., Langevin, R., Freeman, R., Mann, K., & Handy, L. The Clarke SHQ: A clinical sex history questionnaire for males. *Archives of Sexual Behavior,* 1977, *6,* 421–436.

Rada, R. T. *Clinical aspects of the rapist.* New York: Grune & Stratton, 1978.

Reitan, R. M. *Manual for administration of neuropsychological test battery for adults and children.* Tucson, Arizona, Neuropsychology Laboratory, 1979.

Rekers, G. A., Lovaas, O. I., & Low, B. The behavioral treatment of a "transsexual" preadolescent boy. *Journal of Abnormal Child Psychology,* 1974, *2,* 99–116.

Selzer, M. The Michigan Alcoholism Screening Test: The quest for a new diagnostic instrument. *American Journal of Psychiatry,* 1971, *127,* 1653–1658.

Stoller, R. J. *Perversion: The erotic form of hatred.* New York: Pantheon Books, 1975.

Zuckerman, M. Physiological measures of sexual arousal in the human. *Psychological Bulletin,* 1971, *75,* 297–329.

Zuger, B. Effeminate behavior present in boys from childhood: Ten additional years of follow-up. *Comprehensive Psychiatry,* 1978, *19,* 363–369.

IA SEXUAL AGGRESSION

The three chapters in this section examine rapists and voyeurs. The former are known in some cases to injure their victims physically and in others they appear only to desire sexual intercourse. It has been claimed that rape is not sexual but instead is aggressive. Rapists then may share many features in common with nonsexually aggressive men. Other writers have noted that rape is a sexual anomaly associated with peeping, exposing, touching, and sadism. It has been suggested that these latter behaviors may be precursors of rape. Thus, in detecting them, we have opportunities to prevent the more violent and dangerous offences. Study One evaluates whether rapists are more similar to violent men or to sexually anomalous men. The treatment and disposition of the rapist would differ markedly depending on this result.

1 Are Rapists Sexually Anomalous, Aggressive, or Both?

Ron Langevin,
Daniel Paitich,
Anne E. Russon
Clarke Institute of Psychiatry, Toronto

An important fundamental question has yet to be addressed empirically before we can understand and satisfactorily design treatment programs for sexually aggressive men. Is rape an anomalous sexual act, the forceful taking of normal sexual pleasure by an antisocial individual or a blend of both? Stoller (1975) considered rape, among other ''perversions,'' to be ''erotic forms of hatred'' in which the core desire is to hurt people. Some contemporary exponents of women's rights also express the strong opinion that rape is fundamentally an aggressive act. Brownmiller (1975), for example, stated categorically that from prehistoric times to the present, rape has been a conscious process of intimidation by which *all* men keep *all* women in a state of fear. One might expect from this point of view that rapists would not be different from the average person. Nevertheless she concurred that the typical American rapists is an aggressive hostile youth who chooses to do violence to women. She also noted that the rapists ''borrows'' the characteristics of assaultive and property offenders; he damages another person like assaultive men do, and like the robber, he acquires property; he wants ''to have'' her body. So a female is seen as both a hated person and desired property.

Holmstrom and Burgess (1980), among others, also described rape as ''an act of violence expressing power, aggression, conquest, degradation, anger, hatred, and contempt''.[1] They examined 115 rape victims and reported on the sexual acts performed by the assailants. Although the majority performed vaginal intercourse (96%) and fellatio (22%), up to 5% urinated on the victim or their underwear, placed a knife handle in the vagina or placed semen on the victim's body. Thus, a minority of cases seem sadistic, but the majority could be satisfying strictly conventional albeit ''stolen'' sexual needs.

17

Groth and Birnbaum (1979) described rape as a ''pseudosexual act'' address-ing issues of anger and power more than passion. They considered it a misconcep-tion that the rapist is a lusty male, is sexually frustrated, or harbors ''perverted'' desires.[2] They go so far as to say rape is *always* and *foremost* aggressive. They identified three types of rape: anger rape in which sex is a hostile act; power rape which is an act of conquest; and sadistic rape in which anger and power are eroticized. The incidences of each type in their study were 55% power, 40% anger, and 5% sadistic rapes. Other researchers express similar views.

Levine and Koenig (1980) summarized detailed interviews with 10 convicted rapists. They construed rape as nonsexual and suggested some dynamics under-lying the ''hostility.'' Their resulting hypotheses were that rapists are: (1) sexu-ally ignorant and have no understanding of female sexual arousal; (2) generally hate women as a group and want to punish them; (3) see their own sexuality as inseparable from aggression; (4) use rape solely to establish their masculinity; their own pleasure is dissociated from the act; and (5) they are self centered and do not see sex as mutually gratifying.

Some writers have argued that rape may be a byproduct of general crimi-nality. Conceivably the force or threat in rape may be an instrumental act much as a thief might use to obtain his victim's property. As Amir (1971) noted, rape is carried out by aggressive men *who are used to taking what they want*. Thus, it is no accident that rapists are also frequently common thieves as well.[3]

Other writers have stressed the sexually anomalous nature of rape. Freund (1976; Freund, Scher, & Hucker, 1983) aligned rape with voyeurism, exhibi-tionism, frotteurism, obscene calls, and toucheurism as one of the ''courtship disorders,'' noting that in literature reports, the behaviors frequently co-occur. Each represents a disturbance of normal courtship in which there are four stages: seeking a partner, pretactile interaction, tactile interaction, and genital union. One can conceptualize the anomalous man investing most of his sexual energy at one of these stages; the voyeur at seeking, the exhibitionist at pretactile interac-tion, the toucheur at tactile interaction, and the rapist at intercourse or genital union. Their sexual energy builds up quickly and they express it impulsively perhaps because they cannot await the usual social graces. Freund (1976) only considered the ''pathological rape pattern'' to be a courtship disorder. In this case force is an essential component of the act. In an unknown number of rapists, no sexual anomaly may be present.

Freund et al (1983) examined the co-occurrence of voyeurism, exhibitionism, obscene calls, toucheurism, and rape in 139 patients with sexual anomalies. Of 23 rapists, 4% engaged in exhibiting, 4% obscene calls, and 13% in touch-eurism. The majority (83%) only raped. One additional person, an exhibitionist, had also raped, representing 1% of that group. Thus, although there was some overlap of courtship disorders, rape tended to be a discrete outlet. Paitich, Langevin, Freeman, Mann, & Handy, (1977) found that rapists characteristically showed multiple sexual anomalies but their sample size was small. Some rapists

have been labelled sadists but their number among the rapists is unknown (see Rada, 1978). Bizarre acts leading up to murder in some cases may be critical to the sexual anomaly.[4]

Rada stated that sadism in rape is a sexual anomaly. He too pointed out that the frequent association of rape with other anomalies such as voyeurism and fetishism suggests its sexually anomalous nature. However he recognized that a range of motives may be operative in rape and that there is a continuum from purely aggressive to purely sexual behavior. Gebhard, Gagnon, Pomeroy, and Christenson (1965) also described a range of aggressiveness in sex offenders from the sadist through the "thief" to the ordinary man with poor judgment. Clark and Lewis (1977) noted that rapists in many cases use only the degree of force necessary to achieve the rape, but some use more than necessary. In their 1978 study, they reported that 28% of 156 founded cases of rape involved extreme violence. At the same time they indicated that the average male confuses seduction with rape. They suggested that social mores and the law are important factors in the commission of rape. Christie, Marshall, and Lanthier (1978) on the other hand found that 71% of rapists used unnecessary physical force and it was related to a history of nonsexual assault. Fifty-four percent had previous convictions for nonsexual violence.

The full gamut of opinions has been expressed but to date only Gebhard et al. (1965) have reported a controlled study using a standardized sex history interview of imprisoned sex offenders. There is no published study using a self administered standardized sex history questionnaire although some instruments are available (Derogatis, 1978; Paitich et al., 1977).

Aggressiveness in rapists also has been described in terms of gender identity and role (e.g., Clark & Lewis, 1977, 1978). The rapist is believed to see the forceful taking of women as "masculine." Burton (1947) compared the masculinity-femininity scale of the MMPI in an attempt to diagnose rapists, homosexuals, and nonsex offenders but found no significant differences. Little attention has been paid to this question since his study although the MMPI has been used subsequently to study rapists.

The present study examined the relative contribution of aggressiveness and sexual anomalies to rape. In order to do this, the four groups in Table 1.1 were compared on the extent of similarities in personality, criminal and aggressive history, parent child relations, and sexual history. Available findings on rapists for each measure now will be reviewed briefly. The interested reader may find more detail in Rada (1978).

The MMPI personality profiles have been reported for aggressive individuals and rapists, usually, separately (Armentrout & Hauer, 1978; Huesmann, Lefkowitz, & Eron, 1978; Karacan, Williams, Guerrero, Salis, Thornby & Hursch, 1974; Panton, 1978; Rader, 1977). Characteristically aggressors have a 4-8 profile (Psychopathic Deviate-Schizophrenia) but rapists have varied profiles although the Psychopathic Deviate scale is prominent and there are some signifi-

TABLE 1.1
Design of the Sexual Aggression Study

		Aggression	
		Absent	Present
Sexual Anomaly	Absent	Normal Controls	Nonsexual Assaulters
	Present	Nonassaultive Sexual Anomalies	Rapists

cant elevations on Depression, Schizophrenia, and Paranoia. Rada (1978) has pointed out that rapists typically are grouped with other sex offenders which may obscure the results.

Antisocial personality diagnoses are reported for 30% to 40% of rapists although it is often uncertain if men exhibiting incest and pedophilia are included in the sample (Rada, 1978). Nor are we certain that the diagnoses are reliable. Nevertheless, the suggestion remains that rapists and aggressors have similar personalities. Theft and nonsexual assaults are also reported for rapists and this also may reflect their similarity to assaultive men in general.

The family environment of the rapist is frequently one of violence and alcohol abuse. One third of rapists' parents are chronic abusers of alcohol or drugs or, at least, are heavy drinkers. One third of rapists themselves are heavy drinkers or alcoholics and half are drinking at the time of their offence (Rada, 1978). These findings suggest that their upbringing seems no different from one that would generate a generally assaultive or criminal individual.

Sexual history may seem to be the discriminating axis along which to polarize sexual and nonsexual assaulters. Perhaps rape is defined by the presence of an anomalous sexual preference in an aggressive personality. A few phallometric studies have shown that rapists are equally or more aroused by descriptions of rape than of consenting intercourse (Abel, Barlow, Blanchard & Guild, 1977; Barbaree, Marshall & Lanthier, 1979; Quinsey, Chaplin & Varney, 1981; Quinsey & Chaplin, 1982).[5] Nonrapists, on the other hand, are more aroused by descriptions of consenting intercourse. Moreover, the ratio of penile responses to rape divided by those to consenting intercourse, the *rape index*, is positively correlated with the degree of force used in the sexual offence. However, results are still experimental and some problems need resolution.[6]

Some studies showed that rapists manifest multiple sexual anomalies (Gebhard et al., 1965; Paitich et al., 1977, Rada, 1978). Groth and Birnbaum (1980) suggested that some rapists suffered from sexual dysfunction and 16% experienced some degree of impotence during their rapes. On the other hand, MacDonald and Paitich (1983) found that rapists were ''superheterosexuals'' and

started dating early and had an extensive sexual history with adult females and age appropriate female peers. We do not know if this is true of nonsexual assaultives and we do not know how many rapists present any unusual sexual behavior outside the act of rape. The present study addresses these questions.

METHOD

Design of the Study

Two major factors considered to be important in rape were systematically examined: history of aggression and the presence of sexual anomalies (Table 1.1). Each factor had two levels: present or absent. There were four groups in the 2 × 2 factorial multivariate analysis of variance classification. Normal men were negative on both factors and rapists were presumably positive on both. The other two groups were positive on only one factor. The nonsexual assaultive men had a history of aggression and the nonaggressive sexually anomalous men had some nonviolent sexual anomaly.

If the rapist is basically an assaultive person he should be more similar to the common assaultive group than to the other two groups. If he is sexually unusual rather than aggressive, he should resemble the nonaggressive sexually anomalous group more than the other two groups. On the other hand, if rape is a fusion of aggression and sexual anomaly, there should be an interaction effect for the dependent variables in the analysis so the rapist is different from all the other groups although sharing features in common.

Subjects

There were 40 rapists, 40 nonviolent sex offenders, 40 normal controls, and 25 nonsexual assaultive offenders. All were male, at least 18 years of age, and admitted to their offense. Most were being seen as part of a pretrial assessment on the Forensic service of our psychiatric hospital. The cases were selected from a forensic data bank of psychological test information described previously (Langevin, Paitich, Freeman, Mann, & Handy, 1978). The rapists were charged with rape or attempted rape involving a female victim 16 years of age or older. Cases involving rape-murder and rapes of children or men were omitted because they would make the groups too heterogeneous for study. The nonassaultive sex anomaly group (hereafter sexual anomaly group) were men charged with or concerned about their multiple sexual anomalies. They were mainly exhibitionist-voyeurs but they also engaged in other sexually anomalous acts. They too were selected from the data bank for being charged with a sexual offense involving a female victim 16 years of age or older but they had no history of violence. They were chosen over other sexually anomalous categories as the best control

group because in previous pilot work we found that rapists appeared to manifest multiple sexual anomalies, generally of the courtship disorder type. The group of nonsexual assaultive men (hereafter assaulters) had a history of violence but they were sexually normal. They faced charges of common assault and assault causing bodily harm but homicide cases were omitted. Again available information suggested that homicides may be qualitatively different from nonhomicidal assaults and their inclusion might make the group too heterogeneous. Cases involving assaults on girlfriends or wives that may have been sexually motivated were also excluded. The presence of any sexually anomalous behavior led to the exclusion of a case from this group. It was difficult to find such men and this is why only 25 appear in this group. The 40 normal community volunteers (hereafter controls) had no psychiatric or criminal history, no history of violence, and no sexual anomaly. A comparable supplementary control group of 22 males who had been administered the new Sex History Questionnaire (see Appendix A) was also used in some comparisons.

There were no significant group differences in age (mean age range 24–26 years) but there were differences in education, intelligence, and marital status. The controls were more educated[7] averaging 15 years of school in contrast to the other three groups averaging 9–11 years. There were no significant differences in the latter. The pattern of results was similar for both verbal intelligence (VIQ) and performance intelligence (PIQ).[8] The controls were brighter than the other three groups who did not differ from each other (average VIQ 118 versus range 103–104 and average PIQ 119 versus range 103–110). Most scores for the patient groups were within normal limits. Although approximately 32% of IQ scores can be expected to fall outside one standard deviation about the mean, this was the case for 24% of rapists, 24% of assaultives, 23% of sexual anomalies, and 68% of controls. Most of the variance however, was at the upper end of the distribution. Only 3% of rapists, 8% of assaulters, and 3% of sex anomalies had VIQs below 90. None of the research participants was considered mentally retarded.[9]

There were differences in the marital status of the groups as well.[10] Seventy nine percent of normal controls were single compared to 45% rapists, 68% assaulters, and 46% of the sexual anomaly group. The rapists were more like the sex anomaly group in this respect with 37% versus 36% married compared to only 12% for assaulters and 16% for nonpatient controls.[11]

Materials and Procedure

All research participants had been administered the Clarke Sexual History Questionnaire (SHQ) for Males (Paitich et al., 1977), the MMPI, the Cattell 16PF, and the Clarke Parent Child Relations (PCR) Questionnaire (Paitich & Langevin, 1976). In addition, the medical records were searched for pertinent information on history of crime and violence and for details of the rape. These items will be reported in the results. Two raters read the files and extent of agreement was

examined by interclass correlation. Unreliable items were omitted. A new SHQ was also used for approximately 25% of the patients in each group and to a group of 22 supplementary normal controls. The questionnaire contains most items from the old SHQ but it also has items about fantasies and anomalies that are not present in the earlier version of the questionnaire. The old questionnaire is not as comprehensive as the new one and for some anomalies does not provide the incidence of orgasmic behavior.

RESULTS

Aggression

Personality. The MMPI results are shown in Table 1.2. The strongest and most consistent finding was the similarity of rapists to the assaultive group. The tables of means (Table 1.3) and T scores over 70 (Table 1.4) show that the two assaultive groups had a wide range of symptoms reflecting strong emotional disturbance. Both groups tended to be depressed, suspicious, ruminating, worry-

TABLE 1.2

Two × Two Factorial Multivariate and Univariate Analysis of
Variance Results for MMPI of Rapists, Assaultives, Sexually
Anomalous and Control Groups

Scale	F Values for 2 × 2 Univariate Analysis of Variance		
	Assault	Anomaly	Interaction
Lie	7.51**	0.41	5.63*
F	41.35****	0.77	0.10
K	33.64****	5.87*	3.63†
Hypochondriasis	9.06**	1.08	0.26
Depression	24.59****	0.20	0.52
Hysteria	1.92	0.02	0.00
Psychopthic de-viate	47.91****	2.91†	7.10**
Masculinity-femininity	3.84†	0.39	4.49*
Paranoia	37.60****	0.44	8.82**
Psychasthenia	27.10****	2.50	1.21
Schizophrenia	29.96****	3.70†	1.02
Mania	14.80***	0.10	3.65†
Social Introver-sion	26.03****	4.61*	0.01
Multivariate F	8.33****	3.87****	3.50****

Note: †$p < 10$, *$p < 05$, **$p < 01$, ***$p < 001$, ****$p < 0001$

TABLE 1.3
MMPI Means and Standard Deviations

Scale	Group Means and Standard Deviations			
	Rape	Assault	Sex Anomaly	Controls
Lie	3.35	2.76	3.47	4.50[a]
	2.24	1.64	1.80	2.16
F	14.50	13.96	8.62	7.47
	6.74	5.75	5.19	4.85
K	10.57	10.96	13.47	16.70
	3.19	3.97	4.98	4.46
Hypochondriasis	15.72	14.48	12.90	12.47
	5.91	3.93	5.25	2.99
Depression	27.47	27.80	22.57	21.22
	7.43	7.44	7.07	5.40
Hysteria	22.97	23.04	21.72	21.87
	5.79	5.81	5.28	3.68
Psychopathic deviate	31.80	32.64	28.07[b]	24.25[a]
	5.22	4.97	5.21	5.16
Masculinity-femininity	27.82[ab]	26.44[b]	27.67[ab]	30.22[a]
	5.35	5.20	5.39	5.82
Paranoia	13.80[b]	16.24[a]	11.67	10.12
	5.00	4.25	3.50	2.89
Psychasthenia	35.70	35.12	30.72	27.47
	8.66	6.81	7.20	5.41
Schizophrenia	39.70	38.28	32.77	28.22
	11.98	8.79	8.71	5.97
Mania	23.52	25.36	21.92	20.60
	5.33	5.07	4.33	4.78
Social Introversion	38.30	34.40	29.20	25.55
	11.65	11.22	10.64	7.50

Note: Means with the same superscript letter are not significantly different for the interaction effect.

ing, confused, and higher in energy compared to nonassaultive groups. Rapists contrasted with assaultive men in having more bodily concerns, being more feminine, somewhat less energetic, and more introverted.

The controls scored slightly higher than the other three groups on the Lie scale. However, every person scored within normal limits and had a valid profile. The control group was also less psychopathic but more feminine than the other three groups. The sexual anomaly group also scored lower on Psychopathic deviation than the other patient groups.

Only in the case of the Paranoia Scale did the assaultive and rapist groups differ. The assaulters were significantly more paranoid than rapists and both were more paranoid than the other two nonviolent groups.

The multivariate analysis of variance on the 16PF (Table 1.5) produced similar overall results to the MMPI although the sexual anomaly factor was nonsignificant. Table 1.6 and Table 1.7 show that the controls were more intelligent (Factor B) and forthright (Factor N) than the patient groups. The assaultive and rapist groups together were less outgoing (Factor A) and less intelligent (Factor B), less emotionally stable (Factor C), were more suspicious (Factor L), more practical (Factor M), shrewder (Factor N), more apprehensive (Factor O), showed less control (Factor Q3) and were tenser (Factor Q4) than the other two groups. Once again the resemblance of rapists was to the assaulters rather than to the sexual anomaly group.

The three clinical groups were compared on psychiatric diagnoses (Table 1.8). Again rapists and assaulters were similar. ICD9 diagnoses were used but unfortunately no reliability was available. Secondary and tertiary diagnoses were examined in addition to the primary. Patients were classified into "personality disorder," "sexual deviation," "other," and "none," a posteriori. The distribution of diagnoses across the three groups was significantly different.[12] Over three quarters of the rapists and a similar proportion of assaulters were diagnosed as personality disorder in contrast to a third of the sexual anomaly group. By no means were all of them antisocial personalities. Twenty percent of rapists, 24% of assaulters, and 3% of the sex anomaly group were so diagnosed. The majority of the sexual anomaly group tended to be diagnosed as sexually deviant but only 13% of rapists were. The assaulters had 8% of diagnoses related to drug abuse and rapists had 3%. The sexual anomaly group had significantly more sexual

TABLE 1.4
Percentage of MMPI T Scores Greater Than 70

Scale	Chi Square	Group			
		Rape	Assault	Sex Anomaly	Controls
Lie	—	0.0	0.0	0.0	0.0
F	****	57.5	56.0	22.5	12.5
K	—	0.0	0.0	5.0	5.0
Hypochondriasis	*	22.5	8.0	7.5	0.0
Depression	****	65.0	60.0	25.0	20.0
Hysteria	—	22.5	24.0	12.5	7.5
Psychopathic deviate	****	85.0	76.0	58.0	20.0
Masculinity-femininity	—	40.0	28.0	27.5	50.0
Paranoia	****	40.0	52.0	10.0	2.5
Psychasthenia	****	67.5	60.0	27.5	12.5
Schizophrenia	****	67.5	72.0	50.0	15.0
Mania	*	32.5	52.0	17.5	17.5
Social Introversion	****	35.0	24.0	12.5	0.0

Note: *p < 05, ****p < 0001.

TABLE 1.5

Two × Two Factorial Multivariate and Univariate Analysis of
Variance Results for 16 PF of Rapists, Assaultives, Sexually
Anomalous and Control Groups

Factor		F Values for 2 × 2 Univariate Analysis of Variance		
		Assault	Anomaly	Interaction
	Md	6.18*	6.74*	0.42
A	Reserved/Outgoing	4.96*	1.66	2.06
B	Less Intelligent/More Intelligent	14.83***	0.77	8.43**
C	Affected by Feelings/Emotionally Stable	10.26**	2.95†	1.57
E	Humble/Assertive	2.24	0.17	0.01
F	Sober/Happy-go-lucky	2.49	0.13	0.70
G	Expedient/Conscientious	3.27†	0.24	1.53
H	Shy/Venturesome	2.51	3.75†	1.31
I	Tough-minded/Tender-minded	3.50†	6.11*	3.17†
L	Trusting/Suspicious	5.47*	1.19	0.03
M	Practical/Imaginative	5.68*	4.18*	1.54
N	Forthright/Shrewd	7.36**	3.11†	5.30*
O	Self-assured/Apprehensive	11.97***	1.00	0.08
Q1	Conservative/Experimenting	1.01	9.56**	1.55
Q2	Group dependent/Self-sufficient	2.16	1.89	0.24
Q3	Undisciplined self conflict/Controlled	5.76*	0.97	1.77
Q4	Relaxed/Tense	12.79***	1.86	0.10
	Multivariate F	2.81***	1.70	1.78*

Note: †$p < 10$, *$p < 05$, **$p < 01$, ***$p < 001$.

deviation diagnoses and fewer personality disorder diagnoses than the other groups. Once again they contrasted with the assaulters and rapists.[13] Considering the importance attributed to alcohol in rapes and assaults, it is surprising that only 28% of assaulters and 10% of rapists had any diagnosis related to alcohol. None of the sexual anomaly group did. In terms of the general order of the effects for personality, the strongest similarities were assaulters and rapists versus the other nonassaultive groups.

Criminal History. The 40 rapists had a total of 276 convictions compared to 242 for the assaulters and 133 for the sexual anomaly group (Table 1.9). The rape group had carried out 36 rapes and 8 attempted rapes but had 58 other sexual offences, mainly indecent assault, compared to 92 for the sex anomaly group, and none for the assaulters. The legal labels do not reflect the quality of the rapists' acts. Their indecent "assaults" were either precursors of rape, for example, grabbing females on the street or are attempts at rape, unprovable rapes, or forced oral genital and anal contact which to not qualify legally as rape in

Canada. Rapists had eight convictions for indecent exposure but the sexual anomaly groups had 88. All the indecent exposures for the rape group were attributable to two men and once again the quality of the act is not conveyed in the criminal label. For example, one man exposed totally nude with a stocking over his head while carrying a rifle. Most of the sexual anomaly group only

TABLE 1.6
16 PF Means and Standard Deviations

Factor		Group Means and Standard Deviations			
		Rape	Assault	Sex Anomaly	Controls
	Md	5.35	7.23	7.17	8.30
		2.30	2.35	2.80	3.16
A	Reserved/Outgoing	6.38	6.31	6.80	8.22
		2.98	2.69	2.60	2.01
B	Less Intelligent/More Intelligent	3.73	3.15	4.00	5.07[a]
		1.31	1.14	1.36	1.46
C	Affected by Feelings/Emotionally Stable	4.88	6.54	7.37	7.62
		2.61	3.53	2.06	2.81
E	Humble/Assertive	6.46	6.61	5.63	5.90
		2.35	2.53	2.61	2.44
F	Sober/Happy-go-lucky	6.15	5.54	6.53	6.77
		2.49	2.96	2.36	2.34
G	Expedient/Conscientious	6.46	6.85	6.17	5.27
		2.47	1.99	2.36	2.69
H	Shy/Venturesome	5.08	5.54	5.33	7.12
		3.01	2.93	3.02	2.40
I	Tough-minded/Tender-minded	4.65	5.00	4.70	6.82
		2.55	1.87	2.25	2.55
L	Trusting/Suspicious	6.19	5.77	5.20	4.62
		1.92	2.20	2.38	2.20
M	Practical/Imaginative	5.15	5.54	5.70	7.27
		1.91	1.20	2.60	2.53
N	Forthright/Shrewd	6.04	6.31	5.83	3.80[a]
		2.44	3.01	2.80	1.74
O	Self-assured/Apprehensive	6.96	6.54	5.10	4.35
		2.89	3.12	2.35	2.96
Q1	Conservative/Experimenting	6.15	7.08	6.03	8.20
		1.91	1.80	2.47	2.76
Q2	Group-dependent/Self-sufficient	7.27	6.85	6.80	5.90
		1.93	1.82	2.32	2.64
Q3	Undisciplined self conflict/Controlled	5.27	6.38	7.07	6.90
		1.78	3.04	2.56	2.39
Q4	Relaxed/Tense	7.65	7.08	5.87	4.95
		2.81	2.46	2.34	2.74

Note: Means with the same superscript letter are not significantly different for the interaction effect.

TABLE 1.7
Percentage of 16 PF Sten Scores Less Than 3 and Greater Than 8

			Group						
		Rape		Assault		Sex Anomaly		Controls	
Factor	Chi Square	<3	>8	<3	>8	<3	>8	<3	>8
Md	***	57	0	52	0	42	3	15	10
A Reserved/Outgoing	****	57	5	60	4	40	8	5	12
B Less Intelligent/More Intelligent	****	35	0	52	0	27	3	2	15
C Affected by Feelings/Emotionally Stable	****	52	0	60	4	30	3	7	17
E Humble/Assertive	**	37	7	48	12	27	15	2	10
F Sober/Happy-go-lucky	****	45	3	64	4	35	0	5	5
G Expedient/Conscientious	—	42	2	48	0	32	3	20	2
H Shy/Venturesome	****	55	3	64	4	47	3	5	12
I Tough-minded/Tender-minded	****	40	5	52	4	27	10	5	40
L Trusting/Suspicious	—	35	17	52	12	35	15	17	12
M Practical/Imaginative	****	40	2	48	0	32	15	0	30
N Forthright/Shrewd	*	42	7	56	8	35	12	25	0
O Self-assured/Apprehensive	**	35	27	56	28	27	10	17	20
Q1 Conservative/Experimenting	****	35	5	48	16	25	12	0	52
Q2 Group-dependent/Self-sufficient	—	45	2	56	0	45	3	40	0
Q3 Undisciplined self conflict/Controlled	**	57	0	64	0	35	0	22	0
Q4 Relaxed/Tense	**	37	25	48	20	25	12	12	7

Note: *p < 05, **p < 01, ***p < 001, ****p < 0001.

exhibited their genitals and some masturbated while exposing.[14] The assaultive group had more convictions for assault than the other patient group. For some rapists, their charges were reduced to common assault from rape. However they also physically attacked other men. The aggressiveness and substance abuse of the assaulters and rapists is reflected in miscellaneous convictions (e.g., careless driving, drunk and disorderly behavior, possession of drugs and weapons, etc.). The results are interesting for property offences, especially break and enter and theft. The rapists has 93 convictions compared to 108 for the assaulters and 24 for the sexual anomaly group. Overall the rapists appeared very similar to the assaulters in pattern of criminality.[15]

Parent Child Relations. The results of multivariate and univariate analysis of variance for the Clarke Parent Child Relations Questionnaire appear in Table 1.10. In general the assaulters and rapists reported the most similar pattern of

TABLE 1.8
Diagnoses of Rapists, Assaultives, and the Sexual
Anomaly Groups

Diagnoses	Percent of Group		
	Rapists	Assaultives	Sex Anomaly
Personality Disorder	78	68	33
Sexual Deviation	13	0	58
Other	30	60	13
None	10	20	25
	Selected Diagnoses		
Antisocial Personality	20	24	3
Alcoholism	10	28	0
Drug Abuse	3	12	0

Note: An individual could be assigned more than one diagnosis so percents do
not total 100%.

parent child relations. The largest effect was a lower identification with mother
but there was also a prominent if less powerful effect showing lower father
identification. Fathers of assaulters and rapists appeared to be aggressive to
mother and son and the latter reciprocated in kind. The offenders reported that
affection from both parents to them as children was low and their strictness was
high.

The sexually anomalous and rape groups were similar in considering that their
mothers were less affectionate to them and that both parents were less indulgent
to them than the other groups reported.

Individual supplementary items from the Clarke PCR indicated that, compared to nonassaulters' parents, both the assaulters' and rapists' fathers were
more often in trouble with the police[16]; both their fathers and mothers were more

TABLE 1.9
Criminal Convictions for Rapists, Assaulters
and Sexually Anomalous Groups

Charge	Number of Charges		
	Rape	Assault	Sex Anomaly
Sex Offences	102	0	92
Assault	44	61	0
Break & Enter, Theft	93	108	24
Miscellaneous	37	73	17
Total	276	242	133

TABLE 1.10
Two × Two Factorial Multivariate and
Univariate Analysis of Variance of the Parent
Child Relations Questionnaire Scales

	F Values for 2 × 2 Univariate Analysis of Variance		
Scale	Assault	Anomaly	Interaction
MAS	2.43	1.83	0.19
FAS	11.16**	3.30†	0.71
SAM	2.14	0.01	0.98
SAF	5.48*	0.00	1.93
MAF	3.16†	0.86	0.33
FAM	6.59*	0.13	0.06
MC	0.48	0.00	0.02
FC	0.06	0.46	2.67
MAff	16.09****	3.92*	0.52
FAff	7.36**	0.86	0.01
MStr	5.07*	1.31	0.18
FStr	9.22**	1.19	1.69
MId	28.51****	0.01	2.49
FId	17.65****	0.05	0.75
MInd	0.09	5.99*	0.14
FInd	0.24	4.22*	2.91†
Manova	3.26****	1.76*	1.38

Note: The name of each scale can be constructed using the following
key. M = Mother, F = Father, S = Respondant, A = Aggression,
C = Competence, Aff = Affection, Str = Strictness, Id = Identification, Ind = Indulgence.
    †p < .10, *p < .05, **p < .01, ***p < .001, ****p < .0001.

often drunk[17] and the offenders followed in their footsteps, indicating at admission that they drank too much.[18] Rapists and assaulters more often ran away
from home as children[19] perhaps as a reaction to their hostile environment. There
was no evidence of parental sexual abuse or incest but the assaulters more often
overheard parents having sex than controls did.[20] They were also more likely to
be jealous of some sibling who was father's favourite although that sibling was
not necessarily a male.[21] Taking all items together, the greatest similarity among
the four groups was between rapists and assaulters.

Fighting.   Rapists and assaulters were more often in fist fights prior to age
16 than the other groups.[22] Interestingly, after age 16, they continued to engage
in more fist fights than the other two groups[23] but rapists engaged in fewer fights
than the assaulters although still in significantly more fights than the nonassaultive groups.[24] One might hypothesize that rapists direct their hostility to
acts of rape after this age.

Alcoholism was a problem for the violent groups. More assaulters chronically abused alcohol than rapists who in turn did so more often than the other two groups. The same pattern of results held true for alcohol consumption at the time of the presenting offence.[25] Sixty percent of the rapists were drinking at the time of the offence compared to 78% of the assaultives and 18% of the sexual anomalies group. Fifty-four percent of the rapists had a chronic drinking problem compared to 75% of the assaultives and 28% of the sex anomalies group. Once more rapists and assaulters are most similar.

Erotic Preference

Sexual History.   Analysis of variance results for the SHQ are shown in Table 1.11. The rapists resembled both assaulters and the sexual anomaly group as well as showing trends to being unique sexually.[26]

The greatest number of similarities was between rapists and the sexually anomalous men. Both groups exposed, peeped, made obscene calls, and frottaged (rubbed against females in crowds). There was little pattern in the frequency with which the anomalous behaviors co-occurred in the rape group. In fact the associations were no greater than expected by chance. The same was true of the sexual anomaly group. Both groups also had sexual contact with females 13 to 15 years of age after they themselves were 21, including dating them. The latter may reflect a wide ranging sexual appetite or psychological immaturity. Both groups also more often had sexual experiences outside their marriages, including

TABLE 1.11

Two × Two Factorial Analysis of Variance Results for Sex History Scale Scores of Rapists, Assaultives, Sexually Anomalous, and Control Groups

| Scale | *F Values for 2 × 2 Univariate Analysis of Variance* | | |
	Assault	*Anomaly*	*Interaction*
Adult Female Frequency	14.41***	0.02	0.04
Female Child Frequency	1.66	4.70*	0.73
Pubescent Female Frequency	0.13	4.62*	0.00
Anal Activity	0.68	9.67**	2.68
Exhibiting Frequency	3.32†	10.65**	2.86†
Exhibiting Behavior	13.94***	10.91**	1.36
Voyeurism[a]	4.25*	1.21	0.68
Frottage	0.57	5.49*	0.10
Rape	2.37	4.28*	3.10†
Obscene Calls	2.88†	4.97*	2.42
Transvestism	1.35	4.06*	2.78†

Note: †p < 10, *p < 05, **p < 01, ***p < 001.
[a]Old SHQ only.

affairs with married women. A surprising finding was the incidence of men who masturbated while dressed in female attire (transvestism). Both rapists and the sexually anomalous group did it but there was a trend for the rapists to do it more than any other group.

Table 1.12 shows the percentages of rapists and sexual anomaly groups that had ever engaged in the sexual behaviors in question. The results are broken down by old and new Sex History Questionnaire. Although only 25% of the groups answered the new questionnaire, some differences are noteworthy. Occasional peeping is a common behavior in the male population at large but it is rarer when considered as an orgasmic outlet (see Chapter 3 and Gebhard et al; 1965). Therefore the 17% figure for rapists who peep on the new SHQ would appear to be more accurate than the 67% figure found with the older instrument. The second feature that differs from the old to the new SHQ is the frequency of rape without the presence of other sexual anomalies. The old SHQ offers a figure of 11% but the new SHQ shows 42%. Using the old SHQ one can infer that sexual anomalies are a constant feature of rapists. However, using the new SHQ, the conclusion is more tenuous.

The main similarity between rapists and assaulters is in sexual energy reflected in frequency of outlets and the early onset of sexual contacts. Both groups showed a higher frequency of conventional sexual outlets with adult females than

TABLE 1.12
Percentage of Various Sexual Anomalies in the Rapist and Sex
Anomaly Groups

	Rapists		Sex Anomalies Group	
Sexual Behavior	Old SHQ	†New SHQ	Old SHQ	New SHQ
Exhibiting	15	17	90	80
Peeping	67	17	50	70
Frottage-Toucheurism	30	8	23	0
Obscene Calls	15	0	23	0
Transvestism	26	25	20	20
Heterosexual Pedophilia	15	8	3	10
Heterosexual Hebephilia	22	33	10	10
Homosexual Pedophilia	0	0	0	10
Homosexual Ephebephilia††	0	0	0	10
Androphilia	19	8	3	10
Sadomasochism	—	17	—	0
Only Rape	11	42	—	—

†Incidences of orgasm accompanying a behavior are calculated from the new SHQ while the old SHQ does not always ask this question. Exhibiting is an exception in which all incidences were computed for the new SHQ.

††Ephebephilia refers to sexual interaction with 13 to 15 year old boys.

nonassaulters did. In fact they started their sexual contact as teenagers 13–15 years old both with female peers as well as with older females.[27]

Rapists were unique, of course, in having been sexually aggressive and having raped.[28] They were selected on this basis. However the numbers who only engaged in this act are substantial. Moreover, their tendency to crossdress more than the remaining groups is surprising.

There were no differences among the four groups in the self reported incidence of impotence (inability to have erections) or of premature ejaculation (ejaculating before penetrating female). There was an absence of sexual experience or interest in men and boys by the majority of subjects in all groups. Overall rapists shared features with both assaulters and sexually anomalous men but they also tended to be unique.

Body Image.   Rapists were like the sexual anomaly group and unlike the assaulters in having some problems with body image. They would like to be stronger,[29] have a more athletic build, and be more athletic.[30] They also thought there was something wrong with their private parts and that they were less attractive to females.[31] They were more often ashamed to be nude with other boys or men, were more often thought of as sissies, and they wanted to be more forceful.[32]

Amount of Force in the Offence.   The amount of force used in the rapes and assaults was scored by two raters[33] and correlated with the other measures used in the study. The use of alcohol at the time of the offence was unrelated to the amount of force used.[34] On the MMPI there was a tendency for force to be correlated positively with psychopathology in the rapists: F (.42), K (−.37), Depression (.35), Psychopathic deviate (.48), Paranoia (.39), Psychasthenia (.33), Schizophrenia (.37) and Social Introversion (.38) scales. The amount of force used in the crime correlated with low mother identification (−.32) and low father identification (−.37) and on the SHQ to more frequent masochistic fantasies (.32) and to sadistic fantasies (.48).

DISCUSSION

Rapists in the present study were a mixed group. Clearly they most resembled assaulters in personality and diagnosis, pattern of criminality, parent child relations, history of fighting, alcohol use and abuse, and even to some extent on sexual history. Both groups were "superheterosexuals" who had a higher than average frequency of conventional sexual outlets. For a substantial number of rapists there appeared to be no unusual sexual outlet outside the rape. Based on the new SHQ, 42% raped but showed no other anomalous sexual behavior. Freund et al. (1983) reported an even higher incidence of this pattern (83%). One

must wonder why the sexual aggressives raped and common assaulters did not. Further investigation evidently is needed.

Three fifths of rapists did manifest some sexually anomalous behavior outside the rape. In general they engaged in just about every heterosexual behavior that is possible. Nevertheless, the cooccurrence of each anomalous behavior with the others was not different from what would be expected by chance. Moreover, the frequencies of the behaviors are small and may represent no more than a high level of sexual energy or curiosity. Therefore searching for a pattern in these behaviors may be midleading. Even rape itself involved an appropriate stimulus and sexual response. It is the circumstances under which it is carried out which constitutes the abnormality. It may be considered more similar to a theft than to a sexual anomaly. On the other hand, the aggressive nonsexual motivation for rape, described by Groth and Birnbaum (1980) and others may be operative. In any case the rapists in the present study were clearly a mixture of types.

The so-called courtship disorders of exhibiting, peeping, obscene call, toucheurism, and rape cooccurred in the rapists, supporting Freund et al.'s (1983) theory. Nevertheless, one must also explain why these men engage in a range of other sexual behaviors, most prominently, in transvestism and hebephilia. Transvestism has been associated with sadomasochism and fetishism and possibly the latter are operative in rapists.[35] The relationship of degree of force used and sadomasochistic fantasies may reflect a more dangerous individual, perhaps at its extreme representing sadism or a tendency to rape murder.[36] Dressing in female attire for erotic gratification does seem incongruous with the picture of the rapist as a "macho" male who must make conquests or assert his masculinity (Don Juan Complex).

Another striking feature of the rapists' profile was the presence of hebephilia or an inordinate interest in 13-to 15-year-old females. Girls in this age bracket are emotionally immature in general but they are usually physically mature or, at least, developing. The incidence of rapists' dating relationships with them is interesting. Thirty three percent interacted in conventional ways such as dating but only 8% engaged in the more typical form of hebephilia in which there was a casual encounter. Thus this sexual outlet may more appropriately be part of a wide ranging heterosexual interest rather than a fixed erotic preference for immature females, more characteristic of pedophiles.

Some theories of rape were not supported by this study. There was no evidence that homosexuality was of concern nor was impotence and flagging interest in women a factor. In fact, rapists seemed to cope quite well with women and to engage in a wide range of heterosexual outlets. Contrary to expectation, they were not ultra-masculine. If anything, they were feminine and even engaged in transvestism. Their violent history, abuse of alcohol, poor socialization as children, and their higher sexual "drive" would seem to be major factors that predispose them collectively to rape.

REFERENCES

Abel, G. G., Barlow, D. H., Blanchard, E. B., & Guild, D. The components of rapists' sexual arousal. *Archives of General Psychiatry*, 1977, *34*, 895–903.

Amir, M. *Patterns in forcible rape*. Chicago: University of Chicago Press, 1971.

Armentrout, J. A., & Hauer, A. I. MMPIs of rapists of adults, rapists of children, and non-rapist sex offenders. *Journal of Clinical Psychology*, 1978, *34*, 330–332.

Barbaree, H. E., Marshall, W. L., & Lanthier, R. D. Deviant sexual arousal in rapists. *Behavior Research & Therapy*, 1979, *17*, 215–222.

Brittain, R. The sadistic murderer. *Medicine, Science & The Law*, 1970, *10*, 198–207.

Brownmiller, S. *Against our will: Men, women and rape*. New York: Simon & Schuster, 1975.

Burton, A. The use of the Masculinity-Femininity Scale of the MMPI as an aid in the diagnoses of sexual inversion. *Journal of Psychology*, 1947, *24*, 161–164.

Christie, M. M., Marshall, W. L., & Lanthier, R. D. *A descriptive study of incarcerated rapists and pedophiles*. Unpublished manuscript, 1978 Canadian Penetentiary Services, Kingston, Ontario.

Clark, L., & Lewis, D. *Rape: The price of coercive sexuality*. Toronto: The Women's Press, 1977.

Clark, L., & Lewis, D. *A Study of rape in Vancouver & Toronto*. Toronto: Centre of Criminology, University of Toronto, 1978.

Derogatis, L. R., *DSFI (Derogatis Sexual Functioning Inventory)*. Leonard R. Derogatis, Ph.D., 1228 Wine Spring Road, Baltimore, Md 21204, 1978.

Freund, K. Diagnosis and treatment of forensically significant anomalous erotic preferences. *Canadian Journal of Criminology & Corrections*, 1976, *18*, 181–189.

Freund, K., Scher, H., & Hucker, S. The courtship disorders. *Archives of Sexual Behavior*, 1983, *12*, 369–379.

Gebhard, P. H., Gagnon, J. H., Pomeroy, W. B., & Christenson, C. V. *Sex offenders: An analysis of types*. London: Heinemann, 1965.

Gosselin, C., & Wilson, G. *Sexual Variations: Fetishism, sadomasochism and transvestism*, New York: Simon & Schuster, 1980.

Groth, A. N., & Birnbaum, H. J. *Men who rape*, New York: Plenum Press, 1979.

Groth, A. N., & Birnbaum, H. J. The rapist: motivations for sexual violence. In S. L. McCombie (Ed.), *The rape crisis intervention handbook*. New York: Plenum Press, 1980.

Holmstrom, L. L., & Burgess, A. W. Sexual behavior of assailants during reported rapes. *Archives of Sexual Behavior*, 1980, *9*, 427–439.

Huesmann, L. R., Lefkowitz, M. M., & Eron, L. D. Sum of MMPI scales F, 4, and 9 as a measure of aggression. *Journal of Consulting and Clinical Psychology*, 1978, *46*, 1071–1078.

Huhner, M. Rape and satyriasis. *American Journal of Urology & Sexology*, 1918, *14*, 362–371.

Karacan, I., Williams, R. L., Guerrero, M. W., Salis, P. J., Thornby, J. I., & Hursch, C. J. Nocturnal penile tumescence and sleep of convicted rapists and other prisoners. *Archives of Sexual Behavior*, 1974, *3*, 19–26.

Langevin, R. *Sexual strands: Understanding and treating sexual anomalies in men*. Hillsdale, N.J.: Lawrence Erlbaum Associates, 1983.

Langevin, R., Paitich, D., Freeman, R., Mann, K., & Handy, L. Personality characteristics and sexual anomalies in males. *Canadian Journal of Behavioral Science*, 1978, *10*, 222–238.

Langevin, R., Paitich, D., Ramsay, G., Anderson, C., Kamrad, J., Pope, S., Geller, G., Pearl, L., & Newman, S. Experimental studies of the etiology of genital exhibitionism. *Archives of Sexual Behavior*, 1979, *8*, 307–331.

Levine, S., & Koenig, J. *Why men rape: Interviews with convicted rapists*. Toronto: Macmillan Co., 1980.

McDonald, A., & Paitich, D. Psychological profile of the rapist. *American Journal of Forensic Psychiatry*, 1983, *111*, 159–172.

Paitich, D., & Langevin, R. The Clarke Parent-Child Relations Questionnaire: A clinically useful test for adults. *Journal of Consulting and Clinical Psychology*, 1976, *44*, 428–536.

Paitich, D., Langevin, R., Freeman, R., Mann, K., & Handy, L. The Clarke Sex History Questionnaire: A clinically useful sex history questionnaire for males. *Archives of Sexual Behavior*, 1977, *6*, 421–436.

Panton, J. H. Personality differences appearing between rapists of adults, rapists of children and non-violent sexual molesters of female children. *Research Communications in Psychology, Psychiatry, and Behavior*, 1978, *3*, 385–393.

Quinsey, V. L., & Chaplin, T. C. Penile responses to nonsexual violence among rapists. *Criminal Justice & Behavior*, 1982, *9*, 372–381.

Quinsey, V. L., Chaplin, T. C. & Varney, G. A comparison of rapists' and non-sex offenders' sexual preferences for mutually consenting sex, rape, and sadistic acts. *Behavioral Assessment*, 1981, *3*, 127–135.

Rada, R. T. *Clinical aspects of the rapist*. New York: Grune and Stratton, 1978.

Rader, C. M. MMPI profile types of exposers, rapists, and assaulters in a court service population. *Journal of Consulting and Clinical Psychology*, 1977, *45*, 61–69.

Ruff, C. F., Templer, D. I., & Ayers, J. L. The intelligence of rapists. *Archives of Sexual Behavior*, 1976, *5*, 327–329.

Stoller, R. J. *Perversion: The erotic form of hatred*. New York: Pantheon Books, 1975.

Vera, H., Barnard, G. W., & Holzer, C. The intelligence of rapists: New Data. *Archives of Sexual Behavior*, 1979, *8*, 375–378.

Williams, A. H. Rape-murder. In R. Slovenko (Ed.), *Sexual behavior and the law*. Springfield, Ill.: C. Thomas Co., 1965.

ENDNOTES

Note 1. See their article for other references supporting their viewpoint.

Note 2. For contrast see Huhner (1918) who associated rape with satyriasis and discussed older theories and findings such as those of Krafft-Ebing.

Note 3. See also Gebhard et al., 1965.

Note 4. See Brittain (1970) and Williams (1965) for example.

Note 5. See Langevin (1983) for a critique of these studies.

Note 6. See Chapter 2 for more details.

Note 7. Analysis of variance, $F = 30.03$, $p < 0001$ for the interaction effect.

Note 8. Analysis of variance, $F = 18.74$, $p < 0001$ and $F = 5.61$, $p < 05$ respectively for the interactions.

Note 9. There is some debate about the intelligence of rapists (cf. Ruff, Templer, & Ayers, 1976; Vera, Barnard, & Holzer, 1979) with the suggestion that they are not as bright as the average person. However, more empirical data is needed.

Note 10. Chi Square $= 19.64$, $df = 6$, $p < 001$.

Note 11. Within cell correlations of education, marital status (single versus other), VIQ and PIQ with the major dependent variables (discussed later), were examined and selected covariance analyses were done. In the majority of cases there were no significant correlations of dependent variables and covariates.

Interpretation of results as discussed in the results section were unaffected by covariance analysis.

Note 12. Chi Square = 26.69, df = 6, p < 001 primary diagnosis only. It is not legitimate to compare Chi Square on repeated measures. However the goodness of fit Chi Squares for all diagnoses excluding sex deviation diagnosis are informative.

Rapists versus Assaultive	$\chi^2 = 21.47***$
Rapists versus Sex Anomalies	$\chi^2 = 92.59***$
Assaultive versus Sex Anomalies	$\chi^2 = 208.04***$

Although all are significant, the smallest difference is rapists versus assaultives.

Note 13. Overall the rapists contribute 24% to the Chi Square, the assaultors 20%, and the multiple anomalies 56%.

Note 14. See Langevin et al. (1979, 1983) for more details about the "typical" exhibitionist.

Note 15. The total number of offences for the three groups differ obviously. However when the *pattern* of offences for the groups is compared, the similarity of rapists to assaulters is striking. Two separate Chi Square tests were used to compare rapists to assaultive and sex anomalies groups respectively. When the rapists were compared to assaulters, sex offences were omitted since they would distort results. Thus on property offences, person offences and miscellaney, the two groups did not differ, $\chi^2 = 4.66$, df = 2, p > .05. However when rapists are compared to the sex anomalies group on pattern of offences, omitting charges against the person and totalling sex offences, they still are grossly different, $\chi^2 = 23.48$, df = 2, p < .001. The significant result is mainly attributable to differences in both the frequency of property and sex offences (98% of the Chi Square value).

Note 16. F = 18.03, p < 0001.

Note 17. F = 13.56, p < .001 and F = 5.20, p < .05 respectively.

Note 18. F = 18.03, p < .0001.

Note 19. F = 6.50, p < .05.

Note 20. F = 4.37, p < .05.

Note 21. Chi Square = 5.04, p < .05.

Note 22. F = 15.51, p < .0001.

Note 23. F = 46.13, p < .0001.

Note 24. F = 5.63, p < .05.

Note 25. F = 25.75, p < .0001, and F = 17.76, p < .0001 for chronic consumption and drinking at the time of the offence respectively.

Note 26. Empty cells on the 27 scales of the Clarke Sex History Questionnaire for Males made a multivariate analysis of variance impossible without a significantly reduced sample size. Considerable variance in the types of acts tended to obscure differences in the 4 groups on many scales. Therefore only univariate analyses are reported in Table 1.11. Most empty cells reflected the lack of any

sexual experience and interest in men and boys by the majority of men in all four groups.

Note 27. F = 5.28, p < .05 and F = 12.84, p < .001 respectively.

Note 28. Even the results for the rape scale were weak (p < .10). This was due to the scale having only 2 items, one of which was nonsignificant. The better item did show a statistically significant interaction effect in which rapists scored higher than the other three groups, as expected.

Note 29. F = 4.80, p < .05.

Note 30. F = 9.97, p < .01, and F = 7.90, p < .01 respectively.

Note 31. F = 7.40, p < .01, and F = 5.00, p < .05 respectively.

Note 32. F = 8.29, p < .01, and F = 5.56, p < .05 and F = 5.69, p < .05 respectively.

Note 33. Agreement interclass correlation rk = 0.84. Description of the offence was derived mainly from offenders' lawyer and the prosecution but also from police reports in some cases.

Note 34. Rapist plus assaultive groups: Pearson correlation, r = .08, p > .05, rapists only r = .11, p > .05.

Note 35. See Gosselin and Wilson (1980, p. 167).

Note 36. See the cases reported by Williams, (1965) for example.

2 Sexual Aggression: Constructing a Predictive Equation A Controlled Pilot Study

Ron Langevin
Mark H. Ben-Aron
Robert Coulthard
Gerald Heasman
John E. Purins
Lorraine Handy
Stephen J. Hucker
Anne E. Russon
Clarke Institute of Psychiatry, Toronto

David Day
University of Windsor

Vincent Roper
Ontario Correctional Institute

Jerald Bain
George Wortzman
Mount Sinai Hospital, Toronto

Christopher David Webster
Metfors, Toronto

The results of Study 1 raised many questions, some of which are examined in the next chapter. Why do rapists appear to have a high sex drive and to be generally aggressive? Possibly there are hormone abnormalities. Both sex drive and aggressiveness are believed to be related to elevated serum testosterone levels in men but a complete spectrum of sex steroids has yet to be examined.

The most surprising finding in the foregoing chapter was the number of rapists who engaged in transvestism. The latter has been associated traditionally with passivity and feminine gender identity. Transvestism also has been associated with brain pathology and sadomasochism that may be associated with violence in general. The incongruous results for the rapists suggest that their sexual history be re-examined and that a measure of gender identity be scrutinized too.

Finally, the abuse of alcohol by assaultive men including rapists was expected. However in the case of sexual aggression, we

face a paradox. Alcohol presumably reduces erectile potency. How then is rape possible by men who, in substantial numbers, abuse alcohol and are drinking at the time of their offence?

In the following chapter, alcohol and drug use, sex hormones, brain damage, aggressiveness, and sexual arousal to rape stimuli are examined in an attempt to predict future violence and recidivism.

SEXUAL AGGRESSION

A number of factors and their complex interaction have been considered important in the commission of sexually aggressive acts including rape.[1] Often quoted or used in psychiatric assessments of sexual aggressives are : sexual arousal to deviant and aggressive stimuli, alcohol and drug abuse, sex hormone levels, brain pathology, and a history of aggressiveness.[2] Collectively, they are the most important variables in evaluating treatment, disposition, dangerousness, and future acting out. Because of the limited number of existing controlled investigations, the purpose of the pilot project reported here was to evaluate each factor as a predictor of dangerous sexual aggression. Each of these predictors in Table 2.1 will be considered in turn.

Sexual Arousal to Rape Stimuli

A complicating factor in studying rape is that physical abuse in sexual assaults ranges from none, threats only, through some shoving and slapping mostly for the sake of compliance, to the infliction of minor injuries, serious life threatening force, and even to killing in the case of the sadist. Some rapists may be sexually

TABLE 2.1
Indices of Dangerousness in Sex Offenders

Dangerousness	
Predictors	*Criteria*
Sexual Arousal to Rape Stimuli	Repeated Forced Sexual Acts
Alcohol and Drug Use/Abuse	Degree of Force Used
Sex Hormone Levels	
Brain Pathology	
History of Aggression	

conventional and "steal" intercourse (Chapter 1) but others need violence and some force as an integral part of their sexual arousal pattern.

Sexual sadism is an anomaly in which erotic gratification is derived by controlling, humiliating, terrorizing, injuring, and even destroying another person (see MacCulloch, Snowden, Wood & Mills, 1983). Although the anomaly generally has been relegated to the realm of fantasy and pretend role playing (cf. Langevin, 1983a), actual injuries to victims obviously do occur (cf. Brittain, 1970). The sadist is particularly dangerous because, not only is the victim's injury sought out, it is an essential part of his sexual arousal pattern so that whenever he is sexually aroused he will want to hurt someone. Some means of identifying this group therefore would be important.

Common sense suggests that rapists are more sexually aroused than the average man by committing acts of rape and perhaps less aroused by engaging in consenting intercourse. In order to investigate this reasonable hypothesis, Abel and his associates (Abel, Barlow, Blanchard, & Guild, 1977) compared the penile circumference changes of rapists and nonrapists to audio descriptions of consenting sexual intercourse and of rape. The ratio of responses to rape versus intercourse was defined as the *rape index*. This index could discriminate the rapists from the nonrapists. Moreover, the more extreme the index score, the more aggressive and frequent were the rapes. Thus, the rape index should identify the more violence prone sadists. Barbaree, Marshall & Lanthier (1979) and Quinsey, Chaplin & Varney (1981) later replicated the findings of Abel et al. (1977). Their three studies constitute the only experimental literature on rapists in which penile reactions were measured. As with most first studies, there are problems indicating that the method should be refined before accepting clinical application. First, the audiotaped stimuli used by all three authors, suggested to the subjects that they were responding sexually to the described scenes. Demand characteristics therefore may have been an important factor in the results. Second, all authors measured penile circumference and the findings should be examined with the more sensitive penile *volume* (cf. Freund, Langevin, & Barlow, 1974). Third, in Abel's data, the two largest of four reactions were chosen and this could distort the results. Fourth, in some cases, there were no neutral stimuli for comparison. Many of the reactions of the rapists to aggression were in the range of penile circumference change which has been reported in other studies to be typical of neutral stimuli. Fifth, no author used the appropriate multivariate analysis. Instead, univariate analyses of variance and t-tests were used which do not take into account the correlation of responses within persons. Finally, Quinsey and Chaplin (1982), in a continuation of their earlier study (Quinsey, Chaplin & Varney 1981), examined the rape index and found it was not significantly correlated with the degree of force used in offences committed by a group of 44 rapists. However, penile arousal to nonsexual violence in the narratives did relate to degree of force used in the offence. Moreover, Malamuth (1981) exam-

ined penile reactions of college students to stimuli of rape and consenting inter-course under a variety of experimental conditions and found no significant stim-ulus effects. In the present project we attempted to overcome the limitations of the existing studies and to replicate their promising findings.

Little has been said in the professional literature about the sexual history or gender identity of sexually aggressive men. Chapter 1 presented the surprising finding that about a sixth of rapists engaged in orgasmic crossdressing, a behav-ior usually associated with femininity and/or feminine gender identity in men. There are no studies to our knowledge that examine gender identity in rapists, and in fact, gender behavior is studied very little other than in effeminate or androphilic men. It remains an open question whether gender identity distur-bance is not common to many sexual anomalies. In any case, theorists have maintained that rapists are extremely masculine and aggressive. Only Brittain (1970), it seems, noted that sadistic murderers may appear effeminate and that homosexuality may be suspected in some cases. He further stated that many sadists dress up in female clothing at times but he did not elaborate further. MacCulloch et al. (1983) also noted the case of a sadist who was transvestitic. Crossdressing and gender identity were scrutinized in the present project.

Alcohol and Drugs

Many writers have stressed the importance of alcohol in the etiology of various forms of violence (e.g., Greenland, 1970, 1971; Rada, 1978). Alcohol intoxica-tion presents peculiar problems for sexual aggression. Certainly, it has been accepted widely that chronic intoxication is a factor in sexual aggression. How-ever, the exact nature of its involvement has not been thoroughly studied to date. In his book, *Clinical Aspects of the Rapist,* Rada (1978) noted that approximately half of rapists were drinking at the time of their offence and a third of them were chronic alcoholics. Paradoxically, it is commonly thought that alcohol may increase sexual desire but it reduces potency.[3] How then is rape possible? Do minor amounts of alcohol not affect penile erection?

There are only six studies directed to this question all having been reported since 1976. Half of those studies suggest that erectile ability declines in a linear fashion with increases in blood alcohol level (BAL). This supports the notion that the sexual aggressive should be less able to have an erection when drinking than when he is sober. These studies are discussed in chapter 4 in this volume, "The Effect of Alcohol on Penile Erection." We found that the role of alcohol in sexual aggression needs serious reevaluation since relatively large amounts of alcohol did not reduce penile erection, contrary to current beliefs. These results at least explain how moderately intoxicated men can rape. Since one third of rapists are chronic alcoholics, it is an additional important fact that *tolerance to alcohol can develop as a function of prolonged exposure.* Although tolerance may vary with recency of drinking; it is expected that a chronic heavy drinker

will show fewer subjective and behavioral effects than an inexperienced drinker who has consumed the same amount of alcohol (cf. Mello & Mendelson, 1978). One may similarly expect that penile erection is less influenced by alcohol consumption in chronic abusers. It may be assumed that in the six experimental studies examining the effects of alcohol on penile erection, most of the university students serving as research subjects were not chronic abusers of alcohol. It therefore would be interesting to see the effect of increasing amounts of alcohol on rapists who are in substantial numbers, heavy drinkers. Such an investigation was attempted in this study.

Alcohol consumption further may interact with aggressiveness. Mello and Mendelson (1978) indicated that there is no consistent relationship between BAL and emotional responsivity but the prolonged use of alcohol appears to increase feelings of dysphoria, despondency, and social isolation so that intoxication can be associated with the facilitation and perhaps the induction of violent and aggressive behavior.

Drugs have not been discussed but are certainly important in some cases. Carter and Davis (1983) have reviewed the literature describing the effect of drugs on sexual arousal and performance. They noted that our knowledge is limited and we must turn to anecdotes and case reports for information. In general it is believed that sexual behavior increases with moderate doses of central nervous system stimulants and decreases with the use of depressants. Marijuana, amphetamines, and amyl-nitrate may have aphrodisiac properties. Amphetamines also may stimulate aggression (Kalant, 1973). Cocaine may induce sexual exhilaration and psychedelics like LSD may reduce sexual inhibitions. Use of narcotics like heroin, on the other hand, reduces sexual interest and potency. The intended role of drugs in sexual aggression can only be surmised at present. They may be used to enhance sexual pleasures or the crime may be a side effect of drug abuse. We recorded drug use in the present study. Both alcohol and drug use have been generally reported without the aid of standard questionnaires. The use of instruments like the MAST (Michigan Alcoholism Screening Test, Selzer, 1971) and the Clarke Drug Survey would add greatly to a uniform evaluation of the part played by alcohol and drugs in sexual aggression.

Sex Hormones

Sex hormones play an important but not fully understood role in anomalous sexual arousal and in aggression. A number of writers have implicated higher plasma testosterone levels as a factor in men who are violent. Ehrenkranz, Bliss, and Sheard (1974), for example, compared 12 chronically assaultive prisoners with 12 who were not and 12 who were socially dominant. They found that assaultive prisoners had significantly higher plasma testosterone levels compared to the other groups. Scaramella and Brown (1978) found that serum testosterone in 14 college hockey players correlated significantly with amount of body con-

tact, response to threat, and global aggressiveness as rated by their coaches. However, Monti, Brown, and Corriveau (1977) did not find a significant relation between testosterone and aggressiveness as measured by the Buss-Durkee Hostility Inventory in 101 university students nor did Doering, Brodie, Kraemer, Moos, Becker, & Hamburg (1975) in a sample of normals. Other studies present inconsistent results, however, leaving an overall impression that testosterone is positively related to aggressiveness and to sexual arousability (Doering, Brodie, Kraemer, Becker, & Hamburg, 1974; Kreuz and Rose, 1972; Mendelson, 1977; Mayer-Bahlburg, Nat, Boon, Sharma, & Edwards, 1974; Persky, Smith, & Basu, 1971; Persky, O'Brien, Fine, Howard, Khan, & Beck, 1977; Rada, Laws, & Kellner, 1976; Rose, 1975). Most studies have not followed sound assay procedures nor have the ratings of aggressiveness been assessed for reliability or, in many cases, for validity. Most important, significant findings tend to occur in studies that have clear marker groups, for example, prisoners with a history of assault, but nonsignificant findings tend to be from studies using normal university students with no obvious history of aggression.[4] This suggests that the latter may be too restricted a group for studying testosterone and aggression or that the tests on which "aggressiveness" is based may lack validity.

The relation of other sex hormones and testosterone has not been adequately explored in connection with sexual arousal or aggression and more information is available in this regard for homosexual and transsexual men (cf. Meyer-Bahlburg, 1977, 1980; Rose, 1975, for reviews). There may be interesting relations between aggression and sex steroids other than testosterone (cf. Mendelson, Dietz, & Ellingboe, 1982). For example, Sheard, Marini, and Giddings (1977) studied 66 male prisoners for the effect of lithium on serum testosterone and luteinising hormone (LH) in aggression. With a reduction in serious aggressive behavior, there was a significant rise in serum LH but there was no change in testosterone. One may also wonder about crossdressing in rapists (Chapter 1) and a possible link with femininity although, in general, no hormone has been clearly linked to femininity in men (see Meyer-Bahlburg, 1977, 1980 and Chapter 10 for comprehensive reviews). Buhrich, Theile, Yaw, and Crawford (1979) reported pertinent data. They studied 26 predominantly heterosexual members of a transvestite club and 22 controls. They found that levels of plasma testosterone, serum LH, and FSH (Follicle Stimulating Hormone) were similar in both groups but six transvestites had FSH levels above the upper limit of normal (16mIU/ml) and seven had LH levels above average (86ng/ml). One had an XYY chromosome constitution. Other studies of transsexuals and transvestites have not produced convincing evidence that femininity or transvestism are related to sex hormone levels. However, it seems that, for a complete examination of the problem, we need to consider a more comprehensive hormone profile than has been done to date. For sound methodology we need repeated samples of blood as well (cf. Mello & Mendelson, 1978).

The one group that studied hormones in rapists was thorough. Rada et al. (1976) compared 52 rapists and 12 pedophiles on the Buss-Durkee Hostility Inventory, the Megargee Overcontrolled Hostility Scale, the Michigan Alcoholism Screening Test (MAST), and plasma testosterone levels. Rapists were grouped according to the degree of violence used in the rapes. Rada et al. found that testosterone levels in the rapist population were within normal limits, but there was a positive association between degree of force in the offence and testosterone level. Alcoholic rapists also had higher plasma levels of testosterone than nonalcoholic rapists. In general alcohol history has not been reported in studies of hormones and aggressiveness. One has to wonder if the many studies examining testosterone in aggressive men would show a positive relationship between degree of alcoholism and testosterone. In a follow up study of 18 rapists, 26 pedophiles, and 11 controls, Rada, Laws, Kellner, Stivastava, & Peake (1983) examined plasma testosterone, dihydrotestosterone, and LH levels, and a similar set of psychological tests. This time there were no group or alcoholism differences among the hormones. Obviously more work is needed on this question. In the present study, total testosterone, LH, FSH, estradiol. dehydroepiandrosterone sulfate (DHAS), prolactin, cortisol, and androstenedione were assayed three times in each subject.

Brain Pathology

A fourth factor to be considered in sexual aggression is brain pathology which may be aggravated by the use of alcohol and/or drugs and interact with poor socialization and a history of multiple sexual anomalies. Both nonsexual aggression and sexual anomalies have been associated with brain pathology. Since rape has been identified as both violent and sexual, one may expect that brain pathology would play some role in this group. The pathology can be manifested in a number of ways; as structural damage to the brain (e.g., head injuries), as functional and electrical abnormalities as seen on electroencephalograms (EEGs), or as biochemical abnormalities. In any case, little has been done on rapists or sexual aggressives per se.

Temporal lobe abnormalities have been reported for some sexual anomalies. Epstein (1961) and Blumer (1970) studied cases of fetishism and transvestism that were related to temporal lobe epilepsy and to other pathologies such as brain tumors. Although findings in general were positive, the studies did not report adequate sexological or forensic information. Hoenig and Kenna (1979) also found temporal lobe EEG abnormalities in transsexual-transvestites, and Kolarsky, Freund, Machek, and Polak (1967) reported the converse, that is, the presence of sexual anomalies in temporal lobe epileptics. Taylor (1969) also noted the decline of sexual interest in two thirds of 100 cases referred for temporal lobe surgery and 15% showed some sexual anomaly.

The findings of Chapter 1 suggest a connection between transvestism and sexual aggression. One sixth of the sexual aggressives sampled crossdressed and masturbated. Conversely, some transsexuals are aggressive and have a history of criminal behavior (See Langevin, Paitich, & Steiner, 1977, and Chapter 12 of this volume). The relationship of transvestism, transsexualism, masochism, fetishism, and sexual aggression has not been studied adequately to date but results suggest they be examined for common brain pathology, especially in the temporal lobes.

A number of writers have indicated that some form of brain pathology is more likely in prisoners and patients with a history of aggressive acting out than in other prisoners and patients.[5] In practice, one must be concerned that the brain pathology relates to the behavior in a meaningful way. Visual motor damage is not as important as limbic system damage which has been shown in lower animals to relate to aggressive behavior.

Sex steroids are functional in the brain and may serve as neurotransmitters. In animal research at least, receptor sites for steroids are evident in areas characteristically associated with sexual behavior. Much has yet to be learned about human sex hormones in the brain and much is inferred from animal research.[6] The relationship of higher levels of testosterone in aggressive men may be linked to brain pathology.

It is expected that in accordance with the literature, we would find a higher incidence of brain damage in the sexual aggressives (SAs) than in control patients and since it is critical in their sexually anomalous behavior, there will be more trauma localized in the temporal lobes than elsewhere. On the other hand, if the damage is diffuse or not in the lobes mentioned, it may simply reflect alcohol and drug abuse or the trauma their brains have endured as a result of receiving some of the aggression they have administered to others who live in a climate of violence.

History of Aggression

Rada (1978) has indicated that rapists are characterized by a history of violence, petty crime, and common assault. We found in Chapter 1 that SAs certainly were likely to engage in theft, to commit common assault, to show a history of truancy, to run away from home, to fight frequently as children and as adults, and to have extensive criminal records. However, they did not really differ from nonsexual aggressives in this respect. Only the sexual aspect of the crimes clearly distinguished the two groups.

A number of theorists have proposed that rape results from aggression rather than from sexual needs and perhaps from a hatred toward women. The impression gained from Chapter 1 was that many sexual aggressives are normal in preferring intercourse with an adult female but they are willing to "steal" it if it is not otherwise available. Existing measures of aggressiveness are poor[7] which

makes the task of examining sexual aggression more difficult. This is complicated by the fact that the terms aggression and hositility have many meanings. We will focus on physical violence in which an attempt is made to bodily injure another person in face to face contact. In the present study the Buss-Durkee Hostility Inventory was used because of its apparent validity and previous use with rapists (Rada, 1975, 1978; Rada, Laws, Kellner, Stivastava, & Peake, 1983) but we developed our own questionnaire to assess history of aggression as well.

Evaluating Dangerousness and Recidivism

Among the most pertinent questions about sexual aggression for the clinical criminologist are: "Will the offender do it again?" and "Is he dangerous?" Tennent (1971) has made it clear that dangerousness means many things and there is confusion in the literature about what exactly is being discussed. Systematic studies are few in number and because of definitional ambiguities, results should be considered with caution.[8] However, as Quinsey (1979) has indicated, much more progress has been made and will be made in the area of sexual offences because we have a clear criterion for evaluating dangerousness, namely sexual acting out. We will be implying something very specific when it comes to sexual aggression, namely acting out in a sexual way and/or injuring the victim. Moreover, the "danger" must be predicted for the foreseeable future (Rubin, 1972).

METHOD

Design

Each predictor in Table 2.1 was examined in detail separately first, and then they were correlated with criterion ratings of dangerousness.

Subjects

Twenty sexual aggressives (hereafter SAs) of the Forensic Service, Clarke Institute of Psychiatry and Ontario Correctional Institution, Brampton, who were charged with rape, attempted rape, or indecent assault were tested. All cases admitted to their most recent offence or to a previous similar one. A group of 20 nonviolent nonsex offenders (hereafter controls) were matched to the SAs on age and education. This group faced charges of theft, fraud, and possession of drugs. In most cases for both groups, the offenders had been convicted and were not facing charges. The SAs average age was 26.75 years, SD 5.17, and the controls, 24.50, SD 7.87. SAs' average education was 10.05 years, SD 2.28, and controls', 10.55, SD 1.43. None of the differences were statistically significant.

The SAs were also broken down into sadists (N = 9) and nonsadists (N = 11) since the former occurred more frequently than reported in the literature. Assignment to the sadist group was based on erotic preference for or inordinate arousal to control of victims, their fear, terror, destruction, torture, and/or unconsciousness. Seven of the nine cases admitted to such arousal and were readily assigned to the sadist group. In two additional cases, circumstances of the offence suggested sadism but the subjects did not clearly admit to sadistic preferences. All subjects were reimbursed for their time. In some cases it was not possible to test subjects on a certain procedure or a subject was excluded because of experimenter error. This will be noted for each measure.

PREDICTOR 1 - SEXUAL AROUSAL TO RAPE STIMULI

Phallometric Comparison of Rape and Consenting Intercourse: The Rape Index

The design of the phallometric study is shown in Table 2.2. There were four classes of audiotaped stimuli: (1) normal consenting sexual interourse; (2) intercourse plus aggression (i.e. rape); (3) aggression to a female with no sex contact; and (4) neutral statements. There were five stimuli in each category in fixed random blocks so that each type of stimulus appeared in each block.[9] The 20 stimuli were audiotaped by a female, so that each stimulus lasted 100 seconds and was segmented into 10 second intervals to pinpoint the aspects of the stimulus that were important. This method was devised and used successfully by Abel, Barlow, Blanchard & Guild (1977). Subjects were pre-relaxed with a 10 minute relaxation tape-recording used in reciprocal inhibition therapy, because it increases overall responsiveness (Langevin & Martin, 1975).

The dependent variables were penile volume change in the first 10 seconds (start of the stimulus sequence) and at maximum volume change in the 100 second interval. A 2x4x5 multivariate analysis of variance was used to assess the effects of group (2), stimulus class (4), and blocks (5) on the dependent variables. In addition, Abel's rape index was computed by dividing the total re-

TABLE 2.2
Experimental Paradigm in the Phallometric Study
of Sexual Aggression

Subjects	Stimuli	Repeats	Dependent Measure
20 Sexual Aggressives	Rape	5	Maximum penile volume
	Consenting Sex	5	changes during the 100
	Nonsexual Violence	5	second stimulus.
20 Controls	Neutral	5	

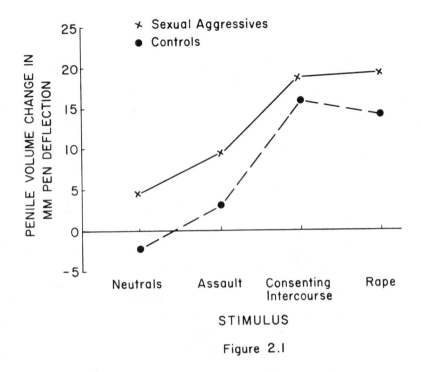

Figure 2.1

sponse to rape stimuli by the total response to the intercourse stimuli. Three Ss were not tested. One in each group refused phallometric testing and one SA was deaf.

Results.   The SAs tended to react more in general than controls but not differentially to rape and consenting intercourse.[10] Figure 2.1 shows the reactions of the two groups to the four types of stimuli. SAs did not differ from controls on any stimulus but both groups reacted more to rape and consenting intercourse descriptions than to nonsexual violence and in turn, than to neutral stimuli.[11]

When the SAs are broken down into sadists and nonsadists, the results were the same.[12] The results are depicted in Fig. 2.2. In *no* case did any group react differentially to rape and consenting intercourse. Each group reacted significantly more to rape and consenting intercourse than to violence or neutrals. Results are distorted by variance and total responsiveness of the three groups. Nonsadistic sexual aggressives had twice the penile output of controls. Sadists responded least and showed a flatter curve.

The rape index was computed for the three groups (Table 2.3) and there were no significant differences. The assault index (sum of penile responses to nonsexual assault divided by sum of responses to consenting intercourse) was com-

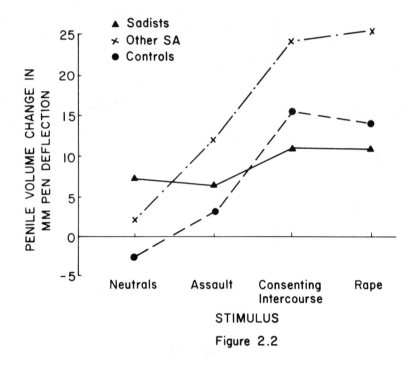

Figure 2.2

puted. Results were nonsignificant. The rape index and assault index were not significantly correlated with degree of force used in the sexual offence (-0.00 and $+0.20$ respectively). Overall the results suggest that the rape index and stimuli used to depict rape and consenting intercourse were not useful in discriminating SAs and controls.

TABLE 2.3
The Rape Index Results

	Mean	S.D.
Sadists (N = 7)	0.85	0.57
Nonsadist SAs (N = 9)	2.30	3.78
Controls (N = 15)	1.41	2.26

Note: F = 0.65, p > 05 for three groups but inhomogeneity of variance was a problem. When sadists were removed, cells were homogeneous but results were still nonsignificant. There was no problem for total SAs vs. controls: t-test = 0.27, p > 05. An assault index = Sum Assault/Sum Consenting Intercourse was computed but was nonsignificant. Also computed was (R-N)/(I-N) where R = sum responses to rape stimuli, N = sum responses to neutrals and I = sum to intercourse stimuli. It too was nonsignificant.

TABLE 2.4
The Derogatis Sexual Functioning Inventory (DSFI) T-Scores for
Sadists, Nonsadistic Sexual Aggressives and Controls

Scale	Sadists (N = 7)		Nonsadist SAs (N = 10)		Control (N = 17)	
	%T < 30	%T > 70	%T < 30	%T > 70	%T < 30	%T > 70
Information	17	0	13	50	7	7
Experience	20	0	0	60	14	14
Drive	0	20	0	56	0	71
Attitudes	43	0	20	20	6	18
Symptoms	43	14	38	25	19	6
Affects	17	50	10	20	0	53
Gender Role	14	14	50	10	24	24
Fantasy	0	57	0	50	0	29
Body Image	14	0	20	20	6	24
Satisfaction	71	0	56	0	41	0

Note: The number of cases fluctuates somewhat because scores were not computed if any item on a scale was not answered.

TABLE 2.5
Clarke Sex History Scales for Sadists, Nonsadist SAs and Controls

	Mean		
	Sadists (N = 7)	Nonsadist SAs (N = 11)	Controls (N = 17)
1. Heterosexual Adult Frequency	10.86	14.17	16.35
2. Heterosexual Pedophilic Frequency	3.14	0.00	0.06
3. Heterosexual Pubescent Frequency	2.43	1.58	0.00
4. Homosexual Adult Frequency	0.14	1.58	0.71
5. Homosexual Pedophilic Frequency	0.00	0.00	0.00
6. Homosexual Pubescent Frequency	0.00	0.00	0.00
7. Crossdressing	1.14	0.83	0.47
8. Voyeurism	0.86	1.33	0.94
9. Obscene Calls	0.14	0.33	0.00
10. Toucheurism and Frottage*	1.29[a]	0.75[ab]	0.23[b]
11. Sadism and Masochism*	1.00[a]	0.42[ab]	0.06[b]
12. Group Sex	0.14	0.50	0.82
13. Exhibition Frequency*	1.29[a]	0.42[ab]	0.06[b]
14. Exhibiting Behavior**	4.14[a]	1.92	1.00

Note: Maximum scores are respectively, (1) 20, (2) 23, (3) 23, (4) 13, (5) 13, (6) 13, (7) 12, (8) 6, (9) 2, (10) 6, (11) 14, (12) 2, (13) 5, (14) 11.
*p < .05, **p < .01. Means with same superscript are not significantly different.

Sex History

Two inventories were used to compare the groups, the Derogatis Sexual Functioning Inventory (DSFI, Derogatis, 1978) and the Clarke SHQ (Paitich, Langevin, Freeman, Mann, & Handy, 1977).

Results. Table 2.4 shows the results for the DSFI. There were no group mean differences on any scale but trends in the distribution of the T-scores are of interest. A large proportion of nonsadistic SAs rated as more informed than

TABLE 2.6
SHQ Items Comparison of Sadists, Nonsadistic SAs and Controls

	Sadists (N = 8)	Nonsadist SAs (N = 11)	Controls (N = 18)
% Any Contact			
Adult Female	100	100	100
Female 12 and Under	13	0	0
Female 13–15	13	9	0
Adult Male	0	18	11
Male 12 and Under	0	0	0
Male 13–15	0	0	0
% Responses Ever			
Heterosexual Intercourse†	75	82	100
Crossdressing—underwear	25	18	11
Crossdressing—underwear—orgasmic	13	18	0
Peeping	38	27	22
Peeping—orgasmic*	13	27[a]	0
Obscene Calls	13	18	0
Obscene Calls—orgasmic†	0	18	0
Exhibiting	25	18	0
Exhibiting—orgasmic	0	9	0
Frottage & Toucheurism‡	38	55	0
Frottage & Toucheurism—orgasmic	13	27	0
Sadism:			
Hurt, Humiliate, Embarrass	25	9	0
Hurt, Humiliate, Embarrass—orgasmic	0	0	0
Threaten or Frighten†	25	0	0
Threaten or Frighten—orgasmic	13	0	0
Beat	0	9	0
Beat—orgasmic	0	9	0
Someone Unconscious/Unable to move	25	18	0
Someone Unconscious/Unable to move—orgasmic	0	9	0
"Rape" (Attempt Intercourse)**	63[a]	45[ab]	0[b]
"Rape"—orgasmic	25	18	0

Note: ‡These acts occur in lonely places rather than public ones.
†p < .10, *p < .05, **p < .01. Means with the same superscript are not significantly different.

TABLE 2.7
Self Reported Incidence of Sexual Dysfunction Among Sadists,
Nonsadist Sexual Aggressives and Controls

	% Group		
	Sadists (N = 8)	Nonsadist SAs (N = 11)	Controls (N = 18)
Impotence	25	9	33
Premature Ejaculation	0	18	6
Retarded Ejaculation	25	18	6
Considers Self Sexually Inadequate**	63[a]	45	28
Considers Self Sexually Abnormal**	63	64	11[a]
Losing Interest in Sex*	38[a]	9[ab]	0[b]
Worry About Latent Homosexuality[†]	38	9	6

Note: *p < .05, **p < .01. Means with same superscript are not significantly different.

average about sex, had more experience than the other two groups and like controls had a higher sex drive. Fantasy was higher in both SA groups than in controls but all groups were dissatisfied with their sexual outlet at present, most likely due to incarceration.

Four of the Clarke SHQ scales were significant (Table 2.5). All groups showed a lack of sexual experience with men of any age and with female minors.[13] The groups differed in toucheurism and frottage, sadomasochism, exhibiting frequency, and exhibiting behavior. Sadists scored highest on all four scales but there was overlap of mean scores with those of nonsadists. There was also a trend for sadists to less often have experienced heterosexual intercourse and more often be sexually aroused by threatening or frightening their victims and to have attempted intercourse in their "rapes" (Table 2.6). Both groups of SAs were polymorphous in the sexual outlets they had tried. Four of the sexual aggressives (two sadists and two nonsadists) dressed in female clothes for sexual gratification. Although the number of cases is small, they suggest that fetishism, bondage, stealing the garments, their texture, or that the garments were worn previously by a female, played a role in this erotic act.

Forty four percent of sadists were married, 55% of nonsadist SAs, and 30% of controls were. The difference was not statistically significant. A Marital Relations Questionnaire (cf. Paitich, 1973) provides six scores; overall marital adjustment, companionship, consensus, affectional intimacy, partner accommodation, and a halo effect. There were no significant group differences. There were no group differences in the reported incidence of impotence, and premature, or retarded ejaculation (Table 2.7). Both SA groups considered themselves sexually inadequate and abnormal significantly more often than controls. Sadists worried that they were losing interest in sex.

Many claims have been made about sexual aggressives' attitudes to women. A collection of 16 items did not support the stereotype of the Don Juan, the sexist

TABLE 2.8
Attitudes About Women Among Sadists, Nonsadist Sexual
Aggressives and Controls

| | %| | |
	Sadists (N = 8)	Nonsadist SAs (N = 11)	Controls (N = 18)
1. Intercourse is more exciting—if woman resists	25	27	6
2. —if woman is forced	13	0	0
3. —if I hit her	0	0	0
4. Women divide into pure and good vs. dirty and cheap	25	9	33
5. Men approach women for dates but they have all the say	63	55	39
6. Women have more control than men in their relationships	75	36	28
7. Men and Women's roles should be kept separate with no overlap	38	18	11
8. Men should not do women's work	38	0	11
9. I have to decribe myself as possessive in relationships with women	63	45	67
10. I believe a man should have as many sex partners as possible	13	0	22
11. I like to tell other men about my sexual experiences	13	18	17
12. Sex outside marriage is o.k. for men but a woman should be a virgin when she marries	25	0	6
13. I find it difficult to talk to women*	75	36	11
14. I don't like to flirt with women	63	18	22
15. Outside of sex, I have little in common with women	13	27	0
16. Women tend to make me angry*	38	9	0

Note: *p < .05.

bigot, or the angry male since only two items were significant (Table 2.8). Sadists differed from the other two groups on the two items. They found it difficult to talk to women who also tended to make them angry. There are trends in the data, however, which suggest the items be examined again in a larger sample.

Feminine Gender Identity and Androgyny

The Bem (1974) Sex Role Inventory (BSRI) and the Feminine Gender Identity Scale (Freund, Langevin, Satterberg, & Steiner, 1977) were used to examine androgyny and gender identity.

TABLE 2.9
A Comparison of the Bem Sex Role Inventory (BSRI)
Scales in Sexual Aggressives and Controls

	Scale Means		
	Masculinity	Femininity	Androgyny*
Sadists (N = 7)	4.54	4.84	−0.30
Nonsadist SAs (N = 10)	4.53	4.26	0.27
Total SAs (N = 17)	4.53	4.50	0.03
Controls (N = 18)	4.69	4.41	0.28

Note: *For Androgyny only, two groups t = 2.78, p < 05, three groups
F = 0.90, p > 05.

Results. The Bem (1974) androgyny scale was significant for the two group
comparison with sexual aggressives being more androgynous (Table 2.9). However, when sadists were separated as a group, the results were nonsignificant
although the sadists showed a trend to greater femininity. The scores for the FGI
scale were clearer.

TABLE 2.10A
Feminine Gender Identity in Sexual Aggressives
and Controls

	Mean Scores		
	Duration*	Intensity†	Sum**
Sadists (N = 7)	−5.14[a]	−6.43	−3.57[a]
Nonsadist SAs (N = 9)	−12.22[ab]	−16.89	−8.33
Total SAs (N = 16)	−9.12	−12.31	−6.25
Controls (N = 15)	−15.80[b]	−19.20	−9.25

TABLE 2.10B
FGI in Study Groups Excluding Crossdressers

	Mean Scores		
	Duration**	Intensity*	Sum*
Sadists (N = 5)	−3.40[a]	−3.60[a]	−3.20[a]
Nonsadist SAs (N = 7).	−10.86[ab]	−14.00[ab]	−7.71
Controls (N = 15)	−15.80[b]	−19.20[b]	−9.25

Note: *Duration is significant for both 2 and 3 group comparisons at p < 05;
†Intensity only for 3 group comparisons at p < .10. **Sum is significant at
p < 05 for two groups, p < 01 for 3 groups. Superscripts a, b are similar to other
use in this chapter.

Two scorings of the FGI scale were used, those reported by Freund et al. (1977) and one described in more detail in Chapter 10. Results were similar for both methods but somewhat stronger for the revised scoring. Only the latter is reported in Table 2.10A and Table 2.10B. The SAs scored higher on all measures and when sadists were sorted out it was thcy who differed most from controls. All groups were masculine identified but the sadists were indifferent/ambivalent or perhaps feminine.[14] When the four men who crossdressed for erotic gratification were excluded, these results remained significant and were similar.

PREDICTOR 2 - BRAIN PATHOLOGY

Brain pathology was assessed in two ways, anatomically by the CT-Scan and behaviorally by the Reitan Battery (Reitan, 1979). The SAs and controls were administered the CT-Scan and Reitan battery in the standard fashion by a trained person. The two groups were compared by Hotelling T-test to offer a multivariate solution to the question. Reitan results were excluded for one SA because he was drinking just before testing. Data from two controls were excluded because of their reading difficulties.

Results.   The CT scans were examined for any pathology and then for temporal lobe damage. Table 2.11 shows that although 45% of all cases had some pathology, there were no significant differences in the two groups. When sadists were compared to nonsadists there was again no overall difference. However, the sadists alone showed significant temporal lobe damage. Fifty six percent of the sadists showed it and it was most often right temporal horn dilation and atrophy or a structural anomaly in being visible on the CT scan when it should not have been.

The overall results for the WAIS and Reitan battery were nonsignificant for SAs versus controls. Only Block Design on the WAIS was significant and results

TABLE 2.11
CT Scan Results of Sexual Aggressives and Controls

	% SA (N = 20)	% Control (N = 18)
Any Pathology	50	39
Temporal Lobe Pathology	30	11

	% Sadists (N = 9)	% Nonsadist SA (N = 11)
Any Pathology	67	36
Temporal Lobe Pathology*	56	0

Note: *p < .05.

TABLE 2.12
Reitan Battery Results for Sadists, Nonsadist SAs and Controls

| Test | Mean Errors/Score | | |
	Sadists (N = 6)	Nonsadist SAs (N = 11)	Controls (N = 17)
Speech Perception*	11.7[a]	4.9	6.2
Rhythm	6.5	2.8	4.2
Aphasia Screening	0.2	0.0	0.1
Tapping Dominant	41.8	46.2	48.9
Tapping Nondominant	37.7	41.3	45.1
Tactile Perception—Time	17.1	12.8	11.8
—Memory	6.0	7.2	6.4
—Location	3.0	3.4	4.4
Sensory Perception	0.0	0.0	0.1
Trails*	173.0[a]	98.0	110.0
Categories	38.5	36.7	25.8
Impairment Index*	0.48[a]	0.23	0.24
% I.I. > 51	33%	8%	18%
% Right Handed	100%	83%	76%

Note: [a]This group is significantly different from the other two.
*p < .05.

were weak with SAs scoring lower than controls (Means 10.3 and 12.1, respectively).[15] Scores were generally within normal limits. Mean IQs were average (sadists 96, other SAs 103, and controls, 105). Although the Reitan Impairment Index was slightly higher in SAs than in controls (0.33 vs. 0.24), results were nonsignificant.

When the SAs are broken down into sadists and nonsadists, some useful information emerges. WAIS results remained nonsignificant but Reitan Speech Perception, Trails, and overall impairment index (I.I.) were significant (Table 2.12). The indices were different for sadists versus the other two groups, but only 33% of sadists had an index over 0.51, the cutoff point for significant brain damage.

The CT scan results suggest that sadists show right temporal lobe abnormalities and there is weak support for that damage on the Reitan battery but not on the WAIS. Results could not be explained on the basis of previous head injury.[16]

PREDICTOR 3—SEX HORMONES

The SAs and controls had blood drawn between 8:00 a.m. and 10:30 a.m.[17] A radioimmunoassay procedure described in more detail in Chapter 10 was used for hormone analysis. Three samples were drawn at approximately 15 minute inter-

vals as suggested by Goldziehr, Dozier, Smith, & Steinberger, (1976). Total testosterone, LH, FSH, estradiol, DHAS, androstenedione, cortisol, and prolactin were assayed along with liver functioning, namely GGT. More details about assay method are presented in Chapter 10. A 3x3 multivariate analysis of variance was used to compare the three groups on three samples using the eight hormone values as dependent variables.

Medical History

The two groups were comparable in their medical history, overall, but marginally significant differences occurred on three items. Thirty percent of SAs reported a history of ulcers, 20% bowel disease, and 20% skin disease such as psoriasis. No control reported these problems. The sadists were the ones reporting problems. There were no other significant differences including head injuries. One SA case had corrective surgery for hypospadias. In general the groups were healthy at the time of examination.

Hormone Results

The results for one sadist were eliminated before the analyses reported here because they caused statistical problems. He was a suspected Klinefelter's Syndrome or had a testicular anomaly in which LH and FSH were both over 80 IU/1 although testosterone was average at 483 ng/dl.[18] A second case was eliminated because of lowered testosterone, likely from medication. He had hypospadias

TABLE 2.13
A Comparison of Mean Hormone Levels for Sadists,
Nonsadist SAs and Controls

Hormone	Unit of Measure	Sadists (N = 6)	Nonsadist SAs (N = 9)	Controls (N = 16)
Testosterone	ng/dl	793	917	786
Androstenedione	nM/l	7.43	9.71	7.46
DHAS*	uM/l	13.43[ab]	14.35[b]	9.65[a]
LH	IU/l	12.43	10.19	13.04
FSH	IU/l	8.84	8.93	10.24
Estradiol	ng/dl	46.43	57.50	52.58
Prolactin	ug/l	10.74	11.45	13.81
Cortisol	ug/dl	13.77	19.70	16.67
GGT††	I.U.	28.00	28.87	29.63

Note: *p < .05. Means with the same superscript are not significantly different.

††This is not a hormone but an enzyme used as an index of liver functioning. Group results were nonsignificant and were not significantly correlated with hormone values.

and other ureteral abnormalities but had only been off medication (provera 100 mg/daily + major tranquillizers) for three days prior to the blood sample. We therefore thought his results might be confounded and excluded them.

Manova was significant for the three group comparison, but not for trials or for the group by trial interaction.[19] Mean values for the three groups are presented in Table 2.13. In univariate analysis only DHAS was significant and both SA groups scored higher than controls. Discriminant analyses showed that the trends in the data for prolactin and cortisol also contributed to the multivariate effect distinguishing the three groups.

The results suggest that adrenal production of sex hormones may be important in sexual aggressives. Although the sample size is too small to permit any firm conclusions, the results indicate that further investigation of sex hormones in SAs is worthwhile. Second, results suggest that sex hormones other than testosterone may hold important information about sexual aggression.

PREDICTOR 4—SUBSTANCE ABUSE

Alcohol

The two groups were compared on the MAST scale (Selzer, 1971) and on penile reactions to erotic stimuli. The SAs and controls were administered sufficient alcohol to produce a BAL of 50 mg.% and then shown the erotic slides. The stimuli varied from neutral and weak erotic valence through five levels to strong valence. No one who was alcoholic was solicited for the study and this presented one limitation for ethical reasons. Only nine cases were used. Unfortunately the most important cases could not be examined. The dependent variables were maximum penile volume change within 30 and 60 seconds after stimulus onset.[20]

Results.   Initially we had the expectation that alcohol would reduce penile output to erotica. As Fig. 2.3 shows, both SAs and controls reacted more than expected to the alcohol condition. We therefore conducted the study reported in Chapter 4 on 48 normal community volunteers. The group from the study in the 50 mg% condition are shown in Fig. 2.3. Both SAs and offender controls reacted even more than these community volunteers. However, the numbers are small, the variance in response is large, and the penile output of the offenders is confounded with the effect of alcohol. All that can be said at this time is that small amounts of alcohol may increase (or at least, not reduce) penile erection, and SAs are no exception to that finding. A further investigation would have to control for base rate penile reactivity as well as drinking history to sort out the influence of alcohol per se on reactions to erotica.

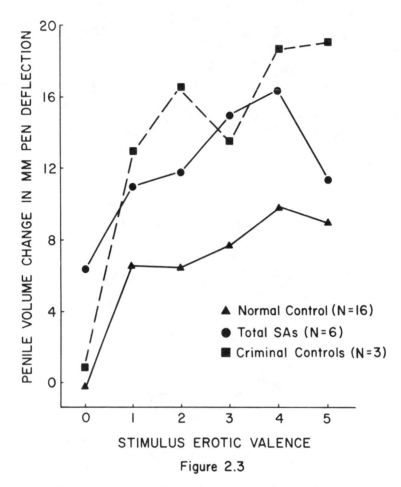

Figure 2.3

Effect of 50 mg % Alcohol on Penile Volume Changes
to Erotica in Sexual Aggressives & Controls

There were no significant group differences on the MAST.[21] However, significant numbers of cases in each group scored in the alcoholic range (Table 2.14) indicating that alcoholism was a serious problem in all groups.

Drugs

Results. Our survey asked about the current frequency, maximum frequency ever, and the affect accompanying the use of a variety of drugs listed in Table 2.15. The control group significantly more often used tranquillizers, cocaine, and hallucinogens than sexual aggressives collectively did. Of those using any

TABLE 2.14
MAST Scores for Sadists, Nonsadist SAs and Controls

	MAST Scores					
	Mean	SD	Minimum	Maximum	% Over 5	% Over 8
Sadists (N = 6)	6.5	5.2	0	15	50	33
Nonsadist SAs (N = 11)	18.4	12.7	4	36	82	64
Controls (N = 17)	12.6	10.8	0	35	76	53

Note: A score over 8 was used to define "alcoholic". χ^2 for "5" cut off = 2.16, df = 2, p > .10 and for "8" χ^2 = 1.77, df = 2, p > .10. Total "alcoholics" with "5" cutoff 74% and with "8" cutoff, 53%.

drug listed in Table 2.15, the current frequency of use and past maximum use were not significantly different in any case. The controls tended to feel pleasant or happy more often than sexual aggressives did on minor tranquillizers and marijuana and more often to feel superior on alcohol. However controls more often felt depressed as the effects of alcohol wore off.

A three group comparison was also made. The sadists differed from the other two groups only in using marijuana, amphetamines, and hallucinogens less often. The nonsadistic SAs were much more comparable to controls on use of

TABLE 2.15
Drug Usage by Sexual Aggressives and Controls

	Percent of Cases		
Drug Used	Sadists (N = 8)	Nonsadist SAs (N = 11)	Controls (N = 17)
Minor Tranquillizers	25	25	59
Marijuana Derivatives**	13	75	71
Alcohol	75	92	94
Amphetamines†	13	42	59
Barbiturates	13	8	29
Cocaine	13	9	41
Narcotics	14	9	24
PCP	13	17	35
Hallucinogens*	13	42	65
Solvents	0	0	6
Bolt, Rush & Bang	0	0	12

Note: †p < 10, *p < 05, **p < 01. For SAs combined versus controls, minor tranquillizers, cocaine and hallucinogens were significant, all p < 05. Number of cases may vary slightly from drug to drug.

these drugs when sadists are separated out. Obviously sample size is influencing results but further investigation appears warranted.

At the time of the offence, 62% were under the influence of drugs or alcohol but there was no significant group difference in their use (56% SAs, 69% controls). However, only 25% of sadists were using drugs or alcohol compared to 80% of nonsadistic sexual aggressives. They differed significantly from the other two groups.[22]

PREDICTOR 5—AGGRESSION

The Buss-Durkee Hostility Inventory, MMPI, and our own questionnaire were used to offer a perspective on aggressive tendencies. The two groups were compared by one-way multivariate analysis of variance and discriminant analysis.

Results.   The Buss-Durkee Hostility Inventory (Buss & Durkee, 1957) offers eight scales: assault, indirect hostility, irritability, negativism, resentment, suspicion, verbal hostility, and guilt. SAs scored higher only on assault.[23] All scales of the inventory were nonsignificant when the three groups were compared.

Clarke History of Aggression Test.   Nested in our own exploratory 186 item questionnaire on personal background were 62 items on aggression, predominantly reflecting the use of physical force currently, in the past, or as part of family upbringing. Of the 62 items, only six were statistically significant and the

TABLE 2.16
Aggression History of Sadists, Nonsadistic Sexual Aggressives
and Controls

Item	*Mean*		
	Sadists *(N = 8)*	*Nonsadist SAs* *(N = 11)*	*Controls* *(N = 18)*
1. Physical Punishment for Bed Wetting*	2.12	1.18	1.22
2. Ever Hit a Brother*	1.25[a]	2.82	2.39
3. Number of Times Injured Others in Fights*	1.25[a]	2.27	2.55
4. Women Tend to Make Me Angry*	1.62[a]	1.90[ab]	2.00[b]
5. Collects Weapons*	2.00	1.50[a]	1.83
6. Punished for Having Temper Tantrums As A Child*	1.75[ab]	1.30[a]	1.83[b]

Note: *$p < 05$. Means with same superscript are not significantly different. No superscript = range effect only. Items are a 5 point scale: 1 = none, 2 = a little, 3 = some, 4 = quite a lot, 5 = a great deal. For item #4–6, 1 = true, 2 = false.

TABLE 2.17
The MMPI Scores of Sadists, Nonsadistic SAs and Controls

Item	Mean		
	Sadists (N = 8)	Nonsadist SAs (N = 10)	Controls (N = 17)
L**	6.0[b]	4.2[ab]	3.5[a]
F*	15.2[a]	8.2	7.7
K	12.7	15.1	13.0
Hypochondriasis	13.7	14.9	11.8
Depression	25.9	22.5	20.7
Hysteria	22.0	22.9	19.7
Psychopathic Deviate	26.6	31.0	28.0
Masculinity—femininity	28.7	26.6	26.1
Paranoia	14.4	11.7	10.6
Psychasthenia	32.7	29.3	27.4
Schizophrenia*	39.4[b]	32.8[ab]	27.0[a]
Mania	24.1	23.2	24.3
Social Introversion	34.5	28.0	25.8

Note: *p < .05, **p < .01. Means with same superscript are not significantly different.

effects were weak (Table 2.16). One can readily interpret this finding to mean that SAs in general do not differ from nonviolent criminals and the term "sexual aggressive" is a misnomer. Ironically the group sexually aroused by force, the sadists, reported the least aggression on the six items, compared to the other groups.[24]

Personality was examined for aggressiveness.[25] In particular, MMPI profile types were scrutinized. Results (Table 2.17) showed that only MMPI, Lie, F, and Schizophrenia scales were significant, with sadists scoring highest in each case. The trend was for sadists to be more devious and confused in their thinking. T-score results supported only the L scales mean findings although p < 0.10 for F, Schizophrenia, and masculinity-femininity. Again sadists stand out with higher scores than the other two groups showing somewhat more confusion and femininity. There was a broad spectrum of MMPI profile types, but there was a trend for controls to have more 4-9/9-4 (Psychopathic Deviate-Mania) profiles (35% controls versus 9% nonsadistic SAs and 0% sadists). No one had a 4-3 (Psychopathic Deviate-Hysteria) profile and one control and one nonsadist SA had a 4-8 (Psychopathic Deviate-Schizophrenia) profile. In general findings from the literature were not supported.[26]

Violence. The traditional indicators of violence, enuresis, firesetting, and cruelty to animals (Table 2.18), did not differentiate the three groups. However, the incidence of firesetting and weapon collecting among the SAs is noteworthy.

There were no significant differences in parent child relations among groups as measured by the Clarke Parent Child Relations Questionnaire but the frequency of disturbed relations in all groups is noteworthy.

CRITERION VARIABLES - DANGEROUSNESS

Three psychiatrists each independently assessed the SAs in the study for: amount of force used in the offence, likelihood of recidivism, the extent of force likely to be used in *foreseeable future* offences, a global rating of dangerousness, and scores on a Dangerousness Rating Scale (Slomen, Webster, & Butler, 1979). Reliability of ratings were assessed by interclass correlation. Each psychiatrist had access to the same materials. The composite ratings from the three psychiatrists were correlated with those items showing significant group differences.

Results.   There were 26 items assessed on the Dangerousness scale plus the three predictor items. Only 14 items were reliable[27] and are listed in Table 2.19. Of these, only four were statistically significant at p < .05 in the three group comparison. Even in the latter cases, differences were weak. Nonsadistic SAs

TABLE 2.18
Indicators of Violence Proneness in Sadists, Nonsadistic Sexual
Aggressives and Controls

	% Group		
Item	Sadists (N = 8)	Nonsadist SAs (N = 11)	Controls (N = 18)
Enuresis after age 5	13	0	0
Firesetting	37	18	6
Cruel to Animals	13	27	33
Torture or Kill Cat	13	9	11
Torture or Kill Dog	0	0	11
Truancy†	25	27	67
Weapon Collecting†	0	45	17
Any Stealing As A Child	37	73	83
Contact with Police			
—before 12 years of age	0	18	6
—12–16 years old	71	55	61
Juvenile Court	14	27	33
Visit to Psychiatrist			
—before 12 years of age	14	0	11
—12–16 years old	43	9	50

Note: †p < .10.

TABLE 2.19
Psychiatric Ratings of Dangerousness for Sadists, Nonsadist SAs
and Controls

Item	Sadists	Nonsadist SAs	Controls
Hostility**	4.12	4.65	3.45
Anger**	4.19	4.65	3.41
Emotional Overcontrol	4.18	4.17	4.65
Emotional Undercontrol	3.88	4.13	3.52
Tolerance†	4.12	3.52	4.43
Environmental Support	3.71	3.78	4.28
Dangerousness Increased Under Alcohol*	4.80	5.36	4.21
Dangerousness Increased Under Drugs*	5.57	4.72	3.76
Patient Manipulative During Interview	3.25	3.09	3.41
Danger to Self at Present	3.59	2.65	2.79
Danger to Self in Future	4.12	3.09	3.07
Amount of Force Used in Rapes (Sex Assaults)	2.18	1.61	—
Likelihood of Using Force of Same Kind in Foreseeable Future	2.47	1.70	—
Likelihood of Acting Out Sexually, in Forseeable Future	2.53	1.61	—

Note: The last three variables mainly concern SAs. No comparisons were statistically significant. When total SAs are compared to controls on hostility and anger, results were significant. When sadists and nonsadist SAs are compared, only "danger to self at present" was significant $F = 6.76$, $p < .05$.
  †$p < .10$, *$p < .05$, **$p < .01$.

scored highest on hostility, anger, and on "dangerousness increased under alcohol." The trend was for sadists to use more force in sexual assaults and they were rated as more likely to use similar force and to act out in the foreseeable future. Group differences were nonsignificant, however and it is noteworthy that some sadists worked at containing their sexual impulses.

Reliable ratings of: (1) "degree of force used in the rape", (2) "likelihood of using similar force in the foreseeable future"; and (3) "likelihood of acting out sexually in the foreseeable future" were correlated with all predictor variables. Noteworthy was the fact that no aggression measure, gender identity, parent child relation, or SHQ item correlated significantly. Reitan Tapping and Verbal IQ minus Performance IQ score correlated significantly with all three measures (range, $r = .43$ to .57). Degree of force used correlated also with "stealing as a child" (.42), WAIS Information ($-.44$), Vocabulary ($-.45$), MMPI Hypochondriasis (.54), Hysteria (.44), and Paranoia (.42). Likelihood of using force or sexually acting out correlated with nonuse of tranquillizing drugs ($-.42$ and $-.40$ respectively). Likelihood of future force correlated also to MMPI Hypoc-

hondriasis (.48), Paranoia (.42), and Reitan categories scores (− .42). In general there was some relationship of brain pathology to criterion variables but overall the predictors and criteria were unrelated.

DISCUSSION

At the outset, it must be clear that pilot data of the foregoing sort is inadequate and a full scale study must be done on a large sample. However, it has served a useful purpose. Because so little is known about sexual aggressives, the study has pointed out the direction for further investigation.

The findings may be summarized as follows:

Rape Index	Does not discriminate rapists and nonrapists.
Sex History	Sadists show more toucheurism and frottage, exhibiting and sadomasochism. Some SAs crossdress orgasmically.
Gender Identity	Sadists are feminine identified or undifferentiated.
Alcohol & Drugs	Abuse common in all groups, but least in sadists.
Sex Hormones	LH and FSH may be abnormal in some sadists. DHAS, cortisol and prolactin may be elevated in rapists in general.
Brain Pathology	Right temporal lobe abnormalities in sadists.
Aggression	Not discriminating.

The sex history of the SAs in our sample was surprising. Sadists were more common than in many other samples (45%). The nature of their acts has been relegated to fantasy but clearly actual force and even destruction of the victim are important in many cases. We know that control, fear and terror, injury, and unconsciousness play a role but we are ignorant about the relative importance of each of these components and what other factors may be important. The postulated lack of experience and information in rapists appear to be incorrect. The opposite in fact may be true such that they have an inordinate interest in and need for sex.

The rape index and the relative arousal value of rape versus consenting intercourse were not useful in the present study. This may be for two reasons. First, many rapists prefer sexual intercourse with an adult female and there is nothing inherently attractive about rape—it is stolen sex. Therefore one may not expect differential reactions to rape and consenting intercourse. Second, some other factors appear operative in the SAs who do manifest a sexual anomaly. The sadists derive some gratification from rape that is more than the pleasure of intercourse but we have not clearly mapped its features to date. Thus rape descriptions can be hit and miss.

The consistent finding of orgasmic crossdressing is also incongruous and does not fit our stereotype of the SA. Although peeping, exhibiting, touching, and rape cluster together as courtship disorders (Freund, Scher, & Hucker, 1983), crossdressing does not make sense. It runs across both sadists and nonsadists. Its meaning and role for the sexual aggressive are unknown. Feminine gender identity or ambivalence about gender is also an important feature of SAs not previously reported.

Sex hormone results were interesting because alcohol and drug abuse were associated with normal testosterone levels. One may expect that substance abuse will not dampen sex drive, at least in young men. In fact some substances like alcohol may enhance sexual experiences. This finding merits careful further investigation. The results of LH and FSH suggest Klinefelter's Syndrome in one case of a sadist. His testosterone level was normal. It was the incongruous levels of *both* testosterone and LH/FSH that was informative. It is clear that previous studies that only examined testosterone may have missed this information. The significant DHAS findings have not been reported previously in this group. A complete hormone profile on a large group of rapists would be informative. One may also wish to pursue genetic investigation in this area because there was one case (5% SAs, 11% sadists) with suspected Klinefelter's Syndrome that may relate to a brain anomaly and possibly to a hormonal abnormality in some sadists since no gross insult to the cortex was obvious in this group.[28]

Brain pathology in the form of a right temporal lobe abnormality may be important in understanding sadism. Uncontrolled case and group studies have suggested that: (a) many sexual anomalies are associated with temporal lobe abnormalities; (b) the temporal lobe is associated with sexual arousal (see Chapter 5); and (c) impotence and/or aggressiveness are associated with temporal lobe epilepsy. All findings suggest further investigation of cortical activity and structure in relation to sexual arousal in sadists. It remains to be shown whether the temporal horn abnormality found in this study is peculiar to sexual sadism or is shared with other sexual anomalies and with nonsexual "sadism".

It is noteworthy that the new CT scan detected the temporal lobe anomaly in sadists but WAIS and Reitan findings were only suggestive. It appears the latter could be dropped in future investigations. The cause of the temporal horn abnormality in sadists is unknown at present. There was no obvious head injury reported but a more thorough examination of early hospital records including information on birth difficulties may be more revealing. The temporal horn is especially susceptible to reduced energy production by asphyxia, carbon monoxide poisoning, respiratory failure, and hypoglycemia (Green, 1964). According to Pincus and Tucker (1978), as a possible consequence of this susceptibility, the hippocampus has the lowest seizure threshold in the cortex. However, one does not see a preponderance of epilepsy in sexually anomalous men but a brain abnormality may be operative nonetheless.

Very little work has been done on sex hormone levels in rapists. Understandably cost is an important consideration in hormone assays, but there were interesting findings in our study on LH, FSH, and DHAS. Sex "drive" level has not been satisfactorily studied in connection with sex hormones.[29] Testosterone correlates with frequency of sexual outlet or penile reactivity in the .30 to .40 range (e.g., Langevin, Paitich, Ramsay, Anderson, Kamrad, Pope, Geller, & Newman, 1979; Salmimies, Kockott, Pirke, Vogt, & Schill, 1982) . Some rapists appeared to have very high drive levels and complained that they masturbated several times a day. One has to wonder whether satyriasis is not a key factor in rape. Green (1964) noted that damage to Ammons horn is associated with increased adrenocorticoid output. It might be fruitful to examine the adrenal gland further in reference to sex drive.

Alcohol and drug abuse were prominent in SAs but also in controls. It is therefore difficult to ascribe sexual aggression to substance abuse per se. However, alcohol in particular may interact with a high sexual reactivity to increase the probability of sexual acting out. We can surmise that alcohol increases sexual reactivity and elicits erotic reactions that are indiscriminate (See Chapter 4). At the very least alcohol does not reduce penile reactivity. The role of tolerance is not well understood. Certainly the results indicate that the role of alcohol is important and its relation to sexual arousal has been oversimplified and/or misconstrued.

The study of aggression in our sample was problematic. As indicated in the introduction, there are almost no psychometrically acceptable measures of aggression/violence proneness. In the present study most scales of the Buss-Durkee Hostility Inventory proved unacceptable. Our own collection of aggression items formed a reliable scale but there were few differences in SAs and controls. Thus the issue is: are measures of general aggression/violence inadequate or are sexual aggressives not really generally aggressive after all? A satisfactory scale to examine aggression is needed before an answer can be provided. It is also possible that SAs do not perceive the extent to which they are violent. Living in an aggressive environment may dull their sensitivity. It may be fruitful to contrast their self report of aggression to those of external observers in order to test the hypothesis.[30]

The SAs divided into two groups: sadists and nonsadistic SAs. They were characterized by:

Sadists	*Nonsadistic SAs*
1. Sexual arousal to sadistic stimuli/courtship disorders	Normal sex/courtship disorders
2. Less alcohol/drug abuse	More alcohol/drug abuse
3. Sex hormones—DHAS elevated; LH and FSH in one case	Higher DHAS

Sadists	Nonsadistic SAs
4. Feminine gender identity/ ambivalence	Normal—masculine
5. Aggression high in sex acts	Aggression less or used for compliance in the rape
6. Right temporal lobe abnormal	Nonspecific brain pathology—alcohol/drug abuse related

Many hypotheses have been generated from this pilot investigation of sexual aggression. The present results suggest that sadism is a separate sexual anomaly. It seems it is part of an *erotic violence syndrome* and future work can establish its construct validity. Nonsadistic SAs may be normal men with a high sex drive and an antisocial history that allows them to act out their needs in socially unacceptable ways. A full range of sexological investigation is needed first and foremost to understand the problem.

ACKNOWLEDGMENTS

This study was supported by NIMH grant #1 R01 MH 34430-01 and a grant from the Clarke Foundation. Portions of the study were presented at the annual meeting of the International Academy for Sex Research, Copenhagen, Denmark, August, 1982.

REFERENCES

Abel, G. G., Barlow, D. H., Blanchard, E. B., & Guild, D. The components of rapists' sexual arousal. *Archives of General Psychiatry*, 1977, *34*, 895–903.

Adebimpe, V. B. Physical violence in the concept of dangerousness: A case report. *American Journal of Psychiatry*, 1977, *134*, 203–204.

Armentrout, J. A., & Hauer, A. L. MMPI's of rapists of adults, rapists of children, and non-rapist sex offenders. *Journal of Clinical Psychology*, 1978, *34*, 330–332.

Bain, J. Personal communication, 1982.

Barbaree, H. E., Marshall, W. L., & Lanthier, R. D. Deviant sexual arousal in rapists. *Behavior Research and Therapy*, 1979, *17*, 215–222.

Bem, S. The measurement of psychological androgyny. *Journal of Consulting and Clinical Psychology*, 1974, *42*, 155–162.

Blumer, D. Changes of sexual behavior related to temporal lobe disorders in man. *Journal of Sex Research*, 1970, *6*, 173–180.

Brittain, R. The sadistic murderer. *Medicine Science and The Law*, 1970, *10*, 198–207.

Buhrich, N., Theile, H., Yaw, A. & Crawford, A. Plasma testosterone, serum FSH and serum LH levels in transvestism. *Archives of Sexual Behavior*, 1979, *8*, 49–53.

Buss, A. H., & Durkee, A. An inventory for assessing different kinds of hostility. *Journal of Consulting Psychology*, 1957, *21*, 343–349.

Carter, C. S., & Davis, J. M. Effects of drugs on sexual arousal and performance. In J. Myer, C.

Schmidt, & T. Wise, (Eds.) *Clinical management of sexual disorders*. Baltimore: The Williams & Wilkins Company, 1983.

Cocozza, J. J., & Steadman, H. J. Some refinements in the measurement and prediction of dangerous behavior. *American Journal of Psychiatry*, 1974, *131*, 1012–1014.

Cormier, B. M., & Simons, S. P. The problem of the dangerous sexual offender. *Canadian Psychiatric Association Journal*, 1969, *14*, 329–335.

Crabtree, J. M., & Moyer, K. E. *Bibliography of aggressive behavior: a reader's guide to the research literature*. New York: A.R. Liss Inc., 1977.

Derogatis, L. *The Derogatis Sexual Functioning Inventory* (DSFI), Leonard R. Derogatis, 1228 Wine Spring Lane, Baltimore, Md., 21204, 1978.

Dix, G. E. Determining the continued dangerousness of psychologically abnormal sex offenders. *The Journal of Psychiatry and Law*, 1975, *3*, 327–344.

Doering, C. H., Brodie, H. K. H., Kraemer, H., Becker, H., & Hamburg, D. A. Plasma testosterone levels and psychologic measures in men over a 2 month period. In R. C. Friedan, R. M. Richart, R. L. Vandeviele, & L. D. Stern (Eds.), *Sex differences in behavior*. New York: Wiley, 1974.

Doering, C. H., Brodie, H. K. H., Kraemer, H., Moos, R. H., Becker, H. B., & Hamburg, D. A. Negative affect and plasma testosterone: A longitudinal human study. *Psychosomatic Medicine*, 1975, *37*, 484–491.

Ehrenkranz, J., Bliss, E., & Sheard, M. H. Plasma testosterone: Correlation with aggressive behavior and social dominance in man. *Psychosomatic Medicine*, 1974, *36*, 469–475.

Epstein, A. W. Relationship of fetishism and transvestism to brain and particularly to temporal lobe dysfunction. *Journal of Nervous & Mental Disease*, 1961, *133*, 247–253.

Freund, K. Diagnosis and treatment of forensically significant anomalous erotic preferences. *Canadian Journal of Criminology and Corrections*, 1976, *18*, 181–189.

Freund, K., Langevin, R., & Barlow, D. Comparison of two penile measures of erotic arousal. *Behavior Research & Therapy*, 1974, *12*, 355–359.

Freund, K., Langevin, R., Satterberg, J., & Steiner, B. Extension of the gender identity scale for males. *Archives of Sexual Behavior*, 1977, *6*, 507–519.

Freund, K., Scher, H., & Hucker, S. The courtship disorders. *Archives of Sexual Behavior*, 1983, *12*, 369–379.

Goldzieher, J. W., Dozier, T., Smith, K., & Steinberger, E. Improving the diagnostic reliability of rapidly fluctuating plasma hormone levels by optimized multiple sampling techniques. *Journal of Clinical Endocrinological Metabloism*, 1976, *43*, 824.

Green, J. D. The hippocampus. *Physiological Reviews*, 1964, *44*, 561–608.

Greenland, C. *Research strategies in the evaluation of violent and dangerous behavior associated with mental disorders*. Paper presented at the 13th GWAN Meeting, Committee on Violence and its Social Aspects, Montreal, 1970.

Greenland, C. Evaluation of violence and dangerous behavior associated with mental illness. *Seminars in Psychiatry*, 1971, *3*, 345–356.

Hoenig, J., & Kenna, J. EEG abnormalities and transsexualism. *British Journal of Psychiatry*, 1979, *134*, 293–300.

Huesmann, L. R., Lefkowitz, M. M., & Eron, L. D. Sum of MMPI Scales F, 4, and 9 as a measure of aggression. *Journal of Consulting and Clinical Psychology*, 1978, *46*, 1071–1078.

Kalant, O. J. *The amphetamines: Toxicity and addiction*, Toronto: University of Toronto Press, 1973.

Kolarsky, A., Freund, K., Machek, J., & Polak, O. Male sexual deviation: association with early temporal lobe damage. *Archives of General Psychiatry*, 1967, *17*, 735–743.

Kreuz, L. E., & Rose, R. M. Assessment of aggressive behavior and plasma testosterone in young criminal population. *Psychosomatic Medicine*, 1972, *34*, 321–332.

Langevin, R. *Sexual strands: Understanding and treating sexual anomalies in men.* Hillsdale, N.J.: Lawrence Erlbaum Associates, 1983(a).

Langevin, R. *Clinical investigations into violent behavior.* Paper presented at the annual meeting of the Canadian Psychiatric Association, Ottawa, 1983(b).

Langevin, R., & Martin, M. Can erotic responses be classically conditioned? *Behavior Therapy,* 1975, *6,* 350–355.

Langevin, R., Paitich, D., Ramsay, G., Anderson, C., Kamrad, J., Pope, S., Geller, G., & Newman, S. Experimental studies in the etiology of genital exhibitionism. *Archives of Sexual Behavior,* 1979, *8,* 307–331.

Langevin, R., Paitich, D., & Steiner, E. The clinical profile of male transsexuals living as females vs. those living as males. *Archives of Sexual Behavior,* 1977, *6,* 143–154.

Lothstein, L. M., & Jones, P. Discriminating violent individuals by means of various psychological tests. *Journal of Personality Assessment,* 1978, *42,* 237–243.

MacCulloch, M. J., Snowden, P. R., Wood, P. J. W., & Mills, H. E. On the genesis of sadistic behavior: The sadistic fantasy syndrome. *British Journal of Psychiatry,* 1983, *143,* 20–29.

Malamuth, N. M. Rape fantasies as a function of exposure to violent sexual stimuli. *Archives of Sexual Behavior,* 1981, *10,* 33–47.

McCreary, C. P. Trait and type differences among male and female assaultive and nonassaultive offenders. *Journal of Personality Assessment,* 1976, *40,* 617–621.

McEwen, B. Neural gonadal steroid actions. *Science,* 1981, *211,* 1303–1311.

Megargee, E. I. The prediction of dangerous behavior. *Criminal Justice and Behavior,* 1976, *3,* 3–22.

Mello, N. K., & Mendelson, J. H. Alcohol and human behavior. In L. L. Iversen, S. D. Iversen, & S. H. Snyder, (Eds.), *Handbook of psychopharmacology.* New York: Plenum Press, 1978.

Mendelson, J. H. Endocrines and aggression. *Psychopharmacology Bulletin,* 1977, *13,* 22–23.

Mendelson, J. H., & Mello, N. Biologic concomitants of alcoholism. *New England Journal of Medicine,* 1979, *301,* 912–921.

Mendelson, J. H., Dietz, P. E., & Ellingboe, J. Postmortem plasma luteinizing hormone levels and antemortem violence. *Pharmacology, Biochemistry & Behavior,* 1982, *17,* 171–173.

Meyer-Bahlburg, H. F. Hormones and homosexuality. *Psychiatric Clinics of North America,* 1980, *3,* 349–364.

Meyer-Bahlburg, H. F. Sex hormones and male homosexuality in comparative perspective. *Archives of Sexual Behavior,* 1977, *6,* 297–325.

Meyer-Bahlburg, H. F., Nat, R., Boon, D. A., Sharma, M., & Edward, J. A. Aggressiveness and testosterone measures in man. *Psychosomatic Medicine,* 1974, *36,* 269–274.

Monti, P. M., Brown, W. A., & Corriveau, D. P. Testosterone and components of aggressive and sexual behavior in man. *American Journal of Psychiatry,* 1977, *134,* 692–694.

Paitich, D. A comprehensive automated psychological examination and report (CAPER). *Behavioral Science,* 1973, *18,* 131–136.

Paitich, D., Langevin, R., Freeman, R., Mann, K., & Handy, L. The Clarke SHQ: A clinical sex history questionnaire for males. *Archives of Sexual Behavior,* 1977, *6,* 421–436.

Panton, J.H. Personality differences appearing between rapists of adults, rapists of children and non-violent sexual molesters of female children. *Research Communications in Psychology, Psychiatry and Behavior,* 1978, *3,* 385–393.

Persky, H., O'Brien, C. P., Fine, E., Howard, W. J., Khan, M. A., & Beck, R. W. The effect of alcohol and smoking on testosterone function and aggression in chronic alcoholics. *American Journal of Psychiatry,* 1977, *134,* 621–625.

Persky, H., Smith, K. D., & Basu, G. K. Relation of psychologic measures of aggression and hostility to testosterone production in man. *Psychosomatic Medicine,* 1971, *33,* 265–277.

Pincus, J. H., & Tucker, G. J. *Behavioral neurology.* New York: Oxford University Press, 1978.

Quinsey, V. L. Assessments of the dangerousness of mental patients held in maximum security. *International Journal of Law & Psychiatry*, 1979, *2*, 389–406.

Quinsey, V. L., Chaplin, T. C., & Varney, G. A comparison of rapists' and non-sex offenders' sexual preferences for mutually consenting sex, rape and sadistic acts. *Behavioral Assessment*, 1981, *3*, 127–135.

Quinsey, V. L., & Chaplin, T. C. Penile responses to nonsexual violence among rapists. *Criminal Justice & Behavior*, 1982, *9*, 372–381.

Rada, R. T. Alcoholism and forcible rape. *American Journal of Psychiatry*, 1975, *132*, 444–446.

Rada, R. T. *Clinical aspects of the rapists.* New York: Grune & Stratton, 1978.

Rada, R. T., Laws, D. R., & Kellner, R. Plasma testosterone levels in the rapist, *Psychosomatic Medicine*, 1976, *38*, 257–268.

Rada, R. T., Laws, D. R., Kellner, R., Stivastava, L., & Peake, G. Plasma androgens in violent and nonviolent sex offenders. *Bulletin of the American Academy of Psychiatry and the Law*, 1983, *11*, 149–158.

Rader, C. M. MMPI profile types of exposers, rapists, and assaulters in a court services population. *Journal of Consulting and Clinical Psychology*, 1977, *45*, 61–69.

Reitan, R. M. *Manual for administration of neuropsychological test battery for adults & children.* Tucson, AZ: Neuropsychology Laboratory, 1979.

Rose, R. Testosterone, aggression and homosexuality: A review of the literature and implications for future research. In E. J. Sachar (Ed.), *Topics on psychoendocrinology.* New York: Grune & Stratton, 1975.

Rubin, B. Prediction of dangerousness in mentally ill criminals. *Archives of General Psychiatry*, 1972, *27*, 397–407.

Salmimies, P., Kockott, G., Pirke, K. M., Vogt, H. J., & Schill, W. B. Effects of testosterone replacement on sexual behavior in hypogonadal men. *Archives of Sexual Behavior*, 1982, *11*, 345–353.

Scaramella, T. J., & Brown, W. A. Serum testosterone and aggressiveness in hockey players. *Psychosomatic Medicine*, 1978, *40*, 262–265.

Selkin, J. Rape. *Psychology Today*, 1975, *8*, 71–76.

Selzer, M. The Michigan Alcoholism Screening Test: The quest for a new diagnostic instrument. *American Journal of Psychiatry*, 1971, *127*, 1653–1658.

Sheard, M. H., Marini, J. K., & Giddings, S. S. The effect of lithium on luteinizing hormone and testosterone in man. *Diseases of the Nervous System*, 1977, *38*, 765–769.

Slomen, D., Webster, C. D., & Butler, B. T. *Assessment of dangerous behavior: Two new scales.* Working paper in forensic psychiatry, #14, Toronto: METFORS, 1979.

Spellacy, F. Neuropsychological differences between violent and nonviolent adolescents. *Journal of Clinical Psychology*, 1977, *33*, 966–969.

Spellacy, F. Neuropsychological discrimination between violent and nonviolent men. *Journal of Clinical Psychology*, 1978, *34*, 49–52.

Taylor, D. C. Sexual behavior and temporal lobe epilepsy. *Archives of Neurology*, 1969, *21*, 510–516.

Tennent, T. G. The dangerous offender. *British Journal of Hospital Medicine*, 1971, *6*, 269–274.

ENDNOTES

Note 1. In this paper, we discuss sexual aggression (SA) against adult females which includes cases of indecent assault as well as attempted rape and rape. The main feature of concern is that some form of erotic body contact was *taken by*

force or threat. Since legal definitions of rape often require that the female victim's vagina be penetrated by the male's penis, demonstrated rape is a relatively infrequent aspect of sexual aggression. In fact, Selkin (1975) indicated that intercourse occurred in less than half of the "rape" cases in Denver during the year of his study. Oral-genital sex and anal intercourse were often forced but they may only result in a charge of indecent assault.

Note 2. See Rada (1978) for a review of those factors in rape.

Note 3. Shakespeare has been quoted as evidence of this longstanding belief. In Act II, Scene III of Macbeth, Macduff asked the porter what drink especially provokes. The porter notes: ". . . lechery it provokes and unprovokes. It provokes the desire but takes away the performance." In contrast, it is interesting that Carter and Davis (1983) note the frequency with which medical books of 1890–1920 list alcohol as an aphrodisiac.

Note 4. See Rose (1975) and Doering et al. (1975) for examples.

Note 5. See Crabtree and Moyer (1977) for a bibliography of this extensive literature.

Note 6. See McEwen (1981) for a review.

Note 7. See Langevin (1983b) for more details.

Note 8. See also Adebimpe (1977), Dix (1975), and Cormier & Simons (1969), Cocozza & Steadman, (1974), Megargee, (1976).

Note 9. In previous work, we found that this procedure effectively counters fatigue effects and confounding of results from repetition of stimulus classes.

Note 10. The response in the first 10 seconds (R1) and the maximum response in 100 seconds (RMax) were used. Only three effects were significant - blocks of trials, stimulus, and stimulus by blocks. F tests results were: for stimulus R1 $F = 2.17$, $p > 05$; R Max $F = 42.40$, $p < 0001$; App $F = 20.29$, $p < 0001$; for blocks R1 $F = 4.76$, $p < 001$; R Max $F = 2.69$, $p < 05$; App $F = 3.25$, $p < 001$. For stimulus by Block R1 $F = 2.14$, $p < 05$, R Max $F = 1.23$, $p > 05$ App $F = 1.59$, $p < 05$. R1 appeared to be more sensitive to subject's expectations. In general all effects should be nonsignificant but individual variation was great and in some cases subjects were extremely reactive.

Note 11. The group by stimulus interaction should be significant but it was not $F < 1$ for R1, R Max and App F. It should be noted that gross inhomogeneity of variance was a problem, F max > 1000. Data transformations were tried with Z scores within persons being best, reducing F max $= 21.42$, still excessive but closer to acceptable limits. Results were the same with a trend to larger F values for the significant effects.

Note 12. Block and stimulus effects remained significant but the stimulus by block effect was nonsignificant and there was now a significant group by stimulus interaction. The block effect $F = 2.96$, $p < .05$ and the stimulus effect $F = 46.64$, $p < .0001$, group by stimulus effect $F = 9.58$, $p < .01$. Only univariate analyses on R Max are reported here.

Note 13. The variability in sexual experience is noteworthy within all groups on the SHQ. This creates problems of homogeneity of variance in analysis of variance. Such was the case on scales 2, 4, 11, and 13 in Table 2.5.

Note 14. On the older scoring, they would be called more feminine but see Chapter 10 for a discussion of this point.

Note 15. This result may have been influenced by previous testing. Psychologists often use block designs alone as an indicator of IQ or of work habits and brain damage. Some men had been administered it before, some were unsure if they had. Hotellings T values for SAs vs controls and Wilks Lambda for the two and three group comparison were nonsignificant for WAIS but significant for the Reitan in the three group analysis.

WAIS   2 groups   T=1.10, p > .05   3 groups Approx.   F=0.79, p > .05.
Reitan   2 groups   T=0.74, p > .05   3 groups Approx.   F=1.87, p < .05.

Note 16. Three of the SAs (1 sadist and 2 nonsadists) had serious head injuries or brain diseases during their lives and four controls did. Group differences were statistically nonsignificant. SAs versus controls $\chi^2 = 0.11$; for sadists, other SAs and controls $\chi^2 = 0.20$, both p > 05. Injuries were not systematically related to CT scans or Reitan results but the numbers of cases are so small, this conclusion is tentative.

Note 17. During the course of drawing blood we became aware that the SA group had a fear of needles beyond normal expectation. Four of them did and one SA refused to give blood compared to only one control. Two nonsadistic SAs were very distressed but insistent that blood be taken. One conveyed a macho male image throughout his stay with us which may have made him insistent about giving blood. However he threw up after. The other nonsadist SA said he would rather be punched in that face than have a needle stuck in him but he too was insistent. He blanched and almost passed out. The two sadists who showed some fear surprisingly were both borderline mentally retarded. The finding was unexpected and we have been looking at it since the study. It appears to be a phobia of neurotic proportions associated with anxiety states, hypochondriasis, and night terrors. The SAs' behavior is complex and an examination of neurotic traits may prove worthwhile.

Note 18. Klinefelter's Syndrome was suspected but could not be confirmed by karyotyping for ethical considerations. This man's testicles were small but not diminutive as usually seen in Klinefelter cases. There was not gynecamastia evident but then he was very thin.

Note 19. The results with all available cases analyzed were grossly distorted by one case noted in the paper. His values for LH and FSH were so discrepant (88.0 and 97.6 vs. 12.43 and 8.84 for the rest of his group) they caused inhomogeneity of variance. A second case was eliminated because he had been administered provera and elavil among other major tranquillizers which affect hormone values. When the two cases were eliminated, results were:

	Group F	Time Sample F	Interaction F
Estradiol	0.18	2.99	0.32
LH	0.71	1.19	1.31
FSH	0.41	0.52	0.91
Prolactin	1.10	4.24*	1.41
Cortisol	1.59	1.98	0.43
DHAS	4.54*	0.71	0.29
Androstenedione	1.43	6.24**	0.32
Testosterone	0.89	1.46	1.60
Manova App.F	1.95*	1.28	0.92

*$p < .05$, **$p < .01$. Both prolactin and androstenedione values decreased for second and third samples but they were still highly correlated with the initial sample. Results were essentially the same for a two group comparison of all SA cases versus controls. Estradiol was not included in the Manova in order to keep the number of cases higher in an already small sample.

Note 20. See Chapter 4 for more details about method.

Note 21. A check on the internal consistency of the MAST showed alpha reliability to be 0.86.

Note 22. $\chi^2 = 6.31$, df = 2, $p < .05$.

Note 23. Unfortunately, some scales lacked internal consistency. In the present study Alphas were:

Scale	Alpha
Assault	0.14
Indirect Hostility	−0.14
Irritability	0.46
Negativism	0.66
Resentment	0.64
Suspicion	0.62
Verbal Hostility	0.50
Guilt	0.70

For the two group comparison on the Assault scale, t = 2.05, $p < .05$, Mean SA 6.06, controls 4.33. Buss-Durkee's mean for college men on the Assault scale, 5.07, maximum score 10. There were no other significant differences in the two group comparison.

Note 24. The 62 items were examined for scale properties and alpha for the five point items was 0.85. The three groups did not differ significantly on total scores.

Note 25. Diagnosis was reported by three psychiatrists but since interrater agreement was unsatisfactory, the results will not be discussed here. Psychiatric

diagnosis is notorious for its unreliability but the problem was compounded here because of the preponderance of personality disorder diagnoses and alcohol/drug abuse. Even DSM III catergorization of personality disorders is incomplete and adequate validation and reliability for a system of evaluating personality disorders remains a task for the future. The line between substance abuse, experimentation, and regular heavy use is also a hard one to define. This contributed to disagreements for those diagnoses. Diagnostic validity and reliability in this problem area of sexual aggression is a large one in itself. Diagnosis should be considered with caution, especially when reliability is not reported.

Note 26. $\chi^2 = 5.12$, df = 2, p < .10. There is some dispute about the exact profile to be expected by aggressive men, some suggesting 4-3, others the 4-8 or 4-9 type (Armentrout & Hauer, 1978; Huesmann, Lefkowitz, & Eron, 1978; Lothstein & Jones, 1978; McCreary, 1976; Panton, 1978; Rader, 1977; Spellacy, 1977, 1978). In some reports it seems that mean group scores were used to compute profile type and the more clinically useful frequency of code types in each group was not computed. The former could distort results. The issue of profile type for aggressive men remains an open question.

Note 27. A generous cutoff point of alpha = 0.50 was used for inclusion and only 14 items met the criteria. Only three nonincluded items showed a group by rater interaction effect. The alphas for included items were: hostility, 0.68; anger, 0.61; emotional overcontrol, 0.65; emotional undercontrol, 0.56; tolerance, 0.73; environmental support, 0.67; dangerousness increased under alcohol, 0.73; dangerousness increased under drugs, 0.78; patient manipulative during interview, 0.74; global rating of: dangerousness to self at present, 0.54; to self in future 0.76; degree of force used in rape 0.84; likelihood of force in future, 0.92; likelihood to act out sexually in foreseeable future, 0.96.

Note 28. During the course of preparing this Chapter, one sadist was readmitted for assessment and he faced another rape charge. A chromosonal study showed him to be XYY. It is interesting that his testosterone levels were normal. Pilot investigation into other cases has begun as part of replication of the findings in this chapter.

Note 29. Some psychological theorists object to classification of sexual outlet as a drive along with hunger or thirst. There is no clear need satisfied by sex as there is for hunger in which individual survival is at stake. It is perhaps the complusive quality of sexual needs that has led to its common description as a "drive." In any case there are marked individual differences in sexual desire and outlet that need studying.

Note 30. We asked a series of questions on paper about the rapes. Many men said they did not rape even though they admitted to their charge. Some men redefined it out of their repertoire as "involving unnecessary force" or "seriously hurting someone" or by saying "I just wanted to make love." No one in our study blamed their victims for what happened but many seemed unaware of the psychological effect that the sexual attack could have on the women.

3 Voyeurism: Does It Predict Sexual Aggression or Violence in General?

Ron Langevin,
Daniel Paitich,
Anne E. Russon
Clarke Institute of Psychiatry, Toronto

Rapists are recognized as a dangerous group but often too late. It is believed that earlier identification may be evidenced in behaviors such as peeping or breaking and entering. Voyeurs in their own right are believed to be violent and dangerous. However no one, to our knowledge, has systematically examined them in a controlled study to test that hypothesis. Moreover, peeping is so common that it is difficult to distinguish the normal and abnormal individual doing it. If the average man peeps, it is a surrogate outlet, chance, or curiosity. When a sexually aggressive male does it, a sexual deviation label is applied. Could the peeping not serve the same purpose for both groups? In the two studies that follow, we are asking: Are voyeurs necessarily violent? Do they show tendencies to rape or carry out sexually aggressive acts?

MAJOR THEORIES

Although voyeurism has played a prominent part in several theories of sexual anomalies, there is almost no systematic research on the behavior. This is not surprising in one sense, because it is a difficult entity to isolate (cf. Gebhard, Gagnon, Pomeroy, & Christenson, 1965). Widespread public interest in pornography and strip shows attests to the power of visual experience to elicit sexual arousal in normal people. However, some theorists consider voyeurs (or "peepers") to be aggressive, to engage in break and enters, and even to rape. For some writers (see Smith, 1976) the object of peeping is also rather broad because

the men may watch solitary females undressing, watch the act of intercourse between male and female, or they may express an interest in filth (mysophilia), feces (coprophilia), and urine (urophilia). Since these latter anomalies are so rarely encountered in clinical settings and rarely reported in journals, examining their relationship to voyeurism is difficult. If we hope to identify violent voyeurs or those who will later become violent, it would seem important to clearly define a sexual anomaly rather than to accept all incidences of sexualized visual experiences as voyeurism. To be a sexual anomaly, there must be an *inordinate* interest in peeping such that total sexual energy (orgasm) is invested in the act of looking and it is preferred over sexual intercourse.[1] The present report examines both the sexual and violent nature of voyeurism. Smith (1976) and Yalom (1960) have reviewed the major theories and Gebhard et al. (1965) have conducted the only extensive empirical study in the professional literature on "peeping" per se. Therefore, the major theories need be reviewed only briefly.

Erotic Preference

Freud (in Saul, 1952) linked voyeurism and exhibitionism as two facets of scoptophilia (literally, love of looking). He indicated that they were aspects of the same problem in which sexual energy, normally invested in genital union, is totally used in the act of looking. More recently, Freund, Scher, and Hucker (1983) theorized that voyeurism along with exhibitionism, obscene calls, toucheurism, frotteurism, and rape were facets of a common underlying courtship disorder. The normal sequence of courtship is: seeking a partner, pretactile interaction, tactile interaction or foreplay, and finally intercourse. The sexually anomalous behaviors are progressive disorders of the courtship stages. Voyeurism represents an unusual searching stage; exhibiting and obscene calls, represent pretactile interaction; toucheurism and frottage, tactile interaction; and rape, a distortion of genital union. It is perhaps excessive investment of libido at the searching stage that forces the voyeur to act the way he does.

The studies of Gebhard et al. (1965), Freund et al. (1983), and Langevin, Paitich, Ramsay, Anderson, Kamrad, Pope, Geller, Pearl, and Newman (1979) suggest that voyeurism is related most to exhibitionism and perhaps to toucheurism, frotteurism, or rape. In Chapters 1 and 2 peeping was associated to some extent with rape. Seventeen percent of the rapists studied in Chapter 1 engaged in peeping with accompanying orgasm compared to 70% of a nonviolent multiple sexual anomaly group. In Chapter 2, 27% of nonsadistic rapists engaged in orgasmic peeping. Langevin et al. (1979) found that exhibitionists and heterosexual pedophiles were the two groups that engaged most in orgasmic voyeurism.

Freund et al. (1983) examined 139 sexually anomalous patients. Twenty four percent of the sample had peeped, most of whom were labelled exhibitionists (16%). Interestingly, only seven (5%) were considered voyeurs and five had no other reported sexual anomaly. However, two engaged in exhibiting and touch-

eurism and one in obscene calls. None of the 23 rapists in the sample had peeped, suggesting voyeurism is not linked to sexual violence.

Smith (1976), argued that some men are voyeurs because they lack the courtship skills needed to establish a relationship with a female. Presumably this means that such men really desire intercourse but do not know how to get it and must settle for less. Gebhard et al.'s (1965) study supported Smith's hypothesis because they concluded that voyeurs generally have inadequate heterosexual lives. Those men whose peeping activity was habitual tended to have more inadequate sex lives. Gebhard et al. noted the high incidence of homosexual acts among peepers and related this to their "stunted heterosexuality." The latter was reflected in fewer peepers having female friends and marrying, or if they married, having fewer extramarital affairs than other sex offenders.

Some facts suggest that voyeurism may not exist as a distinct clinical entity. First, it is extremely common that normal men peep, albeit not with accompanying orgasm. Second, there are very few empirical studies of the behavior indicating its rarity or the inability of clinicians to sort it out from normal acts. Third, Paitich, Langevin, Freeman, Mann and Handy (1977) examined a sample of over 400 sexually anomalous men who came to their forensic clinic during a 6 year period. They found so few cases of pure voyeurism that they wondered if it existed on its own at all.

Aggression

Voyeurism has been linked to crimes of violence, namely murder and arson, as well as to burglary (Yalom, 1960). One might expect that the night prowler who is looking for houses to burglarize will encounter, by chance, instances of sexual acts and of women undressing for bed. However, the association with homicide and arson is less obvious. Yalom (1960) indicated that voyeurism can be considered sadistic since the intention of the voyeur is to injure or humiliate the victim. He and Karpman (1957) stressed that it is the *forbiddenness* of voyeurism that makes it gratifying. According to these authors, voyeurs are not interested in strip shows because it is being *undetected* that is exciting. Similar pleasure is derived from burglary.

Karpman (1957) suggested that voyeurs have an unusual lack of curiosity. They may have been stifled in childhood and then later their curiosity was channelled into peeping. One may equally postulate the opposite; that from the beginning, they had a very high level of sexual curiosity since they observe and engage in a wide variety of sexual acts.

Karpman did not think voyeurism is related to assault but Yalom suggested that it is a defense against aggression. Evidently, some voyeurs do not contain their aggressive urges. Gebhard et al.'s (1965) empirical evidence questions these assertions because, although some peepers tended to have an extensive criminal history, 45% were convicted solely for sexual offenses. The majority of

their other offenses were minor in nature with burglary being the main felony, which the authors noted, is readily associated with peeping. Exhibitionism was the most common other sexual offense. It occurred in 43% of the cases but a noteworthy 20% of the offenses involved force. Thus, a minority of voyeurs may manifest aggressive tendencies.

Moncrieff and Pearson (1979) compared exhibitionist-voyeurs who had been sexually assaultive with men who were only exhibitionists. They reported that MMPI profiles were 4-8-9 (Psychopathic Deviate-Schizophrenia-Mania) for the assaultive exhibitionist-voyeurs and 8-2-4 (Schizophrenia-Depression-Psychopathic Deviate) for the nonassaultive group. The presence of elevated Psychopathic Deviate and Schizophrenia scale scores in the assaultive group was noteworthy compared to exhibitionists who looked relatively normal. Unfortunately a pure group of voyeurs was not examined.

Because voyeurism has been linked to violence, it merits careful scrutiny as a possible precursor and predictor of more serious aggression. Gebhard et al. described peepers as a mixed group including sociosexually underdeveloped men, mental defectives, situational cases, and drunks among other varieties. One can expect violence to be associated at least with some of their behaviors, aside from peeping. Perhaps the "voyeurism" seen in these men is normal behavior but it is given clinical significance because of their other behaviors. In the following two studies, the foregoing findings and speculations were examined.

STUDY ONE

Subjects

Because there were no exclusive voyeurs in a sample of 422 sexually anomalous men tested in a forensic clinic over a 6 year period, non-exclusive voyeurs were used. Three groups of men were compared. First, a normal nonpatient control group was selected from the data bank described earlier by Paitich et al. (1977), and the incidence of peeping ascertained. In all cases, these were nonorgasmic fotuituous instances of peeping and the frequencies were small. On the basis of discriminant analysis, a cutoff point was defined and two further groups were specified. A group of voyeurs who had at least 10 instances of peeping or secretly watching intercourse was first selected. The voyeurs had answered positively the question "Have you ever watched a man or women having sexual relations, since you were 16? How many times?"or "Since you were 16 have you ever secretly tried to see women undressing by looking in windows or by other means? How many times?" After the pertinent cases had been derived from the data bank, the fact that the patients had engaged in voyeurism and admitted engaging in this behavior was verified in their medical records. Six

TABLE 3.1A
Study 1: Composition of Voyeur
Group

Peeped more than other anomalous behavior	38%
Peeped as often as other anomalous behavior	27%
Peeped over 100 times	22%

cases in which this could not be confirmed or in which the information was
ambiguous were excluded. A third group of sexually anomalous men was randomly selected with the proviso that there be no evidence of peeping. All nonvoyeur patient controls were selected from a multiple sexual anomaly group
since this best matched the voyeurs to our knowledge.

In the end, there were 45 voyeurs, 52 sexually anomalous controls, and 52
nonpatient normal controls. Of the 45 voyeurs, 38% engaged in peeping more
often than in other sexually anomalous outlets and an additional 27% did it as
frequently as some other behavior. Twenty-two percent peeped over 100 times
(Table 3.1A).

There were significant group differences in age, education, and intelligence
(Table 3.1B). The voyeurs and anomalous contols were significantly older than
normal controls but the patient groups did not differ from each other. The patient
groups were significantly less educated than nonpatients. The voyeurs were also
less educated than the sexually anomalous control group. Although the majority
of patients showed average or slightly above average IQ, they were less intelligent than controls.[2] Thirty one percent of voyeurs were single compared to 62%
of anomalous controls and 87% of nonpatients.[3] This is contrary to Gebhard et
al.'s (1965) finding that voyeurs tended to be single.

TABLE 3.1B
Study 1: Age, Education and Intelligence Scores for Voyeurs and
Control Groups

		Group Mean		
		Voyeurs	Controls	Sexual Anomalies
Number of cases		45	52	52
Age in years	***	30.35	24.27[a]	29.77
Education in years	****	9.56[c]	14.86[a]	11.08[b]
Verbal IQ	****	103	117[a]	104
Raven IQ	**	106	119[a]	110

Note: **p < .01, ***p < 001, ****p < 0001. Means with same superscript are not significantly different.

Materials and Procedure

All research participants were administered the MMPI, 16PF, the Clarke Sex History Questionnaire for Males (Paitich et al., 1977), and the Clarke Parent Child Relations Questionnaire (Paitich & Langevin, 1976). Most also had a Vocabulary Test and the Raven Standard Progressive Matrices as well as other information described in more detail elsewhere (Paitich et al., 1977). Appropriate data will be noted in the results.

Five scales, derived from the MMPI Handbook (Dahlstrom & Dahlstrom, 1972–1975), were used to measure hostility and curiosity. *Acting Out Hostility*[4], *Manifest Hostility*[5], *Overcontrolled Hostility*[6] and two scales developed by the first author as face valid measures of curiosity: *Range of Interests*[7] and *Diversive Curiosity*[8]. All scales except Overcontrolled Hostility had satisfactory internal consistency but the former was used in spite of this problem because of its long research history. The curiosity measures were selected for their face validity although a more refined study is clearly needed.

RESULTS

The three groups were compared on sexual history, personality, parent child relations, and criminal history.[9]

Erotic Preferences

Sex History.   Summary data appear in Table 3.2 Compared to both patient and nonpatient controls, voyeurs had more overall heterosexual experience, heterosexual pedophilia, exhibiting, frottage, toucheurism, obscene phone calls, rape, outdoor masturbation, more overall masturbation, and a trend toward more crossdressing. They also had more homosexual experience than nonpatient controls but not more than the other sexually anomalous group. The homosexual outlets included pedophilia. The overall experience of both sexually anomalous groups was predominantly heterosexual but there was considerable individual variation in the frequencies of behaviors. The sexual histories of the voyeurs present a multifaceted picture that suggests that voyeurism is not a distinct entity.

A stepwise discriminant analysis was used to compare the major categories of sexually anomalous behaviors, *excluding* voyeurism. Exhibitionism best identified the voyeur group. Sixty two percent of the men in the three groups could be correctly classified with one item alone. The practice of masturbation while exhibiting characterizes voyeurs more so than the other patient group. The addition of the following, in order of power, increased the percentage correctly identifed to 74%: fellating 16-to 20-year-old males, heterosexual intercourse, frottage, and obscene calls. The association of peeping and exhibiting would seem to be a close one as noted elsewhere (Langevin et al., 1979).

TABLE 3.2
Study 1: Percent of Voyeurs and Control Groups Engaging in
Various Sexual Behaviors

Item		Percent of Cases		
		Voyeurs	Controls	Sex Anomalies
1. Heterosexual Intercourse	**	93	81	64
2. Heterosexual Pedophilia: Girls 12 or younger	****	35	2	12
3. Heterosexual Pedophilia: Girls 13–15 years old	**	36	2	23
4. Masturbation at least weekly in the past three months	**	100	83	94
5. Homosexual Pedophilia: boys 12 or younger	*	11	0	23
6. Homosexual Pedophilia: boys 13–15 year old	**	11	0	23
7. Homosexual Androphilia: 16–20 year old males	****	18	2	31
8. Homosexual Androphilia: men 21 or older	****	31	2	23
9. Crossdressing: Dress/Skirt	**	24	2	17
Undergarments		38	4	14
Stockings	*	27	0	12
Shoes		0	0	4
Jewellery		4	2	6
Wig		13	4	4
10. Voyeurism—at Intercourse	***	56	12	0
—at females undressing	****	96	25	0
11. Obscene Calls	***	22	2	6
12. Frottage	****	49	6	21
13. Toucheurism	****	44	8	10
14. Rape	*	22	0	6
15. Outdoor Masturbation	****	73	19	52
16. Exhibiting	****	56	0	39

Note: *p < .05, **p < .01, ***p < .001, ****p < .0001.

Voyeurs tended to start sexual play earlier in life than nonpatient controls but so did nonvoyeur patients. The former more often had sex play before the age of 12 with girls four to five years older or with grown up women. When they were 13-to 15-year-old, they were more likely to engage in similar experience but also to have had sex play with girls their own age. Contrary to expectation, voyeurs attended and enjoyed as many strip shows as controls did. Of the married men, 81% of voyeurs compared to 50% of patient controls had extramarital affairs.

The two spearate SHQ items used to identify voyeurs, peeping at intercourse and peeping at females disrobing, were not significantly correlated (r = −.25). The two items tended to relate to different clusters in the sex history questionnaire. Contrary to expectation, peeping at intercourse was related to increased heterosexual experience and peeping at females disrobing related to less homosexual experience. Only four men had peeped solely at intercourse and 14 solely at disrobing females. The majority had done both.[10]

Body Image.   Twelve questions about body image were administered:

1. Have you ever been ashamed to appear in a bathing suit?
2. Have you ever felt that you would like to change your physical appearance in some way?
3. Have you ever felt that you would like to be taller?
4. More muscular?
5. Stronger?
6. Heavier?
7. Have a more athletic build?
8. Be more athletic?
9. Do you think that you are reasonably attractive to the opposite sex?
10. Have you ever been ashamed to appear in the nude with persons of your own sex around?
11. Have you ever wished that you had a larger penis?
12. Do you think that your penis is smaller than average?

Four items were significant. Voyeurs less often were ashamed to appear in a bathing suit than the other two groups.[11] They wished more often that they were more muscular[12] and stronger.[13] They and nonpatients differed from the sex anomaly group in wishing less often that they were heavier.[14] Both patient groups wished more often than controls that their penises were larger[15] but did not think theirs' was smaller than average. Both patient groups also were afraid at some time that there was something wrong with their penises[16] but no control cases felt this way. In general, there was little that distinguished body image of voyeurs from the remaining groups.

Aggression

Personality.   Results for the MMPI appear in Table 3.3. All scales were significant with the exception of masculinity-femininity, the one scale often significant in sex research. The voyeurs scored higher than the other two groups on most scales reflecting greater overall pathology. Results were similar for T scores less than 70 versus those 70 or greater (not presented). Prominent elevations distinguishing voyeurs from the other two groups were F, Depression,

TABLE 3.3
Study 1: Mean MMPI Scale Scores for Voyeurs, Sexually Anomalous
and Normal Control Groups

Scale		Mean K Corrected Scores		
		Voyeurs	Normals	Sexual Anomalies
Lie	****	2.44[a]	4.61[c]	3.33[b]
F	****	6.89[a]	5.75	4.80
K	****	10.67[a]	16.56[c]	12.83[b]
Hypochondriasis	***	6.25[a]	3.18	4.63
Depression	****	27.35[a]	21.08	23.67
Hysteria	**	24.82[a]	22.02	21.17
Psychopathic deviate	****	31.58[c]	24.15[a]	27.42[b]
Masculinity-femininity		29.84	29.54	29.65
Paranoia	****	14.13[c]	10.29[a]	12.35[b]
Psychastenia	****	35.80[c]	27.50[a]	31.69[b]
Schizophrenia	****	40.87[c]	28.40[a]	33.65[b]
Mania	**	23.73[a]	20.56	21.21
Social introversion	****	34.42	25.02[a]	32.26

Note: *p < 05, **p < 01, ***p < 001, ****p < 0001. Means with the same superscript are not significantly different.

Percent of Ss correctly assigned to their own group in discriminant analysis: Overall 59%, Voyeurs 56%, Normals 83%, Sexual Anomalies 38%.

Hysteria, Psychopathic Deviate, Psychasthenia, and Schizophrenia which suggests serious emotional disturbance and a trend to psychosis. However on the 16PF (see Table 3.4) voyeurs were generally like the sexually anomalous control group and unlike the normal controls. Most voyeurs scored within normal limits, but they differed from the other two groups in responding more scrupulously (MD), in showing less emotional stability (Factor C), more shrewdness (Factor N), and less control (Factor Q3).

Diagnoses assigned by examining psychiatrists reflected a trend to greater pathology in the voyeurs than in the patient controls.[17] Although approximately half of the diagnoses were character disorders in both groups, 20% of the voyeurs had psychotic diagnoses compared to 2% of the patient controls. Only 2% of voyeurs had no diagnosis compared to 11% of patient controls[18] Thirteen percent of voyeurs were given a diagnosis of exhibitionism compared to 28% of patient controls. Only one voyeur (2%) had a diagnosis of voyeurism and 22% were polymorphous sexual deviation. No control had these latter two diagnoses.

The overall pathology shown on the MMPI and by diagnosis was also reflected in the significantly greater frequency of suicide attempts among the voyeurs compared to the other groups (range 0–6 attempts for voyeurs versus 0–3 for sex anomalies and none for nonpatient controls).[19] The voyeurs scored

significantly higher on the Acting Out Hostility and Manifest Hostility scales[20] than nonvoyeur patients, who in turn scored higher than normal controls. Voyeurs scored lower in Overcontrolled Hostility[21] than the other two groups and there were no other differences. There were no significant differences in either curiosity measure. Voyeurs, as a group, were more hostile than controls but average in curiosity.

Parent Child Relations.   Voyeurs reported more disturbed parent child relations than the other two groups did (Table 3.5). They, more than the men in the other two groups, considered their mothers and fathers to be aggressive to each other and to them. Voyeurs reported reciprocating aggression to their fathers but not to their mothers whom they also believed were less competent. Affection from both parents was considered low and strictness from mother was high although not different from strictness reported by the other sexually anomalous men. Finally, identification with both parents was reported as significantly lower in voyeurs than in the other two groups.

TABLE 3.4
Study 1: Mean Raw 16 PF Factor Scores for Voyeurs, Sexually
Anomalous and Normal Control Subjects

Factor			*Means*		
			Voyeurs	*Normals*	*Sexual Anomalies*
Md		****	5.78[a]	8.60[c]	7.23[b]
A	Reserved/Outgoing	**	6.67	8.00[a]	6.94
B	Less Intelligent/More Intelligent	***	4.29	5.13[a]	4.00
C	Affected by Feelings/Emotionally Stable	**	6.04[a]	7.85	7.17
E	Humble/Assertive		6.44	5.86	5.35
F	Sober/Happy-go-lucky		6.80	6.54	6.17
G	Expedient/Conscientious		5.73	5.58	6.38
H	Shy/Venturesome	****	5.02	7.21[a]	5.40
I	Tough-minded/Tender-minded	****	4.47	6.69[a]	5.33
L	Trusting/Suspicious	*	5.64[b]	4.40[a]	4.86[ab]
M	Practical/Imaginative	****	5.82	7.42[a]	5.35
N	Forthright/Shrewd	****	6.62[c]	4.11[a]	5.54[b]
O	Self-assured/Apprehensive	*	5.29	4.06[a]	5.60
Q1	Conservative/Experimenting	****	5.49	8.19[a]	5.71
Q2	Group dependent/Self sufficient	**	7.64	6.04[a]	7.44
Q3	Undisciplined self conflict/Controlled	***	5.60[a]	7.29	7.08
Q4	Relaxed/Tense	**	6.51[b]	4.60[a]	5.65[ab]

Note: *p < 05, **p < 01, ***p < 001, ****p < 0001. Means with the same superscript are not significantly different.

Percent of Ss correctly assigned to their own group in discriminant analysis: Overall 60%, Voyeurs 51%, Normal 77%, Sexual Anomalies 50%.

TABLE 3.5
Study 1: Mean Parent Child Relations Scale Scores for Voyeurs,
Sexually Anomalous, and Normal Control Subjects

Scale		Means		
		Voyeurs	Normals	Sexual Anomalies
MAS	**	8.78[a]	5.23	6.27
FAS	**	10.33[a]	6.23	7.40
SAM		3.64	2.81	2.94
SAF	*	3.84[b]	2.79[a]	3.08[ab]
MAF	*	11.71[a]	8.40	8.40
FAM	*	4.60[a]	3.33	3.25
MC	**	11.82[a]	14.65	15.15
FC		12.62	14.11	13.85
MAff	**	7.87[a]	9.98[b]	8.86[ab]
FAff	*	5.15	7.29[a]	5.77
MStr	**	6.04	4.00[a]	5.25
FStr		5.71	4.42	4.79
MId	****	3.20[a]	4.67	4.46
FId	**	3.09[a]	4.33	3.85
MInd		3.35	2.69	3.13
FInd		1.71	1.35	1.83

Note: $*p < 05$, $**p < 01$, $***p\ 001$, $****p < 0001$. Means with the same superscript are not significantly different. The name of each scale can be contructed using the following key. M = Mother, F = Father, S = Respondant, A = Aggression, C = Competence, Id = Identification, Ind = Indulgence.

Percent of Ss correctly assigned to their own group in discriminant analysis: Overall 58%, Voyeurs 67%, Normals 73% and Sexual Anomalies 35%.

Disturbance in the voyeur's family environment was further suggested by the more frequent occurrence of mental illness in mothers[22] as well as in fathers.[23] As children, voyeurs reported more often running away from home[24] and being in fist fights more often both before and after the age of 16.[25] Both parents were more often drunk[26] and father was more likely to be in trouble with the police.[27] Voyeurs less often than the other groups reported seeing their mothers nude to the waist[28] but there was considerable variation in this experience. They reported less often than the other groups that they remembered having their private parts washed by their mother.

The voyeurs displayed assaultive features that seem to be typical of rapists (Chapter 1). Contrary to Gebhard et al.'s (1965) findings there were no significant differences in number of brothers, of sisters, birth order, or of only children among the three groups.

Criminal History. Voyeurs and nonvoyeur patients did not differ in the frequency of sex offense convictions (range 0–7, average 1.27) but they did

differ in the frequency of other convictions. Voyeurs averaged 2.00 convictions (range 0–18) versus 0.32 for nonvoyeurs (range 0–5). The largest categories of charges for voyeurs were theft (22%), assault (18%), and breaking and entering (13%), and the largest for nonvoyeurs were drinking (9%) and drug charges (4%). Prowl by night charges (9%) also reflect the voyeur's combined peeping and theft activities. Significantly, 18% of voyeurs had assault charges including one wounding and arson. Four percent had charges related to carrying a concealed or illegal weapon and one individual was charged with abduction and indecent assault. The nonvoyeurs had low incidences of assault (2%), theft (2%), and weapon charges (2%). Thus theft and aggression appear to be minor but significant aspects of the voyeurs' behavior.

DISCUSSION

The voyeurs appeared to suffer more overall clinical pathology and were violent more often than the other groups. Their sexual histories were multifaceted which suggests that voyeurism is not a primary clinical entity in itself but an aspect of several other heterosexual behaviors. However the Sexual History Questionnaire items used in the study did not ascertain whether the voyeurism involved was orgasmic. In Study Two this fact was determined and a more discrete grouping was expected.

STUDY TWO

Subjects

Thirty four voyeurs were selected from a second data bank of admitting sex offenders using the same two peeping items used in Study One. Three cases were excluded because of unreliable information, leaving a total of 31. A nonvoyeur sexually anomalous control group was matched to the voyeurs, as far as possible, on the basis of diagnostic erotic preferences as described in the introduction (cf. also Langevin, 1983, Chapter 2). That is, for every "voyeur" labeled as a heterosexual pedophile or as an exhibitionist, and so on, a corresponding individual was selected from that diagnostic group with the proviso that he had not

TABLE 3.6A
Study 2: Composition of Voyeur
Group

Peeped more than other anomalous behavior	23%
Peeped as often as other anomalous behavior	23%
Peeped over 36 times	26%
Orgasmic peeping	26%

TABLE 3.6B
Study 2: Age, Education and Intelligence Scores for Voyeurs and
Control Groups

		Group Mean		
		Voyeurs	*Normals*	*Sexual Anomalies*
Number of cases		31	22	20
Age in years	*	31	24[a]	29
Verbal IQ	**	105[ab]	110[a]	105[b]

Note: *p < .05, **p < .01. Means with the same superscript are not significantly different.

peeped. There were only 20 individuals selected. However both voyeur and nonvoyeur groups had comparable proportions of men from each diagnostic group. The voyeurs, compared to the total sample in the data bank, had representative diagnoses as well. A third group of 22 normal controls was used for comparison. Of the 31 voyeurs, peeping was the most frequent or dominant outlet for only seven (23%). Another seven peeped as frequently as doing some other anomalous act (Table 3.6A).

There were significant group differences in age and intelligence but not in marital status (Table 3.6B). Fifty three percent of the voyeurs were single compared to 64% for controls and 40% of the sexually anomalous control group. There were no significant differences in age for the two patient groups but controls were younger. There was considerable overlap in the distribution of ages among the groups. Although nonpatients were significantly brighter than patients on the average, the distributions of scores overlapped considerably. There were no other significant differences.

Materials and Procedure

All research participants were administered the MMPI as well as the new Sex History Questionnaire (Appendix 1) which is more comprehensive than the old version used in Study One. It ascertains whether orgasm occurs in conjunction with a wider range of anomalous behaviors including peeping and it sample behaviors missed in the older instrument. Criminal record and medical record disgnosis were also available.

RESULTS

Erotic Behavior

Sex History. The sexual history profile of the three groups was different from that found in Study One. The voyeurs showed wide ranging behaviors again but they did not differ as markedly from the sexual anomaly control group. Both

groups engaged in sexual acts with females under 12 years of age, and with adult males more often than normal controls did but there was considerable variation in experience. Moreover the frequencies of these behaviors generally were low (Table 3.7). There were no significant differences in crossdressing although there was a trend for more voyeurs to try on female undergarments. There were no significant differences in toucheurism, frottage, rape, or obscene calls although voyeurs again showed a trend toward higher frequencies. The following

TABLE 3.7
Study 2: Sex History Results

		Percent Any Contacts		
Item		Voyeurs	Controls	Sex Anomalies
1. Heterosexual Intercourse		84	82	85
2. Heterosexual Pedophilia: Girls 12 or younger	*	32	0	20
3. Heterosexual Pedophilia: Girls 13–15 years old		26	0	20
4. Masturbation per week in the past three months				
5. Homosexual Pedophilia: boys 12 or younger		3	0	5
6. Homosexual Pedophilia: boys 13–15 year old		3	0	0
7. Homosexual Androphilia: 16–20 year old males		0	0	0
8. Homosexual Androphilia: men 21 or older	*	19	0	10
9. Crossdressing:				
Dress/Skirt		16(7)	14(0)	10(5)
Undergarments		36(23)	18(9)	15(10)
Stockings		23(10)	0(0)	0(0)
Shoes		16(3)	5(0)	0(0)
Jewellry		13(0)	14(0)	0(0)
Wig		16(3)	18(0)	10(0)
10. Voyeurism—at Intercourse	**	68(35)	14(0)	0(0)
—at females undressing	****	87(55)	23(0)	0(0)
11. Obscene Calls		16(13)	5(0)	5(0)
12. Frottage		32(10)	27(0)	15(5)
13. Toucheurism		26(6)	9(0)	5(5)
14. Rape		0(0)	5(0)	5(0)
15. Outdoor Masturbation	**	77	9	43
16. Exhibiting	***	74	0	70

The items of Study 2 refer to men 16 and older whereas those in Study 1 differentiate 16–20 and 21 or older. The values in brackets indicate the percent of behaviors accompanied by orgasm.
*p < .05, **p < .01, ***p < .001, ****p < .0001.

behaviors were absent in all groups: sexual arousal from hurting, threatening, frightening, beating someone, or having these acts done to the respondant, to seeing someone unconscious or unable to move, to animals, to fire, and the occurrence of incestuous acts with parents or siblings.

The two sexually anomalous groups contrasted with nonpatient controls in the frequency of exhibiting and outdoor masturbation. Voyeurs and community controls were similar in having more sexual experience with adult females than the sex anomaly control group did but differences among the three groups were nonsignificant. None of the groups had homosexual fantasies but voyeurs most often had fantasies of exposing to a female and of peeping. Again there was considerable overlap of average scores which made group discriminations difficult. When discriminant analysis was performed on key SHQ items, the results were similar to Study One. The best predictors were exhibiting items on which voyeurs scored highest. Contrary to expectation, frequency of peeping was not significantly related to heterosexual experience in the voyeur group.

The two items on peeping used to select the voyeur group were positively correlated in this study ($r = 0.52$). Peeping at intercourse was related to heterosexual pedophilia items, crossdressing, frottage, toucheurism, and exhibiting. Peeping at solitary females disrobing related to similar clusters of items with correlations of the same order of size (in the .30's).

TABLE 3.8
Study 2: Mean MMPI Results for Voyeurs and Control Groups

MMPI		K Corrected Raw Means		
		Voyeurs	Normals	Sexual Anomalies
Lie		3.40	3.82	4.67
F		10.57	7.26	8.33
K	*	10.93[a]	14.77[b]	14.11[ab]
Hypochondriasis		12.77	12.73	13.44
Depression		24.73	21.14	24.28
Hysteria		20.53	20.41	22.94
Psychopathic Deviate	**	29.10	23.91[a]	27.83
Masculinity-Femininity		29.13	28.32	26.94
Paranoia		12.40	9.82	12.28
Psychastenia		31.83	28.27	30.06
Schizophrenia	*	9.52[b]	7.28[a]	8.89[ab]
Mania		22.77	21.18	22.78
Social Introversion	**	33.80[b]	24.73[a]	30.00[ab]

Percent of Ss correctly assigned to their own group in discriminant analysis: Overall 54%, Voyeurs 87%, Normals 54%, Sexual Anomalies 0%.

*p < .05, **p < .01. Means with same superscript are not significantly different.

Aggression

Personality. Analyses were the same as those used in Study One. The MMPI findings for the three groups appear in Table 3.8. With the exception of the K Scale on which there was a trend for voyeurs to score lowest, there were no significant differences in the two patient groups and there was considerable overlap with nonpatient controls. The discriminant analysis produced nonsignificant results. Moreover there were only four significant scales in the univariate analysis and much less evidence of personality pathology in the voyeurs here as compared to Study One. There were no significant group differences in curiosity or in Overcontrolled Hostility but both Manifest Hostility and Acting Out Hostility scales were significant.[29] Voyeurs scored highest and significantly more so than the other groups on Manifest Hostility. They did not differ from patient controls on the Acting Out Hostility Scale.

There were no significant differences in the pattern of diagnoses for the two clinical groups as reported by examining psychiatrists (Table 3.9A and Table 3.9B). Only 10% of the voyeurs were considered psychotic and none neurotic but no control patient had these diagnoses. Sex deviation diagnoses were more prominently used in this sample with approximately 45% of both groups so labelled. Only 19% of voyeurs and 15% of controls had personality disorders and 16% and 23% respectively had no diagnosis. Of the sex deviations mentioned in

TABLE 3.9A
Study 2: Diagnosis of Voyeurs and Offender Controls

	% Voyeurs	% Sexual Anomalies
Psychotic	10	0
Neurotic	0	0
Personality Disorder	19	15
Sexual Deviation	45	46
Other	10	15
None	16	23
Selected Sexual Deviation Diagnoses		
Exhibitionism	61	54
Voyeurism	23	0
Polymorphous	3	8

TABLE 3.9B
Criminal Charges

Sex offence only	45	46
Theft/B&E	10	23
Violence	3	23
None	19	15

Percent may not total 100% due to rounding error.

primary, secondary, or tertiary diagnoses, 61% of voyeurs were considered exhibitionists, 23% voyeurs, and 3% polymorphous sex deviation. The percentages were 54%, 0%, and 8% respectively for patient controls. No one had an exclusive diagnosis of voyeurism.

Criminal History. Voyeurs did not differ from nonvoyeurs in frequency of sex offenses (mean 1.42 vs. 1.54, ranges 0–8 vs. 0–4, See Table 3.9B), but in this sample voyeurs had fewer nonsex offenses (mean 0.32) than nonvoyeur controls (mean 1.08). Forty five percent of the voyeurs had only sex offences in their records and 19% had no charges. Results were comparable for controls. More controls (23%) had charges of break and enter and theft than voyeurs (10%). Contrary to expectation only 3% of voyeurs had a violence related charge and 23% of controls did.

A COMPARISON OF THE TWO STUDIES

It appears from the two studies combined that voyeurism is a broad class of behaviors that can be present in almost any heterosexual anomaly. However there are puzzling differences in the two studies in terms of the presence of psychopathology in Study One and its relative absence in Study Two. In an earlier study, Langevin, Paitich, Freeman, Mann, and Handy (1978) found that gross personality disturbance was associated with a greater number of diverse sexual outlets. This seemed a ready explanation for the discrepancy in the two studies reported here. The total number of outlets was analyzed in both studies for patient groups only. There was a significant difference in the voyeurs and patient controls in Study One but it was not as large in Study Two.[30] Voyeurs in Study One had significantly more outlets than the control patients (mean 4.56 vs. 2.54, SDs 1.82 vs. 1.27 respectively, excluding voyeurism per se). The direction of results was similar in Study Two (means 2.70 vs. 1.70, SDs 1.55 and 1.08) but the voyeurs in Study One contrasted with all other groups in both studies in having more outlets.

When the number of diverse outlets was convaried for the MMPI and suicidal behaviors in Study One, the significance of the results was greatly reduced and the items on the attempts at suicide and suicidal ideation were now nonsignificant. The PCR results were nonsignificant after covariance analysis, with the exception of Mother Competence and Mother Identification. Thus, the differences in the outcome of the two studies may be explained on the basis of a greater incidence of polymorphous sexuality or group heterogeneity in Study One. When this incidence is lower, as in Study Two, the voyeur is not distinct from the multiple sexually anomalous patient. So one may conclude that both in sexual behavior and personality the voyeur does not appear to be discrete clinically and information on this problem would seem less pertinent than the other sexual manifestations.

For Study One a comparison was made of results for voyeurs in whom peeping equalled or exceeded other outlets versus those in whom it did not, and separately for the group who peeped over 100 times versus those who did it less. There were very few differences. In Study Two an additional comparison with voyeurs who were orgasmic was undertaken. Results showed that voyeurism and exhibitionism were the only consistently significant clusters of sexual behavior. Comparing cases in which voyeurism was a *dominant* outlet and those in which it was not, offered the weakest discrimination of both peeping frequency and exhibitionism. Orgasmic voyeurism was the best discriminator of both peeping frequency and exhibitionism items. Clinically, the use of orgasmic voyeurism appears more practical because it is so difficult to define a pathological cutoff point using frequencies of peeping alone.

DISCUSSION

The experimental evidence summarized in Table 3.10 suggests that the majority of clinical assumptions about voyeurism appear to be unfounded. Only the association of voyeurism with exhibitionism was relatively consistent. Some results were directly opposite to expectation. Moreover the evidence suggests that voyeurism only rarely exists as a discrete entity by itself. First there were almost no pure cases of voyeurism in a sample of over 600 sexually anomalous men who appeared at a forensic clinic over a 10 year period. Of the men examined in

TABLE 3.10
A Comparison of Hypotheses on Voyeurism and The Outcomes of
Studies One and Two

Hypothesis	Study One	Study Two
1. Voyeurism and exhibitionism are linked.	Supported but voyeurism also linked to most heterosexual anomalies.	Same as Study 1.
2. Voyeurism, exhibitionism, toucheurism and rape co-occur as courtship disorders.	Exhibiting is most related to voyeurism. Relationship of other courtship disorders to voyeurism appears to be a chance one.	Only related to exhibiting.
3. Voyeurs lack satisfactory courtship skills with females.	Negative. They tend to have more overall sexual experience with adult females than both control groups.	Same as Study 1.

(continued)

TABLE 3.10   (*Continued*)

Hypothesis	Study One	Study Two
4. Voyeurs less often marry.	Not supported.	Not supported.
5. The more habitual the peeping, the less adequate the voyeur's sex life.	Negative. The more they peep at intercourse, the more heterosexual experience they have.	No relationship at all.
6. Voyeurism is associated with murder, arson and burglary.	Best link is to theft and this is weak. No murder cases and 1 arson case among voyeurs.	Not supported.
7. Voyeurism is sadistic.	Not tested.	Negative.
8. Voyeurs are uninterested in strip shows; it is the forbiddenness of peeping and being undetected which is exciting.	Negative. No difference in voyeurs and controls.	Not tested.
9. Voyeurism is a defense against aggression.	Show higher scores on Acting Out and Manifest Hostility and lower scores on Over-Controlled Hostility. 18% had violence related charges.	Higher Manifest Hostility. No difference in Overcontrolled Hostility. 3% had violence charges. Controls had more.
10. Voyeurs have a higher incidence of homosexual acts than nonvoyeurs.	Not supported.	Not supported.
11. Voyeurs have an interest in filth, feces, and urine (mysophilia, coprophilia, and urophilia).	Not tested but no evidence reported in medical records.	Same as in Study 1.
12. Voyeurs have an unusual lack of curiosity.	Negative. They seem normal.	Negative.
13. Voyeurs have few sisters; tend to be only children or youngest child.	Not supported.	Not tested.
14. Voyeurs' parents were normal and got along well with their child but not with each other.	PCR disturbed in the direction similar to aggressive sex offenders. Parents tend to be mentally ill.	Not tested.

Studies One and Two, only a fifth showed voyeurism as the most frequent outlet. One may still argue that the foregoing studies did not examine voyeurism proper. Certainly we cannot prove pure voyeurism does not exist, only that it seems very rare. Second, voyeurism was randomly related to almost every sexual anomaly presented, although exhibitionism seemed to have a relatively special status. Some exhibitionists have described peeping as a surrogate activity when exposing is not possible or when it is too risky. They may perceive the female who fails to pull down her shade while undressing as "exposing" (cf. Langevin, 1983 and Langevin et al., 1979). Third, it is very difficult to separate voyeurism as a clinical entity from normal sexual looking behavior. This suggests that one may be witnessing "normal behavior" in these clinical cases that have some other problem as a major focus. It may be a surrogate for many behaviors that are too easily detected (e.g., pedophilia or exhibitionism). It may be no more than curiosity or deprivation in a male with a high sex "drive" or an unwillingness to risk incarceration. Certainly the "voyeurs" studied here did not differ from the controls in two general measures of curiosity. One could argue that their level of *specific* sexual curiosity was higher than average because of the greater number of diverse sexual outlets they displayed. A more refined measure is needed to test this hypothesis. Possibly there are many cases of voyeurism that go undetected and since it is so "normal," there is less need for clinical attention. This remains to be proved.

Men who engaged in peeping showed signs of aggression including criminality but results were weak and inconsistent (Table 3.10). The presence of other factors such as number of sexual outlets and psychopathology were important confounding factors. The association of peeping with violence, sexual or otherwise, was not supported to the extent theory or clinical case studies would lead us to believe. If the data from the two foregoing studies were used to predict rape proneness, about 1 in 5 voyeurs and 1 in 20 nonvoyeurs would be identified in Study One and no voyeur versus 1 in 20 nonvoyeur in Study Two. Even though prediction has some, albeit weak, merit in the former case, one would better predict rape from the absence of voyeurism in the second study. The prediction of nonsexual violence is similar. Eighteen percent of voyeurs had assault convictions compared to 2% of nonvoyeurs in Study One. However, results were reversed in Study Two. Three percent of voyeurs had assault convictions, whereas 23% of nonvoyeurs did. Thus, using voyeurism to predict tendencies to violence or rape is very limited.

Voyeurism may be a surrogate for many activities, a gateway for the imaginary expression of a wide range of socially unacceptable sexual impulses. The value of treating it as a discrete sexual anomaly or as an indicator of future rape or other aggressiveness appears to be very limited. It may prove more useful to examine the content of sexual fantasies during peeping as indicators of violent sexual preoccupation.

REFERENCES

Dahlstrom, N. G., & Dahlstrom, L. E. *An MMPI handbook.* Minneapolis, MN: University of Minnesota Press, 1972–1975.

Freund, K., Scher, H., & Hucker, S. The courtship disorders. *Archives of Sexual Behavior,* 1983, *12,* 369–379.

Gebhard, P. H., Gagnon, J. H., Pomeroy, W. B., & Christenson, C. V. *Sex offenders.* New York: Harper & Row, 1965.

Karpman, B. *The Sexual offender and his offences.* New York: Julian Press Inc., 1957.

Langevin, R. *Sexual strands: Understanding and treating sexual anomalies in men.* Hillsdale, NJ: Lawrence Erlbaum Associates, 1983.

Langevin, R., Paitich, D., Ramsay, G., Anderson, C., Kamrad, J., Pope, S., Geller, G., Pearl, L., & Newman, S. Experimental studies of the etiology of genital exhibitionism. *Archives of Sexual Behavior,* 1979, *8,* 307–331.

Langevin, R., Paitich, D., Freeman, R., Mann, K., & Handy, L. Personality characteristics and sexual anomalies in males. *Canadian Journal of Behavioral Science,* 1978, *10,* 222–238.

Moncrieff, M., & Pearson, D. Comparison of MMPI profiles of assaultive and non-assaultive exhibitionists and voyeurs. *Corrective & Social Psychiatry & Journal of Behavior Technology: Methods & Therapy,* 1979, *25,* 91–93.

Paitich, D., & Langevin, R. The Clarke Parent-Child Relations Questionnaire: A clinically useful test for adults. *Journal of Consulting Clinical Psychology,* 1976, *44,* 428–436.

Paitich, D., Langevin, R., Freeman, R., Mann, K., & Handy, L. The Clarke SHQ: A clinical sex history questionnaire for males. *Archives of Sexual Behavior,* 1977, *6,* 421–436.

Saul, L. J. A note on exhibitionism and scoptophilia. *Psycho-Analytic Quarterly,* 1952, *21,* 224–226.

Smith, S. R. Voyeurism: A review of literature. *Archives of Sexual Behavior,* 1976, *5,* 585–608.

Yalom, I. Aggression and forbiddenness in voyeurism. *Archives of General Psychiatry,* 1960, *3,* 305–319.

ENDNOTES

Note 1. Gebhard et al. (1965) use the term "peeper" to indicate a sexual anomaly. "Voyeur" is then a more general class of behavior in which anyone can engage. The present writers use the terms peeping and voyeurism interchangeably. The only clear indicator of a sexually anomalous preference is the act of peeping associated with orgasm.

Note 2. These measures were covaried where appropriate with the variables of interest but the main results were not affected significantly.

Note 3. $\chi^2=31.25$, df=2, p < .001 for single versus other marital status.

Note 4. Dahlstrom & Dahlstrom (1972–1975) #184 alpha reliability, a=0.75, Study One and a=0.75, Study Two.

Note 5. Dahlstrom & Dahlstrom (1972–1975) #223, a=0.82, Study One and 0.83, Study Two.

Note 6. Dahlstrom & Dahlstrom (1972–1975) #186, a=0.40, Study One and 0.34, Study Two.

Note 7. MMPI items #1, 4, 6, 12, 25, 78, 81, 92, 126, 132, 133, 140, 144, 173, 204, 219, 221, 223, 261, 423, 434, 546, 552. a=0.64, Study One and a=0.68, Study Two.

Note 8. MMPI items #8, 52, 99, 100, 111, 116, 146, 164, 171, 180, 181, 196, 207, 229, 254, 295, 300, 312, 318, 351, 353, 372, 391, 394, 403, 428, 429, 445, 446, 449–451, 453, 479, 482, 497, 547, 561, 566. a=0.80, Study One and a=0.68, Study Two.

Note 9. One way univariate analysis of variance and multivariate discriminant analyses forcing all pertinent variables into the analyses were used. Results for a direct solution are reported. Stepwise solutions were also examined but made little difference to results reported here, so they are not discussed.

Note 10. The results for the subgroup of men who peeped over 100 times and who peeped more than they engaged in other sexual anomalies were similar to those reported here for the total sample of voyeurs.

Note 11. $F=4.40$, $p < 05$.

Note 12. $F=4.10$, $p < 05$.

Note 13. $F=5.88$, $p < 01$.

Note 14. $F=3.53$, $p < 05$.

Note 15. $F=4.12$, $p < 05$.

Note 16. $F=8.94$, $p < 001$.

Note 17. $\chi^2=10.40$, df=5, $p < 10$.

Note 18. A comparison of psychotic diagnosis, no diagnosis, and other diagnoses for the two groups was significant; $\chi^2=9.39$, df=2, $p < 01$.

Note 19. $F=9.19$, $p < 001$. The sexual anomaly and control groups did not differ significantly.

Note 20. $F=35.46$, $p < .0001$ and $F=18.95$, $p < 0001$ respectively.

Note 21. $F=3.50$, $p < 05$.

Note 22. $F=3.92$, $p < 05$. Voyeurs report 13% of their mothers were mentally ill compared to 4% for the other patient group.

Note 23. $F=3.81$, $p < 05$. Voyeurs report 29% of their fathers were mentally ill compared to 12% for the other patient group.

Note 24. $F=11.83$, $p < 0001$.

Note 25. $F=6.62$, $p < 01$ and $F=13.82$, $p < 0001$ for before and after 16 years of age respectively.

Note 26. Father $F=3.98$, $p < 05$ and mother $F=4.52$, $p < 05$.

Note 27. $F=4.99$, $p < 01$.

Note 28. $F=3.49$, $p < 05$.

Note 29. $F=4.10$, $p < 05$ and $F=3.45$, $p < 05$ respectively.

Note 30. $F=86.12$, $p < 0001$ and $F=14.64$, $p < 0001$ respectively.

B RELATED FACTORS IN SEXUAL AGGRESSION: ALCOHOL AND THE BRAIN

When difficulties are encountered in testing hypotheses on patients, it is often useful and more economical to turn to clinical analog studies using community volunteers as research participants. Such is the case for alcohol and brain pathology as factors in sexual aggression. We know that alcohol abuse plays some part in rapists' sexual behavior but its exact role is unclear. In theory, excessive alcohol consumption should make rape impossible. The few available research studies examining the effect of alcohol on penile erection are contradictory but they tend to support this belief. Possibly rapists are peculiar and do not lose sexual potency even if they are extremely intoxicated. In Chapter 2 we attempted to study the effect of alcohol on rapists' penile responses to erotic stimuli, and were surprised that they seemed to react more than expected, based on previous information about the stimuli. However, controls who were not sexually aggressive reacted similarly. Moreover, alcoholic rapists could not be tested for ethical reasons. Results were so contrary to existing belief that the next study was done.

4 The Effect of Alcohol on Penile Erection

Ron Langevin
Mark H. Ben-Aron
Robert Coulthard
Stephen J. Hucker
John E. Purins
Anne E. Russon
Clarke Institute of Psychiatry,
Toronto

David Day
University of Windsor

Vincent Roper
Ontario Correctional Institute

Christopher David Webster
Metfors, Toronto

Alcohol certainly plays some role in violent acts including sexually aggressive ones.[1] It has been implicated in about half of known rapes and, in some studies, in nonviolent sexual crimes (e.g., Rada, 1976). However, its exact influence on sexual arousability still is uncertain. A number of studies have been conducted to determine the effects of alcohol on erotic arousal, but only the six studies outlined in Table 4.1 have actually measured penile erections. Three of these latter studies agreed that increasing amounts of alcohol reduce the degree of penile tumescence to erotica. The other three studies found no difference due to alcohol dose but did show that the *expectation* of receiving alcohol influenced responsiveness.

The results of the studies that suggest alcohol reduces penile erections present a paradox in understanding sexual acts such as rape. If the offender is drinking, how is rape possible? Some men are drinking so excessively that they should not be able to have erections at all.

Tolerance to alcohol may be a major explanatory factor distinguishing the college research subjects in the six studies in Table 4.1 and the sex offenders in question. The seasoned drinker may not react as nondrinkers or light drinkers do (Mendelson, 1977). Although one may assume that no research subject was an alcoholic, actual drinking history was not reported in four of the six studies in Table 4.1. Only Farkas and Rosen (1976) noted that their subjects were "moder-

TABLE 4.1
Studies Examining Effect of Alcohol on Penile Erection

Study	Within S Design	Order Effects	Repeat Same Stimulus	Expectancy Effect	Alcohol Effect
Briddel & Wilson 1976	No	Unknown	Yes	No	Yes
Farkas & Rosen 1976	Yes	Yes	Yes	Not measured	Yes
Rubin & Henson 1976	Yes/Mixed	Yes	Yes	Not measured	Yes
Wilson & Lawson 1976	No	No	No	Yes	No
Briddel, Rimm et al 1978	No	No	No	Partial	No
Lansky & Wilson 1981	No	Unknown	No	Partial	No

ate drinkers consuming alcohol two or three times weekly'' and, Lansky and Wilson (1981) reported that their subjects drank an average of 120 ounces of beer per week.

The belief that one has consumed alcohol may also play a role. The expectation that alcohol will be ingested is believed to influence the individual psychologically and reduce his sexual arousal (cf. Mendelson & Mello, 1979). However, four of the six studies in Table 4.1 that examined the role of expectation are inconsistent. Expectancy increased the degree of penile responsiveness in one study, reduced it in another, had no effect in a third, and it interacted with subject's report of guilt over sex in the fourth. Briddell and Wilson's (1976) results were not significant but Wilson and Lawson's (1976) and Briddell, Rimm, Caddy, Krawitz, Sholis, and Wunderlin's (1978) were. However, in the last study, there was a statistical interaction effect of expectation of receiving alcohol and actually getting it. Those who actually had alcohol, reacted more when it was expected. Lansky and Wilson (1981) examined the role of sex guilt as measured by Mosher's (1966) Questionnaire. He found that only the subjects who were high in sex guilt reacted more when they expected alcohol. The expectancy effect may be more evident when small amounts of alcohol are given and the drinkers have fewer subjective signs of intoxication. Large amounts of alcohol would obviate the fact they actually had received it. Evidently further work is needed to understand the role of expectancy.

Contrary to the foregoing information, the following facts suggest that alcohol in moderate amounts may actually *increase* or at least not affect the sexual reactivity of normal men. (1) Rubin and Henson (1976) found that although alcohol suppressed penile reactions in their study, six of 11 subjects reported believing that the alcohol had enhanced their sexual responding. (2) Farkas and Rosen (1976) found a nonsignificant trend for small amounts of alcohol to increase sexual responding although, in general, alcohol reduced the degree of penile erection. (3) The existing studies showing that alcohol produced significant decrements in penile responding all have important flaws that could distort the effect of alcohol on sexual arousal. (4) Three of the six studies in Table 4.1 found no effect of alcohol on penile tumescence. Two of these three show the

fewest study design problems. As indicated in Table 4.1, studies showing a significant effect due to alcohol suffer one or more problems. Some use a totally within subject design which means that several amounts of alcohol were compared, but each person had all of them. Poulton (1975) has pointed out the serious limitations of such designs in many contexts and recommended that a between subject design is preferable. That is, only one dose of alcohol is administered to each person. However a totally between person design is not practical; erotic and neutral stimuli must be compared.

Another limitation of the studies, connected in part to the use of a within subject design, was the repeating of the same stimulus to each subject in the several alcohol dose conditions. Continued presentation of erotic materials often results in a response decrement. This means that the order of the sessions may interact with the amount of alcohol. Such order effects were noted in some of the studies. This makes the results on the amount of alcohol per se less certain. The three studies free of these problems found no overall effect of alcohol dose (Briddel et al., 1978; Lansky & Wilson, 1981; Wilson & Lawson 1976). (5) Finally, all studies measured penile circumference rather than penile volume changes. Freund and others have shown that, at best, penile volume and circumference correlate 0.7 (i.e., one is predictable from the other with approximately 50% accuracy).[2] Thus, significant reactions may have been missed with the circumference measures, particularly in the mild range of arousal (cf. Freund, Langevin, & Barlow, 1974).

In the present study the effect of alcohol on penile tumescence was examined: (1) using a between subject design; (2) presenting the erotic stimuli only once per person; (3) measuring penile volume; (4) varying the erotic valence of the stimuli to determine if they are differentially affected by alcohol; (5) controlling the expectation of receiving alcohol; and (6) recording the subject's drinking history.

METHOD

Subjects

Forty eight paid volunteers were recruited for the study by notices placed in community colleges, universities, and newspapers. All were male with a mean age of 27 years, standard deviation six years. Any who had a history of mental illness, were treated for alcoholism, or, had a drinking problem were excluded for ethical reasons.

Apparatus

Stimulus slides developed by Freeman (1976) and reported by Langevin, Paitich, Ramsay, Anderson, Kamrad, Pope, Geller, Pearl and Newman (1979) were used. Verbally rated categories of erotic valence formed a linear relationship

with penile volume in our earlier work. New slides were added to increase the range of erotic valence. Slides were projected with a Kodak caroussel projector and controlled automatically by a timer.

A Grass Model 7 polygraph with PT 5A transducer and Preamplifier 7P1 A were used to measure penile volume changes as reported earlier (Langevin & Martin, 1975). The device was adapted from Freund, Sedlacek, and Knob (1965). The Alert Model J3D Breathalyzer was used to measure aveolar alcohol.[3]

Procedure

The study design is presented in Fig. 4.1. Three groups of 16 men were randomly assigned to 0, 50, or 100 mg.% blood alcohol level groups (hereafter BAL groups). There were six categories of stimuli with four repeats of each for a total

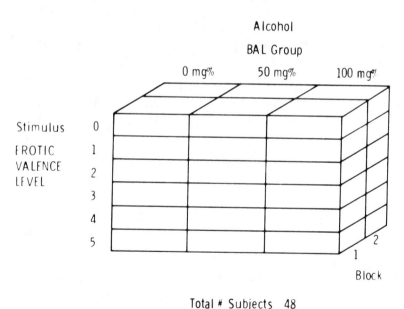

Figure 4.1
Alcohol Study Design

Total # Subjects   48
Total # Stimuli   24

Measures

Maximum Penile Volume Change in 30 seconds
Maximum Penile Volume Change in 60 seconds
Latency to Maximum Penile Volume Change in 60 seconds

of 24 different stimuli shown to all subjects. The stimulus categories were neutral or zero erotic valence and five other levels of erotic valence from weak to strong, or 1 to 5 in Fig. 4.1.

To control for order effects and fatigue, the stimuli were presented in two blocks of 12 stimuli with each erotic valence level represented twice in each block. The stimuli were shown for 30 seconds each in a fixed random order in each block for all subjects. For each stimulus presentation, there were three measures: (a) maximum penile volume change in 30 seconds; (b) in 60 seconds after stimulus onset; and (c) the latency to the start of the largest volume change occurring within 60 seconds.

Once volunteers were screened for mental illness or alcoholism, they were administered sufficient vodka mixed with orange juice and spices to disguise the alcohol taste and to bring the breathalyzer reading within the range of 50 or 100 mg.% BAL. The 0 mg.% BAL group had the same drink without vodka. All drinks were prepared out of subjects' sight.

The men were generally tested in the morning and on an empty stomach. In a few cases, this was not possible and testing was arranged at the volunteer's convenience. One additional person was excluded because he was ill before testing. An initial breathalyzer reading served to instruct subjects in its use and to ensure a 0 BAL reading before starting. BAL was recorded every 15 minutes from the start to the end of the session. Subjects were not informed of readings until after the experiment. To control for expectancy effect, all subjects were led to believe they had received alcohol. They were told "Some people think alcohol reduces sexual arousal and others think it increases it. Keep an open mind and let your body react the way it will. Do not force any reactions when they are not there and don't try to block any reactions that may happen. Just let go and relax and respond naturally." All volunteers appeared to believe they were given alcohol. When the desired breathalyzer reading was obtained, the slides were presented. The session lasted 30 to 60 minutes.

Initially the breathalyzer readings of 50 and 100 were overshot somewhat so that about midsession the level would be close to 50 or 100 mg.%. A check on the effectiveness of the experimental procedures involved analysis of actual amount of alcohol given and BAL readings at the start of slide presentation, midsession, and at the end. Time to reach initial BAL, midsession BAL, and to come down below 20 mg.% were also analyzed.

Table 4.2 shows that the manipulation was successful. Mean midsession values were within three points of desired BAL. However, the time to achieve initial BAL differed significantly and may have influenced participants' expectations.

Standard precautions were taken to test phallometric apparatus and to ensure that the subject was at zero baseline penile volume before presentation of the next stimulus.[4] Subjects were not released until BAL was less than 20 mg.% and they were sent home via transit or in a taxi.

TABLE 4.2
Blood Alcohol Information On The Three Groups

	Mean Scores for BAL Groups		
	0 mg.%	50 mg.%	100 mg.%
1. Actual alcohol given (in oz.)	0	5	9
2. BAL at start of stimulus presentation (in mg.%)	0	56	104
3. Midsession BAL readings (in mg.%)	0	51	97
4. End session BAL readings (in mg.%)	0	42	91
5. Time to achieve initial BAL (in minutes)	36 P	60	103
6. Time to midsession BAL reading (in minutes)	17	22	22
7. Time from midsession to end of study (in minutes)	28	125	242

Note: All measures are significant at p < 0001 except #6 in which times are usual running times for the study.

P: This time includes administration of nonalcoholic drink and BAL readings plus usual set up time for the study.

RESULTS

The maximum volume changes within 30 seconds and within 60 seconds were scored. In order to score latency to response, the point at which 10% maximum volume change occurred was marked and the time from stimulus onset to that 10% point recorded. This is an adaptation from a procedure used by engineers to measure slopes of slow changing functions. The penile volume changes (PVC) were the dependent variables in a 3x6x2 multivariate analysis of variance. Latency was examined separately and in general produced no significant results. The results for PVC in 30 seconds and 60 seconds were essentially identical and will be discussed together.[5]

Stimulus Erotic Valence Effects.   Results were as expected. All erotic slides were more arousing than neutral slides and reactions more or less increased in size with increasing erotic valence.

Effect of Blood Alcohol Level.   Figure 4.2 shows the reaction profile for the three BAL groups and there are several noteworthy features.[6] All points for the 100 mg.% group are below those for 0 BAL which in turn are all below those for 50 mg.% with exception of the highest point. All groups show similar profiles but the 50 and 100 mg.% groups show a slight but nonsignificant drop off in response at the highest level.[7]

In no case was the 100 mg.% BAL group statistically and significantly distinct from 0 BAL. With the exception of reactions to neutral stimuli, the 50 mg.% BAL group responded more to every class of stimulus than the 100 mg.% group. There was a trend for the 50 mg.% group to react more than the 0 BAL group to every erotic stimulus level but only valence level three was significant.

It is noteworthy that there were no overall BAL group differences in penile output for any dependent measure. However there were differences in reactions to the erotic stimulus categories that are informative. The 0% BAL group reacted more or less as expected with four overlapping levels of erotic response: (a)

FIGURE 4.2

THE EFFECT OF BLOOD ALCOHOL LEVEL ON PENILE ERECTION

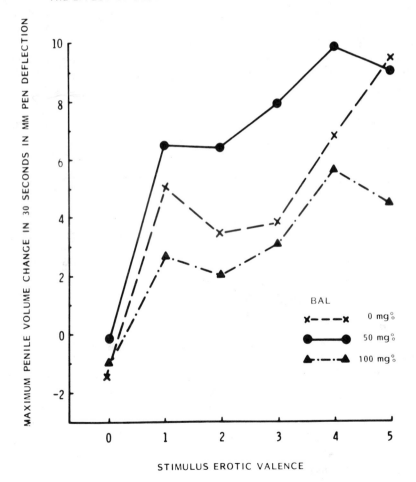

neutral; (b) erotic valence class 1, 2, 3; (c) class 1 and 4; and finally (d) class 4 and 5. The 50 and 100 mg.% BAL basically showed a two level response: neutral and nondiscriminate reaction to all erotic classes. However, similar trends to the means of the 0 mg.% group are evident.

Responding Over the Course of the Session. The group that received no alcohol responded similarly to participants in our previous work. They showed no systematic change in penile response from the first to the second block of stimulus presentations. However, the 50 mg.% group showed a significant decrement in reactivity during the second block and the 100 mg.% group showed a nonsignificant increase. This difference did not occur for the 60 second measure. It seems the trend to increased reactivity of the 50 mg.% group is short lived and disappears when the stimulus is removed. However, contrary to expectation, in no case was their reactivity depressed below the level of the 0 BAL group. Similarly, the 100 mg.% group reacted significantly less than the other two groups during the first block of trials but they did not differ from the 0 BAL group in the second block. Thus, if alcohol had any suppressing effect for them, it was weak and short lived, or perhaps, it only occurred when the stimulus was present.

Immediate Memory. Digit span from the Wechsler memory scale was examined for half the subjects. There were no significant differences pretest but the difference scores post test were (p < .05). The 50 mg.% group showed an improvement of 1.00 point but the 0 mg.% group declined 0.50 point and the 100 mg.% group declined 0.71 point. The 50 mg.% group differed significantly from the other two groups. There were no other significant differences.

Drinking History. There were no significant BAL group differences in age, Michigan Alcoholism Screening Test (MAST, Selzer, 1971) scores (mean 2.04, S.D. 2.0) or in weekly consumption of alcohol. The amount of beer, wine, and spirits consumed weekly was corrected for amount of alcohol (respectively 5%, 10%, and 40% by volume approximately). A 100% pure alcohol equivalent consumed weekly was computed. The average was 5.46 oz., S.D. 5.57 oz./ week, range 0–19 oz.

The effect of drinking habits was examined by comparing those subjects who drank the average weekly intake of alcohol equivalent (5.46 oz.) or less versus those who drank more. The following measures were examined: MAST scores, Digit span, blood alcohol levels during the study, rate of metabolism, and penile reactions. There was only one difference in the heavier and lighter drinkers. Heavier drinkers metabolized the alcohol faster and showed a more rapid reduction in BAL over the course of the session. However, since subjects were randomly assigned to conditions, this did not interact with the measures of interest nor did it influence the interpretation of results presented here.

DISCUSSION

The results were interesting for a least two reasons: large amounts of alcohol did not significantly reduce penile responsiveness but when the subjects were drinking they showed a trend to react nondiscriminately to erotic materials regardless of their usual valence.

The three studies in Table 4.1 with the fewest design problems and the present study agreed in showing that alcohol per se does not affect penile reactions substantially in the average person. This in itself offers a ready explanation of how men can engage in sexual acts when they are drinking. Some researchers have shown that ejaculation is delayed by consumption of alcohol but this may serve only to enhance and prolong the pleasure derived in the sexual arousal which is not diminished by alcohol. Nor did current weekly consumption rate of alcohol influence the results. Although there were no alcoholics in the study, there were some heavy drinkers. However, even among chronic alcoholics, weekly intake has not produced consistent loss of libido or other endocrine side effects (cf. Mendelson, 1977; Van Thiel & Lester, 1974).

Most noteworthy about the results of the present study is the more or less indiscriminate reactions to erotica by drinking subjects. Although the 50 mg.% BAL group reacted most, both they and the 100 mg.% BAL group showed a trend to react to erotic materials indiscriminately and more so than to neutral materials. Thus mild erotic materials elicited greater reactions than they ordinarily do, perhaps due to cortical disinhibition produced by alcohol. In the context of a sexually anomalous man, drinking may result in a greater tendency to act out sexual impulses, even though the erotic stimulus provoking him is mild. Rape carried out by a drinking male is no longer paradoxical if one accepts the present results. One may hypothesize that the rapist's ability to have an erection while drinking is not impaired even at relatively high BALs and he is more likely to react to milder erotic stimuli than when he is sober. Tolerance to alcohol may extend the erotic reactivity range of rapists over even higher BALs. Thus alcohol in general may serve a disinhibiting facilitative role in sexual arousal.

The results of this study should not be treated as conclusive even though they can explain sexual acts performed under the influence of alcohol. Only relatively mild stimuli were examined so that strong erotica may produce different results. Controlling time to reach initial BAL may produce different results as well. The outcome also may be different in men with unusual sexual behavior, either of an anomalous or aggressive type (cf. Pihl, Zeichner, Niaura, Nagy, & Zacchia, 1981, and Chapter 2 for examples). In addition, the stimuli used in the present study need refinement so that the levels of erotic valence represent a wider range of more discrete response levels. Although the results are not definitive, they do indicate that the stereotype of alcohol "increasing desire but reducing erectile ability" is too simplistic and that further studies are clearly desirable. It would be

informative, for example, to examine sexual arousal to pictures of children in normal men as an analog to pedophilia or incest. Since we know that normal men show weak erotic reactions to female children who are as young as 6-years-old, alcohol may increase responsiveness, as it did in the present study. Sex offenders who have attributed their behavior to drink have been dismissed as lying in some cases. The present results suggest that we should seriously reexamine their claims.

ACKNOWLEDGMENTS

This study was supported by NIMH Grant #1 R01 MH 34430-01. Portions of the study were presented at the annual meeting of the International Academy for Sex Research, Copenhagen, Denmark, August, 1982.

REFERENCES

Briddell, D. W., & Wilson, G. T. Effects of alcohol and expectancy set on male sexual arousal. *Journal of Abnormal Psychology,* 1976, *85,* 225–234.

Briddell, D. W., Rimm, D. C., Caddy, G. R., Krawitz, G., Sholis, D., & Wunderlin, R. J. Effects of alcohol and cognitive sex on sexual arousal to deviant stimuli. *Journal of Abnormal Psychology,* 1978, *87,* 418–430.

Farkas, G. M., & Rosen, R. C. Effect of alcohol on elicited male sexual response. *Journal of Studies on Alcohol,* 1976, *37,* 265–272.

Freeman, R. *The role of subject content and stimulus variables in determining evaluative and behavioral reactions to explicit depiction of human sexual behavior.* Unpublished Masters of Arts thesis, University of Waterloo, 1976.

Freund, K., Sedlacek, F., & Knob, K. A simple transducer for mechanical plethysmography of the male genital. *Journal of Experimental Analysis of Behavior,* 1965, *8,* 169–170.

Freund, K., Langevin, R., & Barlow, D. Comparison of two penile methods of measuring mild sexual arousal. *Journal of Behavior Research and Therapy,* 1974, *12,* 355–359.

Langevin, R., & Martin, M. Can erotic responses be classically conditioned? *Behavior Therapy,* 1975, *6,* 350–355.

Langevin, R., Paitich, D., Ramsay, G., Anderson, C., Kamrad, J., Pope, S., Geller, G., Pearl, L., & Newman, S. Experimental studies of the etiology of genital exhibitionism. *Archives of Sexual Behavior,* 1979, *8,* 307–331.

Lansky, D., & Wilson, G. T. Alcohol, expectations, and sexual arousal in males: An information processing analysis. *Journal of Abnormal Psychology,* 1981, *90,* 35–45.

Mendelson, J. H. Endocrines and aggression. *Psychopharmacology Bulletin,* 1977, *13,* 22–23.

Mendelson, J. H., & Mello, N. K. Biologic concomitants of alcoholism. *The New England Journal of Medicine,* 1979, *301,* 912–921.

Mosher, D. L. The development and multitrait-multimethod matrix analyses of three measures of three aspects of guilt. *Journal of Consulting Psychology,* 1966, *30,* 25–29.

Pihl, R. O., Zeichner, A., Niaura, R., Nagy, K., & Zacchia, C. Attribution and alcohol-mediated aggression. *Journal of Abnormal Psychology,* 1981, *90,* 468–475.

Poulton, E. C. Range effects in experiments on people. *American Journal of Psychology,* 1975, *88,* 3–32.

Rada, R. T. Alcoholism and the child molester. *Annals of the New York Academy of Science,* 1976, *273,* 492–496.

Rada, R. T. *Clinical aspects of the rapist.* New York: Grune & Stratton, 1978.

Rubin, H. B., & Henson, D. E. Effects of alcohol on male sexual responding. *Psychopharmacology,* 1976, 47, 123–134.

Selzer, M. The Michigan Alcoholism Screening Test: The quest for a new diagnostic instrument. *American Journal of Psychiatry,* 1971, *127,* 1653–1658.

Van Thiel, D. H., & Lester, R. Sex and alcohol. *The New England Journal of Medicine,* 1974, *291,* 251–253.

Wilson, G. T., & Lawson, D. M. Expectancies, alcohol, and sexual arousal in male social drinkers. *Journal of Abnormal Psychology,* 1976, *85,* 587–594.

ENDNOTES

Note 1. See Rada (1978) and Chapters 1 and 2 for more detail.

Note 2. Technically, it is more precise to say they share 50% of their true variance.

Note 3. Alcohol Countermeasure Systems Inc., Mississauga, Ontario.

Note 4. See Langevin and Martin (1975) for details.

Note 5. The multivariate analysis showed only significant effects for stimulus erotic valence and the BAL group by block interaction. Both univariate analysis for PVC at 30 and 60 seconds were significant for the same effects but also for the BAL group by stimulus erotic valence interaction. The latter are discussed because of their interesting implications but the purist may wish to ignore them because the multivariate results were nonsignificant. They can however still be considered as trends. The multivariate solution may be nonsignificant because of the high correlation of the two dependent measures. However one must still contend with the correlation of responses within subjects and cells. There is no simple answer to this problem.

Z score transformations produced similar results only univariate group by stimulus interactions also were nonsignificant.

Latency presents logical problems in its analyses. When there is no response, is the latency 0, or trial time of 60 seconds, or infinite? The results were examined two ways: number of responses and latency for trials on which there was *some* response. Neither was significant for the amounts of alcohol used in this study. Response latencies reflected individual differences but not stimulus or alcohol effects.

Note 6. Penile volume is presented as millimeters of pen deflection. One mm = 0.02 cc volume change. Pen deflections form a linear scale with penile volume.

Note 7. The significant interaction effect was attributable to a range effect of group means.

5 Brain Correlates of Penile Erection

John E. Purins
Ron Langevin
Clarke Institute of Psychiatry, Toronto

Our motivation for the last and the next clinical analog study was similar. In Chapter Two the discovery of a subtle CT scan abnormality in the temporal horn of sadists was an exciting finding. It was detected by CT scan but not by neuropsychological testing. We did not examine electroencephalograms (EEGs) which may have been informative. We wondered why 56% of sadists showed the CT scan abnormality and 44% did not. It was possible that more cases could be identified if other measures like EEG were employed. More specifically, it would be useful to demonstrate that the temporal horn in man was important in sexual behavior. Knowing this, we could examine sadists as well as other rapists to see how, and if, they differed. Unfortunately very little work has been done relating EEG or other brain measures to sexual arousal in man. So we turned to community volunteers and a clinical analog study to do some of the ground work necessary for a further study of sexually aggressive men. The next chapter examines whether there are recognizable EEG correlates of penile erection. Power Spectral analysis of the EEG during sexual arousal is reported for the first time in a controlled study.

INTRODUCTION

Animal Research

Much of our information about brain correlates of sexual behavior must be inferred from animal research. Experimental study of the central nervous mechanisms regulating sexual behavior in primates dates from the seminal experiments

of Kluver and Bucy first reported in 1939. These investigators described a syndrome, which now bears their names, associated with bilateral temporal lobectomy in old-world monkeys. A component of this syndrome which is of specific interest to the present topic involves profound changes in sexual behavior emerging fully 3 to 6 weeks postoperatively. Bilaterally lobectomized monkeys showed a striking increase of overt sexual behavior whether kept alone or in the presence of other animals. Kept alone, males had an almost continuous erection or semi-erection, engaged in frequent sucking or licking of the penis, in yawning similar to that observed in normal copulatory behavior, in rubbing of the hindquarters on the bars of the cage and in ''presenting'' to an approaching observer. In the presence of a female, the males attempted or actually engaged in protracted and repeated copulation. In the presence of a second bilaterally lobectomized male, attempts at copulation, mutual exploration of the genitals, and biting of the extremities without fighting were observed. All of these behaviors were either absent or occurred under circumscribed and specific conditions in males without lesions, in those with non-temporal cortical lesion, and in those with unilateral temporal lesion.

Schreiner and Kling (1953) subsequently observed similar behavioral disinhibition in temporally-lesioned cats and Gloor (1960) has suggested that lesions to the amygdalae are sufficient to produce the behavioral disinhibition associated with this syndrome.

MacLean (1962) using surgical ablation and intra-cranial stimulation and recording, identified major components of the functional neuroanatomy of sexual behavior in the limbic lobe, medial forebrain, and brain stem of the squirrel monkey. He noted that: (1) the release of sexual behaviors was attendant specifically on ablation of the amygdalae; (2) stimulation of the rostral diencephalon and septum caused erection and produced reciprocal after-discharges in the hippocampus; and (3) stimulation of the hippocampus modified excitability of the immediate septral-diencephalic erectile system. MacLean further noted abnormal spiking in the hippocampus following after-discharge from septal/diencephalic stimulation. In observing that the mammilothalamic tract is phylogenetically the newest area where stimulation may elicit erection, MacLean suggested that it may be a pathway for mediation of complex sociosexual behavior.

HUMAN EPILEPSY AND SEXUAL AROUSAL

Based on both the direct investigation of functional sexual neuroanatomy in lower animals, and on extrapolations from a substantial series of case reports on the effects of temporal lobe lesions in man, Blumer and Walker (1975) have indicated the afferent and efferent systems they concluded are responsible for sexual arousal in man. Afferents from the spinal cord lead through the ventromedial thalamus via the internal capsule to the paracentral lobule of the cortex. Paracentral representation of the perineal-genital areas is thought to be

somato-motor in a manner analogous to that of other somatic systems. A collateral pathway projects, via the inferior thalamic peduncle, to the amygdala. Medial temporal structures project to the cirgulate gyrus and hence via the fornix, to the hypothalamus. Thus, two cortical representations are involved. The paracentral lobule serves as a somato sensory/motor area and the inferior temporal areas as a mediator of libidinal arousal.

Limbic involvement in erotic arousal appears, then, to be twofold. Hippocampal activity seems to be involved in a "bias-setting" relationship to septal excitability, and hence, central mediation of the erectile function proper. On the other hand, amygdaloid activity appears to mediate the cognitive/perceptual initiators of erotic arousal.

Terzian (1957) has described a series of clinical cases with neoplastic or surgical lesion to one or both temporal lobes. In reviewing the behavioral concomitants of bitemporal lobecotomy in man, he described a hypersexuality analogous to that demonstrated in monkeys by Kluver and Bucy. He concluded that this component of the syndrome is specifically associated with insult to the amygdaloid complex and pyriform cortex.

In the context of the postulated role of the temporal lobes, the hypersexuality attendant on bilateral lobectomy may be seen as a release phenomenon in the Jacksonian sense, as was suggested originally by Kluver and Bucy (1939). Hence, temporal structures may be regarded as inhibitory mediators of diencephalic mechanisms in sexual arousal.

The postulated dynamic relationship between temporal and diencephalic structures may be valuable to the understanding of the somewhat enigmatic but widely reported coincidence of temporal lobe (limbic) epilepsy (i.e., *neural hyperactivity*), with a global hyposexuality and various paraphilias in man. Gastaut and Collomb (1954) reported the first substantial series of cases demonstrating hyposexuality, that is, diminution or absence of libidinal interest, gentio pelvic arousal, decrease in sexual fantasies, and frequency of masturbation or coitus. Subsequently, numerous additional series have been reported. The major studies are summarized in Table 5.1. It is beyond the scope of this article to review these series of epileptics in detail. Moreover, the unavoidable heterogeneity of the clinical cases presented with respect to every parameter of concern prevents drawing generalizable conclusions. Nevertheless, two durable and noteworthy coincidences emerge. First, global hyposexuality is identified in 30% to 60% of the cases reported. Second, remission of hyposexuality appears to depend on therapeutic success in controlling temporal hyperactivity, either by chemotherapeutic or surgical intervention. A particularly striking case demonstrating both a paraphilia and hyposexuality is reported by Mitchell, Falconer, and Hill (1954). These authors showed electroencephalographically the onset of temporal seizures in a male who had a fetish for safety pins. The subject himself reported that fantasizing about safety pins could reliably precipitate seizures and that he had strong urges to look at them when either sexually aroused or anxious.

TABLE 5.1
Sexual Behavior and the Temporal Lobe

Study	Hill, Pond, Mitchell and Falconer (1957)	Savard and Walker (1965)
Experimental Group (N of Cases)	16 Total	23 Male 16 Female 39 Total
Control Group (N of Cases)	—	—
Neurological Abnormality in Experimental Group	Temporal Lobe Epilepsy	Temporal Lobe Epilepsy
Basis for Neurological Diagnosis in Experimental Group	Clinical Workup	Clinical Workup
Sexual Abnormality in Experimental Group	Preoperative abnormality not reported.	Failure to "enjoy" sexual activity, feeling "sexually dead"
Basis for Identifying Sexual Abnormality	—	Self-report, collateral report from close relative
Neurological Treatment of Experimental Group	Unilateral temporal lobectomy removing anterior temporal lobe including uncus, hippocampal gyrus hippocampus and amygdala	Unilateral temporal lobectomy
Change in Sexual Abnormality After Treatment	1 S started to masturbate compulsively, 3 lost "perverse" sexual tendencies and showed normalization of libido 1 S who was preoperatively promiscuous showed normalization. 1 S became impotent. Authors state that libido and/or object choice altered in a total of 14/16 Ss.	11/39 (28.2%) reported new enjoyment of sexual activity, increased arousability (all were treatment successes from neurological perspective). 5/39 claimed "decrease in sexual arousal."

Study	Hierons and Saunders (1966)	Blumer and Walker (1967)
Experimental Group (N of Cases)	N = 15 Males	17 Males 4 Females 21 Total
Control Group (N of Cases)	—	—
Neurological Abnormality in Experimental Group	Variously temporal lobe epilepsy, neoplasm or vascular anomaly	Temporal Lobe Epilepsy

(continued)

TABLE 5.1   (*Continued*)

Study	*Hierons and Saunders (1966)*	*Blumer and Walker (1967)*
Basis for Neurological Diagnosis in Experimental Group	Clinical Workup	Clinical Workup
Sexual Abnormality in Experimental Group	"Impotence" but no complaint of global hyposexuality	11 of 21 clearly hyposexual preoperatively
Basis for Identifying Sexual Abnormality	Self-report, collateral report from spouse in at least one case	Self-report, report of close relative, observation
Neurological Treatment of Experimental Group	Variously surgery and/or chemotherapy	11 L temporal lobectomy 10 R temporal lobectomy mean age 33 y.o. at operation
Change in Sexual Abnormality After Treatment	Only 5 cases reported in detail (2 unimproved with medication, 1 unchanged and no treatment reported for 2.	Follow up ½ to 14 years after surgery (mean 5½ years) 4 of 11 persistently hyposexual 4 of 11 (36%) with lasting improvement, 3 of 11 (27%) with temporary improvement. Improvement in sexuality coincided with reduction or elimination of seizures.

Study	*Kolarsky, Freund, Machek & Polak (1967)*	*Taylor (1969)*
Experimental Group (N of Cases)	49 Males 15–43 y.o.	63 Males 37 Females 100 Total
Control Group (N of Cases)	37 Males 15–43 y.o.	None
Neurological Abnormality in Experimental Group	Temporal Lobe Epilepsy (Extra-temporal focii for control group)	Temporal Lobe Epilepsy (Median onset at 10 y.o.)
Basis for Neurological Diagnosis in Experimental Group	Neurological Workup results rated by neurologist in blind procedure.	Hospital neurological workup to evaluate for surgery.
Sexual Abnormality in Experimental Group	Variously voyeurism, exhibitionism, fetishism, homosexuality, sadism, masochism, frotteurism, pedophilia, "feminine	Frigidity, impotence correlated ($r = 0.533$), with early onset of epilepsy also "polymorphous" deviance, sadomasoch-

(*continued*)

TABLE 5.1   (*Continued*)

Study	Kolarsky, Freund, Machek & Polak (1967)	Taylor (1969)
	identification'', hypersexuality and unspecified disturbances of sexual behavior in $^{31}/_{49}$ of experimental group. $^{13}/_{37}$ of controls—hyposexuality not reported for either group.	ism, bizarre fantasy, exhibitionism.
Basis for Identifying Sexual Abnormality	Structured interview by sexologist	Rated from psychiatric notes on 5-pt. scale
Neurological Treatment of Experimental Group	No data reported.	Anterior temporal lobectomy by standard procedure but functional impairment unknown.
Change in Sexual Abnormality After Treatment	No data reported.	22 cases improved. 14 cases worsened. 50 remained poor. 14 remained good degree of seizure relief same for 14 who worsened and 14 who remained good. 50 who remained poor had least seizure relief.

Study	Blumer (1970a) (1970b)	Walker (1972)
Experimental Group (N of Cases)	42 Males _8 Females 50 Total 17–65 y.o. mean age 35.3 years	47
Control Group (N of Cases)	None	None
Neurological Abnormality in Experimental Group	Temporal Lobe Epilepsy	Temporal Lobe Epilepsy
Basis for Neurological Diagnosis in Experimental Group	Clinical Workup	Localized unilateral epileptic focus in temporal lobe by EEG
Sexual Abnormality in Experimental Group	29 of 50 *Ss* globally hyposexual	Global hyposexuality in $^{32}/_{47}$ exhibitionism in $^{1}/_{47}$ sexual arousal with psy-

(*continued*)

TABLE 5.1 (*Continued*)

Study	Blumer *(1970a)* *(1970b)*	Walker *(1972)*
		chomotor attack in ¼₄₇ and postictally in ⁴⁄₄₇ "periods of homosexuality" in ²⁄₄₇.
Basis for Identifying Sexual Abnormality	Self report, report of spouse to psychiatrist	Clinical notes, self report and observation
Neurological Treatment of Experimental Group	Unilateral anterior temporal lobectomy with removal of "medial limbic structures" in 42 of 50 (8 *Ss* not operated) 24 of 29 *Ss* with hyposexuality were operated.	Anterior temporal lobectomy (unilateral) removing anterior temporal cortex, amygdala and part of hippocampus
Change in Sexual Abnormality After Treatment	6 & 18 month follow up postoperatively. 8 of 24 (33%) operated *Ss* showed permanent improvement of sexuality and improvement of elimination of seizures Transient hypersexuality in 1 *S* ictally, 1 *S* postoperatively, 5 *Ss* postictally and 1 *S* after anticonvulsant medication.	15 cases showed increased, 33 remained the same and 2 showed decreased sexuality at average 8.3 years after operation. Of 32 preoperatively hyposexual *Ss*, 12 improved.

Study	Hoenig and Kenna *(1979)*	Shukla, Srivastava and Katiyar *(1979)*
Experimental Group (N of Cases)	35 Male 11 Female 46 Total Transsexuals	30 Males over 15 years of age
Control Group (N of Cases)	None	34 non-temporal epileptics over 15 years of age
Neurological Abnormality in Experimental Group	48% of *Ss* showed clear abnormalities and 24% borderline abnormalities 45% of abnormalities in temporal lobe. 75% of females and 38% of	Temporal Lobe Epilepsy

(*continued*)

TABLE 5.1   (*Continued*)

Study	Hoenig and Kenna (1979)	Shukla, Srivastava and Katiyar (1979)
	males with abnormalities.	
Basis for Neurological Diagnosis in Experimental Group	Standard EEG with activation	EEG in both experimental and control group
Sexual Abnormality in Experimental Group	Transsexualism. Family members aware of *Ss'*. Transsexualism earlier in group with EEG abnormalities than in those *Ss* with normal EEG.	$19/30$ were hyposexual. 1 hypersexual (vs. $1/34$ and $0/34$ in non-temporal group).
Basis for Identifying Sexual Abnormality	Psychiatric workup	Structured interview re: sexual fantasies, dreams, nocturnal emissions, masturbation, frequency of sexual relations, extent of pleasure derived, change from earlier level of performance and attitude to absence or decline in sexual performance.
Neurological Treatment of Experimental Group	Not reported	No data reported
Change in Sexual Abnormality After Treatment	Not reported	No data reported

Contemplation of safety pins gradually replaced coitus as the subject's preferred sexual outlet and he complained of becoming increasingly "impotent." Left anterior lobectomy to remove the epileptic focus restored the subject's interest in coitus as well as his ability to perform it and it abolished his desire to look at safety pins.

A study described by Kolarsky, Freud, Machek, and Polak (1967), noteworthy for its experimental rigor, showed that the various paraphilias were overrepresented in a group of temporal lobe epileptics relative to a control group of non-temporal epileptics.

Finally, Hoenig and Kenna (1979) reported EEG results in a group of 46 transsexuals, without undertaking any sexual activation. Their results are consistent with those of Kolarsky et al. (1967) in identifying EEG abnormalities in 48% of their sample, predominantly in the temporal lobe.

An attempt to discern a brain mechanism underlying the foregoing cases is problematic. There are:

1. A lack of appropriate controls.
2. Variability in the nature and focus (if any) of epileptogenic cortical activity.
3. In age of onset of epilepsy.
4. Absence of sound criteria for identifying hyposexuality or paraphilias.
5. Presence of other neurological, endocrine, or genetic abnormalities.
6. Unvalidated bases for neurological diagnosis.
7. Variability in temporal structures removed by surgical treatment, and finally,
8. The absence of empirical information on cortical and limbic involvement in sexual arousal in the normal human.

EEG STUDIES OF SEXUAL AROUSAL

To date, investigations directed at generating normative data on cortical correlates of sexual arousal in normal humans have been limited both methodologically and heuristically. Electroencephalographic (EEG) activation studies represent the bulk of effort in this area. Available studies are summarized in Table 5.2.

Mosovich and Tallaferro (1954) recorded EEG in three male and three female normal volunteers who masturbated to orgasm. Although no quantitative analysis of the EEG record was possible at the time, the authors identified four distinct phases of EEG activity in association with arousal, orgasm, and resolution. EEG changes reported in this study were largely restricted to temporal areas and showed the emergence of low voltage, fast activity associated with sexual self stimulation. A slowing of activity and a voltage increase leading to three Hz waves interspersed with movement artifacts occurred at orgasm. Resolution was accompanied by a second period of low voltage, fast waves, and then a return to baseline concurrent with resolution of sexual arousal.

Heath (1972) and Moan and Heath (1972) reported results on one female and one male, who each had numerous intracranial diencephalic and subdural recording/stimulating electrodes. They were able to monitor central activity associated with sexual arousal produced variously by masturbation, coitus, and chemical stimulation *per cannula*. Unfortunately, movement artifact obscured the cortical phenomena being measured from scalp electrodes. Interestingly, septal recording in the male showed paroxysmal spiking and intensified delta activity in the amygdalae, especially in the right one, and also in the left caudate nucleus in association with orgasm.

Cohen, Rosen, and Goldstein (1976) demonstrated shifts in electrical power through amplitude and frequency changes of parietal EEG from dominant to nondominant hemisphere. There was a 10 Hz pattern predominant in the left hemisphere and 4 Hz on the right, attendant on 8 of 12 orgasms they observed in four male and three female volunteers. These authors reported no rationale for selec-

TABLE 5.2
EEG Studies of Sexual Arousal

Study	Mosovich and Tallaferro (1954)	Heath (1972) and Moan and Heath (1972)	Cohen, Rosen and Goldstein (1976)
Experimental Group (N of Cases)	3 Male 3 Female 6 Total	1 Male 1 Female	4 Male 3 Female 7 Total
Control Group (N of Cases)	Screened for normal EEG	None	None
Method of Sexual Arousal	Masturbation	Saw films and participated in heterosexual intercourse. S was homosexual.	Fantasy followed by masturbation to orgasm.
Measurement of Sexual Arousal	S observed for somatic muscular tension, ejaculation or vaginal lubrication.	Observation, self report	Penile strain gauge or vaginal blood flow
EEG Recording Sites	Frontal, pre-central anterior, mid and posterior temporal and occipital leads.	Numerous mid-brain and sub-dural recording/stimulating electrodes	R & L Parietal Leads Referenced to earlobes
Control of EEG Artefact	Skeletal muscle artefact noted at all sites.	None	1 S masturbated alternately with L & R hands. 1 S faked orgasm. E used data which appeared to be artefact free on inspection.

122

EEG Findings

Found 4 phases of EEG change: I. With onset of stimulation increase in low voltage activity especially in temporal areas. II. At peak of orgasm slowing and voltage increase leading to 3 Hz. waves interspersed with muscle artefact (3 hz. waves observed only in those Ss where evident body tension accompanied orgasm). III. After peak of orgasm, low voltage fast activity returns. IV. Return to baseline.

Self stimulation of septal site by male S led to sexual arousal and compulsion to masturbate. Recording from septal leads immediately prior to orgasm showed spike and wave "epileptiform" activity. At same time delta seen in L amygdala and mixture of delta and spikes in centromedial thalamus. At orgasm both amygdalae showed delta with R greater than L; L caudate nucleus also showed delta; subdural and scalp leads showed only movement artefact in female Ss. Chemical stimulation of septum produced euphoria, A "sexual motive state" and "repetitive orgasms" associated with regular septal spiking in female S.

EEG voltage was integrated and cumulated over 1 second epochs. Found changes in amplitude of R hemisphere relative to L in 8 of 12 orgasms observed, along with (unreported) frequency changes.

tion of parietal recording sites but felt that their results were specific to erotic arousal after controlling for hand used in masturbation by male subjects and recording EEG during a "faked" orgasm by one female subject. Level of arousal was measured using a penile strain gauge and a vaginal blood flow monitor, respectively. The latter now has doubtful reliability and validity (cf. Beck, Sakheim, & Barlow, 1983).

Sarrel, Foddy, and McKinnon (1977) reported EEG changes during orgasm in a female using a single scalp electrode at an unspecified site in the context of a technical study on a system that permitted recording of various physiological parameters in an ambulatory subject. Since this report was directed at demonstrating the practicality of an analog recording system, its findings are of interest to the present topic to the extent they suggested that a distinctive pattern of cortical electrical activity occurs with sexual arousal. These authors reported only that an observable change in scalp EEG accompanied orgasm without further quantitative description.

Recent work by Adamec, Stark-Adamec, Perrin, and Livingston (1980) suggests that indices of limbic activation may be obtainable by non-invasive measures in man. Working initially with cats, these authors identified the coincidence of activation of the amygdala by direct electrical stimulation with an increase in spectral power on the "omega" (31–55 Hz) band of the EEG of the overlying temporal cortex. They argue that, given the known monosynaptic connections between the amygdala and temporal cortex, driving of the cortex by amygdaloid stimulation would occur in the omega band specifically due to the parameters of propogation delays in this monosynaptic circuit. By analogous procedures, Adamec et al. claim to have identified "signature" EEG frequencies in the 15–27 Hz and 74–78 Hz bands for activation of the ventral hippocampus as well. To the extent that similar monosynaptic corticolimbic circuits exist in man (Klingler & Gloor, 1960), similar EEG indices of limbic activity may be observable in humans. Although Adamec et al. (1980) alluded to monitoring EEG in their human subjects concurrently with procaine activation, they reported no findings regarding this aspect of the experiment. Accordingly the presence of "signatures" of limbic activity in human EEG remains an open issue. It is within this heuristic framework that the present study was carried out.

In conclusion, it is clear that anecdotal and observational evidence supports involvement of the limbic, and possibly neocortical structures of the temporal lobe in mediating human sexuality. Developing technology permits noninvasive investigation and quantitative analysis of central nervous system function at an increasingly higher level of detail and precision. The relative paucity of experimental investigation of normal cerebral involvement in sexuality leaves the field open to electroencepholographic and computer assisted tomographic, positron emission, and nuclear magnetic resonance investigation of dynamic relationships in the neural basis of sexuality.

To date our information is based on uncontrolled studies, usually clinical case reports, which leave doubt about the applicability of findings to the general

population. Movement artifacts have also obscured findings in studies involving masturbation. In the present report EEG correlates of erotic arousal in normal males were investigated in a controlled group study. The purpose of the study was: (1) to demonstrate that the temporal area of the brain is primarily involved in sexual arousal; and (2) the right hemisphere is more active. In the study, subjects were aroused with stimuli graded for erotic valence. Nonerotic stimuli were also included. Motion artifacts were minimized and taken into account in analyses. Finally the volume phallometer was used to reliably record degree of erotic arousal and the EEG was subjected to Fourier analyses.

METHOD

Subjects

Male volunteers were recruited by advertisement at the Univeristy of Toronto Placement Service offering payment for participation in a study of "sexual arousal and brain wave recording" of about 2 hours duration. Respondents to the advertisement were screened for gross drug/alcohol abuse, psychological disorder, physical abnormality, and sexual deviation on the basis of self-report. Information was generated in response to the following questions:

1. Do you have any physical abnormalities?
2. Do you have any allergies?
3. How much do you drink in the course of a week?
4. Have you ever been a patient in a mental hospital or institution?
5. Have you ever seen a psychiatrist or other mental health worker?
6. Have you had hallucinations in which you saw or heard things which were not there?
7. Have you tried any psychedelic drugs?
8. Have you ever been charged with a criminal offence?
9. Are you homosexual or heterosexual?

Of the first 24 respondents, five were excluded for the following reasons: one respondent claimed bisexuality, one acknowledged arrest for a criminal offence, and three acknowledged non-medical use of drugs on 15 or more occasions and/or within the month prior to the experiment. Three of the remaining 19 respondents notified the experimenter that they had changed their mind about participating, or they failed to appear for testing.

None of the remaining 16 experimental subjects reported any physical abnormality, history of psychological or psychiatric treatment, use of alcohol exceeding four drinks per week or nonmedical use of psychotropic drugs on more than 14 occasions in total or on more than one occasion in the preceding month. No one had taken drugs of any kind within a week prior to testing. All subjects claimed to be exclusively heterosexual.

Materials and Procedure

A set of sixteen 35 mm. slides was used as stimuli. They previously had been graded verbally into four categories of differential erotic valence (Freeman, 1976) and subsequently shown to correlate positively with penile volume changes (Langevin, Paitich, Hucker, Newman, Ramsay, Pope, Geller, & Anderson, 1979).

Of the slides originally classified by Freeman into four categories, a subset of 12 was selected from the mildly, moderately, and most arousing groups such that no overlap of PVC in the responses of subjects occurred between stimulus categories. The ordered categories of erotic stimuli thus were known to be associated with graded changes in penile volume. The erotic scenes depicted, variously, nude adult females and heterosexual intercourse. Four sexually neutral stimuli were also selected.

The experimental stimuli were presented in the same fixed random order to all subjects. Stimulus order was randomized within blocks of four slides. Each block had one slide from each category of stimulus erotic valence.

EEG, EOG, EMG, and penile volume change (PVC) were measured using a Grass Instruments Model 7 polygraph with 3 model 7P3A, 1 model 7P3B, 2 model 7P5B, and 1 model 7P1A preamplifiers and 6 model 7DAC and 1 model 7DAG driver amplifiers. EEG, EMG, and PVC data were recorded both on the strip chart pen recorder of the polygraph and on a Philips Analog 7 FM data recorder. EOG was recorded only on the data recorder. In addition, a 500 Hz tone was recorded on the voice channel of the FM recorder to mark the ''on'' time of the stimulus projector lamp.

Beckman silver/silver chloride Biopotential Skin Electrodes, (11 mm in diameter), were applied to the subject's scalp in accordance with the International Ten-Twenty system proposed by the International Federation of Societies for Electroencephalographic and Clinical Neurophysiology (see Craib, Perry, & Low, 1972 and Jasper, 1958). However, the frontal and parietal midline sites, F_Z and P_Z were omitted. Electrode sites were prepared using OmniPrep topical cleanser (trademark of D.O. Weaver & Co.). Cambridge Instrument Co. Electrode Jelly was applied to the electrodes and they were attached to the scalp by adhesive disks and elasticized head bands. Additional electrodes were applied to the medial supraorbital area of the right eye, the external canthus of the left eye, the vertex of the cranium, the hyloid cartilage, and over the left and right mastoid processes.

Impedance of each electrode was measured using a Grass Instrument Model EZM3A impedance meter, after application of the complete montage, and again immediately prior to connection to the amplifier terminals. Adjustments to individual electrodes were made as necessary until no impedance was in excess of 10 kilohms and homologous pairs of electrodes had a differential in impedance of no more than 1 kilohm.

EEG was recorded sequentially from blocks of four sites. These blocks were arranged in a Latin square across subjects. The four blocks consisted of the sites: F3, F4, C3, C4; P3, P4, 01, 02; Fp1, Fp2, F7, F8; and T3, T4, T5, T6, respectively.

A battery-operated calibrator producing a sine wave of 10 Hz. and 100 microvolts, peak to peak, was connected to two open channels of the electrode connector board. It was used as a standard signal to calibrate EEG and as a check on subsequent A to D conversion.

Changes in penile volume were measured using Freund's volume phallometer (Freund, 1963; Freund, Sedlacek, & Knob, 1965) adapted for use with a Grass Volumetric Pressure Transducer, Model PT5A, to allow measurement of penile volume change (PVC) in the range 0.02 - 100 cc (Langevin & Martin, 1975). Volumetric measurement of PVC was used in preference to measuring changes in penile circumference because the former method has been shown to discriminate between small differences in PVC produced by stimuli with relatively low sexual arousal value, whereas circumference measurement failed to do so (Freund, Langevin, & Barlow, 1974). The subject placed the phallometer on himself under the experimenter's supervision. The subject sat in a reclining easy chair, and was then covered from the waist down with a sheet and towel.

Electrooculogram (EOG) was recorded, via separate input cable, as the potential difference between the supra-orbital electrode and that at the external canthus of the contralateral eye. Electromyogram (EMG) for movements of the tongue and larynx was recorded, via separate input cable, between the hyloid electrode and the vertex, C_z, of the scalp. All scalp electrodes were referred to the paired leads from the mastoids.

On arrival subjects were shown the laboratory and shielded chamber where the experiment was to be carried out. Both the phallometric equipment and EEG electrodes were shown to subjects and their respective functions and means of attachment were explained. Subjects were told: "The purpose of the study is to identify EEG correlates of mild sexual arousal. The measures, as obtained by the electrode montage and phallometer, respectively, will be recorded on magnetic tape for subsequent quantitative analysis. During the test you will see a variety of slides projected onto a screen in the shielded chamber." The subjects were given an opportunity to ask questions about the study and they were then asked to sign a consent to participate.

Each subject was instructed to watch the screen and refrain from unnecessary movement or speech. He was further told that he would be asked to do various things by the experimenter during the study. The shielded chamber was darkened to an ambient level of approximately 0.25 footcandles, and the subject was left alone in the shielded chamber.

Analog data were obtained by recording four channels of EEG and one channel each of EOG, EMG, and PVC on a Philips Analog-7 FM data recorder. These data were subsequently digitized on a PDP-11/40/Laboratory Peripheral

System (Digital Equipment Corporation) A to D system at 200 samples/ second/channel such that there were 14 sequential epochs, each of two seconds duration. The start of the first epoch coincided with the onset of the experimental stimulus. Thus, the data set for each trial consisted of 400 samples for each of 14 epochs, and on seven channels. The digitized EEG data were then edited for artifacts.

Mean and standard deviations (S.D.) for EOG and EMG were computed. All EEG data for an epoch were discarded if the EOG response during that epoch exceeded 1.00 S.D. or if the corresponding EMG response exceeded 0.67 S.D. This resulted in an overall data loss of about 50%. Subsequently, the edited EEG data vectors were tested for stationarity in the mean within each two seconds epoch, by the RUNS test (Bendat & Piersol, 1971). The 5.87% of data vectors found to be nonstationary were excluded from subsequent analysis. A discrete Fourier transform was then carried out to obtain power spectra on a per-Herz basis. The spectral power values were then grouped into four frequency bands corresponding to delta (1 to 3 Hz.), theta (3.1 to 7 Hz.), alpha (7.1 to 13 Hz.), and beta (13.1 to 50 Hz.) and a mean spectral power value was calculated for each band for each epoch.

RESULTS

Analysis of variance was used throughout to examine penile volume changes and EEG power spectra.

TABLE 5.3
Penile Volume Change and EEG Power Spectra for Delta, Theta Alpha and Beta Bands for Stimulus Erotic Valences

	Erotic Valence Level			
	1	2	3	4
Penile Volume:				
Relative Area**	7[a]	95[ab]	160[b]	186[b]
Power:***				
Delta	19.91[a]	10.85[c]	15.66[b]	13.43[bc]
Theta	2.53	1.79	2.30	2.12
Alpha	1.16	0.94	1.13	1.11
Beta	0.28	0.25	0.27	0.28

Note: **$p < 01$, ***$p < 001$. Means with the same superscript are not significantly different. Smaller power score means more EEG activity.

TABLE 5.4
EEG Power Spectra for Right Versus Left
Hemisphere For Stimulus Erotic Valence

Erotic Valence	Hemispheric EEG Power		
	Left	Right	Total Valence
0	7.23	4.72	5.97
1	4.14	2.78	3.46
2	6.27	3.42	4.84
3	5.15	3.33	4.24
Total Hemisphere	5.69	3.56	

Penile Volume Change

The data in Table 5.3 indicate that the stimuli used were effective in eliciting erotic arousal.[1] However they were not as potent or discrete from each other as we had expected. There was also a fatigue effect since subjects' responsiveness decreased across presentation.[2] Although the number of trials was relatively short, the long preparation time for EEG electrodes appeared to be a factor in the unexpected result. Thus, the stimuli are limited and must be considered weak.

EEG Bands

Table 5.3 also shows that, of the four EEG bands examined, the delta band alone showed changes from nonerotic to erotic stimuli. Although nonerotic stimuli were statistically and significantly different from erotic stimuli, the latter were erratic in the degree of delta activity over the three erotic valences.

Location of EEG Activity

It has been argued that the right hemisphere of the brain is more active during emotional stimulation. One might expect that the same would hold for sexual stimulation. Table 5.4 shows indeed that the right hemisphere was more active generally during the stimulus presentations. Nevertheless, the activity was not peculiar to erotic stimuli.[3] Rather it seems the whole experiment involving visual stimulation was responsible for this result.

When individual brain sites were examined (Table 5.5) it was the frontal lobes that showed least power, compared to the remaining areas.[4] This however is typical of the frontal lobes. There was no site that discriminated better than the others, erotic and nonerotic stimuli.

It seems a general activation of the cortex was elicited by the stimuli used in this experiment.

TABLE 5.5
EEG Power Spectra of Sixteen Individual Sites
For Stimulus Erotic Valence

Site		Erotic Valence Level 1	2	3	4
Frontal					
Fp1	a	32.00	16.92	26.43	21.71
Fp2	b	27.86	14.99	18.23	18.06
F3		5.42	4.07	5.34	3.59
F4		4.81	3.32	5.04	3.22
F7	c	11.28	4.82	9.64	8.16
F8		0.91	0.59	0.57	0.61
Central					
C3		3.00	1.52	2.33	1.83
C4		0.32	0.22	0.26	0.25
Temporal					
T3		1.75	1.69	1.99	1.77
T4		1.51	1.36	1.50	1.68
T5		1.23	1.15	1.80	1.12
T6		0.20	0.18	0.20	0.19
Parietal					
P3		1.62	1.48	1.41	1.48
P4		1.77	1.26	1.21	2.27
Occipital					
O1		1.51	1.47	1.18	1.51
O2		0.31	0.30	0.30	0.31

Note: a, b, c. The Valence by Site interaction was not significant but the main effect for site was. It was Fp1, Fp2 and F7 that differed significantly from each other and all other mean power values for sites.

DISCUSSION

The foregoing analyses of gross EEG spectral power support the inference of a generalized activation effect due to differential arousal by mild erotic versus erotically neutral visual stimuli. There was no support for the hypothesis that the temporal lobes in particular are involved in sexual arousal. Possibly the results reflect the overall low arousal value of the stimulus materials used. Stronger stimuli, nasopharyngeal/sphenoidal records, a different modality of stimulation (e.g., audio recordings), or sexually anomalous subjects may produce different results.

There was no support for the hypothesis that erotic arousal would produce differential hemispheric cortical activation. Although the right hemisphere was more activated during visual stimulation, it did not differ for erotic and nonerotic stimuli. Rather there was a general cortical activation for erotica but it was not focal to either hemisphere or to any particular EEG site. The present results leave

open the question whether other nonsexually arousing stimuli, (e.g., those producing fear, disgust, or anger, etc.), are discriminable from erotic material on the basis of gross EEG power-spectra.

The role of muscle artifact and eye movement as epiphenomenal contaminators of EEG data, particularly in the frontal sites, was clear in the present study. Half our data was lost to artifact. This could influence interpretations and new methods are clearly desirable. Recently proposed methods for digital filtering of oculographic artifact (e.g., by Barlow, 1983 and Gratton, Coles, & Donchin, 1983) may help to separate artifact from effect better. Certainly the artifact contamination of EEG makes "clinical" interpretations problematic.

In summary, the present results suggest that development of a useful electroencephalographic index of erotic arousal may emerge from ongoing refinement of stimulation/recording procedures on the one hand and digital data analytic methods on the other. We are pursuing these refinements in our laboratories at present.

REFERENCES

Adamec, R., Stark-Adamec, C., Perrin, R., & Livingston, K. E. Limbic kindling and complex partial seizures: New strategies for detection of neurobehavioral change. In M. Girgis & L. G. Kilok (Eds.), *Limbic epilepsy and the dyscontrol syndrome.* Elsevier: North Holland Biomedical Press, 1980.

Barlow, J. S. Muscle spike artifact minimization in EEGs by time-domain filtering. *Electroencephalography and Clinical Neurophysiology,* 1983, *55,* 487–491.

Beck, J. G., Sakhein, D. K., & Barlow, D. H. Operating characteristics of the vaginal photoplethysmograph: Some implications for its use. *Archives of Sexual Behavior,* 1983, *12,* 43–58.

Bendat, J. S., & Piersol, A. G. *Random data: Analysis and measurement procedures.* Toronto: Wiley-Interscience, 1971.

Blumer, D. Changes of sexual behavior related to temporal lobe disorders in man. *Journal of Sex Research,* 1970, *6,* 173–180.(a)

Blumer, D. Hypersexual episodes in temporal lobe epilepsy. *American Journal of Psychiatry,* 1970, *126,* 1099–1106.(b)

Blumer, D., & Walker, A. E. Sexual behavior in temporal lobe epilepsy. *Archives of Neurology,* 1967, *16,* 37–43.

Blumer, D., & Walker, A. E. The neural basis of sexual behavior. In F. Benson & D. Blumer (Eds.), *Psychiatric aspects of neurologic disease.* New York: Grune and Stratton, 1975.

Cohen, H. D., Rosen, R. C., & Goldstein, I. Electroencephalographic laterality changes during human sexual orgasm. *Archives of Sexual Behavior,* 1976, *5,* 189–199.

Craib, A. R., Perry, M., & Low, M. D. *EEG handbook.* Vancouver: Beckman Instruments, 1972.

Freeman, R. *The role of subject content and stimulus variables in determining evaluative and behavioral reactions to explicit depiction of human sexual behavior.* Unpublished MA thesis, University of Waterloo, 1976.

Freund, K. A laboratory method for diagnosing predominance of homo- and hetero-erotic interest in the male. *Behavior Research and Therapy,* 1963, *1,* 85–93.

Freund, K., Langevin, R., & Barlow, D. Comparison of two penile measures of erotic arousal. *Behavior Research and Therapy,* 1974, *12,* 355–359.

Freund, K., Sedlacek, F., & Knob, K. A simple transducer for mechanical plethysmography of the male genital. *Journal for the Experimental Analysis of Behavior,* 1965, *6,* 350–355.

Gastaut, H., & Collomb, H. Etude du comportement sexuelle chez les epileptiques psychomoteurs. *Annales Medicopsychologiques*, 1954, *112*, 657–696.

Gloor, P., Amydgala. In J. Field (Ed.), *Handbook of physiology*, Volume 2, 1960. American Physiological Society, Washington, D.C.

Gratton, G., Coles, M. G. H., & Donchin, E. A new method for off-line removal of ocular artifact. *Electorencephalography and Clinical Neurophysiology*, 1983, *55*, 468–484.

Heath, R. G. Pleasure and brain activity in man: Deep and surface electroencephalograms during orgasm. *Journal of Nervous and Mental Disease*, 1972, *154*, 3–18.

Hierons, M., & Saunders, M. Impotence in patients with temporal lobe lesions. *Lancet*, 1966, *ii*, 761–764.

Hill, D., Pond, D. A., Mitchell, W., & Falconer, M. A. Personality changes following temporal lobectomy for epilepsy. *Journal of Mental Science*, 1957, *103*, 8–27.

Hoenig, J., & Kenna, J. C. EEG abnormalities and transsexualism. *British Journal of Psychiatry*, 1979, *134*, 293–300.

Jasper, H. H. The ten-twenty electrode system of the International Federation *Electroencephalography and Clinical Neurology*, 1958, *10*, 371–375.

Klinger, J., & Gloor, P. The connections of the amygdala and of the anterior temporal cortex in the human brain. *Journal of Comparative Neurology*, 1960, *115*, 333–369.

Kluver, H., & Bucy, P. C. Preliminary analysis of functions of the temporal lobes in monkeys. *Archives of Neurology and Psychiatry*, 1939, *42*, 979–1000.

Kolarsky, A., Freund, K., Machek, J., & Polak, O. Male sexual deviation: Association with early temporal lobe damage. *Archives of General Psychiatry*, 1967, *17*, 735–743.

Langevin, R., & Martin, M. Can erotic responses be classically conditioned? *Behavior Therapy*, 1975, *6*, 350–355.

Langevin, R., Paitich, D., Hucker, S., Newman, S., Ramsay, G., Pope, S., Geller, G., & Anderson, C. The effect of assertiveness training, provera and sex of therapist in the treatment of genital exhibitionism. *Journal of Behavior Therapy & Experimental Psychiatry*, 1979, *10*, 275–282.

MacLean, P. D. New findings relevant to the evolution of psychosexual functions of the brain. *Journal of Nervous and Mental Disease*, 1962, *135*, 289–301.

Mitchell, W., Falconer, M. A., & Hill, D. Epilepsy and fetishism relieved by temporal lobectomy. *Lancet*, 1954, *II*, 626–630.

Moan, C. E., & Heath, R. G. Septal stimulation for the initiation of heterosexual behavior in a homosexual male. *Journal of Behavior Therapy and Experimental Psychiatry*, 1972, *3*, 23–30.

Mosovich, A., & Tallaferro, A. Studies on EEG and sex function orgasm. *Diseases of the Nervous System*, 1954, *15*, 218–220.

Sarrel, P. M., Foddy, J., & McKinnon, J. B. Investigation of human sexual response using a cassette recorder. *Archives of Sexual Behavior*, 1977, *6*, 341–348.

Savard, R., & Walker, E. Changes in social functioning after surgical treatment for temporal lobe epilepsy. *Social Work*, 1965, *10*, 87–95.

Schreiner, L., & Kling, A. Behavioral changes following rhinencephalic injury in cats. *Journal of Neurophysiology*, 1953, *16*, 643–659.

Shukla, G. D., Srivastava, O. N., & Katiyar, B. C. Sexual disturbances in temporal lobe epilepsy: A controlled study. *British Journal of Psychiatry*, 1979, *134*, 288–292.

Taylor, D. C. Sexual behavior and temporal lobe epilepsy. *Archives of Neurology*, 1969, *21*, 510–516.

Terzian, H. Observations on the clinical symptomology of bilateral partial or total removal of temporal lobes in man. In M. A. Baldwin (Ed.), *Temporal lobe epilepsy*. Springfield, Ill: Thomas, 1957.

Walker, A. E. The libidinous temporal lobe. *Schweizer Archiv fur Neurologie und Psychiatrie*, 1972, *111*, 473–484.

END NOTES

Note 1. The results of analyses of variance for penile volume change (PVC), as determined by area under the PVC curve were:

	MS	df	F
Subjects	17.73	15	—
Erotic Valence	41.13	3	7.81**
Blocks	20.71	3	3.93**
Valence × Block	4.20	9	<1
Error	5.26	225	—

Multivariate analysis was not done because of cost considerations.

Note 2. The PVC area means for the four blocks of trials were:

Block:	1	2	3	4
Mean:	165[a]	143[ab]	103[ab]	36[b]

There was also an order of presentation effect for EEG power scores. ($F = 4.12$, df = 3, 4017, $p < 05$), which paralleled the decrement in penile responsiveness over blocks of trials.

Note 3. In the hemisphere by erotic valence by EEG band by block analysis of variance, there were no significant interactions at all. The only statistically significant effects were:

	MS	df	F
Hemisphere	179.31	1	646.13***
Valence	1.07	3	3.85**
Band	366.05	3	1319.05***

$**p < 01$, $***p < 001$.

Note 4. A 4 × 16 × 4 × 16 analysis of variance was used to examine power. The factors were erotic valence (4), EEG site (16), EEG band (4) and subjects (16). Results were:

	MS	df	F
Subjects	2483.24	15	—
Valence (V)	1149.33	3	4.51***
Band (B)	49267.37	3	193.41***
Sites	13096.23	15	51.41***
V × B	884.41	9	3.47***
V × S	277.71	45	1.09
B × S	8918.18	45	35.01***
V × B × S	223.33	135	<1
Error within	254.73	3825	

PEDOPHILIA AND INCEST

The following section examines offenders who engage in sexual acts with minors. In practice heterosexual, homosexual, bisexual pedophiles, and incest offenders have been mixed together. The four groups' behaviors have been subjected to a plethora of clinical interpretations but empirical facts about their underlying erotic preferences and aggressiveness, based on controlled research, are few indeed.

Traditionally it has been asserted that men engaging minors in sexual behavior are shy, passive, and unable to relate to adult women. The "passivity" of pedophiles has been assumed in clinical practice, although we do know some of them are sadistic and even kill their victims. Recent research suggests that violence may be a more common and integral part of the lives and sexual behavior of some pedophiles, than previously believed.

This next study examines similarities and differences in erotic and aggressive behaviors of heterosexual, homosexual, and bisexual pedophiles.

Erotic Preference and Aggression in Pedophilia: A Comparison of Heterosexual, Homosexual, and Bisexual Types

Ron Langevin
Stephen J. Hucker
Lorraine Handy
John E. Purins
Anne E. Russon
Clarke Institute of Psychiatry, Toronto

Helen J. Hook
York University, Toronto

INTRODUCTION

Sexual acts committed on children by adults greatly concern the public but much empirical investigation is needed to define even the rudiments of pedophilia.[1] Available studies often mix together heterosexual, homosexual, and bisexual pedophiles, incest offenders, exhibitionists, and even rapists (cf. Langevin, 1983; Lester, 1975; Quinsey, 1977). These groups certainly are of differential concern to the clinician. One needs particularly to identify violence proneness in these various groups both in sexual and nonsexual contexts. The present study asks: what are the similarities and differences in the erotic profiles of heterosexual, homosexual, and bisexual pedophiles? and, are they passive or aggressive men in general?

EROTIC PREFERENCE

Studies of the sexual history of pedophiles raise puzzling questions about their erotic preferences. Nedoma, Mellan, and Pondelickova (1971), for example, studied 100 men convicted or arrested for sexual offenses against children 15 years of age and younger. Although the exact numbers of heterosexual and homosexual offenders was not indicated, 78% had occasional intercourse with a female their own age and only 27% had coitus with minors. The majority (62%) engaged in masturbation and touching. Quinsey, Steinman, Bergersen, and

137

Holmes (1975) also found that stimuli depicting heterosexual petting were very arousing to pedophiles. Along with the relatively high frequency of marriage at least among heterosexual pedophiles (cf. Langevin, 1983), one has to wonder what motivates them to interact with legally and socially sanctioned minors.

Possibly adults are surrogates for the more desired child. Maybe some pedophiles lie about their sexual experiences. However, one may also interpret their behavior to mean that the body characteristics of the child are only important in some cases. In others, behaviors of children which adults do not exhibit may be primary. Possibly both the adult and child are erotically desired, but for different reasons. The common association and confusion of exhibitionism and pedophilia suggests that narcissism may be a factor (cf. Langevin, Paitich, Ramsay, Anderson, Kamrad, Pope, Geller, & Newmen, 1979 and Paitich, Langevin, Freeman, Mann & Handy, 1978). That is, admiration by another person may be sexually arousing and sufficiently gratifying in itself. However, one has to be concerned about the findings of Groth and Birnbaum (1978) in which a fifth of the sex offenders against children used force and about a third penetrated their victims. The association of pedophilia with rape or sadism usually has not been considered. Although there may be a sample bias from the prison setting from which Groth and Birnbaum collected their data, the results warrant further investigation, especially considering the general and frequent claims that pedophiles are passive.

We know that collectively pedophiles react with penile tumescence more to children than normal heterosexual or androphilic (homosexual) men do (Freund 1965, 1967a, b; Quinsey, Steinman, Bergersen, & Holmes, 1975). Nevertheless their reactions are quite variable in fact and some react significantly to adult females. Freund, McKnight, Langevin, and Cibiri (1972) found that non-pedophilic community volunteers showed significant penile tumescence to female children as young as 6 years of age. The size of their reactions increased with the age of the stimulus person, the largest responses being elicited by physically mature adult females. On the other hand, an examination of clinical cases shows that some heterosexual pedophiles react phallometrically most to children, but others react most to adolescent females (hebephiles). Still others react most to the body characteristics of adult females like normal heterosexuals do. There are no significant reactions to the nonpreferred male in any case. Homosexual pedophiles show profiles analogous to those of heterosexual pedophiles, but with largest reactions being to males. Although one is always concerned about faking on phallometric tests (cf. Quinsey & Bergersen, 1976 and Rosen, Shapiro & Schwartz, 1975), many results appear genuine.

Bisexual pedophiles are unique among all the sexual anomalies in showing largest penile reactions to both male and female children which supports their verbal reports of erotic arousal (Freund and Langevin, 1976 & Freund, Scher, Chan & Ben-Aron, 1982). Bisexuals who interact with adults on the other hand, usually show penile tumescence only to males. Their sex histories showed them

to be "super homosexual" with even more male oriented sex outlets than exclusively homosexual men (Langevin, 1983). The sex history profiles of bisexual pedophiles have not been reported to date. This information may cast some light on differences in response preferences and etiology of the three types of pedophilia.

AGGRESSIVENESS

Aggressiveness may be scrutinized by an examination of the offense, criminal record, personality, family background, and substance abuse which often is associated with violence. Each will be considered in turn.

The Offense

Current evidence suggests that violence in pedophilic offenses has been underestimated and it needs serious reexamination. Howells (1981) included aggression-nonaggression as one dimension to be investigated in pedophilia. Christie, Marshall, and Lanthier (1978) reported violence was used in sexual acts by 58% of a mixed group of pedophiles.[2] However, the sample studied may not be representative of pedophiles in general because it was drawn in part from maximum and medium security prison settings. Nevertheless, the findings of the study are so contrary to existing belief that violence was examined in the three groups reported here. Other studies also offer some support for the Christie et al. findings.

Finkelhor (1979) examined reports of victims of offenses against children. More than half involved undefined "force." Groth and Birnbaum (1978) found 20% of 175 offenders against children (including 15% incest cases) used some force, 49% used intimidation or threat, and 30% used seduction and enticement. Peters (1976) reported that children compared to adult victims were less likely to be forced in sexual acts. Of the offenders against children, 54% involved no force at all in contrast to offenses against adults in which 31% of the victims were pushed or shoved, 51% choked or gagged, 17% slapped, and 9% brutally beaten. However, 37% of the children were subjected to forcible rape.

Criminal Record

General criminality of pedophiles has been examined by some writers for the incidence of violent sex offenses. Toobert, Bartelme, and Jones (1959) found that, among 120 incarcerated "pedophiles," 64% were recidivists. Of the repeated offenders, 34% had carried out nonsex offenses. Violence was not mentioned. Christie et al. (1978) found 74% of pedophiles and 84% of rapists they studied had previous convictions for nonsexual offenses. Fifty one percent of pedophiles had previous convictions for sexual offenses. Even 29% of pedophiles and 12% of rapists had immediate family members who were convicted of minor criminal offenses.

Personality

Characteristically the pedophile has been described as shy and unassertive (cf. Howells, 1981; Langevin, 1983; Mohr, Turner & Jerry, 1964). For example, studies by Fisher (1969; Fisher & Howell, 1970) and our clinic (Langevin et al., 1978) showed that heterosexual pedophiles in particular tended to be shy, passive, and unassertive. Recently the passivity of pedophiles has been questioned. Panton (1978) compared the MMPIs of three groups of incarcerated offenders: 30 rapists of adults, 20 rapists of children, and 28 nonviolent pedophiles. Only valid MMPIs were used and psychotic cases were excluded. The two rapist groups did not differ significantly from each other but both were different from nonviolent pedophiles. Both groups of rapists, moreover, showed a mean 4-8/8-4 profile type (Psychopathic Deviate - Schizophrenia) which has been considered characteristic of violent offenders. The nonviolent pedophiles had the 4-2 profile (Psychopathic Deviate - Depression).[3] Panton described the two rapists groups as showing aggravated hostility, resentfulness, social alienation, self-centeredness, and impulsive seeking of immediate gratification. Their offenses were more assaultive than sexual. The nonviolent pedophiles showed self-alienation but also low self esteem, self doubt, anxiety, inhibition of aggression, aversion to violence, need for reinforcement from others, feelings of inadequacy, insecurity, and fear of heterosexual failure. On the Toobert et al. (1959) MMPI Pedophilia scale, the nonviolent pedophiles scored significantly higher than the two rapist groups. Armentrout and Hauer (1978) studied the MMPIs of 13 rapists of adults, 21 rapists of children, and 17 nonrapist heterosexual offenders and found similar results, indicating that some pedophiles are violent in their sexual behavior and in personality.[4]

The results conflict with older MMPI results on prison samples. Toobert et al. (1959) studied the MMPIs of 120 incarcerated sex offenders against children, selected only on the basis of sexually engaging a child 12 years of age or younger.[5] They found few differences between this group and 160 general prisoners. No scale was clinically significant (mean T-score over 70). Only the Psychopathic Deviate scale was close and it was similar in both groups. The authors developed a 24 item Pedophilia scale and crossvalidated it on a further group of 38 "pedophiles" with controls. The authors described the pedophiles as sexually dissatisfied, having strong religious interests, feeling inadequate, expressing much guilt, and as being highly sensitized to the evaluations of others. The pedophiles were not aggressive nor sexually active but showed the unassertive stereotype considered more typical of the sexual anomaly.

Christie et al. (1978) reported that although many of their pedophilic cases were violent in their sexual offenses both rapists and pedophiles scored within normal limits on all MMPI scales except Psychopathic Deviate. The only significant mean group difference was for Mania on which pedophiles scored higher.

The personalities of bisexual pedophiles have not been studied to date. They are of particular interest and concern because they show erotic reactivity to both

sexes (Freund & Langevin, 1976, Freund et al., 1982). Our own earlier work (Langevin, 1983; Langevin, Paitich, Freeman, Mann, & Handy, 1978) suggested that men who interact sexually with both mature men and women were more emotionally disturbed than men who only interact with one sex. Moreover, the more types of sexual outlets an individual had, the more emotionally disturbed his personality was, as measured by the MMPI. Possibly this is true of the bisexual pedophile as well. One aim of the present study was to investigate this possibility.

Family Background

Christie et al. (1978) found that half of both groups of pedophiles and rapists were brought up by mothers alone or someone besides natural parents. Thirty one percent of pedophiles received frequent violent beatings and another 15% had excessive punitive discipline compared to 33% of rapists who were harshly treated. The results are contrary to those of Paitich and Langevin (1976) on groups of heterosexual and homosexual pedophiles. Aggression was not a prominent factor on the Clarke Parent Child Relations Questionnaire scales but pedophiles' mothers were reported by the offenders as more strict and less affectionate than controls' mothers were. Father relationships were within normal limits. Gebhard, Pomeroy, & Christenson (1965) examined how sex offenders against children got along with each parent. Results were not remarkable although the use of force was associated with poorer adjustment to both parents.

Alcohol and Drug Abuse

Christie et al. (1978) found 65% of their pedophilic prison sample and 56% of rapists were problem drinkers or alcoholics. This is somewhat higher than earlier reports of alcohol abuse among "pedophiles" which range about 28% (Swanson, 1968) to 52% (Rada, 1976). The Christie et al. findings showed a high incidence of alcohol abuse compared to Canadians in general.[6] The two groups reported alcoholism in their family. Fifty percent of the pedophiles and 58% of rapists noted that one or both of their parents were alcoholics or had serious drinking problems. At the time of the offense 53% of pedophiles and 56% of rapists were noticeably intoxicated and an additional 23% of pedophiles and 24% of rapists were drinking just prior to the offense. Nine percent of pedophiles and 18% of rapists were using drugs, mostly marijuana or prescribed tranquillizers. Other reports are comparable. Approximately half of pedophilic and other sexual offenders against children are drinking at the time of their offense (Howells, 1981; Peters, 1976; Rada, 1976) indicating that substance abuse may have played some role in the offenses (See Chapter 4). The Rada (1976) study is noteworthy for use of the MAST, offering a standard index that 52% of 203 pedophiles were alcoholic.

In the following report, heterosexual, homosexual, and bisexual pedophiles and community controls were compared on sexual history, personality, diag-

nosis, criminal history, and alcohol and drug use in order to examine their erotic preference and aggression profiles.

METHOD

Subjects

There were four groups of men used in the study for a total of 142 cases. Heterosexual pedophiles (N=32) had had sexual contact with girls 12 or younger since they themselves were 18 or with girls 13 to 15 since they themselves were 21. Homosexual pedophiles (N=40) had such contact; only with boys in the same respective age categories. Bisexual pedophiles (N=16) satisfied the criteria for both homosexual and heterosexual pedophilia. All pedophilic men admitted to their charges and/or to an erotic preference for minors as determined by clinical interview. A fourth group of community controls (N=54) were compared to the three patient groups. The controls had no history of mental illness, crime, or sexual anomaly.

TABLE 6.1A
Mean Age, Education and Intelligence Scores
of Pedophiles and Controls

		Heterosexual Pedophile	Homosexual Pedophile	Bisexual Pedophile	Control
Number of cases		32	40	16	54
Age in years	****	33	33	36	24[a]
Education in years	****	9	11	10	15[a]
Average Verbal Intelligence	****	106	107	108	117[a]
Average Raven's Intelligence	**	110[a]	112[a]	112[ab]	119[b]

TABLE 6.1B
Distribution of IQ Scores For the Pedophiles And Controls

	Heterosexual Pedophile	Homosexual Pedophile	Bisexual Pedophile	Control
Verbal IQ %				
−89	3	5	0	0
90–110	79	63	73	33
111–	17	32	27	67
Raven IQ %				
−89	3	10	0	2
90–110	45	28	47	13
111–	52	63	53	85

Note: In this table and all subsequent tables, *p < .05, **p < .01, ***p < .001, ****p < 0001. a, b—Means with same superscript are not significantly different.

Age, Education, and Intelligence. There were no significant differences among the pedophilic groups in age or education although all were significantly older than controls and significantly less educated (Table 6.1A).

IQ differences among the groups reflected educational achievement although Raven Standard Progressive Matrices showed greater overlap of group mean scores (Table 6.1B). The distribution of IQ scores (Table 6.1B) shows that the majority of pedophiles were in the normal or superior range.[7]

Materials and Procedure

All research participants were administered the MMPI, Cattell 16PF, Clarke Parent Child Relations Questionnaire (PCR), and Clarke Sex History Questionnaire (SHQ) for males (Paitich & Langevin, 1976; Paitich et al., 1977), the Raven Standard Progressive Matrices and Clarke Vocabulary test (as estimates of Performance and Verbal IQ respectively; Paitich, 1973), along with questionnaires to obtain information on drug and alcohol use. Final diagnoses and criminal records also were available from medical records.

RESULTS

Each set of scales (MMPI, 16PF, PCR and SHQ) were analyzed separately.[8]

Erotic Preference

Sexual and Marital History. There were group differences in marital status (Table 6.2). The homosexual pedophiles and the control group were in the majority, single men. On the other hand, the bisexual and heterosexual pedophiles were similar since over one half of each group had married at some time. Although the bisexual group had more divorces than the heterosexuals, the difference was not statistically significant.

TABLE 6.2
Marital Status of the Pedophilic and Control Groups

	% Heterosexual	% Homosexual	% Bisexual	% Control
Single	31	83	38	87
Married	50	8	25	7
Divorced/Separated	13	8	31	2
Common Law	3	3	0	4
Not Known	3	0	6	0

Note: Chi Square test for all groups on single versus other (known) status: $\chi^2 = 36.79$, df = 3, $p < .001$; pedophiles only $\chi^2 = 20.12$, df = 2, $p < .001$ and for heterosexual versus bisexual pedophiles only $\chi^2 = 0.289$, df = 1, p > 05.

The 27 Clarke Sex History scales[9] are presented in Table 6.3. The four groups did *not* differ significantly on the following scales: crossdressing, frottage, rape, and obscene phone calls. The frequencies of these behaviors tended to be low. The controls showed the expected pattern of sexual experience, the greatest being with mature females and the remaining sex-age categories being basically nil. The main group differences occurred for the age and sex of the preferred stimulus persons (Table 6.4).

The heterosexual pedophiles showed a general lack of experience with males of all ages. They differed most from the other groups in sexually acting out with

TABLE 6.3
Sex History Scale Scores for The Pedophiles and Controls

Scale			Heterosexual	Homosexual	Bisexual	Control
				Mean Z Score		
Heterosexual						
Exhibitionistic Behavior		****	48a	−19b	57a	−31b
Exhibitionistic Frequency		***	41b	−18a	58b	−28a
Voyeurism Frequency		*	48b	−18a	09ab	−17a
Frottage Frequency			41	−16	−04	−11
"Rape" Frequency†			42	−15	−03	−12
Obscene Calls Frequency			−11	−11	−11	17
Oral-Genital-Anal Frequency		***	30b	−48a	−26ab	26b
Anal Activity		*	−36a	33b	29ab	−12ab
Adult	—Desire	****	06b	−65c	−17bc	50a
	—Disgust	****	00	50	24	−44
	—Frequency	*	19b	−44a	17ab	16ab
Pubescent	—Desire	****	63a	−27b	79a	−41b
	—Disgust	*	−05ab	−29a	65b	05ab
	—Frequency	*	45b	−12a	16ab	−23a
Pedophilic	—Desire	****	73c	−23b	126d	−63a
	—Disgust	****	−22b	19ab	−126c	36a
	—Frequency	**	11	−22	76a	−13
Homosexual						
Pedophilic	—Desire	****	−58c	107a	64b	−64c
	—Disgust	****	44a	−55b	−98b	44a
	—Frequency	****	−32a	36b	85b	−33a
Pubescent Frequency		**	−24	36	40	−24
Youth (16–20) Frequency		*	−19ab	35b	15ab	−19ab
Androphilic—Disgust		****	39a	−32b	−77b	23a
	—Frequency	*	−17a	39b	7ab	−21a
General	—Desire	****	−30a	59b	96b	−54a
	—Disgust	****	53a	−64b	−118c	51a
Crossdressing Frequency			28	−11	24	−15

Note: *p < 05, **p < 01, ***p < 001, ****p < 0001, †p < .10. Means with same superscript are not significantly different. Two place decimals omitted.

TABLE 6.4
Selected Sexual Outlets with Sex-Age Stimulus Categories

Outlet		Heterosexual Pedophile	Homosexual Pedophile	Bisexual Pedophile	Controls
			% Group		
Adult Female					
Vaginal intercourse	***	91	50	75	81
Cunnilingus	****	72	18	56	63
Fellatio	****	75	23	56	70
Anal intercourse	*	38	10	13	30
Exposing	**	16	3	13	0
Females 13–15 years old					
Touch in sexual way	****	50	3	38	2
Touch between legs	****	41	3	25	7
They touch penis	****	41	5	31	4
Rub against with penis	***	31	5	19	4
Attempt intercourse	***	31	5	19	4
Exposing	**	19	3	19	0
Females 12 and younger					
Touch in sexual way	****	59	5	75	2
Touch between legs	****	66	5	81	2
They touch penis	****	56	0	44	0
Rub against with penis	****	53	5	31	0
Attempt intercourse	****	25	3	19	0
Exposing	****	44	5	19	0
Adult Male 21 or older					
Touch penis	***	16	33	38	4
They touch penis	**	22	40	44	9
Perform fellatio	**	13	25	25	2
Be fellated	***	19	38	31	4
Perform anal intercourse	**	3	18	25	2
Recipient anal intercourse	**	6	28	19	2
Males 16–20 years old					
Touch penis	****	3	50	50	2
They touch penis	****	3	45	44	4
Perform fellatio	****	3	40	25	2
Be fellated	****	3	30	25	2
Perform anal intercourse	***	3	25	25	2
Recipient anal intercourse	****	0	25	25	2
Males 13–15 years old					
Touch penis	****	0	70	63	0
They touch penis	****	0	75	63	0
Perform fellatio	****	0	63	50	0
Be fellated	****	0	45	38	0
Perform anal intercourse	****	0	28	13	0
Recipient anal intercourse	****	0	23	19	0

(*continued*)

TABLE 6.4 (*Continued*)

Outlet		Heterosexual Pedophile	Homosexual Pedophile	Bisexual Pedophile	Controls
		% Group			
Males 12 or younger					
Touch penis	****	6	88	75	0
They touch penis	****	6	75	56	0
Perform fellatio	****	0	60	56	0
Be fellated	****	6	38	38	0
Perform anal intercourse	****	0	33	6	0
Recipient anal intercourse	**	0	13	19	0
Crossdressing					
Skirt or dress		16	8	19	2
Undergarments	*	9	5	25	4
Voyeurism					
At intercourse		34	28	31	24
At female undressing	*	41	20	63	33
Exhibiting					
To adult females	**	16	2	12	0
Outdoor masturbation		38	35	44	19
Touching and Frottage					
Rub strange female in crowd	**	19	2	31	7
Touch strange female in crowd	*	22	0	13	7
Touch strange female in lonely place		13	0	19	7
"Rape"					
Attempts		25	8	13	9
Succeeded		16	2	6	7
Obscene Calls		0	0	0	2

Note: Items with low frequencies were dichotomized into "never" vs. "ever" for computing Chi Square in order to reduce the number of empty cells.
*p < .05, **p < .01, ***p< .001, ****p < .0001.

13-to 15-year-old females. The greatest number engaged in the full range of sexual behaviors with adult females but considerably fewer did with immature females. Touching was the most prominent behavior involving minors.

The homosexual pedophiles, as expected, had less experience with females of all ages and they showed lower frequencies of sexual acting out with them than the other pedophilic groups. Although 50% of them had intercourse with a physically mature female, they were lowest among the four groups in heterosexual experience with adults (Table 6.3). Their oral-genital-anal sexual experiences with males were uniform across the age groups from 12 and younger through adults over 21-years-old. The exception was that more respondents performed fellatio on children than on adults (see Table 6.4). Touching was again the most common behavior with minors.

TABLE 6.5
Background Family Sexuality in Pedophilia

Variable		Heterosexual	Homosexual	Bisexual	Control
1. Saw mother nude to waist ever	*	42[ab]	46[ab]	13[a]	56[b]
2. Saw mother totally nude ever		29	18	7	37
3. Mother washed genitals ever	*	16	15	53[a]	17
4. Sex play with sisters					
—ever—	*	38[b]	15[a]	27[ab]	21[a]
—more than 5 times—		10	0	13	4

Note: *p < .05. Means with the same superscript are not significantly different.

The bisexual pedophiles did not just react to both sexes. They had significantly more experience with female children 12 and younger than heterosexual pedophiles and a trend to more experience with young male children than homosexual pedophiles had (Table 6.3). The types of outlets in which bisexual pedophiles engaged was comparable to the other two pedophilic groups for their preferred sex. The exception was that bisexuals performed anal intercourse on boys 15 and younger less often than homosexual pedophiles did (Table 6.4).

The bisexual group, and to a lesser extent, the heterosexual pedophiles, showed trends to polymorphous heterosexuality. Although dressing in female clothes was infrequent in all groups, the two groups in greater numbers had crossdressed. They, more than the other groups, peeped at females undressing and rubbed against female strangers in crowds. Both pedophilic groups showed the full range of courtship disorders (voyeurism, exposing, obscene calls, frottage, and rape). The bisexuals contrasted with heterosexual pedophiles in showing fewer of their numbers exposing to females 12 and younger, although as a group they were comparable in the frequency of exposing.

The bisexuals differed in their childhood sexual experiences. They least often of any group saw their mothers nude to the waist or fully nude. However, their mothers more often washed their sons' genitals (Table 6.5). The bisexual and heterosexual pedophiles were most likely to engage in sex play with their sisters. There were no significant differences in the incidence of sex play with brothers nor in mother or father handling the offenders' genitals in a sexual way.

Aggression

Personality and Diagnosis. There were no significant differences in the distribution of diagnoses among the three pedophilic groups as reported by examining psychiatrists. The majority were diagnosed as personality disorders and/or sexual deviations (Table 6.6). The immature and inadequate types of

TABLE 6.6
Diagnosis of The Three Pedophilic Groups

Diagnoses	Pedophilic Groups		
	% Heterosexual	% Homosexual	% Bisexual
Personality Disorder	63	70	50
Sexual Deviation	63	98	63
Other	34	20	19
# Cases	32	40	16
# Cases Without Diagnosis	2	0	1
# Diagnoses	57	83	24
Selected Diagnoses			
Personality Disorder: Total #	*21*	*31*	*8*
Immature/Inadequate	9	10	2
Schizoid	0	5	1
Antisocial	0	4	1
Miscellaneous Personality Disorders	12	12	4
Sexual Deviation: Total #	*23*	*41*	*12*
Heterosexual Pedophilia	12	0	2
Homosexual Pedophilia	0	26	3
Mixed/Unspecified Pedophilia	3	8	3
Exhibitionism	4	1	2
Miscellaneous Sexual Deviations	4	6	2
Other: Total #	*13*	*11*	*4*
Alcoholism	3	2	1
Mental Retardation	0	3	0
Psychoses	4	0	2
Neuroses	4	5	1
Miscellaneous Other	2	1	0

Note: Percentages do not total 100% because multiple diagnoses were given in some cases.

personality disorders were most often used for each group and, as expected, pedophilia was the most frequent sexual deviation diagnosed. Of the "other" diagnoses, psychoses and neuroses were few in number and so were alcoholism or mental retardation.

The results of the MMPI showed that there was considerable emotional disturbance among pedophiles (Table 6.7). The Hypochrondriasis, Depression, Psychopathic Deviate, Paranoia, Psychasthenia, Schizophrenia, and Social Introversion scales were significant for the group comparison. In five of those seven scales, there were no significant differences among the pedophilic groups but all scored higher than controls. In the cases of Hypochondriasis and Depression there was considerably greater overlap of scores with controls. Most of the difference between pedophilic groups and controls appeared on the psychotic

TABLE 6.7
MMPI Mean Scores for Pedophilic and Control Groups

Scale		Heterosexual Pedophile	Homosexual Pedophile	Bisexual Pedophile	Control
Lie	*	3.[a]	4[ab]	4[ab]	5[b]
F		11	11	11	7
K	****	11[a]	13[a]	15[ab]	17[b]
Hypochondriasis	*	15	16	16	13
Depression	**	25[ab]	26[a]	25[ab]	21[b]
Hysteria		24	25	24	22
Psychopathic Deviate	****	30	30	30	24[a]
Masculinity-femininity		28	30	30	30
Paranoia	***	14	14	13	10[a]
Psychastenia	***	32	33	33	27[a]
Schizophrenia	***	36	37	37	28[a]
Mania		22	21	22	21
Social Introversion	****	32	35	33	25[a]

Note: *p < 05, **p < 01, ***p < 001, ****p < .0001. Means with the same superscript are not significantly different. Overall 61% of cases were correctly assigned to their own group. 56% of heterosexual pedophiles, 53% of homosexual pedophiles, 0% bisexual pedophiles and 89% of controls were correctly assigned to their actual group.

TABLE 6.8
Percent of MMPI T Scores 70 or Greater for Pedophilic
and Control Groups

Scale		Heterosexual Pedophile	Homosexual Pedophile	Bisexual Pedophile	Control
L		3	3	0	0
F		34	30	38	13
K		6	3	6	7
Hypochondriasis		31	25	25	9
Depression	**	56	53	38	22
Hysteria	*	25	28	38	7
Psychopathic Deviate	****	66	58	63	20
Masculinity-femininity		28	50	44	46
Paranoia	****	38	38	50	7
Psychastenia	***	56	45	44	15
Schizophrenia	****	59	53	56	17
Mania		41	30	38	17
Social Introversion	***	13	23	31	0

Note: *p < .05, **p < .01, ***p < .001, ****p < .0001.

scales. Serious emotional disturbance, confusion, rumination, and suspicion characterized all the pedophilic groups. The T-scores in Table 6.8 basically confirm results for the mean scores indicating that there is significant *clinical* pathology among pedophiles.[10]

The MMPI two point scale codes were examined. The so-called violent person 8-4/4-8 (Schizophrenia-Psychopathic Deviate) code occurred in 19% of heterosexual, 8% of homosexual, and 25% of bisexual pedophiles. The group differences were not statistically significant.[11] No other two point code was outstanding and all were represented by four cases or less. Between 13% and 19% of the three groups had no scale elevations over T=70.

The Toobert et al. (1959) MMPI Pedophilia scale was examined in the four groups. The significant results showed that the three pedophilic groups did not differ from each other but all scored higher than controls.[12]

TABLE 6.9
16 PF Scores for Pedophilic and Control Groups

Factor			Heterosexual Pedophile	Homosexual Pedophile	Bisexual Pedophile	Controls
	Md	**	6[a]	7[ab]	7[ab]	9[b]
A	Reserved/Outgoing	***	7	6	6	8[a]
B	Less Intelligent/More Intelligent	***	4	4	4	5[a]
C	Affected by Feelings/Emotionally Stable	*	6[a]	7[ab]	7[ab]	8[b]
E	Humble/Assertive		6	5	5	6
F	Sober/Happy-go-lucky		6	6	6	7
G	Expedient/Conscientious		7	7	6	6
H	Shy/Venturesome	*	6[ab]	6[b]	5[b]	7[a]
I	Tough-minded/Tender-minded	****	4[a]	6	6	7
L	Trusting/Suspicious		5	5	5	4
M	Practical/Imaginative	***	6	6	5	8[a]
N	Forthright/Shrewd	***	6	6	6	4[a]
O	Self-assured/Apprehensive		5	5	5	4
Q1	Conservative/Experimenting	****	6	5	6	8[a]
Q2	Group-dependent/Self-sufficient	****	8	8	8	6[a]
Q3	Undisciplined self conflict/Controlled		7	7	6	7
Q4	Relaxed/Tense		6	6	5	5

Note: *p < 05, **p < 01, ***p < 001, ****p < 0001. Means with the same superscript are not significantly different. Means have been rounded. Overall 66% of cases were correctly assigned to their own group. 63% of heterosexual pedophiles, 65% homosexual pedophiles, 25% bisexual pedophiles, and 80% of controls were correctly assigned to their actual group.

TABLE 6.10
16 PF Sten Scores Less Than 3 or Greater Than 8 For Pedophilic and
Control Groups

Factor		Heterosexual Pedophile		Homosexual Pedophile		Bisexual Pedophile		Controls	
		<3	>8	<3	>8	<3	>8	<3	>8
	Md	31	3	13	0	25	0	11	9
A	Reserved/Outgoing	22	3	28	5	25	0	9	9
B	Less Intelligent/More Intelligent	0	0	8	10	0	0	2	15
C	Affected by Feelings/Emotionally Stable	16	3	8	13	13	13	7	15
E	Humble/Assertive	0	9	5	5	0	25	2	9
F	Sober/Happy-go-lucky	19	3	15	3	13	13	7	4
G	Expedient/Conscientious	13	3	10	3	13	0	19	4
H	Shy/Venturesome	3	9	5	5	6	6	0	11
I	Tough-minded/Tender Minded**	6	3	0	18	0	19	4	40
L	Trusting/Suspicious	13	16	3	10	13	25	18	9
M	Practical/Imaginative***	6	9	0	15	0	0	0	37
N	Forthright/Shrewd	9	6	5	5	6	13	22	4
O	Self-assured/Apprehensive	9	13	3	18	6	25	17	19
Q1	Conservative/Experimenting****	9	22	5	10	0	0	0	54
Q2	Group-dependent/Self-sufficient***	6	3	15	5	0	6	41	0
Q3	Undisciplined self conflict/Controlled	13	3	20	0	31	0	17	0
Q4	Relaxed/Tense	9	25	8	23	6	25	13	9

Note: **p < .01, ***p < .001, ****p < .0001.

The 16 PF results in Table 6.9 in general, support those of the MMPI. Ten of the 17 scales were significant. On six of these (Factors A, B, M, N, Q1, and Q2) there were no significant differences among the pedophilic groups but all differed from controls. In three other cases (Md, Factors C and H), there was considerable overlap of pedophilic and normal group means. The unexpected finding was that on Factor I, the "femininity" scale of the 16 PF, heterosexual pedophiles scored lower than the other three groups. An examination of deviant sten scores ("standard ten"-scores range from 1 to 10 with average scores being 5 and 6) in Table 6.10 shows that the heterosexual pedophiles were average and the other three groups had more feminine interests. The controls contrasted with the pedophilic groups in being more outgoing, intelligent, imaginative, forthright, experimenting, and group dependent. It is noteworthy that Factors E and H (shyness and assertiveness) were unremarkable. There was a trend to more shyness among all pedophilic groups compared to controls but there were no significant differences in assertiveness (Factor E). Sten scores on shyness were within normal limits for pedophiles. This is contrary to expectation.

Parent Child Relations.   Only six of the 16 Clarke PCR scales were significant but four of the six were mother scales and two were father scales (Table 6.11
and Table 6.12). Mothers were reported to be more aggressive and stricter (MAS
and MStr) by heterosexual and bisexual pedophiles than by the other two groups.
However, there was considerable overlap of group scores. Mothers in all pedophilic groups were reported as less affectionate than mothers of controls were.
The largest differences among the groups were in mother identification. Heterosexual and bisexual pedophiles identified less with mother than the other two
groups did.

The father scales were not as discriminating as the mother scales. Father
identification was marginally weaker in pedophilic groups than in the controls.
Fathers of bisexual pedophiles were reported to be more indulgent than fathers of
the other three groups were. The heterosexual and bisexual pedophiles had more
mothers with a history of psychiatric hospitalization (Table 6.13). Patterns were
similar for their fathers but results were not statistically significant. Their fathers
also were more often in trouble with the police.

TABLE 6.11
PCR Mean Scores for Pedophilic and Control Groups

Scale		Heterosexual Pedophile	Homosexual Pedophile	Bisexual Pedophile	Controls
MAS	**	8[b]	6[ab]	9[b]	5[a]
FAS		8	8	8	6
SAM		3	3	3	3
SAF		3	3	2	3
MAF		12	9	10	9
FAM		10	10	10	8
MC		13	14	14	15
FC		12	13	16	14
MAff	****	7	9	8	10[a]
FAff		6	6	6	7
MStr	**	6[b]	5[ab]	6[b]	4[a]
FStr		5	5	6	4
MId	****	3[a]	5[b]	3[a]	5[b]
FId	*	3	3	4	4
M Ind		2	3	3	3
F Ind	*	2	1	3[a]	1

Note: The name of each scale can be constructed using the following key. M = Mother,
F = Father,   S = Respondant,   A = Aggression,   C = Competence,   Aff = Affection,
Str = Strictness, Id = Identification, Ind = Indulgence.

*p < 05, **p < 01, ***p < 001, ****p < 0001. Means with the same superscript are not
significantly different. In discriminant analysis, overall 55% of cases were correctly assigned to their
own group. 44% of heterosexual pedophiles, 43% homosexual pedophiles, 44% bisexual pedophiles
and 74% of controls were correctly assigned to their actual groups.

TABLE 6.12
Percent of PCR Centile Score 70 or Greater for Pedophilic and
Control Groups

Scale		Heterosexual Pedophile	Homosexual Pedophile	Bisexual Pedophile	Controls
MAS	*	63	40	63	33
FAS		44	45	44	30
SAM		63	50	56	59
SAF		66	53	44	56
MAF		47	30	44	28
FAM		47	43	38	31
MC		16	30	31	35
FC	*	16	30	44	44
MAff	**	18	33	13	54
FAff		16	28	13	33
MStr	**	50	38	69	26
FStr		25	30	38	22
MId	**	16	38	6	41
FId		19	23	25	30
M Ind		44	53	56	41
F Ind	**	34	25	69	22

Note: M = Mother, F = Father, S = Respondant, A = Aggression, Aff = Affection,
Str = Strictness, Id = Identification, Ind = Indulgence.
  $*p < .05, **p < .01$.

There were no significant group differences in number of male or female siblings or in the birth order of the research subjects.

Criminal History, Aggression, and Suicide Attempts.   Among cases for which information was available, 72% of heterosexual pedophiles had some previous conviction compared to 57% of the bisexuals and 54% of the homosexual group.

TABLE 6.13
Miscellaneous Family Background Factors in Pedophilia

Variable		% Group			
		Heterosexual	Homosexual	Bisexual	Control
1. Mother patient in mental hospital	*	9	3	13	0
2. Father patient in mental hospital		7	0	13	2
3. Father ever in trouble with police	*	20	8	20	7

Note: $*p < .05$.

This difference was not statistically significant.[13] There were statistically significant group differences in the incidence of previous violent offenses but not in sexual or other offenses (Tables 6.14A). The violence related charges were few in number, 11 (7%) of 150 charges to all groups but eight of those charges were attributable to heterosexual pedophiles, three to homosexuals, and none to bisexuals. The violence charges involved 22% of the total heterosexual group, and 8% of the homosexual pedophiles. The difference between heterosexual pedophiles and the other two groups was statistically significant. The violence charges for the heterosexual group included one wounding, three common assaults, and four possession of weapons charges. There was also one charge of abduction which was classed as other. In one case a 15-year-old girl was wounded and in another, 14-,15-,and 16-year-old girls were forced to perform fellatio at knife point. The homosexual pedophiles were charged with one arson, one possession of weapons, one common assault, and also with one abduction. There were no other noteworthy differences among the groups.

TABLE 6.14A
Criminal Record Among the Pedophilic Groups

| | Pedophilic Group | | | | | |
| | Heterosexual | | Homosexual | | Bisexual | |
Offence Type	# Cases	# Charges	# Cases	# Charges	# Cases	# Charges
Sexual	12	26	17	29	6	15
Violence	7	9	3	3	0	0
Property	7	12	5	10	5	24
Other	4	9	6	8	3	5
Total # Charges		56		50		44
# Cases Without						
Charges	8		18		6	
Unknown/Not specified	2		1		2	

TABLE 6.14B
Aggression and Suicide Among The Pedophilic Groups

		Heterosexual	Homosexual	Bisexual
Number of Fist Fights:				
Before age 16†	****	12[a]	6	4
After age 16†	***	5[a]	3[b]	4[ab]
Suicide Attempts		1	1	1
Suicidal Thoughts†		2	2	2

Note: †Normal controls were included in these comparisons and averaged 5 fights before 16 and 2[b] after. They averaged 1.18 suicidal thoughts.
***p < .001, ****p < .0001. Means with the same superscripts are not significantly different.

There was significant reported fighting in the background of the offenders (Table 6.14B). Heterosexual pedophiles fought more than the other groups before age 16 and showed a trend to more fighting after age 16. Violence however was not directed inwards and there were no significant group differences in suicide thoughts or attempts.

Alcohol and Drugs. There were no group differences in self reported alcohol use or drunkenness. Between 60% and 70% of the pedophilic groups had never tried any drugs whatsoever but only 30% of controls were inexperienced. The majority of all groups had tried marijuana but little else. Thus, alcohol and drugs were not found to be significant factors for the pedophilic groups in this study.[14]

DISCUSSION

The three pedophilic groups were similar on a number of clinical variables. Compared to controls, they had less education, lower IQ, (although generally normal); had a considerable number of MMPI psychotic scale elevations, and had poor mother relations. Collectively the pedophiles had personality disorder diagnoses; mainly immature and inadequate types. Differences emerged in sexual history, violence, and previous criminal charges (Table 6.15). Although there were few person offenses, the fact that 22% of the heterosexual pedophiles were involved in serious violence is contrary to the existing clinical beliefs about this group and warrants closer and careful scrutiny. The bisexual group showed less criminal violence but there was some aggression in fist fights, personality, and family background. The homosexual group showed least aggression but significantly, it did appear in criminal charges against the person.

Results on aggression contrast both with earlier findings reporting no violence and with more recent findings that it is a prominent feature of pedophilic offenses. Of course, the confusion of sex offender groups may have played some role in the results. Erotic preferences for children have not always been specified clearly so one remains uncertain how many offenses are attributable to "true pedophiles." The differences in settings from which data were collected also may be important. Maximum security prisons such as the one used in Christie et al.'s study may house the more violent cases, whereas minimum security settings like ours would have fewer. Our results still suggest that violence proneness be evaluated in offenses against children and especially in heterosexual pedophiles.

The sexual history profiles of the three groups were different as expected. Only the homosexual pedophiles had a reduced frequency of outlet with adult females, whereas the other pedophilic groups were average. This casts doubt on the theory that pedophiles in general are shy and unassertive with adult females. Their scores on shyness and assertiveness on personality testing were unremarka-

TABLE 6.15
A Comparison of Erotic Preference, Gender Identity, and Aggression
Among The Pedophilic Groups

	Heterosexual Pedophile	Homosexual Pedophile	Bisexual Pedophile
Erotic Preference			
Stimulus	Female Pubescent/ Child	Male/Adult/Pubescent/Child	All ages both sexes
Response	Touching Prominent but full range behavior	Touching, oral genital	Wide ranging response, polymorphous
Gender Role	Normal on MMPI Lower on 16PF	Normal	Normal
Aggression in:			
Criminal Record	Some, noteworthy	Some	None
Fist Fights	Yes	No	Trend
Personality	Some, mixed results	Little	Some, mixed results
PCR	Mother aggression problem	No	Mother aggression problem

ble. If one accepts that the homosexual pedophiles are basically androphilic, it is difficult to argue too that they are shy and unassertive with men because they have substantial sexual experience with men of all age groups. They may simply be disinterested in females.

Overall, the experience of heterosexual pedophiles with all ages of females and of the homosexual pedophiles with all ages of males is more or less comparable. Perhaps they are truly pangynephilic or panandrophilic and enjoy and prefer sexual outlets with all ages of partners rather than only preferring the child. The results may also mean that adults are serving as surrogates for the legally sanctioned child partner. They may enjoy sex with adults to some degree and it is easier to get as well as less risky.

The bisexuals had a wide range of sexual experience although they, more than the other groups of pedophiles, showed greatest number of outlets with children of both sexes. They showed a tendency to be polymorphous. They not only engaged both sexes, but as well, showed crossdressing, voyeurism, and frottage. Thus their characterization as bisexual pedophiles may be too simplistic.

In all groups touching was a predominant outlet but the full range of sexual behavior was evident. It is misleading to describe the pedophiles' behaviors as passive and childlike. In many cases some form of penetration had been desired and acted out. In some cases violence was fused with sexual outlet. The relationship of sadism to pedophilia therefore needs careful empirical investigation.

The present study offered a start into exploring the nature of erotic preferences in the pedophilias. It was limited in that self report measures were used but it

suggested new directions for investigation, some of which are examined in Chapter 8.

REFERENCES

Armentrout, J. A., & Hauer, A. L. MMPIs of rapists of adults, rapists of children and non-rapist sex offenders. *Journal of Clinical Psychology,* 1978, *34,* 330–332.

Christie, M., Marshall, W., & Lanthier, R. *A descriptive study of incarcerated rapists and pedophiles.* Unpublished Manuscript, Canadian Penetentiary Services, Kingston, Ontario, 1978.

Finkelhor, S. D. Sexually victimized children and their families. *Dissertation Abstracts International,* 1979, *39,* 7006–7007.

Fisher, G. Psychological needs of heterosexual pedophiliacs. *Diseases of the Nervous System,* 1969, *30,* 419–421.

Fisher, G., & Howell, L. Psychological needs of homosexual pedophiliacs. *Diseases of the Nervous System,* 1970, *31,* 623–625.

Freund, K. Diagnosing heterosexual pedophilia by means of a test for sexual interest. *Behavioral Research & Therapy,* 1965, *3,* 229–234.

Freund, K. Diagnosing homo- or heterosexuality and erotic age-preference by means of a psychophysiological test. *Behavioral Research & Therapy,* 1967, *5,* 209–228. (a)

Freund, K. Erotic preference in pedophilia. *Behavioral Research & Therapy,* 1967, *5,* 339–348. (b)

Freund, K., McKnight, C. K., Langevin, R., & Cibiri, S. The female child as a surrogate object. *Archives of Sexual Behavior,* 1972, *2,* 119–133.

Freund, K., & Langevin, R. Bisexuality in homosexual pedophilia. *Archives of Sexual Behavior,* 1976, *5,* 415–423.

Freund, K., Scher, H., Chan, S., & Ben-Aron, M. Experimental analysis of pedophilia. *Behavior Research and Therapy,* 1982, *20,* 105–112.

Gebhard, P. H., Pomeroy, W. B., & Christenson, C. V. *Sex Offenders: An analysis of types.* London: Heinemann, 1965.

Groth, A. N., & Birnbaum, H. J. Adult sexual orientation and attraction to underage persons. *Archives of Sexual Behavior,* 1978, *7,* 175–181.

Howells, K. Adult sexual interest in children: Considerations relevant to theories of aetiology. In M. Cook & K. Howells (Eds.), *Adult sexual interest in children.* New York: Academic Press, 1981.

Langevin, R. *Sexual strands: Understanding and treating sexual anomalies in males.* Hillsdale, N J: Lawrence Erlbaum Associates, 1983.

Langevin, R., Paitich, D., Freeman, R., Mann, K., & Handy, L. Personality characteristics and sexual anomalies in males. *Canadian Journal of Behavioral Science,* 1978, *10,* 222–238.

Langevin, R., Paitich, D., Ramsay, G., Anderson, C., Kamrad, J., Pope, S., Geller, G., & Newman, S. Experimental studies in the etiology of genital exhibitionism. *Archives of Sexual Behavior,* 1979, *8,* 307–331.

Lester, D. *Unusual sexual behavior: The standard deviations.* Springfield, Ill.: C. Thomas Co., 1975.

Mohr, J. Turner, R. E., & Jerry, M. *Pedophilia and exhibitionism.* Toronto: University of Toronto Press, 1964.

Nedoma, K. Mellan, J., & Pondelickova, J. Sexual behavior and its development in pedophilic men. *Archives of Sexual Behavior,* 1971, *1,* 267–271.

Paitich, D. A comprehensive psychological examination and report (CAPER). *Behavioral Science,* 1973, *18,* 131–136.

Paitich, D., & Langevin, R. The Clarke parent child relations questionnaire: A clinically useful test for adults. *Journal of Consulting and Clinical Psychology,* 1976, *44,* 428–436.

Paitich, D., Langevin, R., Freeman, R., Mann, K., & Handy, L. The Clarke SHQ: A clinical sex history questionnaire for males. *Archives of Sexual Behavior*, 1977, *6*, 421–436.

Panton, J. H. Personality differences appearing between rapists of adults, rapists of children and non-violent sexual molesters of female children. *Research Communications in Psychology, Psychiatry and Behavior*, 1978, *3*, 385–393.

Peters, J. J. Children who are victims of sexual assault and the psychology of offenders. *American Journal of Psychotherapy*, 1976, *30*, 398–421.

Quinsey, V. L. The assessment and treatment of child molesters: A review. *Canadian Psychological Review*, 1977, *18*, 204–220.

Quinsey, V. L., & Bergersen, S. G. Instructional control of penile circumference in assessments of sexual preference. *Behavior Therapy*, 1976, *7*, 489–493.

Quinsey, V. L., Steinman, C. M., Bergersen, S. G., & Holmes, F. F. Penile circumference, skin conductance, and ranking responses of child molesters and "normals" to sexual and nonsexual visual stimuli. *Behavior Therapy*, 1975, *6*, 213–219.

Rada, R. T. Alcoholism and the child molester. *Annals of the New York Academy of Science*, 1976, *273*, 492–496.

Rosen, R. C., Shapiro, D., & Schwartz, G. Voluntary control of penile tumescence. *Psychosomatic Medicine*, 1975, *37*, 479–483.

Selzer, M. The Michigan Alcoholism Screening Test: The quest for a new diagnostic instrument. *American Journal of Psychiatry*, 1971, *127*, 1653–1658.

Statistics Canada. *Special report on alcohol statistics*, Ottawa, Canada: Health and Welfare Canada, 1981.

Swanson, D. W. Adult sexual abuse of children. *Diseases of the Nervous System*, 1968, *29*, 677–683.

Toobert, S., Bartelme, K. F., & Jones, E. S. Some factors related to pedophilia. *International Journal of Social Psychiatry*, 1959, *4*, 272–279.

ENDNOTES

Note 1. Some writers use the term "child molester" to indicate sexual acts or sexual offenses against children without implying that the offender has an *erotic preference* for children. Although it is important to remember that the sexual acts with minors involve a heterogeneous group of adult men, some of them *non-pedophiles*, we find the term child molester is too perjorative and emotional to be used in scientific investigation. "Offenses against children or minors" has been used for want of a better term.

Note 2. Of the 41 cases labelled pedophiles, 73% were heterosexual, 15% homosexual, and 5% bisexual pedophiles. Seven percent involved incest.

Note 3. The current use of the term "rape" is becoming broader. In Canada it still implies vaginal intercourse but some U.S. writers mean a wide range of sexual contacts. We have used the term sexual aggression to imply forced body contact, usually forced vaginal intercourse, anal intercourse, fellatio, or cunnilingus but the new meaning of "rape" may include all these behaviors and *any* other sexual contacts even those in which the child may willingly participate for money, favors, or other reasons. Panton (1978) and Armentrout and Hauer (1978) appear to use the traditional meaning of rape as forced vaginal intercourse.

Note 4. The calculation of profile type is not always clearly indicated in reports. It appears that the *mean* scores were used to construct a single "profile." However, in all our reports, the *number* of men with each profile type has been computed. That is, the profile of each case was determined separately and then the numbers with each type were computed. Practically, the clinician needs to know the latter rather than the mean profile. As results show later, only a few men may actually satisfy the criteria for the 4-8/8-4 profile so the mean results may be misleading to the practicing clinician who after all, sees people individually. See Armentrout and Hauer (1978) for a further discussion of this issue.

Note 5. This included 20 cases of incest (17%) and 13 (11%) possible incest (sexual contact with a blood relative or a foster child).

Note 6. Statistics Canada (1981) noted that 16% of Canadians are "heavy drinkers" consuming 14 or more alcoholic drinks per week. Seventy-four to eighty-four percent of Canadian men drink. In literature reports in general we do not know what criteria are used for "alcoholism" or "heavy drinking." The same problem applies to use of drugs, especially marijuana. We are currently administering the MAST (Selzer, 1971) and an alcohol-drug survey which asks for current and maximum ever frequency of use of a wide range of substances. Although it does not solve all the problems of defining an addiction, the standardization offers a useful frame of reference which can be understood by patients and which relies on the frequency and quantity of use.

Note 7. Since age, education, and intelligence have often been considered important to sexual behavior, they were statistically covaried for the four psychometric instruments used in the study. They did not affect interpretation of results but some specific effects will be noted later.

Note 8. Stepwise discriminant analysis using Wilks' Criterion with prior probabilities weighted by group size was employed. Data on other variables were examined by oneway analyses of variance. SPSS programs were used on a DEC 2020 computer of the Clarke Institute.

Note 9. On 16 of them there was an inhomogeneity of variance problem due to the wide variation in sexual experiences within the groups. Log and Z score transformation did not correct this problem. The 27 scales were also examined for the 3 pedophilic groups alone which reduced the inhomogenuity of variance. Dichotomizing items also produced interpretable results.

Note 10. Two validity scales were significantly different for the groups; L and K, but there was considerable overlap of group means. It was the controls who tended to score higher than the pedophilic groups, but still within normal limits. T score distributions for the two scales were not different in the 4 groups and only a few cases had clinically significant T scores over 70. The validity scales did not alter the interpretation of results presented here.

Note 11. The Chi Square for 8-4/4-8 versus other was nonsignificant. $\chi^2 = 3.42$, df = 2, p<.20. Nor was "no code" versus –"some code" significant, $\chi^2 = 0.63$, df = 2, .80>p>.70.

Note 12. F = 18.35, df = 3, 109, p < 0001.

	Het. Ped.	Hom. Ped.	Bisexual	Control
Mean	9.71	10.62	11.33	6.33[a]
S.D.	3.70	2.51	3.94	2.50

The Pedophilia scale includes items 16, 20, 53, 57, 67, 76, 95, 106, 132, 133, 160, 179, 202, 201, 219, 248, 260, 276, 332, 390, 435, 458, 490, 556. A check on internal consistency showed alpha = 0.67 which is low but acceptable for further research investigation.

Note 13. χ^2 =2.50, df=2, p>.05.

Note 14. *Effect of Covarying Age, Education and IQ* The scores on verbal and performance IQ along with age and education were covaried for MMPI, 16PF, PCR, and SHQ scales. On the MMPI the Hs scores were nonsignificant after age and education were covaried. On the 16PF, Factor H was reduced to nonsignificance by education. On the PCR, MAS was reduced to nonsignificance by education. There were no other differences which influenced the interpretations presented here. Covariance analysis did not produce any substantive changes to the Sex History Questionnaire results reported here.

7

Are Incestuous Fathers Pedophilic, Aggressive, and Alcoholic?

Ron Langevin
Lorraine Handy
Anne E. Russon
Clarke Institute of Psychiatry, Toronto

David Day
University of Windsor

Pedophiles, like most people, usually are repelled by sexual contact with kin. However, some not only engage children in sexual acts but are involved in incest too. Because of limited empirical information, we are unsure how many incest offenders are pedophiles, violent abusive fathers, disinhibited alcoholics, or even something else. Mental health workers are especially concerned about the association of incest with violence and alcohol abuse. In the last chapter it was found that a significant subgroup of pedophiles were violent although drug and alcohol abuse was unremarkable. The next study compares heterosexual pedophiles and incest offenders for similarities and differences in sexual and aggressive behavior.

INTRODUCTION

Disparate claims have been made about incest offenders' personalities and sexual preferences (cf. Langevin, 1983). The perpetrators include men who are relatively normal and those who are alcoholic, violent, antisocial, and/or pedophilic. The treatment goals and disposition for this mixed group may therefore be quite varied. For example, alcoholism may override all other factors as a first goal of treatment. One may hesitate to return to his family, a man who shows a pedophilic erotic preference, and so on. The extent to which incest offenders have a pedophilic erotic preference, are aggressive and/or abuse alcohol was examined in this study.

161

EROTIC PREFERENCE

The largest single group of incest offenders are fathers who act out sexually with their daughters. Cavallin (1966) suggested that some of these men are paranoid with unconscious homosexual strivings, but the majority of writers have linked incest to child abuse and heterosexual pedophilia. Although incest offenders and pedophiles have often been mixed in research reports, not all incestuous fathers are considered pedophilic (cf. Weinberg, 1962). Gebhard, Gagnon, Pomeroy, & Christenson (1965) reported only 4% of 147 incestuous fathers admitted to a sexual preference for children. Abel, Becker, Murphy, and Flanagan (1979) examined six incest offenders' penile responses to descriptions of erotic interaction with children and adult females. They found that all cases reacted more to stimuli involving children, suggesting that they were pedophiles. On the other hand, Quinsey, Chaplin, and Carrigan (1979) found in a controlled study that incest offenders were similar to community volunteers and showed normal penile reactions to pictures of females. Paitich, Langevin, Freeman, Mann, and Handy (1977) examined the sex history of a mixed group of heterosexual incest offenders. They found little evidence of pedophilia. Thus, the few available studies suggest that in general incest offenders are not pedophilic but some cases clearly are.

AGGRESSION

The aggressiveness of the incest offender has been discussed in terms of the force used in the offense, criminal record, the offender's personality, and parent child relations in his family of origin.

Criminal Record and Violence. The nature of criminal convictions are not usually indicated in reports so the extent of violent offenses is generally unknown. The actual use of force in the incest acts also has been poorly documented. As Gebbard et al. (1965) pointed out, it is difficult to distinguish parental authority from threat. Only 12% to 14% of their samples of incarcerated incest offenders actually used force in the sexual offenses. However criminality was a significant factor since 28% to 50% of their incestuous groups had three or more criminal convictions. Their crimes tended to be "against public order" rather than property or person offenses (e.g., narcotics, gambling, or military offenses such as absence without leave, insubordination, and so forth). Anderson and Shafer (1979) also found 37% of 62 incestuous fathers had a criminal record. On the other hand, Cormier, Kennedy, and Sangowicz (1962), Langevin, Paitich, Freeman, Mann, and Handy (1978), and Weiner (1964) suggested that in general, incest offenders tend to be noncriminals. Nevertheless results of clinical studies have suggested that incestuous fathers may be violent and tyrannical (cf. Cavallin, 1966; Finkelhor, 1978; Tormes, 1968) so the question of violence merits further attention.

Personality.   Cavallin (1966), using uncontrolled group data, claimed that the incestuous father had a borderline personality, was paranoid with unconscious homosexual strivings and that intellectual deficiency and physical constitution played a role in some cases. Weinberg (1962) examined the personalities of incest cases in an uncontrolled study. He indicated that there are three types of incestuous fathers: introverts, psychopaths, and pedophiles. In controlled comparisons, Gebhard et al. (1965) and Langevin et al. (1978) suggested that incest offenders were shy, inhibited, and ineffectual in family relations.

Panton (1979) compared the MMPI profiles of convicted incest offenders and pedophiles. All incest cases involved fathers and daughters. Cases with a psychiatric disgnosis were excluded. Only one scale was significant. Incest offenders were more socially introverted than pedophiles. Both groups had clinically significant, elevated mean t-scores for the Psychopathic Deviate scale. There was no group difference on Toobert, Bartelme, and Jones (1959) MMPI Pedophilia scale. Panton concluded that both incest offenders and pedophiles showed self-alienation, despondency, rigidity, inhibition, feelings of insecurity, and fear of not being able to function adequately in heterosexual relationships but neither group was predisposed to sexual violence. Incest offenders differed from pedophiles in being more introverted and in showing more mature albeit inadequate psychosexual functioning.

Anderson (1976) found that 14 incestuous fathers compared to 14 control fathers had only significantly higher Psychopathic Deviate scores. Kirkland and Bauer (1982) on the other hand, found among 10 incestuous fathers significant elevations on F, Depression, Psychopathic Deviate, Psychasthenia, Schizophrenia, and Social Introversion compared to controls. The average profile type for the incest group was 4-7-8 which is associated with chronic insecurity, social alienation, acting out behaviors, and passive dependency with exaggerated needs for affection and attention, among others. Thus, of the studies reported in the literature, uncontrolled case and group studies suggest a mixture of traits among incest offenders including violent traits. Controlled studies stress introversion and insecurity as major factors in incest.

Family Background of the Offender.   Some writers believe that the incest offender comes from a depriving family background that sets the scenario for incest. The offender's own father was harsh and authoritarian. The son in turn both hated and admired him which resulted in a passive homosexual longing for him (cf. Henderson, 1972; Weiner 1962, 1964). Karpman (1957) described the mother of the offender as dominating her son in their relationship while father was often absent. She extravagantly admired and spoiled her son so he came to think that his passive body was omnipotent. Consequently he developed a perception of himself as unable to respond in a sexually adult fashion. He overidentified with mother who fostered his incestuous behavior.

Once again the better controlled studies suggest a different picture. Gebhard et al. (1965) found little to distinguish the family backgrounds of incestuous and

other sex offenders. Paitich and Langevin (1976) found little familial aggression in incest offenders versus controls and, contrary to expectations, they were lowest of all sexually anomalous groups in mother affection and identification and highest on mother strictness.

Alcohol.   Incest may be associated with alcohol abuse and a low frustration tolerance that has led some theorists to describe the offender as violent and psychopathic. The incidence of alcohol abuse is quite variable in professional reports ranging from 8% to 72% showing chronic alcoholism (Anderson & Shafer, 1979; Gebhard et al., 1965; Kaufman, Peck, & Tagiuri, 1954; Kirkland & Bauer, 1982; Tormes, 1968; Virkkunen, 1974).

Alcohol intoxication or abuse may be instrumental in both violence and incest but at present its role can only be surmised.[1] The large variation in reporting the incidence of alcohol use, as well as of pedophilia and violence, may be biased by the setting in which the assessment was done. More studies of a systematic nature in a variety of settings would be helpful.

In the present study a uniform group of fathers who were incestuous with their daughters was compared to groups of heterosexual pedophiles and normal controls on tests of sexual history, personality, and parent child relations. Additional demographic data and information on history of drinking and criminal record were examined as well. Father-daughter incest was selected for examination because it is the most frequent kind (Bluglass, 1979; Henderson, 1972; Weiner, 1964). Heterosexual pedophiles also were selected for comparison because, like incest offenders, their sexual offenses were against female minors and if incest offenders are pedophiles, it is this group they should most resemble.

METHOD

Subjects

A group of 34 fathers who had sexual contact with their daughters and faced charges of incest were selected from the Institute's forensic data bank. A group of 32 heterosexual pedophiles reported in Chapter 6 who had no history of incest and had sexually interacted with females 12 or younger since they themselves were 16, or, with females 13 to 15 since they themselves were 21, was used for comparison. Finally a group of 54 men used in previous work (Paitich et al., 1977) was included as a control group. They had no history of mental illness, crime, or sexual anomaly.

All incestuous fathers but one had interacted with their daughters from their marriage. In one case, the daughter of a common law relationship was the victim. In some cases there were multiple victims including two sons, one foster child, and a common law daughter. There was multiple incest in 38% of the cases, with up to four victims involved. The age distribution of the 53 incest

TABLE 7.1
Age Distribution of Pedophilia and
Incest Victims

Age	% Incest Victims (N = 53)	% Pedophilia Victims (N = 52)
2	3.77	0.00
4	0.00	3.85
5	1.89	1.92
6	3.77	3.85
7	1.89	1.92
8	1.89	3.85
9	1.89	13.46
10	5.66	5.77
11	3.77	7.69
12	13.21	9.62
13	11.32	11.54
14	15.09	13.46
15	16.98	3.85
16	5.66	1.92
17	5.66	0.00
18	5.66	0.00
Unknown	1.89	17.31

Note: Percentages have been rounded.

victims is shown in Table 7.1. The majority, 57%, were 12-to 15-years-old and 17% were between 16 and 18, but 25% of the victims were younger than 12 and in the victim age range typical of heterosexual pedophilia. Based on victim age, a pedophilic and hebephilic erotic preference could not be ruled out for the majority of incest offenders.

There was a weak but significant difference in the age distribution of incest victims compared to that for the 52 victims of pedophilia.[2] Forty two percent of pedophilic victims were under 12 years of age, 38% were 12–15, and only 2% were over 15. Of course, by definition the pedophiles had to engage females 15 and under, whereas no such restriction was placed on incest cases. Those men engaging females over 15-years-old also had charges involving younger girls. Significant group differences were attributable in large part to unspecified ages for victims of pedophilia, next to the greater number of 15-year-old incest victims, and finally to differences in the numbers of 9-year-old victims. Overall, the incest offenders engaged significantly older victims than pedophiles did (Mean 12.67 years, SD 3.73 for incest, 10.86 years, SD 3.08 for pedophiles).[3]

Age, Education, and Intelligence.   The incest offenders and pedophiles were comparable in being older, less educated, and less intelligent than controls (Table 7.2). The offender groups differed significantly only in verbal intelligence

TABLE 7.2
Age, Education and Intelligence for Incest Offenders
and Control Groups

Mean		Pedophile	Incest	Control
Number of Cases		32	34	54
Age	****	33	37	24[a]
Education	***	9	10	15[a]
Verbal IQ (Mean)	****	106[b]	94[a]	117[c]
−89 (%)		3	14	0
90–110 (%)		79	79	33
111+ (%)		17	7	67
Performance IQ (Mean)	****	110	102	119[a]
−89 (%)		3	10	2
90–110 (%)		45	48	13
111+ (%)		52	42	85

Note: ***$p < .001$, ****$p < .0001$. Means with same letter superscripts are not significantly different. Percents may not total to 100% due to rounding error.

scores although incest offenders were lower on both IQ tests. In general, both groups were in the average or above average range of IQ.[4]

Procedure and Materials

All research participants had been administered the MMPI, Cattell 16PF, the Clarke Parent Child Relations (PCR) and Sex History (SHQ) Questionnaires (Paitich & Langevin, 1976; Paitich et al., 1977), the Raven Standard Progressive Matrices, and a Word List used to assess verbal intelligence (Paitich, 1973). Other information on alcohol and drug use, diagnosis, and criminal record was also available. The patients were administered the tests as part of their pre-trial/presentence assessment and the normal control group consisted of paid community volunteers.

RESULTS

Erotic Preference

Sex History.   The main results of the SHQ are presented in Table 7.3. None of the 10 homosexual scales is presented because all were statistically nonsignificant in the group comparison.[5] Basically, such behaviors were absent. The homosexual desire scale was significant but group differences were weak. Incest offenders in any case did not differ from controls. There were no significant group differences in the incidence or number of men engaging in crossdressing,

frottage, rape, or obscene calls nor in conventional sexual outlets with adult females.

Differences appeared for sexual outlets with female minors. Incest offenders generally were more like the heterosexual pedophiles than like controls. Table 7.3 shows that both offender groups were comparable in the frequency of outlets with both child and pubescent females. However the incest offenders acted out somewhat less often with females under 12. Table 7.4 shows differences in the *type* of sexual acts. Incest offenders exposed less to the female, attempted intercourse and frottage less, and, in the case of females 12 or younger, less often had her touch his penis.

Incest offenders more than the other groups claimed disgust for sexual contact with 13-15-year-old girls. Nonetheless they desired such contact significantly more than controls did. Pedophiles desired the contact even more than incest offenders. The pattern of desire for sex contact with females 12 and younger was the same but incestuous fathers and controls showed more disgust for it than pedophiles did.

Although sexual behavior in the offender's family of origin has been considered etiologically significant in incest, there were no significant differences between incest offenders and community controls in the reported incidence of

TABLE 7.3
The Sex History Questionnaire Scale Score Results

Scale		Z Score Means		
		Heterosexual Pedophile	Incest	Control
Exhibitionist behavior	***	61[a]	−18	−24
Exhibitionistic frequency	*	32[b]	09[ab]	−25[a]
Voyeurism	*	38[a]	−07[ab]	−18[b]
Heterosexual oral-genital-anal		01	03	−03
Heterosexual adult—Desire	****	08[b]	56[c]	−40[a]
—Disgust	**	10	44	−34[a]
—Frequency		10	−20	06
Heterosexual Pubescent				
—Desire	****	65[a]	05[b]	−42[c]
—Disgust	***	−15	54[a]	−25
—Frequency	**	25	26	−31[a]
Heterosexual pedophilic				
—Desire	****	90[c]	00[b]	−54[a]
—Disgust	***	−58[a]	27	17
—Frequency		20	−07	−07
Homosexual desire	*	38[a]	−07[ab]	−18[b]

Note: Two digit decimal points omitted. *p < .05, **p < .01, ***p < .001, ****p < .0001.
Means with the same superscript are not significantly different.

TABLE 7.4
Selected Sexual Outlets

Outlet		% Group		
		Heterosexual Pedophile	Incest	Control
Females 12 or younger[a]				
Touch in a sexual way	****	59	44	2
Touch between legs	****	66	41	2
She touches penis	****	56	26	0
Rub with penis	****	53	29	0
Attempt intercourse	***	25	12	0
Expose	****	44	6	0
Females 13–15[b]				
Touch in a sexual way	****	50	47	2
Touch between legs	****	41	53	7
She touches penis	****	41	32	4
Rub with penis	***	31	35	4
Attempt intercourse	**	31	15	4
Expose	**	19	3	0

Note: [a]Since the respondent was 16 or older.
   [b]Since the respondent was 21 or older.
   $**p < .01$, $***p < .001$, $****p < .0001$.

sex play with sisters and brothers, in the parents handling the respondent's private parts in a sexual way and washing them, or in overhearing and seeing parents having sex (Table 7.5). There were group differences in the incidence of seeing mother nude to the waist and fully nude. However the incest offenders were least likely to see her this way.

The incest offenders were like pedophiles in showing a trend to more sex experience themselves as children under 12 and to more experience with age peer females when they were 13 to 15 years of age.

Aggression

Criminal Record and Violence. Compared to pedophiles, significantly fewer incest offenders had previous criminal records (Table 7.6).[6] Sixty two percent of the incest group had no criminal record prior to their admission involving incest compared to 25% of pedophiles. In one incest and two pedophilic cases, previous criminal record was unknown. The remaining 12 incest offenders faced a total of 28 charges, the pedophiles faced 56. However, among those men who did have a criminal record, there were no significant differences in the distribution of offenses typed as sexual, violent, property, and other.

Violent crimes ranged from common assault to manslaughter. Thus, the majority of incest offenders were noncriminals but 12% engaged in serious violent acts. Previous sexual charges were the most common in both groups. Some of these charges reflect pedophilic activity but cases of ''rape'' were incest related. Property offenses were next most common with theft and robbery dominating. There was no relation between multiple incest and previous criminal record.

Both offender groups engaged in more fist fights than controls did both before and after age 16 (Table 7.7). Prior to age 16, the pedophiles engaged in even more fights than incest offenders. After age 16, this difference disappeared.

Personality and Diagnosis. Significantly fewer incest offenders than pedophiles were given a diagnosis (Table 7.8).[7] Thirty five percent had no diagnoses compared to 6% of the pedophiles. The distribution of diagnoses given also differed significantly for the two groups.[8] Sexual deviation was reported for fewer incest offenders than pedophiles. When incest proper is excluded as a sexual deviation diagnosis, the difference is even larger with only 21% (or seven cases) of the incest group showing some sexual anomaly. Of these seven cases,

TABLE 7.5
Early Sexual Experiences

Item		% Pedophiles	% Incest	% Control
Mother Nude to Waist	**		a	
Never		58	83	44
1		7	14	26
2–5		29	3	19
Over 5		7	0	11
Mother Fully Nude	*	ab	a	b
Never		71	90	63
1		16	10	19
2–5		13	0	11
Over 5		0	0	7
When 12 or younger				
Had sex play with: (% ever)				
Males 18 or older	*	10[ab]	21[b]	4[a]
Females own age	*	69[a]	48	43
Females 4 or 5 years older	*	41[b]	24[ab]	15[a]
When 13–15 years old				
Had sex play with				
Females own age	*	69[b]	50[ab]	40[a]
Sex play with sister	*	38[a]	13	21
Father concerned				
Keep genitals clean	*	39[ab]	48[a]	20[b]

Note: Percentages may not total 100% due to rounding error.
*p < .05, **p < .01. Letters and superscripts denote means are not significantly different.

TABLE 7.6
Previous Criminal Record of Incest Offenders And Pedophiles

Charge	Incest Offenders		Pedophiles	
	# Men	# Charges	# Men	# Charges
Sexual	9 (26%)	13 (46%)	12 (38%)	26 (46%)
Rape/Attempt Rape	3	4	0	0
Indecent Assault	3	5	9	16
Indecent Exposure	2	3	5	7
Contribute Juvenile Delinquency	1	1	2	2
Prowl by night	0	0	1	1
Violence	4 (12%)	4 (14%)	7 (22%)	9 (16%)
Armed Robbery/Robbery with Violence	2	2	0	0
Common Assault	1	1	4	5
Manslaughter	1	1	0	0
Wounding	0	0	1	1
Weapons	0	0	3	3
Property Offences	6 (18%)	10 (36%)	7 (22%)	12 (21%)
Theft/B&E/Robbery	3	7	6	11
Fogery/Uttering	2	2	1	1
Willful Damage	1	1	0	0
Other	1 (3%)	1 (4%)	4 (13%)	9 (16%)
Joyriding	0	0	1	1
Drinking and Driving	1	1	3	4
Liquor Act	0	0	1	1
Possession of Drugs	0	0	1	1
Obstruct Police	0	0	1	1
Abduction	0	0	1	1
None	21 (62%)	—	8 (25%)	—
Unknown	1	—	2	—

Note: The # men add up to more than total cases because some men had more than 1 type of offence. Percentages in brackets are for number of men with the charge relative to total group and for the number of charges relative to total charges for the group. Goodness of fit on # cases, $\chi^2 = 20.43$, df = 4, p < .001; # charges $\chi^2 = 4.91$, df = 3, p > 05. Rounded percentages may not total exactly 100%.

four were pedophiles, one was an exhibitionist, one polymorphous perverse, and one unspecified. Within the personality disorder diagnoses, the largest number (18%) of incest offenders were labelled immature and inadequate personalities compared to 28% of pedophiles. There were no other striking patterns of personality disorder diagnoses. Only one incest offender was considered an antisocial personality. No pedophile was. Among "other" diagnoses, 12% of incest offenders were labelled alcoholic compared to 9% of pedophiles. Thirteen percent of pedophiles were psychotic but none of the incest offenders were.

Discriminant analysis (Table 7.9) of the MMPI scales produced significant results. Both offender groups differed overall from controls but not from each

TABLE 7.7
Incest Study: Fighting Before and After 16 Years of Age

Item		% Pedophiles	% Incest	% Control
Fights Before 16	****	a	b	c
0–1		3	15	22
2–5		22	12	50
6–10		25	29	19
11–20		22	21	6
over 20		28	15	4
Fights After 16	**			
0–1		26	38	80
2–5		48	48	17
6–10		16	7	0
over 10		9	7	4

Note: Percents may not total 100% due to rounding error.
**p < .01, ****p < .0001.
a,b,c Means with same superscript are not significantly different.

other. Nine of 13 MMPI scales were significant. On six scales (Lie, K, Depression, Psychopathic Deviate, Paranoia, and Social Introversion) only controls differed from the other two groups and three (Hypochondriasis, Psychasthenia, and Schizophrenia) showed the same trend with greater overlap of mean scores. T scores over 70 in Table 7.10 showed the same pattern of results but incest offenders scored as somewhat less pathological overall than pedophiles. Nevertheless a quarter to a third of incest offenders showed considerable emotional disturbance, confusion, and suspiciousness. Almost half were seriously depressed.

MMPI profile types were examined. Nineteen percent of the pedophiles and 28% of incest offenders had no elevations over T=70 but in the majority of cases

TABLE 7.8
Diagnoses of Incest Offenders and Heterosexual Pedophiles

	Incest		Pedophile	
	% Diagnoses	% Cases	% Diagnoses	% Cases
Sexual Deviation	37†	38	40	63
Personality Disorder	45	47	37	63
Other	18	18	23	34
No diagnoses	—	35	—	6
Total #	38	34	57	32

Note: †Excluding incest as a diagnosis, this value would change to 21% of the diagnoses for 18% of the cases. Totals do not add up to 100% because some cases have more than one diagnoses.

TABLE 7.9
Mean MMPI Scores for Incest Offenders, Pedophiles and Controls

Scale		Heterosexual Pedophile	Incest	Controls
Lie	**	3	4	5[a]
F		11	9	7
K	****	11	11	17[a]
Hypochondriasis	*	15	15	13
Depression	**	25	25	21[a]
Hysteria		24	23	22
Psychopathic Deviate	***	30	27	24[a]
Masculinity/Femininity		28	27	30
Paranoia	***	14	13	10[a]
Psychastenia	*	32[b]	30[ab]	27[a]
Schizophrenia	**	36[b]	32[ab]	28[a]
Mania		22	20	21
Social Introversion	***	32	31	25[a]

Note: *p < .05, **p < .01, ***p < .001, ****p < .0001. Means with same superscript are not significantly different. In discriminant analysis 68% of the three groups were correctly classified: 41% of the pedophiles, 50% of incest offenders and 94% of controls.

TABLE 7.10
MMPI T Score >70 for Incest Offenders, Pedophiles and Controls

Scale		Heterosexual Pedophile	Incest	Controls
Lie		3	0	0
F	*	31	29	11
K		3	0	4
Hypochondriasis	***	28	18	0
Depression	**	53	47	19
Hysteria	**	25	35	7
Psychopathic Deviate	****	66	47	20
Masculinity/Femininity		28	24	46
Paranoia	**	31	32	6
Psychastenia	***	56	29	15
Schizophrenia	**	53	35	17
Mania		31	18	15
Social Introversion	*	13	15	0

Note: *p < 05, **p < .01, ***p < .001, ****p < 0001.

(53% pedophiles and 59% incest offenders) there were two or fewer men per profile type. The so called violent 8-4/4-8 type occurred in 19% of pedophiles and 9% of incest offenders. The only other type with more than two cases was the 2-4/4-2 with 9% of the cases in each group. The Toobert et al. (1959) MMPI Pedophilia Scale reported in Chapter 6 was also examined here. The significant results showed that incest offenders and pedophiles were not different (means 9.71 and 10.58 respectively) from each other but both scored higher than controls (mean 6.33).[9]

The 16 PF results are interesting because the three groups were different overall (Table 7.11 and 7.12). Twelve of the 17 scales were significant and although seven showed only controls different from the other two groups (on Md, A, C, H, I, L, Q1), five differentiated offender groups. Incest offenders

TABLE 7.11
Mean 16 PF Factor Scores for Incest Offenders,
Pedophiles and Controls

Factor			Heterosexual Pedophile	Incest	Controls
	Md	**	6	7	9[a]
A	Reserved/Outgoing	****	7	5	8[a]
B	Less Intelligent/More Intelligent	****	4[a]	3[b]	5[c]
C	Affected by Feelings/Emotionally Stable	**	6	6	8[a]
E	Humble/Assertive	***	6	4[a]	6
F	Sober/Happy-go-lucky		6	6	7
G	Expedient/Conscientious		7	6	6
H	Shy/Venturesome	**	6[ab]	5[a]	7[b]
I	Tough-minded/Tender-minded	****	4	4	7[a]
L	Trusting/Suspicious	*	5[b]	4[a]	4[ab]
M	Practical/Imaginative	****	6[b]	4[a]	8[c]
N	Forthright/Shrewd	**	6[a]	4	4
O	Self-assured/Apprehensive		5	5	4
Q1	Conservative/Experimenting	****	6	5	8[a]
Q2	Group-dependent/Self sufficient	**	8[a]	6	6
Q3	Undisciplined self conflict/Controlled		7	6	7
Q4	Relaxed/Tense		6	5	5

Note: Means with same superscript are not significantly different. In discriminant analysis 72% of the 3 groups were correctly classified: 63% of pedophiles, 62% of incest offenders and 83% of controls.

Significance: *p < 05, **p < 01, ***p < 001, ****p < 0001.

TABLE 7.12
The 16 PF Sten Scores Less than 3 and Greater than 8 for Incest
Offenders, Heterosexual Pedophiles and Controls

Factor		Heterosexual Pedophiles		Incest Offenders		Controls	
		<3	>8	<3	>8	<3	>8
Md		31	3	29	3	11	9
A Reserved/Outgoing	**	22	3	41	3	9	9
B Less Intelligent/More Intelligent	****	0	0	26	3	2	15
C Affected by Feelings/Emotionally Stable		16	3	21	3	6	15
E Humble/Assertive	**	0	9	21	3	2	9
F Sober/Happy-go-lucky		19	3	26	6	6	4
G Expedient/Conscientious		12	3	21	6	18	4
H Shy/Venturesome	**	3	9	18	0	0	11
I Touch-minded/Tender-minded	****	6	3	18	9	4	39
L Trusting/Suspicious		12	16	23	3	18	9
M Practical/Imaginative	****	6	9	21	0	0	37
N Forthright/Shrewd		9	6	23	6	22	4
O Self-assured/Apprehensive		9	12	15	18	17	18
Q1 Conservative/Experimenting	***	9	22	15	18	0	54
Q2 Group-dependent/Self sufficient	**	6	3	29	0	41	0
Q3 Undisciplined self conflict/Controlled		12	3	23	3	17	0
Q4 Relaxed/Tense		9	25	18	15	13	9

Note: **p < .01, ***p < .001, ****p < .0001.

scored lower than the other two groups on Factors B,E, and M indicating that the former were less intelligent, assertive, and imaginative than the pedophiles and controls were. Pedophiles differed from the other two groups in scoring higher on Factors N and Q2 indicating that they were shrewder and more calculating, more self sufficient, and less group dependent. It was incest offenders who best fit the stereotyped profile attributable to pedophiles. They were as a group shy, unassertive, humble, accommodating, and trusting. However, sten scores in Table 7.12 suggest that this profile would not be useful clinically because there are few deviant sten scores for the group.

Parent Child Relations.   The three groups differed significantly in the total number of sibs in their family of origin.[10] Incest offenders had most (average number 5.74), and pedophiles did not differ significantly from controls (average

number 4.07 vs. 3.52 respectively). There were no differences in the number of
female siblings but incest offenders had more brothers (mean of 3.62) than
pedophiles (mean of 2.64) or controls (mean of 2.24).

The Clarke PCR was used as a self report measure of the offenders' relationships with their own parents. Six of the 16 scales were significant (Table
7.13). Five of the six showed differences only between offender groups and
controls. Four of the six scales were mother related. Heterosexual pedophiles and
incest offenders both reported that their mothers were stricter and less affectionate than controls' mother were and they identified less with them. However,
pedophiles had higher mother aggression scores than the other two groups. Both
offender groups reported less father affection and identification. The centile
scores (Table 7.14) support the findings on mother scales but the father scales
results were not as strong, suggesting that clinically one may expect to see more
significant mother-son problems than father related problems in incest offenders.
Father drunkenness was more commonly reported by the pedophilic group, less
by incest offenders and least by controls.[11] Twenty seven percent of pedophiles'

TABLE 7.13
Mean Scale Scores for PCR of Incest Offenders, Heterosexual
Pedophiles and Controls

Scale		Heterosexual Pedophiles	Incest Offenders	Controls
MAS	**	8[a]	6	5
FAS		8	8	6
SAM		3	2	3
SAF		3	2	3
MAF		12	8	9
FAM		10	8	8
MC		13	14	15
FC		12	14	14
MAff	***	7	8	10[a]
FAff	*	6	6	7[a]
MStr	**	6	6	4[a]
FStr		5	5	4
MId	***	3	3	5[a]
FId	**	3	3	4[a]
M Ind		2	3	3
F Ind		2	2	1

Note: *p < .05, **p < .01, ***p < .001. Means with the same superscript are not significantly
different. In discriminant analysis 67% of the groups were correctly classified overall: 47% of
pedophiles, 65% incest offenders and 80% of controls.

The name of each scale can be constructed using the following key. M = Mother, F = Father,
S = Respondent,   A = Aggression,   C = Competence,   Aff = Affection,   Str = Strictness,
Id = Identification, Ind = Indulgence.

TABLE 7.14
PCR Centiles Greater Than 70 for Incest Offenders, Heterosexual
Pedophiles and Controls

Scale		% Heterosexual Pedophiles	% Incest Offenders	% Controls
MAS	*	63	38	33
FAS		44	47	30
SAM	**	63	29	59
SAF	*	66	32	56
MAF		44	32	26
FAM		47	26	31
MC		16	35	37
FC	**	16	50	44
MAff	**	19	35	54
FAff		16	21	33
MStr		50	44	26
FStr		25	38	22
MId	*	16	21	41
FId		19	12	30
M Ind		44	62	41
F Ind		34	32	22

Note: *p < .05, **p < .01.

fathers were often drunk compared to 15% for incest offenders' fathers and 10% of controls'.

Alcohol and Drug Use.   Self reported alcohol and drug use showed that incest offenders drank too much more frequently than the other two groups.[12] The controls more often tried marijuana but there were no significant differences in the other two groups. Only 12% of incest offenders and 16% of pedophiles reported having tried any drugs whatsoever.[13]

DISCUSSION

The answers to each of the questions raised in the title of this chapter is a qualified yes. Some incestuous fathers are pedophilic, some are alcoholic, and some are aggressive. However, in general, none of these factors seemed predominant.

Many hypotheses about incest were not supported. Family of origin incest, homosexual behavior, and parental seductiveness were not found. In most respects the incest offenders seem normal. Even the object of incest was not sexually anomalous in many instances since a physically mature female was

victim. It is the social relationship that defines the problem. The results suggest than incestuous fathers are a mixed group of pedophiles and gynephilic men, of emotionally disturbed and stable men, of violent criminals and noncriminals. Sex history results showed that some incestuous fathers do have pedophilic erotic preferences. Between a quarter to a third of this sample showed some disturbance of clinical note. A thorough clinical assessment therefore is needed in each case since an overall pattern for this offense is not evident. Phallometric assessment of erotic preference may be valuable in studying incest.

One must be concerned with the bias introduced by the setting in which data is collected. Our minimum security forensic service is described in the introduction to this volume. Our cases have been the humble, accommodating introverted male generally but the present sample of incestuous fathers was quite mixed. Treatment goals in the form of social skills training and family therapy seem to be indicated for this type of offender. However, concern must be raised about the presence of pathological violence, alcoholism, or the existence of a fixed erotic preference for children. Different programs may be required for each type. There are no tested programs for violent sexual offenders although some settings do offer programs. Alcoholism is difficult to treat and it may override all other considerations. "Drying out" the alcoholic father may be necessary before any family therapy can be undertaken. Even a more extensive program for alcoholism may be warranted. Finally, the presence of pedophilia may hamper efforts to treat the incestuous family. The children will continue to be primary sources of erotic arousal to their father since he prefers them over adults sexually. We know of no proven means of changing erotic preference at present so management of such cases may be difficult. However, a variety of approaches should be tried to test empirically how each factor influences treatment.

Because of the heterogeneity of incest offenders, an assessment should include a thorough examination of the variables discussed in this chapter. Although many incestuous fathers will be normal; alcoholism, violent criminal past, personality pathology, and sexual anomalies may play some role in the offense.

REFERENCES

Abel, G. G., Becker, J. A., Murphy, N. D., & Flanagan, B. *Identifying dangerous child molesters.* Paper presented at 11th Banff International Conference on Behavior Modification, March, 1979.

Anderson, L. A. *Personality and demographic characteristics of parents and incest victims.* Paper presented at the Eleventh Annual MMPI Symposium, Minneapolis, Minnesota, March, 1976.

Anderson, L. M., & Shafer, G. The character-disordered family: A community treatment model for family sexual abuse. *American Journal of Orthopsychiatry,* 1979, *49,* 436–445.

Bluglass, R. Incest. *British Journal of Hospital Medicine,* 1979, *22,* 2–15.

Cavallin, H. Incestuous fathers: A clinical report. *American Journal of Psychiatry,* 1966, *122,* 1132–1138.

Cormier, B. M., Kennedy, M., & Sangowicz, J. Psychodynamics of father-daughter incest. *Canadian Psychiatric Association Journal,* 1962, *7,* 203–217.

Finkelhor, D. Psychological, cultural and family factors in incest and family sexual abuse. *Journal of Marriage and Family Counselling*, 1978, *4*, 41–49.

Gebhard, P., Gagnon, J., Pomeroy, W., & Christenson, C. *Sex offenders*. New York: Harper & Row, 1965.

Henderson, D. J. Incest: A synthesis of data. *Canadian Psychiatric Association Journal*, 1972, *17*, 299–313.

Karpman, B. *The sexual offender and his offences*. New York: Julian Press, 1957.

Kaufman, I., Peck, A. L., & Tagiuri, C. K. The family constellation and overt incestuous relations between father and daughter. *American Journal of Orthopsychiatry*, 1954, *24*, 544–554.

Kirkland, K. D., & Bauer, C. A. MMPI traits of incestuous fathers. *Journal of Clinical Psychology*, 1982, *38*, 645–649.

Langevin, R. *Sexual strands: Understanding and treating sexual anomalies in men*. Hillsdale, N. J.: Erlbaum Associates, 1983.

Langevin, R., Paitich, D., Freeman, R., Mann, K., & Handy, L. Personality characteristics and sexual anomalies in males. *Canadian Journal of Behavioral Science*, 1978, *10*, 222–238.

Paitich, D. A comprehensive psychological examination and report (CAPER). *Behavioral Science*, 1973, *18*, 131–136.

Paitich, D., & Langevin, R. The Clarke Parent-Child Relations Questionnaire: A clinically useful test for adults. *Journal of Consulting and Clinical Psychology*, 1976, *44*, 428–436.

Paitich, D., Langevin, R., Freeman, R., Mann, K., & Handy, L. The Clarke SHQ: A clinical sex history questionnaire for males. *Archives of Sexual Behavior*, 1977, *6*, 421–435.

Panton, J. H. MMPI profile configuations associated with incestuous and non-incestuous child molesting. *Psychological Reports*, 1979, *45*, 335–338.

Quinsey, V. L., Chaplin, T., & Carrigan, W. Sexual preference among incestuous and nonincestuous child molesters. *Behavior Therapy*, 1979, *10*, 562–565.

Toobert, S., Bartelme, K. F., & Jones, E. S. Some factors related to pedophilia. *International Journal of Social Psychiatry*, 1959, *4*, 272–279.

Tormes, Y. *Child victims of incest*. Denver: The American Human Association, Children's Division, 1968.

Virkkunen, M. Incest offences and alcoholism. *Medicine, Science and The Law*, 1974, *14*, 124–128.

Weinberg, S. *Incest behavior*. New York: Citadel Press, 1962.

Weiner, I. B. Father daughter incest: A clinical report. *Psychoanalytic Quarterly*, 1962, *36*, 607–632.

Weiner, I. B. On incest: A survey. *Exerpta Criminologica*, 1964, *4*, 137–155.

ENDNOTES

Note 1. See Chapter 1 and Chapter 2 for further discussion of alcohol and violence.

Note 2. $\chi^2 = 27.76$, df $= 16$, p$<.05$.

Note 3. t$=2.53$, df $= 94$, p$<.02$, two tailed test.

Note 4. Age, education, and IQ were covaried for the main factors of interest and will be discussed again later.

Note 5. Fourteen of the 27 scales suffered inhomogeneity of variance in the analysis of variance and this was unchanged with log or Z score transformation. Dichotomizing data helped in examining group differences.

Note 6. Goodness of fit test, $\chi^2 = 18.10$, df-3, p<.001.

Note 7. $\chi^2 = 8.05$, df=1, p<.01.

Note 8. Goodness of fit $\chi^2 = 60.32$, df=2, p<.001. 50% of the Chi Square was attributable to differences in sex deviation diagnosis, 13% to personality disorders and 37% to other diagnoses.

Note 9. F = 17.05, df = 2, 90, p<0001. The alpha reliability was similar to that for the scale in Chapter 6, alpha = 0.68, indicating the scale is weak but within acceptable limits.

Note 10. F = 6.47, df = 2, 94, p<.01.

Note 11. F = 3.39, df = 2, 94, p<05.

Note 12. F=3.67, p<05. Percent who "drink too much" for Heterosexual Pedophiles, 19%, for Incest Offenders, 39%, and for Controls, 19%.

Note 13. *Covarying Age, Education and IQ.* The scores on Verbal and Performance IQ, age and education were covaried for the MMPI, 16PF, PCR and SHQ. The MMPI D and Sc scales were reduced to nonsignificance by education but there were no other noteworthy changes.

The 16 PF was most influenced by Verbal IQ which reduced B, M, and Q1 to nonsignificance. Performance IQ also affected Md, B, and C, making them nonsignificant. Factor B was changed by age and Factors A and Q4 by education, all covaried results being nonsignificant.

The PCR Mother Identification scale was nonsignificant when education and Performance IQ were covaried. On the other hand, Subject Aggression to father was now significant when age was covaried. While the 16 PF was most influenced by the covariance analysis, the pattern of results were basically the same for the MMPI and PCR and SHQ.

8

Why are Pedophiles Attracted to Children? Further Studies of Erotic Preference in Heterosexual Pedophilia

Ron Langevin
Stephen J. Hucker
Mark H. Ben-Aron
John E. Purins
Clarke Institute of Psychiatry, Toronto

Helen J. Hook
York University

One of the most puzzling features of the pedophilias is why children are chosen erotically at all. We know that many pedophilic men desire and sexually interact satisfactorily with adult females. We also know that normal gynephiles (preferring adult females) react erotically to children as young as 6-years-old. What motivates the heterosexual pedophile to act out with female minors when the gynephile can keep his impulses in check? Why do some pedophiles choose victims that are physically, if not emotionally mature? For example, pubescent females are often physically similar to adult females. To risk incarceration for sexually acting out with such minors is incongruous and may involve a powerful urge that encompasses some feature of the child that has been overlooked to date. On the other hand, in such cases, the theory that pedophiles are inadequate gynephiles may be operative. That is, they truly are attracted to adult females and they desire coitus but they are blocked from obtaining that goal so the child serves as a surrogate. It is believed that the pedophiles' shyness and lack of assertiveness prevent them from interacting sexually with mature women. In the next chapter heterosexual pedophiles' assertiveness and erotic desires for adults and children are studied.

INTRODUCTION

Pedophiles have been described in contradictory terms. They characteristically are considered in older writings to be passive, and "lacking in masculinity" (cf. Karpman, 1950, 1957; Langevin, 1983; Mohr, Turner, & Jerry, 1964 for reviews). They may have some fear of, or aversion to, adult females so that children are sought out. Their sexual acts with children are mainly touching and fondling; regressive sexual behavior typical of the "show and tell stage" of childhood development. More recent authors (see Chapter 6) have noted the significant incidence of penetration and aggression in the sexual acts of pedophiles. Some writers call selected pedophiles "rapists of children." However, empirical tests of any theory are still few in number. In this chapter we examined the following hypotheses about heterosexual pedophiles:

1. Pedophiles are unassertive.
2. They have a fear of, or aversion to, the female body, especially the pubic hair.
3. They have a fear of, or aversion to, heterosexual intercourse.
4. Force and domination are important components of pedophilic sexual arousal.
5. The small size and immaturity of the child are important components of their sexual arousal.
6. Like exhibitionists, the pedophiles are narcissists who are passive and erotically aroused by the admiration of others.
7. Regressive play and fantasy are eroticized in pedophiles.

The literature supporting each hypothesis will be reviewed briefly in turn. Heterosexual pedophiles were selected for examination because they are the most common type (cf. Groth & Birnbaum, 1978; Mohr, Turner, & Jerry, 1964).

LACK OF SOCIAL SKILLS

Pedophiles have been described as individuals who are shy and unassertive. They may be shy and passive with everyone, or only with adult females. In either case, because they are unable to relate to the adult female, they interact with the child to whom they may seem mature, competent, and perhaps sexually experienced. Thus, children may serve as surrogate outlets for their emotional and sexual needs (Storr, 1964).

There are a number of uncontrolled group studies and a few controlled studies described elsewhere (Howells, 1981; Langevin, 1983; and Chapter 6) which suggests that this is in fact the case. Langevin, Paitich, Freeman, Mann, and Handy (1978) in fact, found that of all sexually anomalous groups studied, pedophiles were among the most likely to be shy and unassertive. However, the

subjects of their study were examined via the MMPI and the 16PF Personality Test which do not have specific measures of assertiveness per se. Hook (1981) examined a mixed group of 10 pedophiles and controls on two reliable measures of assertiveness, the Assertion Inventory (Alberti & Emmons, 1970) and the Rathus (1973) Assertiveness Schedule. She found that pedophiles were significantly less assertive than controls.

The limited evidence therefore suggests that lack of assertion in pedophiles, which has been discussed in clinical studies and reports, does in fact represent a deviation from the norm. However, more direct measures of assertiveness need to be examined in homogeneous groups of pedophiles. Assertiveness questionnaires of demonstrated reliability were used in the present study to further validate the clinical picture of the pedophile.

FEAR OF ADULT FEMALES

Pedophiles' attraction to children may be the result of a "timid inability" to make contact with adult females (Storr, 1964). There may be a fear of intercourse, a fear of adult females in general, or, an aversion to parts of the mature female body, in particular, to pubic hair as noted by Karpman (1950, 1957). Possibly sexual intercourse with the adult female is desired but her mature behavior is threatening so an avoidance reaction is established. Quinsey, Steinman, Bergersen, and Holmes (1975), measuring penile circumference changes, found that pedophiles were sexually aroused to stimuli depicting intercourse suggesting that the heterosocial potential of the pedophile may be high.

Pedophilia has also been considered a variant of homosexuality (see Karpman, 1957; Langevin, 1983; Noyes & Kolb, 1958). Homosexual men in general were believed in earlier writings to have an aversion to females but Freund and his associates (Freund, Langevin, Cibiri, & Zajac, 1973; Freund, Langevin, Chamberlyne, Deosera, & Zajac, 1974; Freund, Langevin, & Zajac, 1974) did not find empirical support for this hypothesis. Although the aversion hypothesis of pedophilia has not been examined directly, some empirical investigations suggest it is not a significant factor. Freund (1967a,b) examined phallometric responses of pedophiles to movies of nude adults and children of both sexes. He found, like Quinsey, Steinman, Bergersen, and Holmes (1975), that the largest reactions on the average were to children. However, the adult female body did have substantial erotic valence, at least for heterosexual pedophiles.

In fact, reaction profiles of sex offenders against children are quite variable. Theoretically possible types are illustrated schematically in Fig. 8.1. The profile of normal males is depicted in Part A of the figure. They show some erotic arousal to female children as young as 6-years-old but penile reactions increase in size as the stimulus female becomes older. So largest reactions occur to the young physically matured adult female (Freund, McKnight, Langevin, & Cibiri, 1972). Some pedophiles also show this profile suggesting that they prefer the

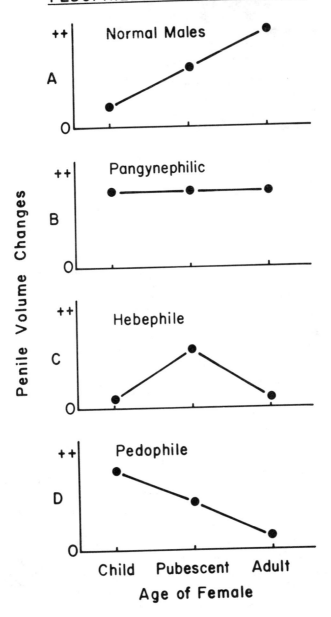

Figure 8.1

PROFILES OF HETEROSEXUAL
PEDOPHILES AND NORMAL MEN

184

body characteristics of adult females. The child may be only a surrogate for them, used sexually at a time of stress. Some pedophiles may be most aroused by the body shape of adult females but they may be aroused even more by some *behavior* of the child, such as submissiveness.[1] Perhaps pedophiles with the normal profile are faking (see Quinsey & Bergerson, 1976; Rosen, 1973).

The flat profile depicted in Part B of Fig. 8.1 indicates that any aged female has similar erotic valence (pangynephilic). The hebephile depicted in Part C shows largest penile responses to the maturing pubescent female and the "true" pedophile in Part D reacts most to the younger children with a decrement in erotic response as the stimulus female becomes increasingly physically mature. Thus, we are dealing with a heterogeneous group and it would be valuable to know the incidence of the theoretical subtypes. Nevertheless in all cases the erotic reaction potential of heterosexual pedophiles to the adult female is high enough to doubt that they have an aversion to her body. Pedophiles also frequently marry and engage in sexual acts with adult females (see Chapter 6 and Langevin, 1983 for more details). Although all these findings are far from definitive, they cast doubt on the aversion hypothesis of pedophilia. In the present study, questionnaire and phallometric responses were examined for the pedophile's aversion to the adult female, to parts of her body, and to vaginal intercourse.

FORCE AND DOMINANCE

The foregoing hypotheses attempt to explain why pedophiles cannot relate to the adult female rather than attempting to determine what attracts them to the child. When one asks how the child differs from the adult, it is the dependency, subservience, and obedience of the child that present obvious differences. Howells (1979) used the Repertory Grid to map the constructs "adult female," "adult male," and "child" in heterosexual pedophiles and controls. He found that pedophiles more often rated adults as overbearing but children were nonthreatening and submissive.

The subordinate role of the child is noteworthy especially in reference to violence inflicted on them. Adults tell children what to do. They hit children with no consequence to themselves—it is part of discipline. In a contemporary national survey in the USA., Straus, Gelles, and Steinmetz (1981) reported that 84% to 97% of all parents used physical punishment on their children at some time during their lives. In their own survey of 2143 families, they noted that 63% of the children between 3 and 17 years of age had at least one violent episode in the year previous to the study. Fifty eight percent were slapped or spanked, on the average, almost once a month. Only in the extreme case of child abuse does society become concerned but as Straus et al. noted, the line between abuse and normal discipline may be difficult to define. Avery-Clarke, O'Neil, and Laws (1981) have further suggested that sexual and physical abuse of children are often

blended. Although we do not wish to imply that all parents may potentially abuse their children sexually, it is clear that North Americans are prone to violence, even in everyday family life. The latter fact may cause us to overlook the meaning that the child has for the pedophile, namely, they are easily dominated and there are few penalties for making them submit.

Pedophilia has been linked to sadism which may be important in sexual anomalies in the broader sense of dominating or controlling another person. This reflects the most common relation between adults and children, described in sadomasochistic relations as "teacher and pupil," or "master and servant." However, the elements of torture and destruction of another person and/or their unconsciousness add components to sadism that are alien to the parenting role.

Some contemporary writers have claimed that pedophiles may be more violent with their victims than previously believed (See Chapter 6). Howells (1981) indicated that there are three important dimensions in pedophilia: whether the act was situational or the result of a fixed sexual preference; whether it was homosexual or heterosexual; and whether it was aggressive or nonaggressive. Stoller (1975) described many sexual anomalies including pedophilia as "erotic forms of hatred," suggesting that one can expect to see aggression in pedophiles in one form or another. Studies discussed in Chapter 6 indicate that at least a subgroup of pedophiles are aggressive and similar to rapists of adults. Whether the force used on children is an integral and necessary part of pedophilic erotic preference has not been systematically examined to date. Penile reactions to rapes of children were examined in the present report.

PHYSICAL FEATURES OF THE CHILD

Perhaps as a corollary to the dominance hypothesis, one may suggest that the small size of the child is sexually arousing to pedophiles. Size, strength, and dominance have been related to sexual attraction in lower animals (Manning, 1981). Generalizations based on animals and applied to humans must always be considered with caution. Nevertheless some parallels are interesting in the present context. Manning (1981) noted that *fitness,* in a Darwinian sense, was an important factor. A female mammal often "selects" a mate on the basis of his fitness to survive which helps perpetuate her own genes and offspring. In many ways the male's attractiveness is reflected in his dominance, strength, size, and age.[2] Female mammals seek out the dominant male who may fight off many others in his territory which is perhaps the most favorable environment for food, shelter, and the overall provision of needs related to survival. He will likely be larger as well and produce more sperm than smaller males; again a reproductive advantage. Age is another index of genetic potency and in part it reflects size and strength but it also correlates with ability to survive (i.e., being able to overcome disease, competition, etc.). Although many other factors such as pheromones or

plumage play a role in sexual attraction among lower animals, size and strength variables may be common to human courtship as well. Cultural influences can direct mating patterns but Dion (1981) noted that sexual attraction is mainly determined on the basis of features that connote strength, vigor, and stamina; a parallel perhaps to the features important in mammals' sexual attraction in general.

Traditionally a human male's social status and power have been most important in his sexual attractiveness and the female's physical features have been salient (Dion, 1981). A long lasting stereotype of female heterosexual attractiveness has been her overall body build and particularly her facial features (i.e., blonde hair, light blue eyes, white soft skin, and red lips). Her figure should be small, well rounded, and her waist small and graceful (Dion, 1981). In short, the male should be "fit" and the female should be "delicate."

Freund et al. (1972) presented data that counterindicated the importance of facial features in sexual attraction. They examined the erotic arousal valence of various parts of the adult female body for community volunteers. Using the phallometric method, they found the order of erotic arousal of males for body areas of the female were most to: (1) the pubic area; then (2) to the breasts and rear end; and last (3) to the face and legs. They have yet to report such data on pedophiles.

The normal pattern of attraction (fitness) and the features of the child that may be erotically attractive to pedophiles have not been examined in a controlled study to date.[3] A review of the available literature was used to construct a questionnaire on normal men and women which in turn was examined in heterosexual pedophiles.

NARCISSISM

Pedophilia often co-occurs with exhibitionism which suggests that they may have a common etiology. Langevin, Paitich, Ramsay, Anderson, Kamrad, Pope, Geller, and Newman (1979) theorized that exhibitionists who are attracted to adult females may be narcissistic and derive their preferred erotic gratification from females admiring their penises. Physical contact is not desired but both male and female exposing and masturbating simultaneously may be the ultimate sexual experience for them. Mohr et al. (1964) noted that the pedophile is distinct from the exhibitionist in desiring body contact with the child. However, to be technically correct, it seems that exhibitionists and pedophiles have different erotic *stimulus* preferences for the adult versus the child respectively but some pedophiles are similar to exhibitionists in having an erotic *response* preference for exposing (See Note 1).

Narcissism may be manifested sexually in at least two ways, autoerotically or interpersonally. In the former, the person is completely self satisfying. He ad-

mires himself and climaxes. Cases of interpersonal narcissism are apparently more common. Admiration by another person while exposing is necessary for sexual gratification, much as an actor needs an audience for artistic gratification while on stage. Interpersonal narcissism appears to be operative in exhibitionists to adult females. Some pedophiles may derive similar satisfaction from children. The hypothesis was tested in the present study.

REGRESSION

Groth and Birnbaum (1978) distinguished two types of pedophiles. The fixated type shows arrested psychological maturation and from the time of puberty is primarily attracted to children. The regressed type shows primitive sexual behavior after more mature forms of expression have been attained. Fixation readily explains why pedophiles interact sexually with children. They are acting out with their mental or emotional age peers. Eighty eight percent of the fixated pedophiles were single and never married compared to only 25% of regressed pedophiles. The two types may be seen to correspond to the "true" pedophile who erotically prefers children (Fig. 8.1) and surrogate cases in which the child provides a temporary sexual attraction.[4]

Mohr (1981; Mohr et al., 1964) described three types of pedophiles based on the age of initial sexual offense. An adolescent group was characterized by delayed development of social-sexual functioning; a middle aged group by regression, and an old group of situational offenders who were reacting to loneliness.[5]

The regressive or fixated nature of pedophilia has also been linked to narcissism. Fraser (1976) theorized that the pedophile engages an idolized child who is pretty and much like himself as a child. He may indulge the child with gifts or attention that he himself received (or would like to have received) at that age.[6] Regressive play as an erotic stimulus for pedophiles was examined in the present collection of studies.

STUDY 1—ASSERTIVENESS

Subjects

There were 14 heterosexual pedophiles defined as: any male 18 years of age or older who showed an erotic preference for females 12 years of age or younger. One bisexual pedophile was included because he was predominantly heterosexual.

A control group of 16 nonsex offenders seen at the same clinic served as a control group. They faced mainly charges of fraud and theft among other property offenses but as far as we could ascertain, they had neither sexual offenses nor

sexual anomalies. All men in both groups admitted to their erotic preference and crimes.

The pedophiles were older than controls averaging 32.17 years (SD 12.25) versus 25.53 years for controls (SD 7.85). Pedophiles were also less educated with a mean of 8.82 years (SD 2.89) versus 10.87 years (SD 1.41) for controls. One pedophile and three controls had some post secondary education.[7]

Materials and Procedure

All subjects were administered the Assertion Inventory (Alberti & Emmons, 1970), and the Rathus (1973) Assertiveness Schedule which showed satisfactory internal consistency.[8]

RESULTS

The two groups' total scores were compared by t-tests. There were no significant group differences on either total scale score in Table 8.1 suggesting that pedophiles are not especially unassertive. There was considerable variation and skewed distribution of scores on both scales for the two groups. Only four items showed any differences of significance. Pedophiles stated that the following item was more uncharacteristic of them: "When I am given a compliment, I sometimes just don't know what to say"; but they more often "pursued an argument after the other person had enough"; asked a person to "stop kicking or bumping their chairs in a movie, etc.," and they more often "got into physical fights, especially with strangers." Of course these results may be artifactual since t-tests on 65 items could produce three significant values by chance. However, it is noteworthy that pedophiles were more assertive and even aggressive compared to controls on the four items. Overall there were no significant differences. Thus, the hypothesis was not supported.

TABLE 8.1
Mean Assertiveness Scores for Pedophiles and Controls

Scale	Pedophiles		Controls	
	Mean	S.D.	Mean	S.D.
Rathus Assertiveness Schedule	11	25	10	28
Assertion Inventory	41	69	70	59

Note: Ns vary slightly with a minimum of 9 cases answering a test. Maximum scores possible, Rathus Scale 90 and Assertion Inventory 140.

STUDY 2—AVERSION TO ADULT FEMALES
AND INTERCOURSE

Subjects

The subjects from Study 1 were used here.

Materials and Procedure

There were two methods used in this experiment: phallometric testing and verbal reports. The phallometric procedure, reported by Freund et al. (1973) was used to examine the aversion of the subjects to parts of the female body and to intercourse. Subjects were prearoused with slides of female children until they attained 1 ml. penile volume increase.[9] Then they were shown one of the following six critical slides for seven seconds: full figure nude female, her nude breasts, or pubic region; heterosexual coitus, "disgusting" slides of skin diseases on human figures; and neutral pictures; usually landscapes without obvious phallic symbols. There were four sets of these six critical slides for a total of 24 stimuli. They were shown in random order within each block. Each type of critical slide was shown in every block.[10]

Penile volume was measured by the phallometer developed by Freund (1963) and modified for the Grass Polygraph by Langevin and Martin (1975). Volume change at 7 and 14 seconds after the critical stimulus onset was recorded.

Three bipolar responses were examined in verbal reports: sexual arousal increase-decrease, pleasantness-unpleasantness, and attractiveness-unattractiveness to the following stimuli: (a) make-up or perfume; (b) breasts; (c) hair on underarms or legs; (d) pubic hair; (e) facial hair or down; (f) clean shaven pubis; (g) rounded hips; (h) maximum and minimum age of partners acceptable; (i) person around your age; (j) maximum and minimum height of a partner acceptable; (k) person around your height; (l) approaching a female sexually; and (m) a female approaching you sexually. The items were administered orally and the stimuli shown on cards to respondants.[11] They were told: "The following characteristics are to be rated in terms of how *sexually arousing* they are to you with respect to the sex of your preferred person and to the age or age range of the person.

Rate:

1. strongly increases sexual arousal.
2. moderately increases sexual arousal.
3. not at all arousing (indifference).
4. moderately decreases sexual arousal.
5. strongly decreases sexual arousal.

Instructions and task were repeated twice and the words "sexually arousing" replaced first by *pleasant* and second by *attractive*. Pedophiles rated children of their preferred age and both groups of subjects rated adult females.

RESULTS

Phallometric results showed no significant differences between pedophiles and controls. Figure 8.2 shows that all slides of the adult female body and vaginal intercourse with her were associated with an increase in penile tumescence; neutrals with little change, and disgusting pictures with a decrement in response. There were no significant differences in breasts, pubic area, full figure, or

Figure 8.2

Penile Volume Changes to Critical Stimuli
Fourteen Seconds After Prearousal

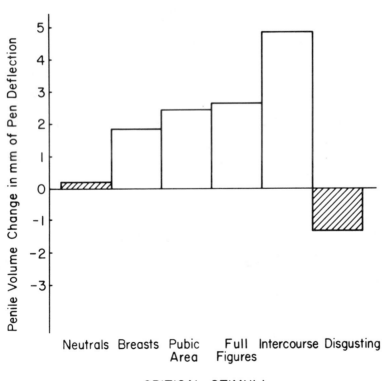

intercourse stimuli. Results suggest that pedophiles do not have an aversion to the female body or to intercourse.[12]

There were no significant group differences on any questionnaire item pertaining to the adult female. The scores for sexual arousal increase-decrease, pleasantness-unpleasantness, and attractiveness-unattractiveness were similar and highly correlated so only results for sexual arousal are presented in Table 8.2. Most items had a positive valence except "hair on underarm or leg" and "hair on face" which tended to decrease sexual arousal, but in both groups comparably. Breasts and rounded hips and the female approaching sexually were most arousing to both groups.

Table 8.3 shows the verbal rating of child versus adult for pedophiles. There were remarkably few differences. Make-up or perfume were less arousing on the child than on the adult. There was a trend for the chest to be less arousing on the child than on the adult. Taller children also tended to be less arousing but the age and height range of most arousing adult and child partners overlapped considerably. In most respects ratings of reaction patterns were quite similar for both female adult and child. The aversion hypothesis was not supported either in verbal or phallometric response.

TABLE 8.2
Verbal Ratings of Sexual Arousal Increases-Decreases from Adult
Females for Pedophiles and Controls

Item	Pedophiles (N = 12)		Controls (N = 14)	
	Mean	S.D.	Mean	S.D.
1. Make up or perfume	2.33	0.89	2.14	0.53
2. Breasts	1.33	0.89	1.57	0.51
3. Hair on leg or underarm	3.50	1.24	3.79	1.19
4. Pubic hair	2.00	0.95	2.14	0.53
5. Hair on face (down)	4.00	0.85	3.78	1.19
6. Clean shaven pubis	2.92	1.38	2.79	0.89
7. Rounded hips	1.75	0.75	1.92	1.00
8. A person around your age	2.00	1.21	1.64	0.74
9. A person around your height	1.83	0.83	2.29	0.73
10. Approaching female sexually	1.92	0.90	1.93	0.47
11. A female approaching you sexually	1.50	0.90	1.36	0.50
12. Maximum age partner arousing	32.42	8.89	32.00	8.31
13. Minimum age partner arousing	18.17	2.62	18.57	2.59
14. Maximum height (cm.) partner arousing	68.58	3.29	68.21	2.49
15. Minimum height (cm.) partner arousing	60.67	5.43	61.93	2.40

Note: Unless otherwise specified, the Scale is 1 = strong arousal increase, through 3 = neither increase nor decrease to 5 = strong arousal decrease.

TABLE 8.3
A Comparison of Sexual Arousal Ratings For
Child and Adult in Pedophiles

Item	Adult		Child		Pearson Correlation
	Mean	S.D.	Mean	S.D.	
1. Make up or perfume*	2.33	0.89	3.25	1.05	0.10
2. Breasts†	1.33	0.89	2.08	1.24	0.30
3. Hair on leg or underarm	3.50	1.24	3.83	1.19	0.49
4. Pubic hair	2.00	0.95	2.42	1.56	0.79**
5. Hair on face (down)	4.00	0.85	3.75	1.21	0.35
6. Clean shaven pubis	2.92	1.38	2.67	1.30	0.79**
7. Rounded hips	1.75	0.75	1.67	0.78	0.62*
8. A person around your age	2.00	1.21	1.87	0.99	0.58
9. A person around your height†	1.83	0.83	2.25	0.75	0.65*
10. Approaching female sexually	1.92	0.90	2.17	1.03	0.31
11. A female approaching you sexually	1.50	0.90	1.92	1.44	0.59*
12. Maximum age partner arousing**	32.42	8.89	19.17	9.07	−0.06
13. Minimum age partner arousing***	18.17	2.62	11.50	2.91	−0.06
14. Maximum height (cm.) partner arousing*	68.58	3.29	65.58	4.05	0.46
15. Minimum height (cm.) partner arousing	60.67	5.43	57.58	10.49	0.87***

Note: †p < 10., *p < 05, **p < 01, ***p < 001.

STUDY 3A—PHYSICAL FEATURES IN EROTIC ATTRACTION

In order to examine how pedophiles differ from the average male, it was first necessary to develop a questionnaire on controls that would ascertain the typical relative erotic valence of various body parts and traits, including size and strength.

Subjects

Sixteen males and 20 females in an undergraduate psychology course served as volunteers.

Materials and Procedure

During class time, the subjects were tested as part of an illustration of research method and questionnaire development. They were free to leave or answer the tests without penalty. They were given group results in a later class.

There were 17 items with the following instructions:

> Rate the following characteristics in terms of how sexually attractive you find them in the opposite sex. Select and circle the number for each item of the type of characteristic you find most sexually attractive. If you cannot decide, mark ''cannot say'' but try to make a decision in each case.

PART A

The Face

1. Head Hair Length
1	2	3	4	5	x
very short	short	medium	long	very long	cannot say

2. Facial hair (beard & moustache in men, down in women)
1	2	3	4	5	x
absent	a little	average	considerable	a lot	cannot say

3. Eyebrows
1	2	3	4	5	x
very thin	thin	average	thick	very thick	cannot say

4. Lip Size
1	2	3	4	5	x
very thin	thin	average	thick	very thick	cannot say

5. Chin Shape
1	2	3	4	5	x
very rounded	rounded	in between	squared	very squared	cannot say

The Body

6. Body hair
1	2	3	4	5	x
absent	little	some	considerable	a lot	cannot say

7. Shoulder Breadth
1	2	3	4	5	x
very small	small	medium	large	very large	cannot say

8. Musculature
1	2	3	4	5	x
not evident	slight	average	evident	very evident	cannot say

9. Weight (in relation to you)

1	2	3	4	5	x
much lighter	lighter	same	heavier	much heavier	cannot say

10. Height (in relation to you)

1	2	3	4	5	x
much shorter	shorter	same	taller	much taller	cannot say

11. Hip Shape

1	2	3	4	5	x
very rounded and flared	rounded & flared	in between	straight	very straight	cannot say

12. Shape of Behind

1	2	3	4	5	x
very rounded	rounded	in between	flat	very flat	cannot say

13. Leg Shape

1	2	3	4	5	x
very smooth & rounded	smooth & rounded	in between	muscular	very muscular	cannot say

14. Pubic Hair

1	2	3	4	5	x
absent	some	average	considerable	a lot	cannot say

Men Only

15. Breast size

1	2	3	4	5	x
very small	small	average	large	very large	cannot say

16. Breast shape

1	2	3	4	5	x
very pointed	pointed	in between	rounded	very rounded	cannot say

Women only

17. Penis size

1	2	3	4	5	x
very small	small	average	large	very large	cannot say

Subjects were also asked to rank the importance of the same items as follows:

Rank the following characteristics from most important in sexual attraction (1) to least important. These are the same characteristics you rated in Part A. Refer to them as necessary. Take into consideration your ratings above. For example, if you

find the absence of facial hair important, how does this compare to the other features you have rated e.g., weight, etc.

Finally a set of nine additional items were examined:

Rate the following behavior and personality characteristics in terms of how sexually attractive you find them in the opposite sex. Select and circle the number for each item of the type of characteristic you find most sexually attractive. If you cannot decide, mark ''cannot say'' but try to make a decision in each case.

PART B

1. Physical strength in relation to you:

1	2	3	4	5	x
much weaker	weaker	same	stronger	much stronger	cannot say

2. Outgoing (Extraversion):

1	2	3	4	5	x
very introverted	slightly introverted	average	extraverted	very extraverted	cannot say

3. Dominating versus Submissive:

1	2	3	4	5	x
very submissive	slightly submissive	in between	slightly dominating	very dominating	cannot say

4. Age in relation to you:

1	2	3	4	5	x
much younger	slightly younger	same	slightly older	much older	cannot say

5. Dress:
   A. Tie and shirt (skirt or dress)
   B. Jeans

6. Grooming:
   A. Clean and neat
   B. Not so clean or neat

7. Masculine—Feminine:

1	2	3	4	5	x
very feminine	feminine	in between	masculine	very masculine	cannot say

8. Overall physical beauty:

1	2	3	4	5	x
much below average	below average	average	above average	very good looking	cannot say

9. Rate yourself on overall physical beauty:

1	2	3	4	5	x
much below average	below average	average	above average	very good looking	cannot say

The Freund, Langevin, Satterberg, & Steiner (1977) FGI scale also was administered and an 81 item questionnaire containing Lie and Social Desirability scales.

RESULTS

In Table 8.4, the only *nonsignificant* differences in male versus female comparisons were for lip size and pubic hair. However, by far the greatest differences

TABLE 8.4
Male-Female Differences in Erotic Valence of
Opposite Sex Body Characteristics

	F	Eta	*Average*	
			Males Prefer	Females Prefer
1. Hair length	13.89***	.30	Long	Medium
2. Facial hair	41.25***	.56	Absent	Average
3. Eyebrows	13.59***	.29	Thin	Average
4. Lip Size	0.26	.01	Average	Average
5. Chin shape	4.32*	.13	Slight rounded	Slight squared
6. Body hair	40.28***	.55	Little	some— considerable
7. Shoulder breadth	46.89***	.59	Medium	Large
8. Musculature	27.01***	.44	Slight	Evident
9. Relative weight	273.83***	.89	Lighter	Heavier
10. Relative height	196.58***	.85	Shorter	Taller
11. Hip shape	127.31***	.80	Rounded and flared	straight
12. Shape of behind	15.03***	.33	Rounded	in between— flat
13. Leg shape	49.99***	.59	Smooth and round	Muscular
14. Pubic hair	0.04	.00	Average	Average
15. Breast size	N/A	—	Large	
16. Breast shape	N/A	—	Rounded	
17. Penis Size	N/A	—		Average

Note: *$p < 05$, ***$p < 001$.
N/A—Not applicable. Items 15 through 17 naturally could not be analysed.

were in relative weight and height. Both sexes wanted the female shorter and lighter than the male. Hip shape was also outstanding in marking sex differences. The characteristic rounded flared female hip attracted males but females desired the straight male hip. The remaining features, although significant, were considerably behind these three in differentiating the sexes.

The ranking of features within sexes is presented in Table 8.5 and a somewhat different picture emerged. For males hip shape, breast shape, and leg shape were primary and for females relative height, weight, and musculature were. Genital size was only ranked 12 by the females.

Finally, seven other nonphysical features (not ranked) were compared for males and females (Table 8.6). Relative strength, age, and masculinity-femininity were most important. Both sexes wanted the female younger, weaker, and feminine compared to the male.

All items were subjected to correlation with social desirability and naive lying but none correlated significantly with lying and only two did with social desirability, outgoingness (-.43, p<.05), and own physical beauty (-.41, p <.05). Most items therefore appear to have discriminant validity from lying and social desirability.

TABLE 8.5
Order of Mean Importance of
Characteristics in Sexual
Attraction

Item	Males	Females
1. Head hair length	7	4
2. Facial hair	11	6
3. Eyebrows	13–14	14
4. Lip size	9	11
5. Chin shape	15	13
6. Body hair	13–14	7
7. Shoulder breadth	12	5
8. Musculature	10	2
9. Relative weight	8	3
10. Relative height	5	1
11. Hip shape	1	9
12. Shape of behind	4	8
13. Leg shape	3	10
14. Pubic hair	16	15
15. Breast size	2	—
16. Breast shape	6	—
17. Penis size	—	12

TABLE 8.6
Miscellaneous Factors in Sexual Attraction

Item	F	Eta	Male	Female
1. Relative strength	343.31***	.91	Weaker	Stronger
2. Outgoing	1.85	.05	Average	Average
3. Dominant—Submissive	13.59***	.29	In between	Slight dominating
4. Relative age	59.48***	.66	Slightly older	Slightly younger
5. Dressed vs. casual	2.55	.07	In between	In between
6. Grooming	0.02	.00	Clean and neat	Clean and neat
7. Masculine-feminine	218.41***	.86	Feminine	Masculine
8. Physical beauty	10.21**	.23	Above average	Average
9. Own physical beauty	8.38**	.20	Above average	Average

Note: **$p < 01$, ***$p < .001$.

The remaining items were subjected to item analysis and principal axes factor analysis to determine the extent to which they formed a scale. Alpha reliability was 0.91 and a single factor explained 46% of the total variance and 70% of the common variance indicating that the items could be used as a scale.

In the factor analysis, highest loadings were on relative physical strength (.96), relative height (.96), masculine-feminine (.95), relative weight (.94), hip shape (.88), and relative age (.81). There were only three items with loadings less than .30, lip size (.12), pubic hair (.06), and grooming (.14) but no other item had a communality less than .59.

DISCUSSION

The relative size, strength, and age of male and female appear to be among the most important factors in human sexual attraction. They may be conditional to allow other features to "fine tune" mate selection (e.g., breast size, chest hair, etc.) However, the results were based on self report. In the next study marriage partners were examined to determine the extent to which the size variables operated in fact.

STUDY 3B—MATE CHARACTERISTICS

Subjects and Procedure

Twenty individuals who were staff on the Clarke Institute were asked to provide the age, height, weight, and hair color of themselves and their mates.

TABLE 8.7A
A Correlation of Age, Height and Weight in Married Couples

	Female		
	Age	*Height*	*Weight*
Male	.367	.232	.326

TABLE 8.7B
Significance Level of Males Versus Females in Age,
Height and Weight

	Men vs. Women in General	*Husbands vs. Wives*
Age	.157	.021
Height	.035	.001
Weight	.002	.001

RESULTS

Hair color was not significant and will not be discussed further. The correlations among the remaining three measures between husbands and wives were small and nonsignificant (Table 8.7A).[13] Men were significantly taller and heavier than women but they did not differ in age. However, when husbands were compared specifically to their wives, the results were even more significant. Husbands were heavier and older than their wives. In only five cases was the husband younger than his wife, none was shorter, and none was lighter.

DISCUSSION

The two studies on normal men and women suggest that relative size, strength, and age of desired sex partners are positively related to erotic arousal and mate selection as they are in lower animals. In fact, they may be the most potent and consistent variables in selective mating. Although hip shape and secondary sex characteristics play a role in sexual attraction, they are less discriminating than size parameters and strength. The questionnaire developed in Study 3A offers a means for comparing the pedophile to the norm. It is perhaps in the realm of size that he shows an exaggerated need for a discrepancy with his partner. These questions were examined next.

STUDY 3C—PHYSICAL FEATURES IN PEDOPHILIC EROTIC AROUSAL

Subjects

The men from Study 1 were used here.

Materials and Procedure

An attempt was made in pilot work to administer the questionnaire used in Study 3A. However pedophiles were confused. Therefore the items were typed on cards and individually administered orally to each subject. The same descriptors were used but some items were added and one removed. Subjects were asked to evaluate head hair texture (thick to thin), hair style (straight, wavy, curly), body frame (large to slight), style of dress (conservative, stylish), timidness (5 point scale), independence, and sexual behavior (intercourse, touching etc.). The item on "age in relation to you" was removed. Instead the preferred age of sex partner was ascertained and the items answered for those preferred partners. Pedophiles answered the questions a second time in reference to adult females so their responses to children and adults could be compared.

RESULTS

Only two items significantly differentiated the groups. Pedophiles found average to pointed breasts on the adult female more sexually arousing and controls rated rounded to very rounded breasts more arousing.[14] Controls were more aroused by "very neat and clean" partners and pedophiles by "neat and clean" ones.[15] Both groups found the lighter, shorter, somewhat weaker adult female most sexually arousing. She should also be slightly timid, submissive, independent, and above average in physical beauty. Vaginal intercourse was the preferred sexual behavior for 93% of controls and 75% of pedophiles. The difference was not statistically significant. One pedophile each preferred anal intercourse, masturbation, and touching, and one control preferred oral-genital sex.

The rankings of relative sexual arousal was similar in the two groups with three exceptions. Big and rounded breasts, and smaller body frame were rated most important in sexual attraction for both groups. They differed in that pedophiles found lip size and chin size less arousing but pubic hair more arousing.[16]

There were only two differences in pedophiles ratings of adults versus children. The child's lips should be thinner and breasts smaller than the adult. There were trends for straighter hair and grooming to be more important in the child than in the adult. There were no significant differences in rankings for adult

versus child. The preferred sexual behaviors were not significantly different for child and adult but the small number of cases may have masked real differences. Only 33% were consistent in desired behaviors from both child and adult. The largest difference was for vaginal intercourse. Seventeen percent desired it from both child and adult but 33% desired touching, 25% oral genital, 17% masturbation from the child, and 8% did not reply.

STUDY 4—AN EXAMINATION OF VIOLENCE, NARCISSISM, AND REGRESSION IN PEDOPHILIC SEXUAL AROUSAL

Subjects

The men from Study 1 were examined here.

Materials and Procedure

Penile volume changes were measured in the same way as Study 2 but subjects listened to audiotaped stimuli instead of viewing slides.

The stimuli were recorded by an adult female and they depicted sexual interaction emphasizing:

a. The size of the female child.
b. Her admiration of the listener's penis while he exposes.
c. Rape.
d. Dominance of her in a state of fear.
e. Regressive play.
f. Heterosexual adult intercourse—male initiated.
g.   —Female initiated.
h. Assault.
i. Sex teacher.
j. Her shock when he exposes.
k. Neutral stimuli.

There were two repeats of each except for (e) and (f) which were only presented once and (k) neutrals for which there were three stimuli. There was a total of 20 stimuli. With the exception of the intercourse items, all referred to young girls and in one case of a neutral statement, to a teenage girl. The stimuli were presented in two blocks in a fixed random order. Penile volume change in each 10 seconds of the 100 second stimulus presentation time was recorded along with the maximum change in the 100 seconds (R max) for each stimulus.

RESULTS

Multivariate and univariate analysis of variance for the responses in the first 10 seconds of stimulus presentation (Ro, baseline) and the maximum response in 100 seconds (R max) were analyzed for the two blocks of trials, the two groups, and the eight classes of stimuli for which there were repeats. Nonrepeated stimuli were analyzed separately. A rape index and an assault index were computed after Abel, Barlow, Blanchard, and Guild (1977) and Quinsey and Chaplin (1982) (See also Chapter 2).

The two groups[17] did not react differentially to any class of stimulus. However the controls reacted more to all erotic descriptions than to neutral stimuli and they showed two levels of penile responsiveness with largest reactions being to consenting intercourse initiated by a female adult (Table 8.8A). Pedophiles did not react differentially to neutrals, nonsexual assault, or exposing-shock stimuli. They did not distinguish among the remaining stimuli although largest reactions were to dominance-fear. The nonrepeated stimuli (Table 8.8B) did not distinguish the two groups either.[18] The Rape and Assault Indices were nonsignificant.[19] Results suggest that, at least in the laboratory, a wide range of sexual interactions with female children is arousing to both pedophiles and controls in similar ways.

TABLE 8.8A
Mean Z Score Penile Volume Changes to Statements Depicting
Erotic Interaction with Female Children

Stimulus	Pedophiles	Controls
1. Neutrals	−0.77[a]	−1.00[a]
2. Assault	−0.62[a]	−0.23[ab]
3. Exposing-Shock	−0.29[a]	−0.20[b]
4. Size	0.17[b]	−0.30[b]
5. Dominance—Fear	0.41[b]	0.11[bc]
6. Exposing—Admiration	0.20[b]	0.49[c]
7. Rape	0.23[b]	−0.05[b]
8. Female Initiated Intercourse	0.29[b]	0.79[c]

Note: Means with same superscript are not significantly different *within each column*.

TABLE 8.8B
Miscellaneous Nonrepeated Stimuli

Stimulus	Pedophiles	Controls
1. Neutral	−1.09[a]	−0.87[a]
2. Sex Teacher	0.40	0.28
3. Male initiated intercourse	0.87	0.91
4. Regressive Play	0.59	0.49

DISCUSSION

When the results are examined as a whole, heterosexual pedophiles remain an enigma. None of the commonly held hypotheses were supported. Pedophiles were *not* unassertive. Introversion, in fact, may be more descriptive of non-violent pedophiles than lack of assertiveness. Extraversion-introversion is a dimension of human personality that can be described as "outgoingness"—how much the individual seeks out or needs the company of others. Some individuals, the introverts, prefer solitary activities that may be the case for a variety of reasons; fear of others, feelings of inferiority, and perhaps not stressed enough, a genuine non-neurotic lack of interest in people. If adult females do not satisfy the erotic needs of pedophiles, they may be ignored or not sought out for this reason. The relative lack of skills may result from disinterest rather than from a "failed attempt to relate sexually in a mature way." The introversion seen in clinical cases of pedophilia as well as in other sexual anomalies, may also relate to "narcissism," a self-centered sexuality.

The pedophiles in this study liked adult females sexually and generally in similar ways to offender controls and community volunteers. They did not show an aversion to adult females or to intercourse and in fact they appeared to enjoy it. Unusual response categories such as rape and exposing were unremarkable in distinguishing pedophiles and controls. However, the trend for "dominating the fearful child" to be most arousing to pedophiles may be important. More refined stimuli may be useful in testing this hypothesis.

Perhaps the *lack* of distinction between child and adult is most important. Normal men react erotically to children as young as 6-years-old in the laboratory but usually do not act out in the community. The lack of inhibition either as a cortical or as a social phenomenon may be operative in pedophiles. Their failure to distinguish physical features of children and adults in their erotic attraction is noteworthy. One may wish to examine stimulus and response generalization in this group. For some reason they may overgeneralize so children are not discrete from adults. Thus pedophiles are not afraid of, or disinterested in, adult females and there may be nothing especially different about the child that they find erotically arousing. They may simply fail to sexually differentiate females on the basis of physical maturity. One may then wonder why they risk so much in acting out with the child since social sanctions are great.

It is possible that the fitness parameters are exaggerated in pedophiles and we were unable to detect differences. Even normal males want the female smaller and lighter than themselves but the *degree* to which the adult male pedophile wants his most desired female partner smaller may have been missed. Perhaps use of silouettes that could be varied on a number of physical parameters would be more discriminating.

The series of pilot studies reported here was limited in sample size and selection among other things. Subjects in other settings may be different. The use

of a female voice in audio-descriptions and the stimuli chosen may also have colored results. They should be replicated with a male voice and other stimuli. Finally, subjects may have distorted results at a time when social pressure against pedophiles is pronounced. Nevertheless, the results suggest that new hypotheses are needed to explain pedophilia.

ACKNOWLEDGMENTS

The authors wish to thank M. Friesen and C. Anderson for assistance in data collection and W. Curnoe for careful data analyses.

REFERENCES

Abel, G. G., Barlow, D. H., Blanchard, E. B., & Guild, D. The components of rapists' sexual arousal. *Archives of General Psychiatry*, 1977, *34*, 895–903.

Alberti, R., & Emmons, M. *Your Perfect Right*. San Luis Obispo, CA: Impact Press, 1970.

Apfelberg, B., Sugar, C., & Pfeffer, A. Z. A psychiatric study of 250 sex offenders. *American Journal of Psychiatry*, 1944, *100*, 762–770.

Avery-Clark, C., O'Neil, J. A., & Laws, D. R. A comparison of intrafamilial sexual and physical child abuse. In M. Cook & K. Howells (Eds.), *Adult sexual interest in children*. New York: Academic Press, 1981.

Cook, M. (Ed.) *The bases of human sexual attraction*. New York: Academic Press, 1981.

Dion, K. K. Physical attractiveness, sex roles and heterosexual attraction. In M. Cook, (Ed.), *The bases of human sexual attraction*. New York: Academic Press, 1981.

Fraser, M. *The death of narcissus*. London: Secker & Warburg, 1976.

Freund, K. A laboratory method for diagnosing predominance of homo- and hetero-erotic interest in the male. *Behavior Research and Therapy*, 1963, *1*, 85–93.

Freund, K. Diagnosing homo- or heterosexuality and erotic age preference by means of a psychophysiological test. *Behavior Research & Therapy*, 1967, *5*, 209–228. (a)

Freund, K. Erotic preference in pedophilia. *Behavior Research & Therapy*, 1967, *5*, 339–348. (b)

Freund, K., Langevin, R., Chamberlyne, R., Deosera, A., & Zajac, Y. The phobic theory of male homosexuality. *Archives of General Psychiatry*, 1974, *31*, 495–499.

Freund, K., Langevin, R., Cibiri, S., & Zajac, Y. Heterosexual aversion in homosexual males, *British Journal of Psychiatry*, 1973, *122*, 163–169.

Freund, K., McKnight, C. K., Langevin, R., & Cibiri, S. The female child as a surrogate object. *Archives of Sexual Behavior*, 1972, *2*, 119–133.

Freund, K., Langevin, R., Satterberg, J., & Steiner, B. Extension of the gender identity scale for males. *Archives of Sexual Behavior*, 1977, *6*, 507–519.

Freund, K., Langevin, R., & Zajac, Y. Heterosexual aversion in homosexual males: A second experiment, *British Journal of Psychiatry*, 1974, *125*, 177–180.

Groth, A. N., & Birnbaum, H. J. Adult sexual orientation and attraction to underage persons. *Archives of Sexual Behavior*, 1978, *7*, 175–181.

Hook, H. *Aversion to adult females in pedophiles*. Honors B. A. Thesis, Psychology Department, York University, 1981.

Howells, K. Some meanings of children for pedophiles. In M. Cook & G. Wilson (Eds.), *Love and attraction: An international conference*. Oxford, England: Pergamon Press, 1979.

Howells, K. Adult sexual interest in children: Considerations relevant to theories of aetiology. In M. Cook, & K. Howells, (Eds.), *Adult sexual interest in children*, New York: Academic Press, 1981.

Hovarth, T. Physical attractiveness: The influence of selected torso parameters. *Archives of Sexual Behavior*, 1981, *10*, 21–24.

Karpman, B. A case of paedophilia (legally rape) cured by psychoanalysis. *Psychoanalytic Review*, 1950, *37*, 235–276.

Karpman, B. *The sexual offender and his offense*. New York: Julian Press, 1957.

Langevin, R. *Sexual strands: Understanding and treating sexual anomalies in men*. Hillsdale, NJ: Lawrence Erlbaum Associates, 1983.

Langevin, R., Paitich, D., Freeman, R., Mann, K., & Handy, L. Personality characteristics and sexual anomalies in males. *Canadian Journal of Behavioral Science*, 1978, *10*, 222–238.

Langevin, R., Paitich, D., Ramsay, G., Anderson, C., Kamrad, J., Pope, S., Geller, G., & Newman, S. Experimental studies in the etiology of genital exhibitionism. *Archives of Sexual Behavior*, 1979, *8*, 307–331.

Manning, A. Sexual attraction in animals. In M. Cook (Ed.), *The bases of human sexual attraction*. New York: Academic Press, 1981.

Mohr, J. Age structures in pedophilia. In M. Cook, & K. Howells (Eds.), *Adult sexual interest in children*, New York: Academic Press, 1981.

Mohr, J., Turner, R. E., & Jerry, M. *Pedophilia and exhibitionism*. Toronto: University of Toronto Press, 1964.

Noyes, A. P., & Kolb, L. C. *Modern clinical psychiatry*. Philadelphia: Saunders & Co., 1958.

Quinsey, V. L., & Chaplin, T. C. Penile responses to nonsexual violence among rapists. *Criminal Justice & Behavior*, 1982, *9*, 372–381.

Quinsey, V. L., Steinman, C. M., Bergersen, S. G., & Holmes, T. F. Penile circumference, skin conductance, and ranking responses of child molesters and ''normals'' to sexual and nonsexual visual stimuli. *Behavior Therapy*, 1975, *6*, 213–219.

Quinsey, V. L., & Bergersen, S. G. Instructional control of penile circumference in assessments of sexual preference. *Behavior Therapy*, 1976, *7*, 489–493.

Rathus, S. A 30 item schedule for measuring assertive behavior. *Behavior Therapy*, 1973, *4*, 398–406.

Rosen, R. C. Suppression of penile tumescence by instrumental conditioning. *Psychosomatic Medicine*, 1973, *35*, 509–514.

Stoller, R. J. *Perversion: The erotic form of hatred*. New York: Pantheon Books, 1975.

Storr, A. *Sexual deviation*. Harmondsworth, England: Penguin Books, 1964.

Straus, M. A., Gelles, R. J., & Steinmetz, S. K. *Behind closed.doors: Violence in the American family*. New York: Anchor Press, 1981.

Wiggins, N., & Wiggins, J. S. A typological analysis of male preferences for female body types. *Multivariate Behavior Research*, 1979, 89–102.

ENDNOTES

Note 1. One can conceptualize erotic behavior in terms of stimulus features of preferred objects or persons and the responses or behavior preferred by the actor and his partner/victim. See Langevin (1983) for more detail about a stimulus response matrix of erotic behavior.

Note 2. One might object to teleological thinking ascribed to lower animals in this theory. However the signs of strength, size, etc. may be attractive to the female and these features are adaptive without the female animal necessarily being aware of it. Human females may be aware of ''fitness'' however, and select mates on this more abstract basis.

Note 3. Hovarth (1981) and Wiggins and Wiggins (1979) have examined the role of torso shape in physical attractiveness for college students, but not size and strength parameters and not for sex offenders. Moreover, the term "attractive" was used in ratings rather than *sexually* attractive so it is not clear what has been rated. As Dion (1981) noted, there is a positive correlation between physical attractiveness and sexual appeal but research indicates that the two terms reflect different dimensions of interpersonal interest. See Cook (1981) for an overview of factors important in human sexual attraction.

Note 4. Karpman (1957) also noted a distinction between fixated and regressed types in his comprehensive review of the literature. Apfelberg, Sugar, and Pfeffer (1944) described pedophilia occurring late in life as "regression to a *homosexual* phase."

Note 5. See Chapter 9 for an overview of the elderly sex offenders.

Note 6. Karpman (1957, p. 104–105) also summarized earlier similar theories. Regression and narcissism may be fused, especially in the homosexual pedophile who seeks out the beautiful male child he wishes he could be.

Note 7. $t = 1.71$, $p = .05$ for age; $t = 2.40$, $p < .05$ for education. The numbers of cases in the two groups with post secondary education were not significantly different.

Note 8. The alpha reliabilities calculated by the SPSS Reliability program for the present study were: Rathus Scale 0.81, Assertion Inventory 0.87.

Note 9. In earlier reports (Freund et al. 1973, Freund, Langevin, Chamberlyne, et al., 1974 and Freund, Langevin, & Zajac, 1974) a criterion of 1.5 or 2.0 ml. was used but this was not possible here since it was very difficult to prearouse the subjects. As a group the pedophiles were older than our earlier homosexual subjects which may explain differences in arousability. Paradoxically one subject was diabetic and a second nonadmittor not included here was too. Since diabetes is often associated with impotence, this can also explain their lack of reactivity in the laboratory but it creates a paradox as to why they would act out with children. Their desire and cognitions surrounding sexual arousal may not be affected but penile arousal is. Alternatively, the diabetes may not affect their sexual arousal at all.

Note 10. Previous work has shown that this procedure prevents significant stimulus class by order of presentation interaction effects in analysis of variance.

Note 11. In pilot work, the questionnaire was first self administered and terms like "aversion" were tried. The respondents were confused and the present prodecure was found by trial and error to be satisfactory.

Note 12. There were only significant block and stimulus effects:

	0 sec.	7 sec.	14 sec.	Manova
Block F	1.36	3.32*	5.86***	3.12***
Stimulus F	2.09†	14.13***	12.73***	6.31***

There were trends for group by block and stimulus by block interactions to be significant as well:

	0 sec.	7 sec.	14 sec.	Manova
Group by Block F	2.44†	1.30	0.67	1.60*
Stimulus by Block F	1.73†	0.48	0.52	1.11

Because of a possible confounding of initial arousal level on aversive responses, the actual prearousal levels (0 sec) were covaried for the 7 and 14 second responses. Only the stimulus effect was significant and it was somewhat stronger now.

	7 sec.	14 sec.	Manova
Stimulus F	18.35***	18.87***	12.89***

It was difficult prearousing subjects in this study, particularly the pedophiles, and rapid fatigue showed up as a block effect. The results still suggested that pedophiles do not have an aversion to the adult female.

The aversion reaction to "disgusting" pictures was not as pronounced as it was in early tests of this hypothesis in homosexual (androphilic) men. The difference between neutrals and disgusting pictures was only significant at $p < .05$ when the main effect was $p < 001$. This may be due to two changes in procedure; the lower level of prearousal and the smaller screen used here to project slides.

Inhomogeneity of variance was not a problem in this study but Z scores were examined as a matter of routine. Results were essentially the same.

Note 13. The correlation of weight of husband and wife implies a constant linear relationship between the two. A perfect correlation between the two would mean that every wife is, say, 7 cm. shorter than her husband. Such an outcome is highly unlikely. The more tenable hypothesis is that wives are shorter than husbands, but *in varying degrees*. It should be examined by t-test or other group comparison statistic rather than by correlation.

Note 14. $t = 2.91$, df = 24, $p < .01$.

Note 15. $t = 3.88$, df = 24, $p < .001$.

Note 16. The actual mean ranks were:

	Pedophiles	Controls	t
Lip Size	17	10	2.13*
Chin Size	19	14	2.69*
Pubic Hair	9	19	3.20**

df = 20 in each case.

Note 17. Most effects were significant. F values were:

	R.	R.Max.	Manova
Group	0.30	0.07	0.34
Stimulus	1.34	10.58***	6.24***
Block	0.00	13.65***	7.30***
Group × Stimulus	1.38	2.25*	1.59†
Group × Block	0.13	0.31	0.18
Stimulus × Block	4.64***	1.23	2.59**
Group × Stimulus × Block	2.09†	1.47	1.80†

The use of Z scores resulted in only 3 significant effects and 1 trend:

	R.	R. Max.	Manova
Stimulus F	1.22	13.69***	7.71***
Block F	1.19	17.11***	10.75***
Stimulus × Block F	3.96**	1.29	2.36**
Group × Stimulus F	1.27	2.08*	1.42

The analysis of penile volume changes is characteristically influenced by order effects, different group responsiveness (irrespective of stimuli) and, inhomogeneity of variance results. Z score transformations usually correct the problems but not always. In the present case, there remained a stimulus by block effect indicating that everyone tended to react less during the second block than the first to erotica but not to neutral stimuli. This is simply fatigue. The group by stimulus interaction was due to a range effect of means and the greater differentiation of stimuli by controls than by pedophiles.

Note 18. Results were only significant for the stimulus effect.

	R.	R. Max	Manova
Stimulus	1.49	23.86***	11.41***

Note 19. For the Rape Index (Rape Responses +50/Intercourse Responses +50), t = 1.24, p>.05 and the Assault Index (Assault Responses +50/Intercourse Responses +50), t = 0.18, p>.05. The scores were incremented by 50 to avoid negative numbers. The rape index (RI) and assault index (AI) values were:

	RI	AI
Pedophiles	0.99	0.76
Controls	0.84	0.74

Z score transformation within subjects did not change the results substantially.

9 Elderly Sex Offenders

Stephen J. Hucker
Mark H. Ben-Aron
Clarke Institute of Psychiatry, Toronto

An unusual feature of pedophilia is its occurrence apparently for the first time in elderly men of "blameless character." Most sex offenses are committed by young men who often "burn out" in their 30s or 40s. Sex offenses by men over 60 are therefore especially interesting to clinicians. Brain abnormalities such as those in senile dementia are believed by some theorists to be operative. On the other hand, the loneliness of many elderly people may also play a role in their offenses. In the next study the relative importance of psychiatric diagnosis and social adjustment in elderly sex offenders is examined.

INTRODUCTION

Most writers who have studied elderly criminals have considered sex offenders to be the most common among this group (Abrahamsen, 1944; Bergman & Amir, 1973; Devon, 1930; Fox, 1946; Schroeder, 1936). However, Roth (1968), drawing upon British official statistics, found that sex offenses constituted only about 12% of all offenses in this age group. Similarly, Keller and Vedder (1968), using the FBI's Uniform Crime Reports, found that sex offenses occupied twelfth position among the "top twenty" crimes in those aged 60 years or older. Epstein, Hills, and Simon (1970) reported in their survey of arrests during one year, that there were only four sex offenders out of 722 aged 60 years or older. It is also worth noting that in most of the widely quoted studies of sex offenders (e.g.,

Gebhard, Gagnon, Pomeroy, & Christenson, 1965; Mohr, Turner & Jerry, 1964; Radzinowicz, 1957) elderly perpetrators were uncommon. It seems likely therefore, that the frequency of sex offenses by the elderly have been distorted by the sources of data employed.

Among sexual offenses committed by the elderly, those involving child victims are generally considered the most frequent (Ellis, 1933; Pollack, 1941; Whiskin, 1967, 1968; Zeegers, 1966, 1978). Most elderly sex offenders are said to be first time offenders with no previous record of sexual or any other offenses (Moberg, 1953; Roth, 1968; Zeegers, 1966, 1978) and they are often described as being of previously "blameless character" (Pollack, 1941; Slater & Roth, 1969).

The most popular theory advanced to explain why elderly men might commit sexual crimes has been that they are suffering from dementia (East, 1944; Ellis, 1933; Henninger, 1939; Rollin, 1973; Rose, 1970; Rothschild, 1945; Ruskin, 1941; Storr, 1964; Sutherland, 1924; Von Krafft-Ebing, 1965; Whiskin, 1968; Zeegers, 1966, 1978). Nevertheless, others have disputed this (Allersma, 1971; Brancale, MacNeil, & Vuocolo 1965; Groth, Burgess, Birnbaum, & Gary, 1978; Hirschmann, 1962; Rothschild, 1945) although some who argued for the importance of organic deterioration conceded that the offense itself might be the "first sign" of senile change (Henninger, 1939). Others have indicated that the more typical features of dementia may be lacking (Ellis, 1933; Roth, 1968). Pollack (1941) noted that the crimes often lack planning and caution, though sometimes the degree of circumspection is surprising (Roth, 1968).

Other explanations of the elderly sex offender's behavior have included "changes in the prostate" (Sutherland, 1924) and "regression" due to emotional factors (Revitch & Weiss, 1962). Many elderly sex offenders who involved children are said to have been intoxicated at the time of the offense (Pollack, 1941). Other authors support the frequent claim of offender's that they were themselves the victim of seduction by a child (Allersma, 1971; Henninger, 1939; Meyers, 1965; Pollack, 1941; Slater & Roth, 1969; Virkkunen, 1975; Zeegers, 1966, 1978).

East (1944) proposed that elderly sex offenders most frequently selected children as victims because the aged are unattractive to adult females by whom they fear rejection. He argued that "fantasy and desire have outlived potency" so that they are capable only of what Whiskin (1968) calls "partial sexual acts" short of intercourse. Whiskin (1968) also suggested that the crime represents an attempt to bolster a flagging sense of masculinity. Children are the chosen victims because they have no prejudice toward the elderly. The "grandfather" image is one that is trusted (Roth, 1968). Other writers have suggested that child victims are chosen because they are less able to defend themselves, easier to bribe, more amenable to threats, and less likely to report the incident (Henninger, 1939).

Hirschmann (1962) considered most elderly sex offenders to have been sexually well-adjusted, whereas Zeegers (1966, 1978) found that, although many had been married, a substantial number were divorced or had experienced marital difficulties; an impression shared by Roth (1968).

The social problems that accompany old age such as loneliness and isolation following the death of friends and separation from family, together with reduced income, have been shown to be prominent factors among elderly sex offenders (Allersma, 1971; Law, 1979; Meyers, 1965; Mohr et al., 1964; Revitch & Weiss, 1962). These factors may contribute to the offense by drawing the elderly to the company of children in settings such as public parks.

Thus, many conflicting assertions are found in the limited literature about the elderly sex offender. The present study was an attempt to examine some of these issues.

METHOD

Subjects

Staff of the Forensic Service of the Clarke Institute of Psychiatry have, since it opened in 1966, examined large numbers of offenders who were referred for psychiatric evaluation. Between July 1, 1966 and December 31, 1979, 70 individuals aged 60 years or older were seen. The group consisted of 43 sex offenders, 16 violent offenders, and 11 miscellaneous cases.

The sample of 43 elderly sex offenders was selected for this study. Because Mohr et al. (1964) suggested that there may be important differences between individuals who commit sexual offenses earlier in their lives and those who offend in old age, a comparison group of 43 individuals aged 30 years or younger was also obtained. The latter were selected at random from sexual offenders of all ages who had been examined at the institute since 1966. No attempt was made to match the groups on legal charges because the available literature indicated that the proportion of certain charges, for example, those involving minors, might be different between the two age groups.

Materials and Procedures

The senior author selected the files of the elderly and young sex offenders and recorded pertinent information. Both authors reviewed the medical records and independently rated selected items for which interrater reliability was calculated. The presence or absence of seven broad diagnostic categories (organic brain syndrome, functional psychosis, neurosis, antisocial personality disorder, other personality disorder, alcoholism, and drug addiction) based on criteria described

TABLE 9.1
Elderly Sex Offenders: Offender
Characteristics

	Elderly Sex Offenders	Young Sex Offenders
N	43	43
Mean Age (In Years)	66.1	22.8
Age Range (In Years)	60–84	18–29
Occupation:		
Unskilled	39.5%	39.5%
Skilled	55.8%	34.9%
Professional	4.7%	11.6%
Student	0.0%	14.0%
I.Q.		
Superior	21.0%	7.0%
Bright Normal	25.5%	34.9%
Normal	34.9%	34.9%
Dull Normal	9.3%	18.6%
Retarded	0.0%	0.0%
Unknown	9.3%	4.6%
*Education**		
Grade 8 or less	55.8%	27.9%
Grades 9–13	34.9%	62.8%
Post Secondary	7.0%	9.3%
Unknown	2.3%	0.0%
*Marital Status****		
Ever Married	86.0%	34.9%
Never Married	14.0%	65.1%
Quality of Marital Relationship (in married subjects)**		
Below Average	70.0%	50.0%
Average	11.0%	50.0%
Above Average	19.0%	0.0%
*Social Contacts****		
None	16.0%	0.0%
Few	61.0%	35.0%
Some	23.0%	56.0%
Many	0.0%	9.0%

Note: *p < 05, **p < 01, ***p < 001, Chi Square Test.

in the International Classification of Diseases, ninth edition (ICD-9) was examined.[1] Multiple diagnoses were therefore possible. Because of the retrospective nature of the study and missing data in some of the files it was deemed impractical to employ the more recent and stricter criteria of the Diagnostic and Statistical Manual, third edition, of the American Psychiatric Association (DSM-III). The senior author's diagnoses and ratings were used in the tables and statistical analyses for simplicity. Other information collected is noted in the tables to follow. Data were mainly analyzed using chi-square.

RESULTS

The Offender

Demographic and clinical information on the experimental and comparison groups are given in Table 9.1.

No striking differences emerged between the two groups with respect to occupation or intelligence. Older offenders were significantly less educated and this probably reflects the better educational opportunities available in more recent years. Elderly sex offenders were more likely than younger offenders to be currently married or to have been married previously. This result may be a function of group selection on the basis of age. Of those who were married at the time of their offense, 70% of the elderly offenders and 50% of the young sex offenders were rated as having a "below average" marital relationship. The elderly sex offenders had significantly fewer social contacts than their younger counterparts.[2]

Table 9.2 shows that the most frequent psychiatric diagnoses in the elderly group were alcoholism, personality disorders other than the antisocial type,

TABLE 9.2
Psychiatric Diagnosis of Elderly Sex Offenders
and Controls

	Elderly Sex Offenders	Young Sex Offenders
Organic Brain Syndrome	14.0%	2.0%
Functional Psychosis	2.0%	2.0%
Neurosis	19.0%	2.0%
Personality Disorder—Antisocial	0.0%	19.0%
Personality Disorder—Other Type	21.0%	63.0%
Alcoholism	21.0%	26.0%
Drug Addiction	0.0%	14.0%

Note: Some patients had multiple diagnoses and others had none so percentages do not total 100%.

neurosis, and organic brain syndrome. In the younger group, the most common diagnoses were personality disorders of both antisocial and other types, alcoholism, and drug abuse.

Only 14% of the elderly offenders and 26% of the younger group were drinking at the time of the offense; none of the elderly and 7% of the younger offenders were intoxicated with drugs, and one younger offender was using both drugs and alcohol. Examining drugs and alcohol intoxication together, it was found that the younger offenders were significantly more likely to be intoxicated than the older group.[3]

TABLE 9.3
Elderly Sex Offenders: Offense Characteristics

	Elderly Sex Offenders	Young Sex Offenders
Legal Charges		
Indecent Assault Female	44.0%	23.0%
Indecent Assault Male	21.0%	9.0%
Contributing to Juvenile Delinquency	18.0%	9.0%
Indecent Exposure/Act	12.0%	37.0%
Buggery/Bestiality	5.0%	5.0%
Attempt Rape	0.0%	12.0%
Rape	0.0%	5.0%
*Nature of Sexual Contact***		
Looking Only	2.0%	2.0%
Exhibiting/Obscene Phone Call	14.0%	35.0%
Touching	63.0%	21.0%
Attempted Intercourse/Fellatio	14.0%	7.0%
Intercourse/Fellatio	0.0%	30.0%
Unknown	7.0%	5.0%
*Use of Force***		
None	70.0%	58.0%
Bribes	26.0%	2.0%
Threats	0.0%	9.0%
Physical Force	0.0%	7.0%
Unknown	4.0%	23.0%
Commonest Location		
Home of Victim/Assailant	51.0%	26.0%
Private Vehicle	7.0%	23.0%
Public Place	40.0%	40.0%
Other	0.0%	2.0%
Unknown	2.0%	9.0%

Note: $**p < .01$, $***p < .001$.

TABLE 9.4
Victim Characteristics

	Elderly Sex Offenders	Young Sex Offenders
Age of Victim(s)[a]***	%	%
1–12 years	67.0%	26.0%
13–15 years	14.0%	16.0%
16+ years	14.0%	49.0%
Unknown	5.0%	9.0%
Victim—Offender Relationship***		
Relative	9.0%	0.0%
Close Friend	7.0%	2.0%
Acquaintance	54.0%	19.0%
Stranger	30.0%	72.0%
Unknown	0.0%	7.0%

[a]Note that the mean age of victims was used in calculations when the offender engaged more than one victim.

***$p < .001$.

While 28% of the elderly sex offenders and 19% of the younger offenders had previous psychiatric histories, the difference was not statistically significant.

The Offense

The list of legal charges in Table 9.3 gives little useful information about the nature of the act that took place. However, the absence of rape and attempted rape in the elderly group is noteworthy. When the nature of the sexual contact is examined, it is clear that the majority of elderly sex offenders were involved usually in rather passive touching and exhibiting, whereas 37% of the younger group attempted or consumated intercourse or fellatio. Similarly, the elderly group in this series never used threats or actual force, whereas 16% of the younger men threatened or actually were aggressive toward the victim. The commonest location for the offense was the home of the offender or of his victim but public places were also frequently used.

The Victim

As shown in Table 9.4, the victim was known to the elderly sex offender in 70% of the cases, whereas a comparable percentage of young sex offenders more often chose strangers. The latter is, however, chiefly a reflection of the large number of exhibitionists and sexual aggressives in the younger group who typically choose female victims who are unknown to them. Generally, the older

group chose child victims but there were no significant differences between the two groups with respect to either sex of victim or number of victims.

Previous and Subsequent Criminal Behavior

Younger sex offenders tended to have more previous offenses than their elderly counterparts despite the fact that the latter had a longer lifetime during which to have accummulated such a record (Table 9.5). However, it should be noted that almost half of the elderly sex offenders had previous records and nearly a quarter of them for sex offenses. The infrequency of subsequent convictions of the elderly group for their current offense is readily apparent from Table 9.5. Of course, the increasingly likelihood of death in the elderly group could account for this small number of re-offenders.

Court Verdict and Sentence

An inspection of Table 9.6 shows that the number of cases for elderly offenders that were adjourned sine die (i.e., indefinitely), or for which charges were dropped, was somewhat greater than those for younger offenders. Although the court found sufficient evidence to render a guilty verdict, a greater proportion of the elderly offenders denied the offense at the time of the assessment compared

TABLE 9.5
Elderly Sex Offenders: Previous &
Subsequent Criminal Behaviour

	Elderly Sex Offenders	Young Sex Offenders
*Previous Convictions***		
Sex Offense	23.0%	35.0%
Violent Offense	7.0%	14.0%
Other Type Offense	19.0%	30.0%
Total	49.0%	79.0%
*Subsequent Convictions****		
Sex Offense	7.0%	26.0%
Violent Offense	0.0%	7.0%
Other Type Offense	0.0%	9.0%
Total	7.0%	42.0%

Note: **p < .01, ***p < .001.

TABLE 9.6
Elderly Sex Offenders: Court
Verdict & Sentence

	Elderly Sex Offenders	Young Sex Offenders
Verdict		
Guilty As Charged	77%	91%
Adjourned Sine Die	5%	2%
Not Guilty	7%	2%
Charges Dropped	9%	0%
Unknown	2%	5%
*Attitude To Offense Of Guilty Offenders***		
Complete Denial	32%	7%
Admits but Minimizes	41%	35%
Fully Admits	21%	52%
Attitude Unknown	6%	6%
Sentence		
Fine/Caution	7%	7%
Suspended Sentence with Probation	61%	58%
Prison Sentence	2%	25%
Not Applicable	23%	5%
Unknown	7%	5%

Note: **p < .01.

with the younger men who were found guilty. Perhaps these elderly men have greater difficulty in acknowledging the offense because of a fear of further social ostracism or in the hope that their credibility and dignity will survive the accusation.

Large numbers from both groups of offenders were dealt with by means of fines, cautions, or suspended sentences with or without probation. Only 2% of the elderly group were sent to prison compared with 25% of the younger group.

Treatment

Treatment was recommended by the assessing psychiatrist for 35% of the elderly sex offenders. Of those cases for which data were available (N=39), 33% received psychotherapy or counselling. Of the young sex offenders 33% were recommended for treatment and 50% actually received it. The greater percentage of young patients were probably treated because of concern for further offenses, whereas the older group were often seen as needing social support rather than psychiatric treatment.

DISCUSSION

This study confirms some of the impressions from the existing literature, refutes others, and leaves a few issues still unresolved.

Certainly, most of the elderly sex offenders in this sample referred for psychiatric examination in relation to their charges had molested children. These victims were usually known to the offender and sometimes were a relative or close friend. The typically non-aggressive nature of the sexual contact is also clear though the fact that other studies noted occasional aggressive sexual behavior in old men needs to be acknowledged (e.g., Whiskin, 1967).

Zeegers (1966, 1978) found in his series of 47 elderly sex offenders that many were either single or, if they had married, that their sexual relationship in many cases had been poor. Our study supports this observation and casts doubt on Hirschmann's (1962) impression that these men were free of sexual problems earlier in their lives. A quarter of our group and a similar number of Zeegers' (1966, 1978) cases had previous convictions for sexual offenses. One may speculate that some of the older offenders have had a life long attraction to children and that they were apprehended only infrequently or that they managed to keep their sexual impulses under control.

The psychiatric diagnoses in the elderly and young sex offenders are worthy of special mention. As noted in the introduction, many authors have regarded sex offenses by elderly men to be a symptom of organic brain deterioration. About 14% of our group of elderly sex offenders were suffering from dementia (Table 9.2) compared, for example, with 49% of Zeegers' (1966, 1978) cases and 60% of Whiskin's (1967, 1968). Community surveys of the prevalence of organic mental disorders in the elderly population tend to give rather similar figures to those in our study. For those suffering from severe brain syndromes combined with those showing "mild mental deterioration" for example, Essen-Möller (1956) quoted 15.8%, Kay Beamish, and Roth (1964), 11.3%; Neilsen (1963), 18.5%, and Sheldon (1948) found 15.6%. Thus, our figures do not suggest that elderly sex offenders suffer from organic brain syndromes to any greater extent than the elderly population in general. The question that then arises is why other authors such as Whiskin and Zeegers found such a high percentage in their studies. Although Whiskin (1967, 1968) diagnosed 9 out of his 15 cases as suffering from organic brain disease, he seemed to admit that the diagnostic criteria he employed were vague and he suggested that "social isolation and attempts at regressive solutions" may contribute to a "pseudo-organic syndrome" (Whiskin, 1967, p.249). Similarly, Zeegers (1978) stated that among his cases, the main features of dementia were not loss of memory or intellectual deficiency, but a "restriction of their 'being-in-the-world'." This use of existential terminology is somewhat puzzling to North American psychiatrists and it seems likely that many of Zeeger's cases of dementia might fail to satisfy modern criteria for organic dementia.

In studying cases of pedophilia in all age groups, Revitch and Weiss (1962) and Mohr et al. (1964) failed to find dementia in most of their elderly cases and saw greater importance in the observation that these offenders are often lonely and socially isolated.[4] Although we were able to confirm this finding, it is known that many elderly persons have these difficulties. We were not able to clarify in our study whether the sex offender group is any more socially isolated than non-offenders of the same age. We tend to agree, however that loneliness and isolation might affect the judgment of these men so that they act upon deviant impulses that they normally kept under better control.

Along with the observation that these men tend to be non-aggressive in their sexual behavior and to suffer notable social and mental problems, the low recidivism rate among elderly sex offenders makes it reasonable for the courts to continue to deal sympathetically with this group of offenders.

REFERENCES

Abrahamsen, D. *Crime and the human mind.* New York: Columbia University Press, 1944.

Allersma, J. Ouderdom en Criminaliteit. *Nederlands Tijdschrift Voor Gerontologie,* 1971, *2,* 285–293.

Bergman, S., & Amir, M. Crime and delinquency among the aged in Israel. *Geriatrics,* 1973, *28,* 149–157.

Brancale, R., MacNeil, D., & Vuocolo, A. Profile of the New Jersey sex offender: A statistical study of 1,206 male sex offenders. *Welfare Reporter,* 1965, *16,* 3–9.

Devon, J. Age and crime. *Police Journal,* 1930, *3,* 118–126.

East, W. N. Crime, senescence and senility. *Journal of Mental Science* 1944, *90,* 836–849.

Ellis, H. *Psychology of sex.* London: W. Heinemann Ltd., 1933.

Epstein, L. J., Mills, C., & Simon, A. Antisocial behavior of the elderly. *Comprehensive Psychiatry,* 1970, *11,* 36–42.

Essen-Möller, E. Individual traits and morbidity in a Swedish rural population. *Acta Psychiatrica Neurologica Scandanavica,* 1956, Supplement 100.

Fleiss, J. L. Measuring nominal scale agreement among many raters. *Psychological Bulletin,* 1971, *76,* 378–382.

Fox, V. Intelligence, race and age as selective factors in crime. *Journal of Criminal Law,* 1946, *37,* 141–152.

Gebhard, P., Gagnon, J. H., Pomeroy, W. B., & Christenson, C. V. *Sex offenders: An analysis of types.* New York: Harper and Row, 1965.

Groth, A. N., Burgess, A. W., Birnbaum, H. J., & Gary, T. S. A study of the child molester: Myths & realities. *Journal of American Criminal Justice Association,* 1978, *41,* 17–22.

Henninger, J. M. The senile sex offender. *Mental Hygeine,* 1939, *23,* 436–444.

Hirschmann, J. Zur Kriminologie der Sexualdelikte des Alternden Mannes. *Gerontologica Clinica Additamentum,* 1962, *4,* 115–119.

Kay, D., Beamish, P., & Roth, M. Old age mental disorder in Newcastle-Upon-Tyne. Part I: A Study of Prevalence. *British Journal of Psychiatry,* 1964, *110,* 146–158.

Keller, O. J., & Vedder, C. B. The crimes that old people commit. *The Gerontologist,* 1968, *8,* 43–50.

Krafft-Ebing, R. Von. *Psychopathia sexualis.* English Trans. by H. E. Wedeck. New York: Putnams Sons, 1965.

Law, S. K. Child molestation: A comparison of Hong Kong and Western findings. *Medicine, Science and Law.* 1979, *19,* 55–60.

Meyers, T. J. Psychiatric examination of the sexual psychopath. *Journal of Criminal Law,* 1965, *56,* 31.

Moberg, D. Old age and crime. *Journal of Criminal Law, Criminal and Political Science,* 1953, *43,* 764–776.

Mohr, J. W., Turner, R. E., & Jerry, M. B. *Pedophilia and exhibitionism.* Toronto: University of Toronto Press, 1964.

Nielsen, J. Geronto-psychiatric period-prevalence investigation in a geographically delimited population. *Acta Psychiatrica & Neurologica Scandanavica,* 1963, *38,* 307–330.

Pollack, O. The criminality of old age. *Journal of Criminal Psychopathology,* 1941, *3,* 213–235.

Radzinowicz, L. *Sexual offences.* London: Macmillan Co., 1957.

Revitch, E., & Weiss, R. The pedophiliac offender. *Diseases of the Nervous System,* 1962, *23,* 1–6.

Rollin, H. Deviant behaviour in relation to mental disorder. *Proceedings of Royal Society of Medicine,* 1973, *66,* 99–103.

Rose, E. F. Criminal responsibility and competency as influenced by organic disease. *Missouri Law Review,* 1970, *35,* 326–348.

Roth, M. Cerebral disease and mental disorders of old age as causes of antisocial behaviour. In: A. V. S. de Reuck & R. Porter (Eds.), *The mentally abnormal offender,* London: J. and A. Churchill, 1968.

Rothschild, D. Senile psychoses and cerebral arteriosclerosis. In: O. Kaplan (Ed.), *Mental Disorders of Later Life,* Stanford: Standford University Press, 1945.

Ruskin, S. H. Analysis of sex offenses among male psychiatric patients. *American Journal of Psychiatry,* 1941, *97,* 955–968.

Schroeder, P. L. Criminal behaviour in the later period of life *American Journal of Psychiatry,* 1936, *92,* 915–924.

Sheldon, J. H. *The social medicine of old age.* London: Nuffield Foundation, 1948.

Slater, E., & Roth, M. *Clinical psychiatry,* 3rd Ed. London: Bailliere, Tindall and Cassell, 1969.

Storr, A. *Sexual deviation.* Harmondsworth, Middlesex: Penguin Books, 1964.

Sutherland, E. H. *Principles of criminology.* Chicago: Lippincott, 1924.

Virkkunen, M. Victim-precipitated pedophilia offences. *British Journal of Criminology,* 1975, *15,* 175–180.

Whiskin, F. E. The geriatric sex offender. *Geriatrics,* 1967, *22,* 168–172.

Whiskin, F. E. Delinquency in the aged. *Journal of Geriatric Psychiatry* 1968, *1,* 242–262.

Zeegers, M. Dementie in Verband Met Het Delict Ontucht. *Tijdschrift voor Strafrecht,* 1966, *75,* 265.

Zeegers, M. Sexual delinquency in men over 60 years old. 1978. Personal Communication.

ENDNOTES

Note 1. The reliability was assessed using the Kappa statistic (Fleiss, 1971). The results were

	% Actual Agreement	% Chance Agreement	Standard Normal Deviate
Organic Brain Syndrome	93	73	4.268**

Functional Psychosis	98	93	1.640
Neurosis	85	65	3.974**
Personality			
Disorder—Antisocial	96	83	3.059**
—Other	81	47	6.331**
Alcoholism	89	56	6.134**
Drug Addiction	94	86	2.200*

Only functional psychosis was nonsignificant. This was due at least in part to the infrequency of the diagnosis

Note 2. Reliability of ratings was again assessed using Kappa (Fleiss, 1971). The results were

	% Actual Agreement	% Chance Agreement	Standard Normal Deviate
Marital Adjustment	90	50	5.680**
Social Contacts	66	41	4.702**

The senior author's ratings are used throughout for simplicity.

Note 3. $\chi^2 = 5.103$, df = 1, p<.05.

Note 4. See also Chapter 6 for a study of pedophiles of all ages drawn from the same setting as the present study.

III HOMOSEXUALITY, TRANSVESTISM, AND TRANSSEXUALISM

Homosexual, transsexual, and transvestitic men are believed to occupy the feminine end of the gender identity spectrum. Being more feminine may also entail having a female sex hormone profile. So the average heterosexual male shows a predominance of androgens but the homosexual, like the female, is expected to show a trend to more estrogens. For some writers, this hormone profile correlates with femininity and passivity, especially in sexual behavior. However, this is an oversimplification. Sexual behavior has been caricatured and empirical data suggest that neither homosexuals nor females are especially passive. Moreover it has been puzzling why so many homosexual men are not feminine identified and apparently never have been. Although 31 studies have examined some sex hormone in reference to homoerotic behavior, the results have been inconsistent. The next chapter examines a number of sex hormones in gay men and, for the first time in such a study, homoerotic preference is validated with a standardized sex history questionnaire and a phallometric test of erotic preference.

10 Peripheral Sex Hormones, Homosexuality, and Gender Identity

R. Michael Sanders
Malcolm Grove Hospital, Maryland

Jerald Bain
Mount Sinai Hospital, Toronto

Ron Langevin
Clarke Institute of Psychiatry, Toronto

In the present report, two questions are addressed:

1. Are there ''resting state'' differences among peripheral sex hormones in homosexual versus heterosexual men?
2. If there are such differences, do they relate differentially to gender identity and sexual orientation?

These questions seem straightforward, and a number of studies have attempted to answer them. However, when the literature is reviewed regarding hormones and human sexuality, conflicting and confusing results are found. This seems related to both methodological and conceptual problems. It therefore seems appropriate to examine carefully the current status of knowledge regarding biological factors in human sexuality. First, the concepts of gender identity and sexual orientation will be discussed and then research problems in the study of sex hormones will be examined.

GENDER IDENTITY AND SEXUAL ORIENTATION

Gender identity as defined here is a psychological construct that reflects the fundamental psychological experience of oneself as belonging to one sex or the other (Stoller, 1968). Sex in turn is taken to indicate the biological and phys-

iological basis of maleness and femaleness with examples of this being 46XY karyotypes, testes, and penis (Meyer, 1982). However, the distinction between gender identity and sex is not so clear cut. Sex researchers increasingly point out that core gender identity itself may represent a confluence of both biological and psychological components (Stoller, 1982; Tyson, 1982) but an understanding of the nature of how these factors coalesce has yet to be established (cf. Freund, 1974; Meyer, 1982; Money & Ehrhardt, 1972; Stoller, 1982; Tyson, 1982).

Gender role reflects the "public expression of one's private experience of gender identity" (Money & Ehrhardt, 1972). As such, it describes interpersonal transactions that appear to be influenced most by social and cultural factors (Stoller, 1982; Tyson, 1982). In spite of the defined relationship between gender role and identity, measures of the two constructs do not overlap as completely as one may expect. Although measures may be at fault, it also appears that gender role is more fluid and dynamic than gender identity. Both constructs often subsume erotic behavior but a distinction needs to be made among these concepts and sexual orientation.

The latter is a psychological construct that represents the acquisition of eroticism in sustained and preferential patterns of sexual arousal. It may be expressed in sexual fantasies or overt behavior (Meyer, 1982). The two major male variants of concern here are heterosexual (or gynephile) and homosexual (or androphile) with more atypical variations being heterosexual and homosexual pedophilic (arousal in relation to the sexually immature), hebephilic (heterosexual arousal in relation to the adolescent who is partially mature), and ephebophilic (homosexual arousal in relation to the adolescent who is partially mature).

As difficult as it may be individually, to define or measure these concepts and specify the experiences they reflect, it is even more difficult to understand how they may interrelate with one another. In most persons there appears to be a certain organized relationship among each of these so that a male gender identity is associated with a masculine gender role that is associated with a heterosexual orientation. However, atypical constellations of these factors also occur. Freund et al. (Freund, Nagler, Langevin, Zajac, & Steiner, 1974, Freund, Langevin, Satterberg, & Steiner, 1977) have demonstrated, for instance, that some homosexually oriented men have a relatively low feminine gender identity (approximately one-third in their study) but others had a much higher feminine gender identity. It was not clearly documented what these subjects demonstrated in terms of gender role but it is suspected that there was considerable variation. It appears possible to demonstrate that each combination of gender identity, gender role, and sexual orientation exists. What is not clear are the determinants of these different combinations and precisely why some are more common than others. More specifically, for the purposes of this study, it is not at all clear, despite considerable experimental studies, what factors might impact on these constructs. Many experimental studies have examined peripheral sex hormones in relation to sexual orientation which seems a logical place to start.

PERIPHERAL SEX HORMONES

Two reviews by Meyer-Bahlburg provide a comprehensive comparative analysis of research studies on sex hormones and homosexuality (Meyer-Bahlburg, 1977, 1980). In those articles, studies were discussed that examined animal and human data, sexual behavior associated with hormone disorders, the effects of steroid treatment on sexual behavior, and the implications of hypogonadism in relation to sexuality. In addition, comments were made on both the behavioral and neuroendocrine indicators of possible prenatal androgen abnormalities in homosexual subjects. Rather than attempting to duplicate such a comprehensive survey, this section will focus only on peripheral hormones in relation to homosexuality.

There are 31 different studies examining one or more hormones in subjects selected for various degrees of homosexuality. These 31 reports resulted in a total of 57 comparisons among the hormones. Table 10.1 summarizes this information.[2] The numbers of cases and mean values listed are only for those subjects within each study who were closest to being exclusive in their sexual orientation. Thus, although Kolodny, Masters, Hendryx, and Toro (1971) for example, reported a research sample of 30 homosexuals, only eight of these were identified as exclusively homosexual ("Kinsey 6", Kinsey, Pomeroy, & Martin, 1948) and only data for those eight subjects have been included. This simplifies and increases the rigor of comparison of different studies, a task that has already been made difficult by differences in hormone sample sources (urine, plasma, serum), assay techniques (chromatography, protein binding, radioimmunoassay), units of measurement (mU/ml, ug/100 ml, ng/ml), and by a considerable variation in the quality of research design.

As a means to facilitate comparison, the studies are organized in Table 10.1 such that similarity is maintained for a given set of studies in relation to hormone levels: (1) being higher in heterosexuals (Het>Hom); (2) lower in heterosexuals (Het<Hom); (3) no different in heterosexual and homosexual cases (Het=Hom). In addition, an estimate of the merits of each study is listed which was determined by the senior author on the basis of five parameters: rigorous patient selection criteria (e.g., nonpatient and nondrug using subjects, exclusive in their sexual orientation), psychological assessment (e.g., some determination by interview or psychometrics of psychological variables), physiological assessment (e.g., physical exam, laboratory studies), adequate technical assay procedures (e.g., radioimmunoassay, multiple samples), and adequate comparative analysis (e.g., use of statistical analysis, adequate number of subjects in each group). Thus a study's merits could vary from 0 to 5 in number with one unit given for satisfaction of each of the criteria above. The merit score was the number of merits divided by five. As a result, if two studies revealed conflicting results, this estimate of merit might assist in assigning a relative degree of credence to the results.

TABLE 10.1

Summary of Studies Examining Hormones in Homosexual and Heterosexual Men

Hormone	# of Comparisons	Het. > Hom.	# Cases*		Merits of Studies	Het. < Hom.	# Cases		Merits of Studies	Het. = Hom.	# Cases		Merits of Studies
			Het.	Hom.			Het.	Hom.			Het.	Hom.	
LH	8	0	—	—	—	2	76	34	0.3	6	66	52	0.5
FSH	4	1	4	4	0.6	0	—	—	—	3	16	27	0.3
Prolactin	2	0	—	—	—	1	50	8	0.2	1	15	2	0.8
Testosterone (bound)	20	4	179	43	0.4	2	30	32	0.5	14	123	73	0.5
Testosterone (free)	4	2	38	35	0.4	1	26	25	0.4	1	18	20	0.8
Dihydro-testosterone	2	0	—	—	—	1	26	26	0.4	1	4	4	0.6
Cortisol	1	0	—	—	—	1	18	20	0.8	0	—	—	—
Androstene-dione	4	0	—	—	—	2	18	20	0.8	2	4	4	0.6
Andros-terone/Etiocho-lanolone	4	3	144	88	0.4	0	—	—	—	1	11	13	0.6
Total Estro-gen	1	0	—	—	—	0	—	—	—	1	109	28	0.4
Estrone	3	0	—	—	—	1	26	26	0.4	2	22	24	0.7
Estradiol	3	0	—	—	—	2	36	50	0.6	1	18	20	0.8
Progesterone	1	0	—	—	—	0	—	—	—	1	4	4	0.6
Total**	57 (31)	10 (9)	365	140	0.4	13 (8)	161	186	0.5	34 (19)	301	188	0.6

Note: abbreviations: Het = Heterosexual, Hom = Homosexual.

*Number of cases = that number of subjects included in a particular study that was closest to being exclusive in orientation (Kinsey 5 or 6).

†Merits of Study = an estimate of the quality of the study from the following criteria: rigorous patient selection criteria, psychological assessment, biological assessment, adequate technical assay procedures, adequate comparative analysis. One point is allowed for each of the above criteria and thus a study's merit can vary from 0 to 5. The average merit was determined by adding all of the positive merits of all of the studies reaching a particular conclusion and dividing by the possible number of positive merits (e.g. LH: study A, $+++ = \frac{3}{3}$, Study B, $-++ = \frac{2}{3}$; merits = $\frac{5}{10} = 0.5$).

**Total number of different studies appear in brackets. Some studies made more than one comparison of hormones with different outcomes. Thus the # comparisons is greater than the # studies.

The available studies examined the following 13 hormone measures: luteinizing hormone (LH), follicle stimulating hormone (FSH), prolactin, bound and free testosterone, dihydrotestosterone, cortisol, androstenedione, androsterone/etiocholanolone ratio, total estrogens, estrone, estradiol, and progesterone.

Nine studies (Evans, 1972; Kolodny, Jacobs, Masters, Tobo, & Daughaday, 1972; Loraine, Adamopoulos, Kirkham, Ismail, & Dove, 1971; Margolese, 1970; Margolese & Janiger, 1973; Newmark et al., 1979; Pillard, Rose, & Sherwood, 1974; Stahl, Dorner, Ahrens, Graudenz, 1976; Starka, Sipova, & Hynie, 1975) reported 10 comparisons of mean hormone values for which heterosexuals were higher than homosexuals. Eight studies (Brodie, Gartrell, Doering, & Rhue, 1974; Doerr, Kockott, Vogt, Pirke, & Dittmar, 1973; Doerr, Pirke, Kockott, & Dittmar, 1976; Friedman, Dyrenfurth, Linkie, Tendler, & Fleiss, 1977; Kolodny et al., 1972; Newmark, Rose, Todd, Birk, & Naftolin, 1979; Rohde, Stahl, & Dorner, 1977; Tourney & Hatfield, 1973) reported in 13 comparisons just the reverse, that is, higher means for the homosexual groups on one or more hormones. Finally 20 separate studies, reporting 34 comparisons, found no systematic differences in relation to one or more of the hormones listed (Barlow, Abel, Blanchard, & Mavissakalian, 1974; Birk, Williams, Chain, & Rave, 1973; Decourt, 1977; Doerr et al., 1973; Dorner, Rohde, Stahl, Krall, & Masius, 1975; Evans, 1972; Friedman, Wollesen, & Tendler, 1976; Friedman, & Frang, 1977; Halbreich, Segal, & Chowers, 1978; James, Carter, & Orwin, 1977; Kolodny et al., 1972; Livingstone, Sagel, Distiller, Morley, & Katz, 1978; Loraine, Ismail, Adamopoulos, & Dove, 1970; Mischel, 1966; Newmark et al., 1979; Parks, Korth Schutz, Penny, Hilding, Dumars, Fraser, & New, 1974; Rohde et al., 1977; Stahl et al., 1976; Tourney & Hatfield, 1973; Tourney, Petrilli, & Hatfield, 1975). The total number of studies referenced (nine, eight, and 20) is greater than the number of separate studies in the literature (31) since some studies reported results on two or more hormones with different directions of results in some cases. If all the protocols examining all hormones are considered: 34 of 57 found no differences. When the merits of the studies reaching different conclusions are compared, it appears that those finding no significant differences were the better designed. Summary of merits of: studies showing no difference = 0.6; studies showing heterosexual means greater = 0.4; studies showing homosexual means greater = 0.5.

These overall findings were reflected in studies of testosterone. There were 20 studies in all that examined this hormone and 14 found no difference, (Barlow et al., 1974; Birk et al., 1973; Decourt, 1977; Doerr et al., 1973; Dorner et al., 1975; Friedman et al., 1977; Halbreich et al., 1978; James et al., 1977; Livingstone et al., 1978; Mischel, 1966; Newmark et al., 1979; Parks et al., 1974; Rohde et al., 1977; Stahl et al., 1976), four found lowered means for homosexuals (Kolodny et al., 1971; Loraine et al., 1970; Pillard et al., 1974; Starka et al., 1975), and two showed increased mean levels in homosexuals (Brodie et al., 1974; Tourney & Hatfield, 1973).

When androgen metabolites are examined, several studies reported the androsterone/etiocholanolone ratio as being higher for heterosexual subjects. Three studies (Evans, 1972; Margolese, 1970; Margolese & Janiger, 1973) reported such results and Tourney and Hatfield (1973) reported a statistical trend in that direction. The weak adrenal androgen, androstenedione, has been examined as well. Friedman, Wollesen and Tendler, (1976) and Friedman, Dyrenfurth, et al., (1977) reported in two studies that homosexual men had increased levels of androstenedione. One of these studies investigated a monozygotic twin pair discordant for sexual orientation (Friedman et al., 1976) and the other compared 20 homosexual and 18 heterosexual subjects (Friedman, Dyrenfurth, et al., 1977). Newmark et al. (1979) and Tourney and Hatfield (1973) did not find any differences in this hormone in two separate studies. Additionally, Friedman, Dyrenfurth, et al.'s (1977) study demonstrated elevated cortisol levels in those same homosexual subjects. This interesting finding has yet to be replicated or contradicted. Friedman et al. speculated that this result may have been due to emotional stress secondary to the experience of the homosexuals belonging to a repressed minority group in a homophobic society. Meyer-Bahlburg (1980) pointed out that there are other alternative explanations both from a psychoendocrine standpoint and from psychological considerations.

Subsidiary issues that have been examined concern whether there could be differences for the biologically active fraction, free testosterone, despite lack of differences in total testosterone levels. Two studies (Rohde et al., 1977; Stahl et al., 1976) found heterosexuals' free testosterone levels above that of homosexuals', one found the reverse (Doerr et al., 1976), and one (Friedman, Dyrenfurth, et al., 1977) found no difference.

A corollary set of questions has to do with degree of effeminacy and preferred sexual role. Although Rohde et al. (1977) reported a tendency toward decreased levels of free testosterone in effeminate compared to non-effeminate homosexual males, this was not statistically significant. Similarly, Pillard et al. (1974) reported no relationship between total testosterone levels and degree of effeminacy. Rohde et al. (1977) also reported higher FSH and LH levels for effeminate versus non-effeminate homosexuals but no statistical test was used. No study has related differences in total estrogens, estradiol, or estrone levels to effeminacy. The one study that addressed preferred partner role (active, passive, alternatively active, or passive) found no correlations with testosterone levels (Doerr et al., 1973).

In summary, there has been considerable variation in results of studies concerning hormones and homosexuality but the majority of studies and the better designed studies indicate no systematic differences between heterosexual and homosexual subjects. As well, there appear to be no specific relationships among hormones and other aspects of sexuality such as degree of effeminacy and preferred partner role. Elevations of androstendione levels in some homosexual

groups and the unreplicated finding of elevated cortisol in homosexuals (Friedman, Dyrenfurth, et al., 1977) are interesting but have yet to be replicated.

Although the findings overall may suggest that the relationship of hormones to homosexuality is not worth pursuing at present, the methodology of existing studies leaves much to be desired. The implications are that the previous studies have yet to define clearly the possible hormone relationships in homosexuality. One particularly pertinent issue is the wide variance in quality of research methodology and design seen in these studies. Among the problems are inadequate assay technique, single versus repeated blood samples, no assessment of gender identity, lack of control for physical health, drug use, and mental illness (see Meyer-Bahlberg's 1977, 1980 reviews for details). In particular, poverty of methodology is evident in assessment of erotic preference. No study to date used a standard sex history questionnaire or phallometry in the evaluation.

Since homosexual acts are quite common in men who do not have a homosexual erotic preference, subjects must be carefully screened. Kinsey et al. (1948), for example, found that 37% of males in the USA had some orgasmic homosexual experience in their lives but only 4% were exclusively homosexual. One must also be concerned that homosexual acts between adults can occur in men who manifest a range of sexual anomalies. In particular, one needs to rule out pedophilia in which sexual acts with adults may be quite common and in which the label ''homosexual'' may be self applied indiscriminately by the subject (see Chapter 6 for example). Freund's (1963, 1965, 1967a, b, Freund, Sedlacek, & Knob, 1965 and Freund, McKnight, Langevin, & Cibiri, 1972) test of erotic preference in which penile tumescence responses are measured to erotic stimuli is especially useful in this respect and it is 90% accurate in identifying homosexual versus heterosexual males.

Thus, a consideration of the limitations of previous studies provides the basis for an attempt to clarify these matters in a new study where methodological rigor is attempted and multiple hormones are studied.

METHOD

Design

The study consisted of three separate but interrelated parts designated Phase I, II, and III (see Fig. 10.1). In each of the phases, a series of measurement procedures led to subjects being either accepted or rejected for further study based upon specific criteria. In Phase I, subjects were screened in reference to specific psychological criteria. In Phase II, subjects not rejected for such reasons were further screened in relation to specific biological criteria. In Phase III, the remaining subjects were assigned to one of three groups based on the criteria of

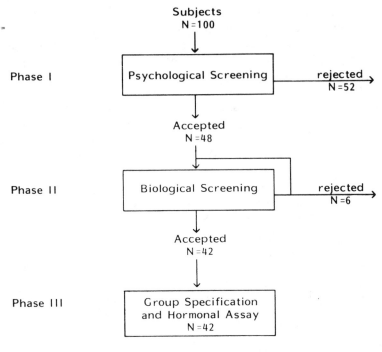

Design of Study in Three Phases

FIGURE 10.1

sexual partner orientation and gender identity. Following this, plasma levels of seven hormones were determined. This design was intended to result in a highly screened subgroup of the original subjects in which important confounding variables were eliminated or controlled to allow more precise specification of sexual behavior and hormonal assay results.

Subjects

Selection Criteria.   All subjects resided in the Metropolitan Toronto area and most were students at the University of Toronto or York University. They responded to printed announcements placed at common points of gathering for students at the University of Toronto and York University, to presentations and discussions held with various gay organizations, and to printed advertisements placed in the local press.

In each instance it was stated that the purpose of the study was to understand psychological and biological factors possibly related to human sexuality. Selection criteria were specified. It was mentioned that there would be paper and

pencil psychological tests and that some subjects would be selected to participate in a more detailed study involving biological tests. Specifics of the biological study were given to those subjects accepted for further investigation after successful completion of the psychological tests in Phase 1. Volunteers were paid for their participation.

Potential subjects completed a telephone interview in which the investigator obtained information related to specified selection criteria. One hundred subjects, 46 of whom identified themselves as heterosexual and 54 as homosexual, entered Phase I after indicating by self-report that they met all of the criteria specified below:

1. Exclusively heterosexual or homosexual in sexual orientation. This was defined as exclusive same sex or opposite sex erotic attraction in regard to both behavior and fantasy all of one's life and was equivalent to Kinsey category 0 or 6.

2. No significant current or past medical history. This was defined as consultation, treatment, or hospitalization for anything other than a minor illness.

3. No significant current or past psychiatric history. This was defined as consultation, treatment, or hospitalization for a psychiatric illness or for any severely disturbed behavior such as suicidal acts or persistent suicidal ideation.

4. No current use or abuse of prescription or illicit drugs. This was defined as no current use whatsoever of any drug including marijuana during the past six weeks. Additional criteria included no significant past history of "hard" drug use or abuse such as more than two or three occasions using barbituates, amphetamines, or LSD and no use whatsoever in the past or currently of injected drugs such as heroin.

5. No current or past involvement with the law or the courts. This was defined as any charge or conviction for anything other than minor traffic violations.

6. Age between 18 and 35.

Thus subjects selected for entry into the study were identified by self-report as young, non-patient, non-disturbed, physically healthy groups of exclusive heterosexuals and homosexuals who were non-drug users and non-offenders.

Age and education for the groups of subjects are presented in Table 10.2. There were no significant differences with the exception of post secondary education. Heterosexuals had more.

Materials

Subjects were administered the Clarke Sexual History Questionnaire (Paitich, Langevin, Freeman, Mann, & Handy, 1977), MMPI, FGI Scale (Freund, Nagler, Langevin, Zajac, & Steiner, 1974 and Freund, Langevin, Satterberg, &

TABLE 10.2
Age and Education of Heterosexual and Homosexual Groups

Variable	Homosexuals N = 54		Heterosexuals N = 46		Total N = 100	
	Mean	S.D.	Mean	S.D.	Mean	S.D.
Age	26.54	5.06	25.24	4.20	25.94	4.71
Secondary Education	12.76	0.61	12.96	0.29	12.85	0.50
Post Secondary Education*	1.39	1.27	2.02	1.31	1.68	1.32

Note: two tailed t-test was used, *p < .05, df = 98. Education is expressed in years. Maximum secondary education is 13 years.

Steiner, 1977), a medical screening questionnaire, and a drug use survey (DST), (Paitich, 1973).

Clinical laboratory tests that are useful in assessing general health screening for hematologic, renal, endocrine, and liver status were employed. They included: (a) complete blood cell count (CBC) and white blood cell determination (WBC) with differential white blood cell count and specification of cell morphology; (b) complete urinalysis (UA); (c) fasting blood glucose (FBS), and (d) gamma glutamyl transferase (GGT).

Volume phallometry described by Freund, Sedlacek, and Knob (1965) was used as a psychophysiologic measure of erotic arousal and functioned as a cross validation of self-report and psychometric assessment of sexual orientation. An abbreviated standard test or erotic preference was used (Freund, McKnight, Langevin, & Cibiri, 1972).

Procedures

Phase I—Psychological Screening.   Subjects who satisfied all the recruitment criteria as specified above, entered the study and validated this information again in writing.

Subjects completed the Sexual History Questionnaire. Responses were checked to insure that the psychometric results confirmed the subject's previous self-report of sexual partner orientation. It was required that items indicating both behavior and desire be exclusive in terms of erotic attraction with no evidence of paraphilic experiences such as pedophilia or exhibitionism. Subjects were rejected for entry into Phase II if there was indication of anything other than exclusive hetero- or homosexual behavior or desire. Seven heterosexuals and 12 homosexuals were so rejected.[3]

Subjects completed the 566 item version of the MMPI. Any subject with either an individual validity or clinical scale score elevation evidencing psychological distress or psychopathology (i.e., T-score above 70) was rejected prior to

entry into Phase II of the study. The exception to this was the MF scale. This score was recorded but elevations above a T-score of 70 were not used as a rejection criteria. Sixteen heterosexuals and 15 homosexuals were rejected on the basis of MMPI test results.[4]

The DST questionnaire was completed. History of significant drug use or abuse, persistent suicidal ideation, or any suicidal acts led to rejection. Report of marijuana use during the past six weeks also led to rejection. All subjects reported some degree of past use of marijuana and this was not by itself a basis for rejection. The degree, however, of past use of marijuana was specifically quantified and the two groups were compared. This was important in view of reports concerning the effects of cannabinoids on various hormone mechanisms including receptor sensitivity (Garmick, 1980; Olugi, 1980; Purohit, Ahluwahlia, & Vigersky, 1980; Rosenkrantz, & Egher, 1980). Thirteen heterosexual subjects were rejected for DST items, seven homosexual subjects were so rejected.[5]

Phase II—Biological Screening.   A total of 52 subjects were rejected as a result of the psychological screening in Phase I. Thus, out of 100 initial subjects 48 were accepted for biological screening in Phase II of the study. One subject from the heterosexual group decided to remove himself from further study on the basis of discomfort regarding the idea of blood being drawn for hormone assay and medical tests. This resulted in 47 subjects entering Phase II.

A full medical history and a complete physical examination were accomplished. The medical history was reviewed and the examination performed by two licensed and experienced physicians. The physical examination included height, weight, all vital signs, and a full examination of the body for general health status. Specific emphasis was paid to any indication of endocrine disorder. In particular the genitalia were examined closely with testicular measurements being made using a standardized technique developed as a rigorous check for gonadal dysfunction (Bain, 1982). History of significant past medical disorder, evidence of impaired current health status, and particularly any indication of endocrinopathy led to subjects being rejected for further study. Sexual history data were collected including time interval since last orgasm and average number of orgasms per week, in order that group comparisons could be made. One subject from the Phase II group of 47 subjects was rejected because of sustained blood pressure readings with diastolic values above 100mm. The subject was from the homosexual group. No subject from the heterosexual group was rejected.[6]

Clinical laboratory tests were accomplished as a further screen for impairment in physical and health status, endocrine, and liver function. These included CBC, WBC, UA, FBS, and GGT. Blood and urine samples were collected on all subjects at a uniform time between 8:00 a.m. and 10:00 a.m. after subjects had fasted from the previous midnight. Blood was drawn by an experienced laboratory technician and assayed according to established procedures in the clinical

laboratory of Mount Sinai Hospital, a 500-bed teaching hospital affiliated with the University of Toronto. Results were reviewed by both physicians. Subjects demonstrating any abnormal results were informed and a repeat procedure performed. Although three subjects demonstrated initial elevations in these tests, all were within normal limits upon retest. Thus no subject was rejected because of clinical laboratory data. Three specimens were drawn from each subject at 15 minute intervals. This was in accordance with techniques reported to improve the reliability of fluctuating plasma hormone levels (Goldzieher, Dozier, Smith, & Steinberger, 1976). After collection, the blood specimens were maintained separately for each time and for each subject. Plasma was separated following clotting then frozen and maintained at least below $-20°c$. until assay.

Subjects were scheduled for phallometric assessment of arousal as a cross-validation of self-report and psychometric data assessment of sexual preference. Subjects were given specific details about the phallometric test and any questions or concerns thoroughly discussed prior to beginning the assessment. A previously established and specially equipped laboratory setting at the Clark Institute was employed. Standard procedures for phallometric assessment were followed as described in detail elsewhere (Freund, 1963, 1965, 1967a, 1967b Freund et al., 1972). Basically the test measures penile volume changes to 14 second movie clips of nude male and female persons in four age categories; 6–8, 9–11, 13–15, and 18–25-years-old. There are 54 movie clips in the full test, including six repeats of each age-sex category and six neutral scenes. Half were used in this project. An experienced technician trained in the procedure performed the test and compiled a permanent record of results. Of the 46 subjects assessed by phallometry, four were identified as non-responders at the completion of testing, two each from the heterosexual and homosexual groups. The self-report and psychometric assessment of sexual partners orientation for each of these subjects were consistent and they were not excluded from hormonal study. Four other subjects were excluded, however, because of phallometric data. One subject from the heterosexual group was identified as demonstrating pedophilic arousal. One subject from the homosexual group also demonstrated pedophilic arousal. Two other homosexual subjects were rejected, one because of indiscriminate arousal and the other because of ephebophilic (adolescent) arousal.[7]

Phase III—Group Specification & Hormonal Assay.   Forty two subjects remained after psychological and biological screening. These subjects were then assigned to groups based on the two independent variables of sexual orientation and gender identity. The identification by the first of these resulted in 19 heterosexuals and 23 homosexuals. Subjects were administered the Freund Feminine Gender Identity (FGI) Questionnaire. By use of an empirically derived FGI cutoff score of 10, the homosexual group was divided into two groups based on low or high feminine gender identity group. Ten homosexual subjects were assigned

to a low feminine gender identity group (mean 7.80, S.D. 2.25) and 13 were assigned to a high feminine gender identity group (mean 15.00, S.D. 3.16). The 19 heterosexuals all scored below 10 and had a mean FGI score of 6.32, SD 3.20.

All subjects then had blood drawn for the following seven hormones: luteinizing hormone (LH), follicle stimulating hormone (FSH), prolactin, testosterone, androstenedione, dehydroepinandrosterone sulfate (DHEA), and estradiol. These hormones were chosen in view of their importance in basic physiologic mechanisms and key metabolic pathways. LH and FSH are the non-steriodal gonadotropins and function in the pituitary-gonadàl axis. LH is responsible for the production of androgenic steroids by the Leydig cells in the testis, and FSH governs spermatogenesis in the Sertoli cells in the seminiferous tubules (Bartke, 1976). Prolactin, also a non-steroidal hormone, has been implicated in certain sexual dysfunction syndromes in which increased levels interfere with the conversion of testosterone to dihydrotestosterone as mediated by 5-alpha-reductase (Margrini, Ebiner, Burckhardt, Felber, 1976).

Testosterone is the prinicipal androgen in the human male and its main precursor is androstenedione (Paulsen, 1974). Dehydroepiandrosterone (DHEA) is the main C-19 product of the human adrenal gland, is the principal precursor of 17-ketosteroids, and is a weak androgen, but to a small extent is metabolized to testosterone thus assuming biologic importance as an androgen itself (Paulsen, 1974). Estradiol, one of the principal estrogens in men, is derived from testosterone by aromatization peripherally in gonadal tissue and in the central nervous system (Paulsen, 1974).

The three assays for all hormones were accomplished in duplicate by radioimmunoassay. Gonadotropins were determined by a Diagnostics Products RIA kit using the second International Reference Preparation as a Standard. Prolactin determination and standard was by the Bio-Rad Lypho Check Kit. The steroid hormones, testosterone, androstenedione, DHEA sulfate, and estradiol were determined by the standard methods of Bain (1982) and used purified preparations as standards. The percent errors of the assays (intra assay variation) were the following: FSH, 2%; LH, 2%; prolactin, 4%; testosterone, 8%; androstenedione, 10%; DHEA sulfate, 10%; and estradiol, 5%. Between assays error is 8–9% LH, 7–14% FSH, 9–10% testosterone, 10–13% androsetenedione, 8–11% DHEA, 6–10% estradiol, and 7–18% prolactin. Interassay variation was minimized by all samples being simultaneously assayed over a short period using the same standard.

Principal statistical analysis was a 3x3 multivariate analysis of variance (MANOVA); independent variables being, three groups (heterosexuals, low feminine gender identity homosexuals, high feminine gender identity homosexuals), measured at three times (each individual blood sample), for seven dependent variables (each individual hormone). The BMD MANOVA was employed and was performed on a Digital DEC 10 system linked to an IBM 370 Computer.

Multivariate analyses of covariance were run similarly to examine possible confounding variables. Wilk's criterion was used as the multivariate statistic.

RESULTS

The multivariate analysis of variance indicated nonsignificant effects for group, time, (i.e., the three blood samples) and the group by time interactions.[8] This indicates that when all seven hormones were simultaneously analyzed for any statistically significant source of variance derived from effects related to the groups, the different sampling times, or any interaction between them, none was found. None of the individual hormones revealed any such significant effects, as indicated by univariate analysis of variance. For comparative purposes, the hormone values from the three sampling times were collapsed into one value and the means and standard deviations are listed in Table 10.3.

The extent of lifetime marijuana/hashish use, as quantified by the DST questionnaire, was greater for the heterosexual subjects than the homosexual subjects making up the final groups.[9] Thus, this was used as a covariate in a multivariate analysis of covariance in order to determine if this might have suppressed the hormone values of the heterosexuals leading to the negative results noted above. This analysis revealed no such effect.[10]

The values of several physical, clinical laboratory, and sexual activity parameters were also used as covariates in a multivariate analysis of covariance in order to determine if any effects from these measures might have also suppressed

TABLE 10.3
Means and Standard Deviations for Seven Hormones for Final
Subjects in Three Groups

Variable	Units	Heterosexuals N = 19		Low FGI Homosexuals N = 10		High FGI Homosexuals N = 13	
		Mean	S.D.	Mean	S.D.	Mean	S.D.
LH+	IU/l	7.46	1.84	8.17	2.20	8.26	2.51
FSH	IU/l	5.21	2.35	6.73	2.50	5.49	1.71
Prolactin	ug/l	7.84	3.09	9.30	4.38	9.38	7.30
Testosterone	ng/dl	899.67	253.76	896.93	281.17	861.44	296.04
Androstenedione	nM/l	4.78	1.49	4.57	2.24	4.57	1.36
DHEA Sulfate	uM/l	14.22	4.82	13.77	3.59	11.89	4.08
Estradiol	ng/dl	6.72	1.46	5.99	1.67	5.90	1.44

TABLE 10.4
Selected Results of Physical Exam, Clinical Laboratory Tests and
Sexual Activity Data: Final Subjects in Three Groups

Variable	Heterosexuals N = 19		Low FGI Homosexuals N = 10		High FGI Homosexuals N = 13	
	Mean	SD	Mean	SD	Mean	SD
Height (cm)	175.47	8.85	174.40	4.60	175.54	5.25
Weight (kg)	69.74	8.67	65.10	4.28	69.46	10.49
Testicular Index	32.38	13.04	27.27	8.22	29.42	11.57
Fasting Blood Glucose (mg/dl)	88.42	8.81	88.90	9.21	89.00	4.38
Gamma Glutamyl Transferase (U/L)	14.42	5.90	17.10	7.66	19.69	7.74
Hours Since Last Orgasm	45.26	27.29	25.80	15.56	41.38	27.18
Average Number of Orgasms/Week†	4.32	2.56	6.70	2.94	6.54	4.43

Note: †$p < .10$, Analysis of variance df = 2, 39.

differences in hormone values. These parameters included age, height, weight, testicular volume estimate,[11] blood glucose value, gamma glutamyl transferase value, interval since last orgasm, and average number of orgasms per week. Analyses revealed no statistically significant effects.

A check was made to determine whether significantly different numbers of subjects were rejected for any of the psychological or biological measures in the screening procedures of Phase I or Phase II. This functioned as a test of whether one of the groups might have been more functionally impaired psychologically or biologically and thus were not comparable in regard to those criteria used as screening measures. Fisher exact tests for the numbers of subjects rejected for each criterion and for each group showed that there were no significant differences in rejection rates for either group in relation to any single psychological, psychophysiologic, or physical criterion or for all criteria combined (see endnotes 3–6).

The results of the physical exam, clinical laboratory studies, and sexual activity data for the final subjects are listed in Table 10.4. One-way analysis of variance indicates no group differences of any statistical significance for any of these parameters, although there was a trend for homosexual men to have more orgasms per week than heterosexuals did.

DISCUSSION

The principal analyses indicated that subjects demonstrated no systematic group differences in relation to any specific hormone studied. How can this be understood in light of the previous studies in the literature? A number of logical possibilities exist.

First there may indeed be no statistically significant differences in resting state peripheral hormone levels that are related to homosexual orientation or gender identity. This is supported by the preponderance of negative studies in the literature, the fact that the better designed studies tended to be the negative ones, and the rigorous design of the current study. It is not supported by the positive and relatively well designed study of Friedman et al. (1977), that revealed differences in androstenedione and cortisol, nor is it supported by the studies showing differences in androstenedione/etiocholanolone ratios (Evans, 1972; Margolese, 1970; Margolese & Janiger, 1973).

The secondary analyses demonstrated no difference in the rejection rates of heterosexual and homosexual subjects and substantiate prior reports that these groups do not necessarily differ in various measures of adaptive functioning. This is of interest particularly since some might object that without "in-depth" knowledge of the subjects no conclusions can be drawn regarding level of functional capacity. Yet the rejection rates represented a composite of multiple assessments of psychological, physical, and psychophysiological function and indicated similar levels of healthy functioning. The final groups appeared to be quite comparable in relation to numerous indices. The comparative description of the accepted and rejected groups supports the importance of careful screening procedures since the degree of psychological distress and drug abuse were considerably higher in the rejected groups; a factor that could have confounded the hormonal results.

Careful specification and assessment of various aspects of sexuality are important if studies such as this are to clarify rather than confuse matters. In addition to sexual orientation, some assessment of gender identity seems useful as a means of more carefully defining subgroups that may have potential bio-behavioral correlates.

There are limitations of the current study that include the relatively small final sample, the select nature of the groups (e.g., mostly university students, living in a metropolitan area), and the degree of past drug use in both groups. Additionally the subjects selected themselves by making a response to the advertisements perhaps biasing the sample. One could observe in particular that the homosexual subjects might be unrepresentative in that they identified themselves as being homosexual by belonging to various social, academic, or religious organizations and by participating in the study at a time when police activity towards homosexuals in Toronto was particularly forceful. Finally, although multiple samples

were drawn for hormone assay they were all taken within a 30-minute time period and might not have identified differences in pulsatile secretion.

It can be concluded from this study that issues of design and methodology are crucial to research of this type. This is demonstrated when 58 of 100 subjects were rejected for various specified criteria. It should be recalled that even to gain entrance to the study, subjects had to satisfy extensive selection criteria by self-report. Yet psychometric, psychophysiologic, and biological validation of these reports resulted in almost 60% being rejected. The most productive screening device was the MMPI which led to 31 of the 58 subjects being rejected. The importance of a non-patient and non-psychologically distressed or disordered sample for research of this type is highly significant. Some may object that psychometric testing reveals little regarding important issues related to interpsychic mechanisms and these objections to some extent are valid. The MMPI is, however, a useful screening instrument and forms the basis for comparative descriptions both between groups within a given study and between studies. Additionally, some validation of self-report of sexual behavior appears to be necessary and at the very least a psychometric validation of sexual orientation by use of some form of sexual history questionnaire is indicated. It would seem an appropriate research strategy that exclusivity in sexual orientation be required and this would further require some form of thorough sexual history questionnaire.

Similar points could be made in relation to the need for exclusion of subjects who are active drug users. Kolodny's studies (Kolodny, Masters et al., 1971, Kolodny, Jacobs et al., 1972) may have been significantly compromised because of this factor alone. This is of note in view of data suggesting cannabinoids influence hormone function in some instances (Garmick, 1980; Olugi, 1980; Purohit et al., 1980; Rosenkrantz & Egher, 1980). The analysis of the present study employing marijuana use as a covariate would tend to support the idea that past use as opposed to current active use will not effect results. This is important since marijuana use is so common that it is difficult to find subjects for study who have not had at least some past use.

In the same fashion, assessment of clinical laboratory tests and a physical exam would seem required for a rigorous design. Although only one case was rejected on this basis in the present study, the potential for physiological confounding of hormone assays is still significant and controls should be used. The results of our study call into question the significance of previous reports and clinical laboratory differences between homosexual and heterosexual subjects such as Evans' study (1972).

The negative results of the current study do not at all indicate that further investigation in this area is unwarranted. Indeed it should only clarify the methodological and conceptual issues necessary to proceed further. For instance, continued exploration in "resting state" peripheral hormone studies are justified since Friedman's findings for cortisol levels have yet to be replicated (Friedman

et al., 1977). Also measures of free testosterone and/or dehydrotestosterone would be of interest as a means to resolve the contradiction in the results of studies by Stahl et al. (1976), Doerr et al. (1976), and Friedman et al., (1977). Finally, studies of certain cortisol metabolites would be useful in clarifying 5-alpha-reductase function in non-intersex subjects with variation in gender identity and sexual orientation as indirectly suggested by Imperato-McGinley's work (Imperato-McGinley, Peterson, Gantier, & Sturla, 1979a,b). Of special interest are the functional studies in which hormonal relationships are examined by provoking or evoking certain functional mechanism. Dorner, Gotz, & Rohde's (1975) and Dorner, Rohde, Seidel, Haas, & Schott's (1976) studies, despite their problems, deserve particular attention. The mechanism of brain differentiation they suggest can be studied in a number of ways and it may have profound implications. The methodological issues should be resolved with stringent patient selection, careful screening assessments, and rigorous hormonal assays. The conceptual problems of viewing these issues from a disease or disorder framework could also be resolved by the concept of biobehavioral diversity. Although these studies imply a functional difference in homosexuality, the possibility exists that there are related structural differences in brain organization as well. Thus studies might eventually employ the more sophisticated scanning techniques such as the CT scan or nuclear magnetic resonance (NMR). Eventually they may have something to offer in understanding more clearly the issues of the relationship between behavior and brain structure and function. Thus this research might ultimately assist in understanding some of the most basic brain mechanisms that underlie human experience.

REFERENCES

Bain, J. 1982. Personal communication.
Barlow, D. H., Abel, G. G., Blanchard, E. B., & Mavissakalian, M. Plasma testosterone levels and male homosexuality: A failure to replicate. *Archives of Sexual Behavior*, 1974, *3*, 571–575.
Bartke, A. Pituitary-testis relationships. *Progress in Reproductive Biology*, 1976, *1*, 136–152.
Birk, L., Williams, G. H., Chain, M., & Rose, L. I. Serum testosterone levels in homosexual men. *New England Journal of Medicine*, 1973, *289*, 1236–1238.
Brodie, H. K. H., Gartrell, N., Doering, C., & Rhue, T. Plasma testosterone levels in heterosexual and homosexual men. *American Journal of Psychiatry*, 1974, *131*, 82–83.
Decourt, J. Sur 91 cas d'homosexualite masculine: etude morphologique et hormonale. *Hormones et Sexualite Probl. Actuals Endocrinol. Nutr.*, 1977, *21*, 129–230.
Doerr, P., Kockott, G., Vogt, H. J., Pirke, K. M., & Dittmar, F. Plasma testosterone, estradiol, and semen analysis in male homosexuals. *Archives of General Psychiatry*, 1973, *29*, 829–833.
Doerr, P., Pirke, K. M., Kockott, G., & Dittmar, F. Further studies on sex hormones in male homosexuals. *Archives of General Psychiatry*, 1976, *33*, 611–614.
Dorner, G., Gotz, F., & Rohde, W. On the evocability of a positive oestrogen feedback action on LH secretion in female and male rats. *Endokrinologie*, 1975, *77*, 369–372.
Dorner, G., Rohde, W., Stahl, F., Krall, L., & Masius, W. A neuroendocrine predisposition for homosexuality in men. *Archives of Sexual Behavior*, 1975, *4*, 1–9.

Dorner, T., Rohde, W., Seidel, K., Haas, W., & Schott, G. On the evocability of a positive estrogen feedback action on LH-secretion in transsexual men and women. *Endocrinology,* 1976, *67,* 20–25.

Evans, R. B. Physical and biochemical characteristics of homosexual men. *Journal of Consulting Clinical Psychology,* 1972, *39,* 140–147.

Freund, K. A laboratory method for diagnosing predominance of homo- or hetero- erotic interest in the male. *Behavioral Research Therapy,* 1963, *1,* 85–93.

Freund, K. Diagnosing heterosexual pedophilia by means of a test for sexual interest. *Behavioral Research & Therapy,* 1965, *3,* 229–234.

Freund, K. Diagnosing homo- or heterosexuality and erotic age preference by means of a psycho-physiological test. *Behavior Research and Therapy,* 1967, *5,* 209–228. (a)

Freund, K. Erotic preference in pedophilia. *Behavior Research & Therapy,* 1967, *5,* 339–348. (b)

Freund, K. Male homosexuality: An analysis of the pattern. In J. A. Loraine (Ed.), *Understanding homosexuality: Its biological and psychological bases.* Lancaster, England: Medical and Technical Publishing Co., 1974.

Freund, K., Langevin, R., Satterberg, J., & Steiner, B. Extension of the gender identity scale for males. *Archives of Sexual Behavior,* 1977, *6,* 507–519.

Freund, K., McKnight, C. K., Langevin, R., & Ciberi, S. The female child as a surrogate object. *Archives of Sexual Behavior,* 1972, *2,* 119–133.

Freund, K., Nagler, E., Langevin, R., Zajac, A., & Steiner, B. Measuring feminine gender identity in homosexual males. *Archives of Sexual Behavior.* 1974, *3,* 249–260.

Freund, K., Sedlacek, F., & Knob, K. A simple transducer for mechanical plethysmography of the male genital. *Journal of Experimental Analysis of Behavior,* 1965, *8,* 169–170.

Friedman, R. C., Dyrenfurth, I., Linkie, D., Tendler, R., & Fleiss, J. Hormones and sexual orientation in men. *American Journal of Psychiatry.* 1977, *134,* 571–572.

Friedman, R. C., & Frang, A. G. Plasma prolactin levels in male homosexuals. *Hormones and Behavior,* 1977, *9,* 19–22.

Friedman, R. C., Wollesen, F., & Tendler, R. Psychological development and blood levels of sex steroids in male identical twins of divergent sexual orientation. *Journal of Nervous Mental Disease.* 1976, *163,* 282–288.

Garmick, M. B. Spurious rise in human chorionic gonadotropin induced by marijuana in patients with testicular cancer. (letter) *New England Journal of Medicine,* 1980, *303,* 1177.

Goldzieher, J. W., Dozier, T., Smith, K., & Steinberger, E. Improving the diagnostic reliability of rapidly fluctuating plasma hormone levels of optimized multiple sampling techniques. *Journal of Clinical Endocrinology,* 1976, *43,* 824.

Halbreich, U., Segal, S., & Chowers, I. Day-to-day variations in serum levels of follicle-stimulating hormone and luteinizing hormone in homosexual males. *Biological Psychiatry.* 1978, *13,* 541–549.

Imperato-McGinley, J., Peterson, R. E., Gautier, T., & Sturla, E. Male pseudohermaphroditism secondary to 5-alpha-reducatase deficiency—a model for the role of androgens in both the development of the male phenotype and the evolution of a male gender identity. *Journal of Steroid Biochemistry,* 1979, *11,* 637–645. (a)

Imperato-McGinley, J., Peterson, R. E., Gautier, T., & Sturla, E. Androgens and the evolution of male-gender identity among male pseudohermaphrodites with 5-alpha-reductase deficiency. *New England Journal of Medicine,* 1979, *300,* 1233–1237. (b)

James, S., Carter, R. A., & Orwin, A. Significance of androgen levels in the aetiology and treatment of homosexuality. *Psychological Medicine,* 1977, *7,* 427–429.

Kinsey, A. C., Pomeroy, W. B., & Martin, C. E. *Sexual Behavior in the Human Male,* Philadelphia: Saunders, Co., 1948.

Kolodny, R. C., Jacobs, L. S., Masters, W. H., Toro, C., & Daughaday, W. H. Plasma gonadotrophins and prolactin in male homosexuals. *Lancet,* 1972, *2,* 18–20.

Kolodny, R. C., Masters, W. H., Hendryx, J., & Toro, G. Plasma testosterone and semen analysis in male homosexuals. *New England Journal of Medicine*, 1971, *285*, 1170–1174.

Livingstone, I. R., Sagel, J., Distiller, L. A., Morley, J., & Katz, M. The effect of luteinizing hormone releasing hormone (LRH) on pituitary gonadotropins in male homosexuals. *Hormone and Metabolism Research*, 1978, *10*, 248–249.

Loraine, J. A., Adamopoulos, D. A., Kirkham, K. E., Ismail, A. A. A., & Dove, G. A. Patterns of hormone excretion in male and female homosexuals. *Nature*, 1971, *234*, 552–555.

Loraine, J. A., Ismail, A. A. A., Adamopoulos, D. A., & Dove, G. A. Endocrine function in male and female homosexuals. *British Medical Journal*, 1970, *4*, 406–408.

Margolese, M. S. Homosexuality: A new endocrine correlate. *Hormone Behavior*, 1970, *1*, 151–155.

Margolese, M. S., & Janiger, O. Androsterone/etiocholanolone ratios in male homosexuals. *British Medical Journal*, 1973, *3*, 207–210.

Magrini, G., Ebiner, J. R., Burckhardt, P., Felber, J. P. Study of the relationship between plasma prolactin levels and androgen metabolism in man. *Journal of Clinical Endocrinol. Metab.* 1976, *43*, 944–947.

Meyer, J. E. The theory of gender disorders. *Journal of the American Psychoanalytic Association*, 1982, *30*, 381–448.

Meyer-Bahlburg, H. F. Sex hormones and male homosexuality in comparative perspective. *Archives of Sexual Behavior*, 1977, *6*, 297–325.

Meyer-Bahlburg, H. F. Hormones and homosexuality. *Psychiatric Clinics of North America*, 1980, *3*, 349–364.

Mischel, W. A social-learning view of sex differences in behavior. In E. Maccoby (Ed.) *The Development of Sex Differences*. Stanford, CA: Stanford University Press, 1966.

Money, J., & Ehrhardt, A. A. *Man and woman, boy and girl*. Baltimore, MD: Johns Hopkins Press, 1972.

Newmark, S. R., Rose, L. I., Todd, R., Birk, L., & Naftolin, F. Gonadotropin, estradiol, and testosterone profiles in homosexual men. *American Journal of Psychiatry*, 1979, *136*, 767–771.

Olugi, S. O. Hyperprolactenemia in patients with suspected cannabis induced gynecomastia. *Lancet*, 1980, *816*, 255.

Paitich, D., Langevin, R., Freeman, R., Mann, K., & Handy, L. The Clarke SHQ: A clinical sex history questionnaire for males. *Archives of Sexual Behavior*, 1977, *6*, 421–435.

Parks, G. A., Korth Schutz, S., Penny, R., Hilding, R. F., Dumars, R. W., Fraser, S. D., & New, M. I. Variation in pituitary gonadal function in adolescent male homosexuals and heterosexuals. *Journal of Clinical Endocrinology*, 1974, *39*, 796–801.

Paulsen, C. A. The testis. In R. H. William (Ed.), *Textbook of endocrinology*. Philadelphia: W. B. Saunders, Co., 1974, p. 323–367.

Pillard, R. C., Rose, R. M., & Sherwood, M. Plasma testosterone levels in homosexual men. *Archives of Sexual Behavior*, 1974, *3*, 453–458.

Purohit, V., Ahluwahlia, B. S., & Vigersky, R. A. Marijuana inhibits dihydrotestosterone binding to the androgen receptor. *Endocrinology*, 1980, *107*, 848–850.

Rohde, W., Stahl, F., & Dorner, G. Plasma basal levels of FSH, LH and testosterone in homosexual men. *Endokrinologie*, 1977, *70*, 241–246.

Rosenkrantz, H., & Egher H. J. Cannabinoid induced hormone changes in monkeys and rats. *Journal of Toxicology and Environmental Health*, 1980, *6*, 296–313.

Sanders, R. M. *Hormones and human sexuality in the adult male*. Master of Science Thesis, University of Toronto, 1984.

Stahl, F., Dorner, G., Ahrens, L., & Graudenz, W. Significantly decreased apparently free testosterone levels in plasma of male homosexuals. *Endokrinologie*, 1976, *68*, 115–117.

Starka, L., Sipova, I., & Hynie, J. Plasma testosterone in male transsexuals and homosexuals. *Journal of Sex Research*, 1975, *11*, 134–138.

Stoller, R. J. *Sex and gender: On the development of masculinity and femininity*. New York: Science House, 1968.

Stoller, R. J. Scientific proceedings-panel reports. *Journal of American Psychoanalytic Association*, 1982, *30*, 185–196.

Tourney, G., & Hatfield, L. M. Androgen metabolism in schizophrenics, homosexuals, and normal controls. *Biological Psychiatry*, 1973, *6*, 23–36.

Tourney, G., Petrilli, A. J., & Hatfield, L. M. Hormonal relationships in homosexual men. *American Journal of Psychiatry*, 1975, *132*, 288–290.

Tyson, P. A developmental line of gender identity, gender role, and choice of love object. *Journal of American Psychoanalytic Association*, 1982, *30*, 61–85.

ENDNOTES

Note 1. This study was part of a Masters of Science dissertation submitted by Dr. Sanders at University of Toronto, 1983.

Note 2. More detailed information is available in Dr. Sanders' (1983) unpublished thesis.

Note 3. Fisher exact test indicated this was a non-significant group difference in numbers of subjects rejected ($p = 0.5285$).

Note 4. Fisher exact test indicated this was a non-significant group difference for rejection ($p = 0.5899$).

Note 5. Fisher exact test revealed no significant group difference in rejection ($p = 0.2932$). The total number of cases rejected is less than the sum rejected for sex history, personality pathology and drug use because some men were rejected for more than one test.

Note 6. Results of Fisher Exact Test were non-significant ($p = 0.8511$).

Note 7. Fisher exact test revealed these numbers of rejections to be non-significant between groups ($p = 0.8205$). The phallometric test is accurate in 90% of cases but the 10% inaccuracy is due mainly to nonresponders who do not react at all and to indiscriminate responders who are so excited that they react to everything, even neutral stimuli. Expectancy of seeing "pornography" can be a major operative variable in producing indiscriminate reactions.

Note 8. Approximate F values were: group $F = 0.92$, df $= 14,16$; samples F $= 0.76$, df $= 14,144$ and the interaction $F = 0.91$, df $= 28,261$. All effects were nonsignificant.

Note 9. The frequency fprevious marijuana use was: heterosexuals Mean 54.68 times, S.D. 39.60, low FGI homosexuals, 18.30, S.D. 30.92, high FGI homosexuals 26.73, S.D. 34.23, $p<.05$.

Note 10. Approximate $F = 0.51$, df $= 14, 61$, $p>.05$.

Note 11. Testicular shape was assumed to be a prolate spheroid: volume $= 4/3$ $(w^2/2 * L/2)$; where W $=$ width and L $=$ length of testicles. Index $= 2$ x volume.

11 Feminine Gender Identity in Homosexual Men: How Common is it?[1]

R. Michael Sanders
Malcolm Grove Hospital, Maryland

Jerald Bain
Mount Sinai Hospital, Toronto

Ron Langevin
Clarke Institute of Psychiatry, Toronto

The foregoing study weakened the hypothesis that an endocrine basis for homosexuality exists. Gay men did not show a female sex hormone profile, at least not in the peripheral blood. Possibly their similarity to women and their cross sex gender identity have been exaggerated, too. The next study examines gender identity and sex partner preferences in homoerotic subjects.

INTRODUCTION

Most men and women have a clear conviction that they are members of their own anatomical sex. Their bodies tell them so. Their socially defined gender behavior and their attraction to the opposite sex tell them so. But what about men and women who are homosexual? It is an old hypothesis that gay men are the intersex between man and woman, so that some of them are more feminine identified. Thus, they should show not only effeminate behavior but they will "feel like they are the opposite sex" in varying degrees. This theoretical formulation has had widespread acceptance and over the years, the differences between men and women in attitudes, preferences, and behaviors have been used not only as markers for masculinity-femininity and gender role scales, but also as indicators of homosexuality and heterosexuality (cf. Burton, 1947). In empirical research, the homosexual male was found to be more feminine.[2] Yet when one asks what is the essence of this "femininity" and "feminine gender identity," the answer is not so clear.

Terman was among the first to define masculinity-femininity empirically by attitudes and preferences of men versus women and the Terman Miles (Terman & Miles, 1936) Scale resulted. If one examines that scale's items today, they seem time and culture bound, for example, Do you like or dislike the book "Daddy Long Legs" by Jean Webster, the person "Aaron Burr," the game "Dare Bare" or "Near Beer"? Other similar attempts were made and several major inventories have masculinity-femininity scales, for example, the California Personality Inventory, (Gough, 1952) and the Minnesota Multiphasic Personality Inventory (MMPI). Lunneborg (1972) examined several widely used measures of masculinity-femininity and found that there was little interrelationship among them. More recent investigations (Bernard, 1981; Bohannon & Mills, 1979; Pearson, 1980) have produced similar results adding to the uncertainty of exacting what is being measured by gender role scales.

Freund and his colleagues (Freund, Nagler, Langevin, Zajac, & Steiner, 1974) attempted to examine the question from another perspective. They developed a scale to measure gender identity rather than gender role. They argued that feminine gender identity in men may be different than that defined by male-female differences. They used transsexual males as a marker group to identify extreme feminine gender identity in men. The transsexuals, who are normal anatomically, claim to have such a longstanding conviction to being the opposite sex that they request sex reassignment surgery to change their physical form to match their emotional-cognitive convictions. The Freund Feminine Gender Identity (FGI) scale proved to be quite a discriminating instrument. Only 3% of homosexual men who did not desire to change anatomical sex had scores that overlapped with those of the transsexual group. The interesting finding for the present study was that, in the large sample, homosexual men's scores were between the heterosexual controls' and the transsexual group's. One third of homosexuals were not distinct from the heterosexual controls on their FGI scores but two thirds showed a greater degree of feminine gender identity.

Freund et al. were not satisfied with the scale because it had too few items and the masculine gender identity end of the scale seemed too undiscriminating. When they tried to extend the scale (Freund, Langevin, Satterberg, & Steiner, 1977) they found that they could not add very many items and, those they did add started to look like gender role items of the earlier scales, such as the MMPI. For example, "In childhood did you ever wish to become a dancer?" or "In childhood, were you very interested in the work of a garage mechanic?" The core of the scale remained the feeling and conviction of being the opposite sex: "Between the ages of 6 and 12 did you wish you had been born a girl instead of a boy?" When one attempts to discuss what this scale means, it simply is a paper and pencil series of items that confirm the desire of the respondent to change sex or to be satisfied with his current anatomical/social sex role. The motivation for and essence of the gender identity are elusive.

Yet the sex role behaviors of children are believed to cause or at least be precursors of homosexuality, albeit it is unknown at present exactly to what extent gender role and identity predict later erotic anomalous preference (cf. Gershman, 1966; Green, 1979, Lewis, 1979; Stoller, 1972; Zuger, 1978). On the other hand, Bell, Weinberg, and Hammersmith (1981) found that few homosexuals said they were feminine while growing up. Langevin (1983) also argued that gender identity and erotic preference as seen in homosexuality may be independent. Therefore there would be less reason to believe gender role or identity would predict erotic preference. We attempted in the present study to clarify the role of FGI in homosexuality in two ways. First, we examined the duration and intensity of the feelings surrounding gender identity conviction. These two variables were not fully assessed in the 1977 version of the FGI scale. One cannot be sure from the questionnaire whether the crossgender feelings were short transitory intellectualizations or strong feelings that persisted over a prolonged period. So we added two items for each existing scale item to tap the duration and intensity of the feelings surrounding gender identity. Second, we scored the FGI scale in a new way. We noted that feminine gender identity was scored as follows on the published FGI Scale:

> prefer male toys   — score 0
> unsure, didn't matter or can't remember — score 1
> prefer female toys   — score 2

In other words, ambivalence or indifference about gender behaviors were scored as one point in the feminine direction. This is certainly one interpretation of that indifference. However, if many items were scored as neutral, the score may seem to be a degree of conviction of femininity rather than indifference. We therefore decided to change the scoring without changing the relative weights so that male identity was a negative score and female a positive score and indifference zero, for example:

> prefer male toys   — score −1
> prefer neither/unsure — score 0
> prefer female toys   — score +1

Thus, many ambivalent scores would result in a 0 score overall, but male gender identity would show a negative score and feminine identity a positive one. Although this does not change the results of the scale items in any way, it is not clear where the homosexuals would fall in overall score.

Gender identity inversion in homosexual men was examined further via erotic preference patterns. In Chapter 8 of this volume a scale was developed to examine the erotically attractive features of sex partners. Heterosexual men and wom-

en showed stereotypic preferences (e.g., the male found women who were shorter, lighter, weaker, younger etc. more sexually arousing). Women preferred the opposite (i.e., men who are bigger and stronger, etc.). If homosexuality does represent gender inversion as well as erotic preference inversion, gay men who are more feminine identified should prefer male partners who are bigger, stronger, and so on, like females do, but gays who are more masculine identified will want their partners smaller, weaker, etc. and so on, as heterosexual men do. However, if gay men are generally ambivalent or indifferent about gender behavior, there may be no pattern to the results or some other features may be primary in their erotic preference.

METHOD

Subjects

The same men used in Chapter 10 were used here. There were 54 heterosexual men, and 46 homosexual men. From these initial groups, three subgroups were also used: heterosexuals (n = 19), low FGI homosexuals (n = 10), and high FGI homosexuals (n = 13). The latter groups consisted of psychologically and physically healthy individuals, selected by extensive screening. Their erotic preference was validated by phallometric testing. The reader interested in more detail may wish to reexamine the method in Chapter 10.

Materials and Procedure

As part of a screening procedure for the Chapter 10 study, the men were administered the FGI scale (Freund et al., 1977) among other tests. For the purpose of this chapter, only the MMPI, BSRI, (Bem, 1974), FGI, and Sex Partners Questionnaire tests are discussed. The Bem scale (BSRI) was included because of recent interest in androgyny in homosexual men (Bernard & Epstein, 1978; Hooberman, 1979; Robinson, Skeen, & Flake-Hobson, 1982; Skrapec & MacKenzie, 1981). A brief investigation of the relationship of androgyny, gender role (MMPI Mf), and gender identity is reported in Appendix D, as a supplement to the present study.

The FGI scale first was administered as described by Freund et al. (1977). When the respondent completed it, he went over the items again to fill in two additional answers for each item: the intensity and duration associated with the answer he had previously checked on the 19 FGI items. Thus there were now 3x19 or 57 items. Intensity was rated as (3) strong, (2) moderate, (1) weak, (0) not applicable or cannot say, and duration was rated as proportion of time (4) 100%, (3) 75%, (2) 50%, (1) 25%, (0) not applicable or cannot say. The FGI scale was scored first in the fashion previously reported by Freund et al. and

TABLE 11.1
A Comparison of Gender Role and Identity Measures in
Homosexuals and Heterosexuals

			Heterosexuals N = 46	Homosexuals N = 54
MMPI	Mf	***	30	35
BEM	Femininity	**	5	5
	Masculinity	**	5	5
	Androgyny	***	−1	−0
FGI	— Standard	***	7	12
FGI	— Intensity	***	7	15
FGI	— Duration	***	9	18
GI	— Revised Scoring	***	−7	−2
GI	— Intensity	***	−11	−2
GI	— Duration	***	−11	−2

Note: Maximum scores are: 30 for FGI Standard 90 Intensity and 120 Duration. For revised GI +19, Intensity +57 and Duration +76.
$**p < 01, ***p < 001$.

TABLE 11.2
Gender Role and Identity Scores of High and Low FGI Androphiles
and of Heterosexuals

			Mean Scores		
			High FGI Homosexuals N = 13	Low FGI Homosexuals N = 10	Heterosexuals N = 19
MMPI	Mf		35	36	29[a]
BEM	Femininity		5[b]	4[ab]	5[a]
	Masculinity	**	5[a]	5[ab]	5[b]
	Androgyny	***	0[a]	−0	−1
FGI	— Standard	****	15[a]	8	6
FGI	— Intensity	****	22[a]	7	7
FGI	— Duration	****	26[a]	8	8
GI	— Revised Scoring	****	1[a]	−6	−8
GI	— Intensity	****	2[a]	−9[b]	−13[c]
GI	— Duration	****	3[a]	−12	−13

Note: Maximum scores are: 30 for FGI Standard 90 Intensity and 120 Duration. For revised GI +19, Intensity +57 and Duration +76.

The GI results in this table are distorted by the preselection of subjects based on GI scores but are used anyway for comparative purposes.

$**p < .01, ***p < .001, ****p < .0001$. Means with the same superscipt are not significantly different.

second, with items keyed positive-negative as described in the introduction. Intensity and duration items were multiplied by the signed FGI scores. The scale was item analyzed and the two groups compared by t-test. The three subgroups, heterosexuals, "masculine identified" homosexuals and "feminine identified" homosexuals also were compared by one way analysis of variance. Because the subgroups were preselected on the basis of the old FGI scoring, they offered marker groups for the new scoring and for the additional items on intensity and duration of gender identity. The questionnaire measuring erotically attractive features in sex partners described in Chapter 8 was also used here. SPSS computer programs were used for analysis.

RESULTS

Gender Identity

Table 11.1 and Table 11.2 show the mean score and the significance levels of t-tests and one way analyses of variance for gender role and identity measures for the total sample and the three subgroups. The pattern of results are essentially the same in the two tables. Homosexual subjects showed more feminine gender

TABLE 11.3
Percent of Cases in Masculine and Feminine Score Range
on the FGI Scale

	Item Scores		Intensity		Duration	
	Het.	*Homo.*	*Het.*	*Homo.*	*Het.*	*Homo.*
FGI						
Standard						
0–10	85	41	76	33	73	35
11–20	13	57	18	33	13	23
21–30	2	2	7	29	7	23
31–50	0	0	0	6	7	19
Actual Maximum Score	24	21	28	46	42	44
GI						
Revised						
−	93	65	93	54	89	48
0	0	6	4	15	4	19
+	7	30	2	31	7	33
Actual Maximum Score	+9	+8	+3	+12	+12	+18

Percent may not total exactly 100% due to rounding error.
Possible maximum score, FGI Standard 30; Intensity 90, Duration 120, GI Revised +19, Intensity +57, Duration +76.

TABLE 11.4
All Homosexuals vs. Heterosexuals on Features of Sex Partner
Preference

Name	P	Homosexuals	Heterosexuals
Head Hair Length	***	2.92	3.70
Facial Hair	***	2.74	1.65
Eyebrows	**	3.11	2.75
Lip Size	—	3.21	3.32
Chin Shape	***	3.64	2.97
Body Hair	***	3.17	2.27
Shoulder Breadth	***	3.64	2.88
Musculature	***	3.67	2.95
Weight	***	3.29	2.12
Height	***	3.44	2.45
Hip Shape	***	3.44	2.48
Shape of Behind	—	2.21	2.07
Leg Shape	***	3.88	2.86
Pubic Hair	*	3.24	2.90
Breast Size	—	2.89	3.11
Breast Shape	—	3.52	3.58
Penis Size	—	3.61	NA
Physical Strength	***	3.47	2.40
Outgoing	—	3.43	3.51
Dominating Vs. Submissive	**	3.35	2.93
Age	***	3.39	2.69
Dress	—	1.75	1.58
Grooming	—	1.05	1.19
Masculine/Feminine	***	3.95	2.12
Overall Physical Beauty	***	3.81	4.46
Your Own Physical Beauty	—	3.39	3.63

Note: $*p < .05$, $**p < .01$, $***p < .001$

identity and femininity. However, in the revised FGI form, it is clear that their scores were not so much feminine as less masculine. That is, the gays had average scores that were negative and they were slightly masculine overall or indifferent about the gender identity axis. Similar results appear for the pre-selected High FGI androphiles in Table 11.2. They showed low scores in the feminine direction but generally scored around zero indicating that indifference or ambivalence was a prominent feature. One finding is unique to the subgroups: the Low FGI gays showed masculine identification but it is less intense than the heterosexuals' and more intense than feminine identification of the High FGI gays.

Table 11.3 shows the percent of each group in the masculine/feminine range. With the revised scoring there is a noteworthy shift to the masculine end of the spectrum. Fifty nine percent of androphiles have significant feminine identifica-

TABLE 11.5
Comparison of Homosexual & Heterosexual Subgroups on Features
of Sex Partner Preference

Name	F/P	High FGI Homosexuals	Low FGI Homosexuals	Heterosexuals
Head Hair Length	—	2.91	3.17	3.69
Facial Hair	****	3.20[a]	1.87	1.12
Eyebrows	—	3.18	2.87	2.75
Lip Size	—	3.16	3.25	3.29
Chin Shape	—	3.36	3.71	3.21
Body Hair	****	3.83[a]	2.75	2.06
Shoulder Breadth	****	3.75	3.87	2.83[a]
Musculature	****	3.92	4.00	2.72[a]
Weight	****	3.33	3.57	2.05[a]
Height	****	3.45	3.71	2.47[a]
Hip Shape	****	3.58	3.75	2.55[a]
Shape of Behind	—	2.25	2.25	2.35
Leg Shape	**	4.00	4.00	2.94[a]
Pubic Hair	—	3.25	3.37	2.94
Breast Size	—	2.92	3.17	3.05
Breast Shape	—	3.70	3.50	3.72
Penis Size	—	3.58	3.62	N/A
Physical Strength	****	3.50	3.43	2.29[a]
Outgoing	—	3.17	3.37	3.78
Dominating/Submissive	—	3.08	3.37	2.88
Age	*	3.70[b]	3.00[ab]	2.75[a]
Dress	—	1.92	1.71	1.62
Grooming	—	1.08	1.00	1.17
Masculine/Feminine	****	4.08	4.00	2.17[a]
Overall Phys. Beauty	—	3.83	4.00	4.44
Your Own Phys. Beauty	—	3.33	3.37	3.56

Note: $**p < .01$, $****p < .0001$.

tion on the standard FGI (scores over 10), comparable to original results (Freund, Nagler et al., 1974). Using the revised scoring, 30% did and, as noted for Table 11.2, it was weak, suggestive of ambivalence or indifference more than of a firm conviction. Discriminant analysis showed that the revised GI scoring was comparable to the old FGI in correctly assigning subjects to their own groups.[3] Further psychometric comparisons of the measures are presented in Appendix D.

Features of Preferred Sex Partner

All heterosexuals and homosexuals were compared. Table 11.4 shows mean scores on a five point scale for the two groups.[4] Most items were significant in the expected direction since heterosexuals were evaluating females as partners

and homosexuals; males. The strongest discriminating items for men versus women were again important. Heterosexuals desired lighter and shorter partners who were physically weaker. The female flared hips were also an important feature. However, the homosexuals were almost indifferent about these factors rather than showing special preferences. Heterosexual versus homosexual comparisons may be misleading here because these results do not distinguish gender identity and erotic preference. A better comparison is presented in Table 11.5 in which subgroups of heterosexuals, low scoring FGI and higher scoring FGI gays were examined.

In this comparison erotic preference was the same in both homosexual groups but gender identity varied. Most differences between the two homosexual groups were nonsignificant. There was a weak trend for feminine identified gays to prefer older partners and a significant preference on their part for men who had more facial and body hair.[5] There were no other differences suggesting that gender identity in homosexual men does not predict partner preference features as well as it does in heterosexual males versus females. The difference in stereotyped patterns of preference between heterosexual men and women does not appear operative within subgroups of homosexual men.

Rankings of features showed homosexuals preferred in order of importance: musculature, weight, shape of behind, height, and facial hair. Hetersexuals rated shape of behind, weight, breast shape, and size, and leg shape as most attractive.

DISCUSSION

There was support for the theory that homosexual men are not feminine identified but are ambivalent/indifferent about gender roles or are masculine identified in general. One could argue that the ambivalence, or indifference leads to a homosexual erotic preference. However, it is also possible to argue that gender identity is only a vehicle used socially to express erotic behaviors. In general, the results suggest that gender identity and erotic preference are certainly not entwined to the extent that early theories of the homosexual "intersex" would lead us to believe. Nor does gender identity in homosexual men relate to features of preferred sex partner in the way it does for heterosexual men versus women. The homosexual erotic choice may be independent of the social vehicle and perhaps homosexuals feel an indifference to gender behavior for this very reason. The homosexual may be confused from the association of the two by the majority of society and so he develops indifference to it as an adaptive response.

The FGI scale could be reconstructed to reflect not just femininity or masculinity, nor their difference (androgyny), but as an axis of gender identity indifference (non-gender identity). Conceivably the male who never feels strong impulses toward male or female behavior patterns may be very different from one who strongly adapts to the feminine or masculine roles. The intensity and

duration of gender identity or the feeling of not belonging may result in very different outcomes. At the very least, the androphile may not incorporate the gender roles to the degree gynephiles do because they are at odds with his erotic needs.

A study of the FGI scores of transsexuals would be informative. It seems this group may be more divergent from homosexuals than originally reported in earlier work (Freund, Langevin, Zajac, Steiner, & Zajac, 1974). Possibly sorting them according to the new FGI scoring used in this study will provide a useful index for successful sex reassignment surgery.

REFERENCES

Bell, A. P., Weinberg, M. S., & Hammersmith, S. K. *Sexual preference: Its development in men and women.* Bloomington, IN: Indiana University Press, 1981.

Bem, S. The measurement of psychological androgyny. *Journal of Consulting Clinical Psychology,* 1974, *42,* 155–162.

Bernard, C. The multidimensional aspects of masculinity-femininity. *Journal of Personality and Social Psychology,* 1981, *41,* 797–802.

Bernard, L. C., & Epstein, D. J. Androgyny scores of matched homosexual and heterosexual males. *Journal of Homosexuality,* 1978, *4,* 169–178.

Bohannon, W. E., & Mills, C. J. Psychometric properties and underlying assumptions of two measures of masculinity/femininity. *Psychological Reports,* 1979, *44,* 431–450.

Burton, A. The use of the Masculinity-Femininity Scale of the MMPI as an aid in the diagnosis of sexual inversion. *Journal of Psychology,* 1947, *24,* 161–164.

Freund, K., Langevin, R., Satterberg, J., & Steiner, B. Extension of the gender identity scale for males. *Archives of Sexual Behavior,* 1977, *6,* 507–519.

Freund, K., Langevin, R., Zajac, Y., Steiner, B., & Zajac, A. The transsexual syndrome in homosexual males. *Journal of Nervous Mental Diseases,* 1974, *158,* 145–153.

Freund, K., Nagler, E., Langevin, R., Zajac, A., & Steiner, B. Measuring feminine gender identity in homosexual males. *Archives of Sexual Behavior,* 1974, *3,* 249–260.

Gershman, H. The role of core gender identity in the genesis of perversions. *American Journal of Psychotherapy,* 1966, *20,* 58–67.

Gough, H. G. Identifying psychological femininity. *Educational Psychological Measurements,* 1952, *12,* 427–439.

Green, R. Childhood crossgender behavior and subsequent sexual preference. *American Journal of Psychiatry,* 1979, *136,* 106–108.

Hooberman, R. Psychological androgyny, feminine gender identity and self esteem in homosexual and heterosexual males. *Journal of Sex Research,* 1979, *15,* 306–315.

Langevin, R. *Sexual strands: Understanding and treating sexual anomalies in men.* Hillsdale, NJ: Lawrence Erlbaum Assocates, 1983.

Lewis, H. B. Gender identity: Primary narcissism or primary process? *Bulletin of the Menninger Clinic,* 1979, *43,* 145–160.

Lunneborg, P. W. Dimensionality of MF. *Journal of Clinical Psychology,* 1972, *28,* 313–317.

Pearson, J. A factor analytic study of the items in three selected sex role instruments. *Psychological Reports,* 1980, *46,* 1119–1126.

Robinson, B. E., Skeen, P., & Flake-Hobson, C. Sex role endorsement among homosexual men across the life span. *Archives of Sexual Behavior,* 1982, *11,* 355–359.

Skrapec, C., & MacKenzie, K. R. Psychological self-perception in male transsexuals, homosexuals, and heterosexuals. *Archives of Sexual Behavior*, 1981, *10*, 357–370.

Stoller, R. J. The "bedrock" of masculinity and femininity: bisexuality. *Archives of General Psychiatry*, 1972, *26*, 207–212.

Terman, L. M., & Miles, C. *Sex and personality: Studies in masculinity and femininity*, New York: McGraw-Hill, 1936.

Zuger, B. Effeminate behavior present in boys from childhood: ten additional years of followup. *Comprehensive Psychiatry*, 1978, *19*, 363–369.

ENDNOTES

Note 1. This study was carried out as part of data collection for Dr. Sanders' Masters of Science dissertation, University of Toronto, 1983.

Note 2. See Langevin (1983) for details and a review of the literature.

Note 3. The old versus new scoring produced the following correct classification of subjects in discriminant analysis:

	% Heterosexual	% Homosexual	% Total
Old Scoring	72	80	76
New Scoring	72	81	77

The subcategories of the Bem Scale were examined, namely masculine, feminine, androgynous and undifferentiated, after Robinson et al. (1982) and using the Stanford University means for males provided by Bem (1974). Results were:

	Undifferentiated	Feminine	Androgynous	Masculine
Homosexual	6.8%	22.7%	61.4%	9.1%
Heterosexual	2.3%	9.3%	58.1%	30.2%

which are significant but weak; $\chi^2 = 8.40$, $p<05$. Differences basically reflect the tendency of homosexuals to be more feminine and heterosexuals to be more masculine. There were no differences in androgyny or undifferentiated categories. Both masculine and androgynous categories were significantly related to tendency to respond in a socially desirable way. The four categories together had little predictive utility in understanding the other gender identity/role scores or sex partner features (see also Bernard & Epstein, 1978; Hooberman, 1979).

Note 4. The alpha reliability of the 26 items of the scale was 0.82, indicating it could be used as a scale. However, in the present paper, individual items were of greater interest, and the scale itself is not discussed.

Note 5. When only the two gay groups are compared, the results are essentially the same. Facial and body hair items were the only ones significant ($p<05$ in both cases).

12

Crossdressing, Erotic Preference, and Aggression: A Comparison of Male Transvestites and Transsexuals

Betty W. Steiner
Ron Langevin
*Clarke Institute of Psychiatry,
Toronto*

R. Michael Sanders
Malcolm Grove Hospital, Maryland

Feminine gender identity and crossdressing may seem to be odd bedfellows for sexual aggression but the link among them may be closer than previously believed. Clinicians expect transvestitic and transsexual men to behave like women who are, in large part, noncriminal and nonviolent compared to males. However femininity may have a different meaning to them. The surprising association of crossdressing and feminine gender identity with rape (Chapter 2), autoerotic asphyxia and sadomasochism, suggests that the question be examined in greater detail than typically has been done. The next study examines erotic behavior and aggressiveness in men traditionally believed to be "passive"; transvestites and transsexuals.

INTRODUCTION

Crossdressing in female attire is a poorly understood phenomenon. Individuals engaging in this behavior usually do not want public or psychiatric attention unless they desire sex reassignment surgery. However, in the past 10 years, more research has been done, especially on transsexualism (cf. Langevin, 1983; Steiner, 1984). In this chapter, heterosexual transvestites and homosexual transsexuals are compared on erotic preference and aggression.

Erotic Preference

There have been few comprehensive investigations of the erotic preference of transsexuals and there are many unanswered questions about the nature of this gender/ sexual anomaly. For example, the homosexual transsexual may want sex reassignment surgery to attract "heterosexual" male partners (Freund, Langevin, Zajac, Steiner, & Zajac, 1974b), but it seems they are willing also to forego erotic arousal for gender needs. Some are heterosexual. Some have been described as "asexual" (cf. Bentler, 1976; Lukianowicz, 1959). However, Langevin, Paitich, and Steiner, (1977) found that transsexual males applying for sex reassignment surgery but still living as males, had considerable sexual experience involving their own penises. The fact that sadists and masochists as well as a variety of psychiatrically disturbed individuals seek sex reassignment surgery creates uneasiness that more attention has not been paid to investigations of their erotic preferences (cf. Berger, Green, Laub, Reynolds, Walker, & Wollman, 1979; Meyer, 1974; Newman & Stoller, 1974; Stoller, 1973).

Although there are many questions about the transsexual's erotic and gender behavior, there are even more about the transvestite's. Why do they masturbate in female attire? Labelling transvestites as fetishists for female clothes seems simplistic. For example, one wonders why only 50% of transvestites in Bentler's (1976) sample described themselves as "fetishists." Wilson and Gosselin (1980) compared 125 fetishists, 285 transvestites and transsexuals, 133 sadomasochists, and 50 normal male controls in a nonclinical sample. Sexual experiences of the three sexually anomalous groups showed an overlap of interests. Eighty eight percent of fetishists shared at least one of the other two outlets of sadomasochism or crossdressing. More than a third of the group was interested in all three outlets and only 37% of the transvestite-transsexual group crossdressed exclusively. Gosselin (1981) further described the most popular fantasies of transvestites on the Wilson Sex Fantasy Questionnaire as including: being forced to do something, being hit or spanked, being hurt by a partner and being tied up, suggesting masochistic tendencies.

Buhrich and Beaumont (1981) compared 126 American and 86 Australian male members of transvestite clubs on erotic behaviors and also found some evidence of masochism. They selected cases on the basis of the crossdressers reporting at least some period in their lives of fetishism to women's clothes. Most sexual behaviors were expected from the definition of transvestism but 28% of the Americans and 41% of the Australians had fantasies of bondage during crossdressing. Most maintained a predominantly or exclusively heterosexual orientation throughout their sexual histories.

Croughan, Sagher, Cohen, and Robins (1981), on the other hand, examined a group of 70 crossdressers who appeared to be predominantly transvestites. They found that only 4% engaged in sadomasochism. Most engaged in transvestism proper and secondarily in heterosexual intercourse while crossdressed.

Some writers have associated transvestism with exhibitionism. Bowman and Engle (1957) and Rosen and Kople (1977) reported cases of men who engaged in exhibitionism while crossdressed. In the former the patient exposed to women, in the latter, to men. The association of the two anomalous behaviors remains unexplained.

One wonders why transvestites seek sex reassignment surgery, although later in life than transsexuals. Meyer. (1974) among others described "aging transvestites" who close the gap between the theoretically discrete anomalies of transvestism and transsexualism. Freund, Steiner, and Chan (1982) reported a systematic investigation on feminine gender identity (FGI) in a mixed group of patients from a gender identity clinic. They found FGI was not as strong in transvestites as it was in transsexuals and it tended to increase with age in the former. Buhrich and McConaghy (1977b) found that, compared to transvestites, transsexuals were significantly younger, single, crossdressed fully, reported homosexual interest, feminine gender identity, and usually desired sex reassignment surgery.

Walsh, Stahl, Unger, Lilienstern, and Stephens (1977) described 43 cases of autoerotic asphyxia in which men derived erotic gratification by hanging or by other means of reducing the oxygen supply to the brain. In 26% of the cases, women's clothes were worn at the time of the apparently accidental deaths. Other writers have described similar cases (for example, Dietz, 1978; Litman & Swearington, 1972; Stearns, 1953). In a living case, Hucker (1983) treated the patient with provera and castration which helped to reduce sexual urges to engage in the acts. Interestingly, this patient showed a strong desire for sex reassignment surgery after castration, although he maintained he always had some interest in it. We also have noted one recent applicant for sex reassignment surgery who served time in penitentiary for rape and another with an extensive history of firesetting. In the present report heterosexual transvestites and homosexual transsexuals were compared on a standard sex history questionnaire.

Aggression

Aggressiveness has seldom been examined in cases of gender dysphoria, perhaps because femininity is seen as "passive" and nonaggressive in nature. However, the association of both transsexualism and transvestism with sadomasochism in Wilson and Gosselin's (1980) sample and the recent association of crossdressing with autoerotic asphyxia (Dietz, 1978; Litman & Swearington, 1972; Stearns, 1953; Walsh et al., 1977) and with rape (see Chapters 1 and 2) suggests that aggressiveness in the two groups be scrutinized.

Transvestites and transsexuals have been studied separately but seldom together (cf. Buhrich, 1976, 1981; Taylor & McLachlan, 1962, 1964) and existing comparisons have tended to focus on relative mental health and personality.

Personality

The single largest body of data on transvestites suggests that they are relatively normal. Bentler and Prince (1969, 1970, Bentler, Sherman, & Prince, 1970; Prince & Bentler, 1972) studied 504 transvestites who read the magazine *Transvestia*. The readers were found to be well adjusted. Seventy six percent had never seen a psychiatrist.

Meyer (1974), on the other hand, described "aging transvestites" seeking sex reassignment as seriously depressed patients who view the surgery as an alternative to suicide or self castration.[1]

Transsexuals have similarly received mixed ratings of mental health ranging from 70% showing some psychiatric diagnosis to most showing a clean bill of health (Derogatis, Meyer, & Vazquez, 1978; Finney, Brandsma, Tondow, & Lemaistre, 1975; Hoenig, Kenna, & Youd, 1970a,b; Langevin et al., 1977; Leavitt, Berger, Hoeppner, & Northrop, 1980; Tsushima & Wedding, 1979). No mention of aggression or violence was made in several empirical studies of transsexuals although emotional disturbance was noted by some writers (Hoenig, Kenna, & Youd, 1970a,b; Langevin et al., 1977; Leavitt et al., 1980; Tsushima & Wedding, 1979). In fact Derogatis et al. (1978) stressed the absence of hostility in the group as measured by his inventory, the DSFI. Nevertheless two features are noteworthy. First, Finney et al. (1975) found that among 20 applicants for sex reassignment surgery five were paranoid schizophrenic and three had paranoid personalities. These diagnoses have been related to violent behavior and even homicide (cf. Langevin, Paitich, & Orchard, 1982). Croughan et al. (1981) examined psychiatrically treated and untreated members of a crossdressing club. They too found that some of their 70 cases had diagnoses often associated with violence. Thirteen percent were antisocial personalities, 4% paranoid schizophrenic, 24% alcoholic, and 23% drug users. However, violence per se was not discussed.

Second, depression is a marked symptom in transsexuals and transvestites presenting at psychiatric clinics and frequently is associated with suicidal tendencies or attempts. We know that suicide is a symptom of depression but it also may be related to sadomasochism. Suicide and homicide have often been considered aspects of the same phenomena, namely aggression. In some cultures the association is quite high, as in Denmark, but in others it is not, as in the USA (cf. Langevin, et al. 1982).

Walinder (1967) noted that 60% of his 30 Swedish cases of male transsexuals had suicidal thoughts and 20% had made attempts. Aggression per se was not noted although 11% were reported for "intemperance" and 18% to child welfare boards for delinquency.

In general, personality results suggest that some violence may be a factor in transsexualism and transvestism but the absence of aggression has been stressed. Differences in results from clinical samples and crossdressing clubs in the com-

munity are noteworthy. One expects to see emotionally disturbed individuals in psychiatric hospitals, transvestites, or otherwise. The "healthy" crossdressers do not come to our attention or, as Wise and Meyer (1980) indicated, the men may find symptom relief in the club itself.

Childhood and Parent Child Relations

The family background of the transsexual has been described as disturbed with the mother dominating and showing some pathology, especially depression (Freund, Langevin, Zajac, Steiner, & Zajac, 1974a; Langevin et al., 1977; Paitich & Langevin, 1976; Weitzman, Shamoian, & Golosow, 1971).

Parker and Barr (1982) examined the parent child relationships of 30 male-to-female transsexual patients and a control group using the Parental Bonding Instrument. The 25 item instrument measures parental care and protectiveness (Parker, Tipling, & Brown, 1979). The two groups did not differ in scores for mothers but transsexuals described their fathers as less caring but more over-protective and discouraging their son's independence and autonomy.

Langevin et al. (1977) compared transsexuals, homosexuals, and heterosexuals on the 16 scales of the Clarke Parent Child Relations Questionnaire. Transsexuals reported their mothers were more indulgent than average but fathers were less competent and affectionate compared to the other groups. There were no group differences in aggressiveness among mother, father, and son. Scores were within normal limits.

Blanchard, McConkey, Roper, & Steiner (1983) developed a scale to measure physical aggressiveness in childhood. They compared transsexual, homosexual, and heterosexual males on the 12 item scale and found that the three groups were significantly different. The transsexuals were least aggressive, the homosexuals more aggressive, and heterosexuals most aggressive. The scale correlated $-.71$ with the Freund (Freund, Nagler, Langevin, Zajac, & Steiner, 1974; Freund, Langevin, Satterberg, & Steiner, 1977) Feminine Gender Identity Scale.

Criminal Record and Violence

Criminality has not been reported in general for transvestites or transsexuals. However, Langevin et al. (1977) compared male transsexuals living as females with those living as men to control groups of homosexuals and heterosexuals. The transsexuals living as females tended to have personality disorder diagnoses, and more often have criminal records that included break and enter and prostitution. The transsexuals living as males showed more emotional disturbance and confusion but less criminality. Although general criminality was a factor in transsexualism, violent crimes were not.

O'Gorman (1982) also noted that three of 21 biological male transsexuals had a criminal record but not of a serious nature. Croughan et al. (1981) reported that

of 70 members of a crossdressing club, 24% had been arrested, most in connection with crossdressing but one case, interestingly, for child molestation.

The occasional report has noted extreme brutality. Bowman and Engle (1957) reported two cases of transvestism associated with murder, but little detail was presented. Levine (1980) also described a transsexual who ''brutally attacked'' female strangers on two occassions. However, he did not report aggression in general in his sample of 39 biological males and 12 females.

Milliken (1982) presented three cases of homicidal transsexuals, two males and a female. All satisfied DSM III criteria for transsexualism but they had other diagnoses as well. Aggression was directed to others in fighting, violent fantasies, one murder, and one attempted murder, but it was also directed inward. In all cases there were suicidal thoughts and the two males had made attempts on their lives and one had performed autocastration.

Sorenson and Hertoft (1982) described the male transsexual having an antiaggressive attitude with ''heavily subdued'' spontaneity in aggressive and libidinal relations. They noted nonetheless that female transsexuals have been described as impulsive and acting out aggressively. However, the ''aggressiveness'' was not of the proportions that result in criminal charges of assault. In some instances ''aggressiveness'' may be an exaggerated caricature of the male much as some male-to female transsexuals enact a stereotype of the female by dressing inappropriately and seductively (see Vogt, 1968, pg. 78, Case #3 for an example of an ''aggressive'' female transsexual).

In the present study, transvestites and transsexuals were compared on sexual history, personality, parent-child relations, and criminal record, to profile differences in erotic preference, gender role, and aggressiveness.

METHOD

Subjects

All men were patients at a gender clinic. Eighteen heterosexual transvestites who were sexually attracted to women and masturbated while crossdressed were compared to 31 homosexual transsexuals who were sexually attracted to men and did not masturbate while crossdressed. All transvestites but only 53% of transsexuals were living as men. Both groups satisfied DSM III criteria with the exception that the homosexual transsexuals had not necessarily lived two years as females but were in the process of doing so as part of a program for sex reassignment surgery.

The transvestites were older than transsexuals but they were also somewhat better educated and had higher Performance IQ but not Verbal IQ scores (Table 12.1). Although more transvestites had postsecondary education than transsexuals, the results were not statistically significant. Most transsexuals were single

TABLE 12.1
A Comparison of Mean Age, Education, IQ and Marital Status In
Transvestites and Transsexuals

		Transvestites (N = 18)	Transsexuals (N = 31)
Age	***	32 (10)	23 (5)
Education	*	12 (1)	11 (2)
Postsecondary education		24%	7%
VIQ		108 (11)	102 (16)
PIQ	*	115 (12)	105 (15)
Marital Status	****		
Single		28%	89%
Married		39%	8%
Divorced		33%	0%
Separated		0%	4%

Note: *p < 05, ***p < 001, ****p < .0001.
Values in brackets are standard deviations. Percent may not total 100% due to rounding error.

and never married in contrast to most transvestites who were married at some
time.

Materials and Procedure

All *Ss* completed the following tests—MMPI, 16PF, Clarke PCR, and Clarke
SHQ (Paitich & Langevin, 1976; Paitich, Langevin, Freeman, Mann, & Handy,
1977). IQ was estimated from the Raven Standard Progressive Matrices and a
Vocabulary test (Paitich, 1973). Information on age, education, marital status,
and history of drug and alcohol use was also available.

RESULTS

The MMPI, 16 PF, PCR, and SHQ scales were each subjected to discriminant
analysis. The more clinically useful T-scores and Sten scores were also compared in the two groups.[2]

Erotic Preference

Sex History results (Table 12.2) showed expected differences in experience with
adult males versus females and lack of difference in frequency of crossdressing
(maximum is 100 times on the questionnaire). However, the transvestites appeared to be more "polymorphous perverse" than transsexuals since they signif-

TABLE 12.2
Sex History Results: Percent of Transvestites and Transsexuals Ever
Sexually Engaging in Stimulus and Response Categories

		Transvestites %	Transsexuals %
Stimulus Categories			
Adult Female	***	100	22
Pubescent Female		28	7
Child Female		11	0
Adult/Male Youth		17	100
Pubescent Male		0	11
Child Male		6	15
Response Categories			
Heterosexual Interest	****	89	26
Exhibitionism	*	17	0
Voyeurism	**	33	0
Crossdressing—Skirt or dress		94	92
—Undergarments		94	92
—Stockings		100	96
—Shoes		94	96
—Jewelery		94	100
—Wig		89	73
Toucheurism	*	22	0
Frottage	**	28	0
Rape		6	0
Obscene Calls		6	0

Note: F test based on dichotomous scores of SHQ behaviors (present/absent) % are presented for
convenience.
*p < .05, **p < .01, ***p < .001, ****p < .0001.

icantly more often peeped, exposed, molested females with their hands, and
rubbed against females in crowds (frottage). Approximately half of the transvestites engaged in one or another of these activities. They also showed a trend to
greater frequencies of acting out sexually with physically immature females. The
discriminant analysis correctly identified 98% of the cases.

Aggression

Personality.   Discriminant analysis of the MMPI (Table 12.3) correctly assigned 83% of the cases to their own group, but only three scales were significant, K, Masculinity-femininity, and Social Introversion. Transsexuals tended to
respond in a more socially desirable way, to be more feminine and less introverted than transvestites. When clinically significant MMPI T-scores were examined, the two groups did not differ at all. However, both groups showed substan-

TABLE 12.3
Mean MMPI Scores for Transvestites
and Transsexuals

	Transvestites	Transsexuals
1 Lie	4	5
2 F	11	9
3 K*	11	14
4 Hypochondriasis	9	9
5 Depression	27	26
6 Hysteria	24	25
7 Psychopathic deviate	23	23
8 Masculinity-femininity*	36	40
9 Paranoia	13	12
10 Psychastenia	26	22
11 Schizophrenia	26	23
12 Mania	19	18
13 Social Introversion*	40	32

Note: *$p < .05$

TABLE 12.4
Mean 16 PF Scores for Transvestites and Transsexuals

	Transvestites	Transsexuals
1 Md**	5	8
2 Reserved/Outgoing	17	9
3 Less Intelligent/More Intelligent	5	4
4 Affected by Feelings/Emotionally Stable	5	6
5 Humble/Assertive	6	5
6 Sober/Happy-go-lucky	6	7
7 Expedient/Conscientious	8	8
8 Shy/Venturesome	4	6
9 Tough-minded/Tender-minded	8	8
10 Trusting/Suspicious	7	5
11 Practical/Imaginative	7	7
12 Forthright/Shrewd	6	5
13 Self-assured/Apprehensive	7	8
14 Conservative/Experimenting	6	7
15 Group-dependent/Self-sufficient	7	6
16 Undisciplined self conflict/Controlled	8	7
17 Relaxed/Tense	7	7

Note: **$p < .01$.

TABLE 12.5
Parent Child Relations Scales, Means and T Scores for Transvestites
and Transsexuals

| | | Mean | | % T Scores > 70 | |
		Transvestites	Transsexuals	Transvestites	Transsexuals
1. MAS		7	7	61	41
2. FAS		8	9	50	52
3. SAM		3	3	50	55
4. SAF		4	4	72	69
5. MAF	*	12	7	39	17
6. FAM		5	5	6	14
7. MC		14	15	28	41
8. FC		12	13	11	28
9. MAff		9	10	28	59
10. FAff		4	5	0	17
11. MStr		5	6	44	45
12. FStr		6	6	50	41
13. MId		4	4	28	41
14. FId		2	1	6	3
15. MInd		3	4	33	52
16. FInd		1	1	11	24

Note: *$p < .05$. The name of each scale can be constructed using the following key. M = Mother, F = Father, S = Respondant, A = Aggression, Aff = Affection, C = Competence, Id = Identification, Str = Strictness, Ind = Indulgence.

tial numbers who were depressed (approximately 55% both groups) and very feminine (78% transvestites and 97% transsexuals).

The MMPI two point codes were examined. The groups did not differ significantly in the distribution of code types. Twenty eight percent of the transvestites had no elevations over 70 (Mf excepted) and 22% had the 2-7/7-2 code (Depression-Psychasthenia). There were three or fewer cases for all other codes. There were 24% of the transsexuals without significant scale elevations and 14% had the 2-7/7-2 profiles. Seventeen percent had the 2-4/4-2 profile (Depression-Psychopathic Deviate) but no transvestite showed this. Depression was the most noteworthy feature in both groups. No transvestite or transsexual had the 4-8 or 4-9 "violent" profile.

The 16 PF (Table 12.4) was slightly more discriminating than the MMPI. Although only Md and Factor A were significant, 90% of cases were correctly assigned to their own groups. Again transsexuals were less open in responding to questions than tranvestites and they were more outgoing. Sten scores for the latter factors were also clinically significant with 25% of transvestites compared to no transsexuals showing extreme sten scores. Noteworthy in both groups was the high degree of "femininity" (Factor I, 67% and 76% for transsexuals and

transvestites respectively), guilt proneness (Factor 0, 58% and 53%) and in transvestites, suspiciousness (Factor L, 42% vs. 18% for transsexuals).

Parent Child Relations. There was only one group difference on the Clarke Parent Child Relations (PCR) questionnaire (Table 12.5) although discriminant analyses correctly classified 79% of the cases. Transvestites more than transsexuals reported that their mothers were aggressive to their fathers but no scale showed group differences in number of centile scores over 70. Nevertheless, both groups reported a considerable exchange of aggression among father, mother, and son and strictness on the part of both parents (Table 12.5). There was a noticeable trend to higher mother affection in the transsexual group over the transvestites and lower father affection in both groups. Although mother identification was average, father identification was low in both groups.

Criminal Record. The transsexuals had faced a total of 21 charges versus the transvestites' 10. They involved 23% of transsexuals and 20% of transvestites.[3] The charges were mainly property offenses (71% and 50% respectively). There were no violent or sex offenses for transsexuals but one transvestite had been convicted of threatening and two for sex offenses (indecent assault and indecent exposure). Transsexuals had one charge for prostitution and one for crossdressing in public. One transsexual and two transvestites had alcohol/drug charges. In general both groups were nonviolent but over a fifth had some criminal record.

DISCUSSION

The transvestites who came to our clinic were older than transsexuals but the two groups showed few clinical differences in personality. Transvestites tended to be more introverted, supporting Wilson and Gosselin's (1980) results. More transvestites married than transsexuals which may in part explain their delay in seeking our attention and/or surgery.

It is noteworthy that the transvestites not only masturbated in female attire but engaged in a range of other sexually anomalous behavior. This suggests that the characterization of transvestites as heterosexual fetishists may be too simplistic. Only extreme groups were examined here and borderline or mixed cases were excluded. The latter may show even more overlap of the sexual behavior clusters.

In Chapter 1 and Chapter 2 of this book, Langevin et al. found that sexually aggressive individuals who were charged with rape showed significant crossdressing behavior. We know that the act of donning women's attire can serve many purposes—pretending one is a woman because of gender identity; humiliating or embarrassing oneself as a masochistic act; pretending the female is

another person in one's control as a sadistic act; as a narcissistic act involving admiration by oneself or others; or fetishism, and possibly others. The relative contribution of each meaning of crossdressing needs to be evaluated in future work with both transvestites and transsexuals.

The act of crossdressing in the male has been assumed to reflect feminine longings and even feminine gender identity. Its association with violence, especially in sadomasochism, has not been stressed. However, the extensive courtship disordered behavior (exhibiting, peeping, frottage, and rape) in transvestites suggests that crossdressing may be multifaceted in nature and may go hand in hand with violent sexuality as noted in the first study in this book. One has to wonder if the transvestite derives similar pleasure from exposing and other sexual behaviors as he does from crossdressing. Future investigation of this question should be informative.

Aggression was not pronounced in the personality profiles of either group but it was noteworthy in parent child relations for both transvestites and transsexuals. This may be reflected in the sexually aggressive acts of some transvestites but it is not clearly related to transsexualism. Some theorists maintain that murder and suicide go hand in hand so that aggression may be readily directed outward to others or inward to the self. The association of sadomasochism with transsexualism has not been investigated extensively to date so this remains an open question. Certainly gender identity clinics need to look more closely at both the erotic profile and history of aggression in patients presenting as transvestites and transsexuals. The desperation of sex reassignment surgery applicants and their selective omission of material, noted by Levine (1980) may make this task difficult. The poor state of measurement in aggression research is also a problem. However, criminal record, family background, violence, or fighting are useful markers with which to start investigations.

ACKNOWLEDGMENT

The authors wish to thank S. Wilkinson and J. Schick for their assistance in data collection.

REFERENCES

Bentler, P. M. A typology of transsexualism: Gender identity theory and data. *Archives of Sexual Behavior*, 1976, *5*, 567–584.

Bentler, P. M., & Prince, C. Personality characteristics of male transvestites: III. *Journal of Abnormal Psychology*, 1969, *74*, 140–143.

Bentler, P. M., & Prince, C. Psychiatric symptomatology in transvestites. *Journal of Clinical Psychology*, 1970, *26*, 434–435.

Bentler, P. M., & Prince, C. Personality characteristics of male transvestites. *Journal of Clinical Psychology*, 1970, *26*, 287–291.

Berger, J. C., Green, R. Laub, D. R., Reynolds, E. L., Walker, P. A., & Wollman, L. *Standards of care: The hormonal and surgical sex reassignment of gender dysphoric persons.* Galveston, TX: Harry Benjamin International Gender Dysphoria Association, 1979.

Blanchard, R., McConkey, J. G., Roper, V., & Steiner, B. *Measuring physical aggressiveness in heterosexual, homosexual and transsexual males.* Gender Identity Clinic, Clarke Institute of Psychiatry, Toronto, Canada. Unpublished Manuscript, 1983.

Bowman, K. M., & Engle, B. Medicolegal aspects of transvestism. *American Journal of Psychiatry*, 1957, *113*, 583–588.

Buhrich, N. A heterosexual transvestite club: Psychiatric aspects *Australian and New Zealand Journal of Psychiatry*, 1976, *10*, 331–335.

Buhrich, N. Psychological adjustment in transvestism and transsexualism. *Behavior Research & Therapy*, 1981, *19*, 407–411.

Buhrich, N., & Beaumont, T. Comparison of transvestism in Australia and America, *Archives of Sexual Behavior*, 1981, *10*, 269–279.

Buhrich, N., & McConaghy, N. The discrete syndromes of transvestism and transsexualism. *Archives of Sexual Behavior*, 1977, *6*, 483–495.

Croughan, J. L., Sagher, M., Cohen, R., & Robins, E. A comparison of treated and untreated male cross-dressers. *Archives of Sexual Behavior*, 1981, *10*, 515–528.

Derogatis, L., Meyer, J., & Vazquez, N. A psychological profile of the transsexual. *Journal of Nervous & Mental Disease*, 1978, *166*, 234–254.

Dietz, P. E. *Kotzwarraism: Sexual induction of cerebral hypoxia.* Unpublished manuscript, Medical Criminology Research Centre, McLean Hospital, Belmont, Massachusetts, 1978.

Finney, J. C., Brandsma, J. M., Tondow, M., & Lemaistre, G. A study of transsexuals seeking gender reassignment. *American Journal of Psychiatry*, 1975, *132*, 962–964.

Freund, K., Langevin, R., Satterberg, J., & Steiner, B. Extension of the gender identity scale for males. *Archives of Sexual Behavior*, 1977, *6*, 507–519.

Freund, K., Langevin, R., Zajac, Y., Steiner, B., & Zajac, A. Parent-child relations in transsexual and non-transsexual homosexual males. *British Journal of Psychiatry*, 1974, *124*, 22–23.(a)

Freund, K., Langevin, R., Zajac, Y., Steiner, B., & Zajac, A. The transsexual syndrome in homosexual males. *Journal of Nervous & Mental Disease*, 1974, *158*, 145–153.(b)

Freund, K., Nagler, Z., Langevin, R., Zajac, A., & Steiner, B. Measuring feminine gender identity in homosexual males. *Archives of Sexual Behavior*, 1974, *3*, 249–260.

Freund, K., Steiner, B., & Chan, S. Two types of cross gender identity. *Archives of Sexual Behavior*, 1982, *11*, 49–63.

Gosselin, C. The influence of special sexual desires. In M. Cook (Ed.), *The bases of human sexual attraction.* New York: Academic Press, 1981.

Hoenig, J., Kenna, J., & Youd, A. A follow up of transsexualists: social and economic aspects. *Psychiatrica Clinica*, 1970, *3*, 85–100. (a)

Hoenig, J., Kenna, J., & Youd, A. Social and economic aspects of transsexualism. *British Journal of Psychiatry*, 1970, *117*, 163–172. (b)

Hucker, S. Personal communication, 1983.

Langevin, R. *Sexual strands: Understanding and treating sexual anomalies in men.* Hillsdale, NJ: Lawrence Erlbaum Associates, 1983.

Langevin, R., Paitich, D., & Steiner, B. The clinical profile of male transsexuals living as females vs. those living as males. *Archives of Sexual Behavior*, 1977, *6*, 143–154.

Langevin, R., Paitich, D., & Orchard, B. Diagnosis of killers seen for psychiatric assessment: a controlled study. *Acta Psychiatrica Scandanavica*, 1982, *66*, 216–228.

Leavitt, F., Berger, J., Hoeppner, J., & Northrop, G. Presurgical adjustment in male transsexuals

with and without hormonal treatment. *Journal of Nervous and Mental Disease*, 1980, *168*, 693–697.

Levine, S. B. Psychiatric diagnosis of patients requesting sex reassignment surgery. *Journal of Sex & Marital Therapy*, 1980, *6*, 164–173.

Litman, R. E., & Swearington, C. Bondage and suicide. *Archives of Psychiatry*, 1972, *27*, 80–85.

Lukianowicz, N. Survey of various aspects of transvestism in the light of our present knowledge. *Journal of Nervous & Mental Disease*, 1959, *128*, 36–64.

Meyer, J. K. Clinical variants among applicants for sex reassignment. *Archives of Sexual Behavior*, 1974, *3*, 527–558.

Milliken, A. D., Homicidal transsexuals: Three cases. *Canadian Journal of Psychiatry*, 1982, *27*, 43–46.

Newman, L., & Stoller, R. Nontranssexual men who seek sex reassignment. *American Journal of Psychiatry*, 1974, *131*, 437–441.

O'Gorman, E. C. A retrospective study of epidemiological and clinical aspects of 28 transsexual patients. *Archives of Sexual Behavior*, 1982, *11*, 231–236.

Paitich, D. A comprehensive automated psychological examination and report (CAPER). *Behavioral Science*, 1973, *18*, 131–136.

Paitich, D., & Langevin, R. The Clarke Parent Child Relations Questionnaire: A clinically useful test for adults. *Journal of Consulting and Clinical Psychology*, 1976, *44*, 428–436.

Paitich, D., Langevin, R., Freeman, R., Mann, K., & Handy, L. The Clarke SHQ: A clinical sex history questionnaire for males. *Archives of Sexual Behavior*, 1977, *6*, 421–435.

Parker, G., & Barr, R. Parental representations of transsexuals. *Archives of Sexual Behavior*, 1982, *11*, 221–230.

Parker, G., Tipling, H., & Brown, L. B. A parental bonding instrument. *British Journal of Medical Psychology*, 1979, *52*, 1–10.

Prince, V., & Bentler, P. M. Survey of 504 cases of transvestism. *Psychological Reports*, 1972, *31*, 903–917.

Rosen, R. C., & Kople, S. A. Penile plethysmography and biofeedback in the treatment of a transvestite-exhibitionist. *Journal of Consulting & Clinical Psychology*, 1977, *45*, 908–916.

Sorensen, T., & Hertoft, P. Male and female transsexualism: the Danish experience with 37 patients. *Archives of Sexual Behavior*, 1982, *11*, 133–155.

Stearns, A. W. Cases of probable suicide in young persons without obvious motivation. *Journal of the Maine Medical Association*, 1953, *44*, 16–23.

Steiner, B. W. (Ed.) *Transsexualism and gender identity*. Springfield, IL: C. Thomas Co., 1984.

Stoller, R. J. Male transsexualism: Uneasiness. *American Journal of Psychiatry*, 1973, *130*, 536–539.

Taylor, A., & McLachlan, D. Clinical and psychological observations on transvestism. *New Zealand Medical Journal*, 1962, *61*, 496–506.

Taylor, A., & McLachlan, D. Transvestism and psychosexual identification. *New Zealand Medical Journal*, 1964, *63*, 369–372.

Tsushima, W. T., & Wedding, D. MMPI results of male candidates for transsexual surgery. *Journal of Personality Assessment*, 1979, 43, 385–387.

Vogt, J. H. Five cases of transsexualism in females. *Acta Psychiatrica Scandanavica*, 1968,*44*, 62–88.

Walinder, J. *Transsexualism: A study of forty-three cases*. Copenhagen, Denmark: Scandanavian University Books, 1967.

Walsh, F. M., Stahl, C. J., Unger, H. T., Lilienstern, O. C., & Stephens, R. G. Autoerotic asphyxial deaths: A mediolegal analysis of forty-three cases. In C. H. Wecht (Ed.), *Legal medicine annual*. New York: Appleton-Century-Crofts, 1977.

Weitzman, E. L., Shamoian, C. A., & Golosow, N. Family dynamics in male transsexualism. *Psychosomatic Medicine*, 1971, *33*, 289–299.

Wilson, D., & Gosselin, C. Personality characteristics of fetishists, transvestites and sadomaso-
chists. *Personality and Individual Differences,* 1980, *1,* 289–295.
Wise, T. N., & Meyer, J. K. Transvestism: Previous findings and new areas for inquiry. *Journal of
Sex & Marital Therapy,* 1980, *6,* 116–128.

ENDNOTES

Note 1. See Walinder (1967) for a review of older studies that suggest that the risk of autocastration and suicide is high in transsexuals.

Note 2. The SPSS program Discriminant was used. Both direct and stepwise solutions were tried. The number of cases compared to the number of variables is clearly inadequate. However the procedures used are still the most conservative. The need for replication of the study is evident but the difficulty of obtaining suitable cases for investigation is a limiting factor.

Note 3. The difference was not significant. $\chi = 0.05$, df $= 1$, p$>.05$.

Summary, Conclusions, and Speculations

The studies in this book have provided a number of new findings that raise many questions about sexual anomalies. The results were novel in many cases, and it is interesting to speculate on their meaning.

SEXUAL AGGRESSION

Rapists were found to be a mixed group of men exhibiting combinations of aggressiveness, antisocial personality, and sexual anomalies. Chapter 1 showed that they were more like assaultive than sexually anomalous men. Many were sexually conventional in their choice of erotic stimulus and response, that is, they desired heterosexual intercourse with the adult female. The unusual feature was their tendency to *steal* sex. Contrary to the current belief of some writers, the rapists studied in Chapter 1 had more sexual experience than average and could be labelled "superheterosexuals." The sexual aggressives in Chapter 2 tended to have higher sex drive as well as sexual knowledge that was average or better. Chapter 3 showed, contrary to expectation, that most voyeurs were not violent or predisposed to rape. Predicting future violent behavior based on a past history of voyeurism alone was poor.

A surprising finding was the amount of orgasmic crossdressing carried out by rapists. This result was confirmed in Chapter 1 and Chapter 2 and appeared to reflect fetishism. Nonsadistic rapists as a group had somewhat higher penile arousal potential perhaps reflecting higher sex drive. Substance abuse was a prominent factor in both studies with alcohol being abused most.

Results of Chapter 4 suggested that alcohol does nothing to reduce sexual arousal *level* and in fact may *help* in instigating rape or other sexual acts.

The studies of Section 1A and Section 1B indicate that the following hypotheses need careful empirical examination:

1. Alcohol may increase sexual arousal to weak erotic stimuli.

2. Even large amounts of alcohol may not influence penile responsiveness in average drinkers.

3. Young, heavy, and tolerant drinkers may show increased sexual responsiveness when consuming large amounts of alcohol or at least they may show no change from their typical nonalcoholic condition.

4. Mood dysphoria especially aggressiveness, may be increased in the chronic abuser of alcohol.

5. Testosterone level may be increased in the young heavy drinker and it may exacerbate already heightened sexual needs.

6. Alcohol may aggrevate brain pathology, already associated with an aggressive sexual anomaly, to produce more aggression.

7. Finally, alcohol may set up an interaction of testosterone, other hormones, brain damage, and chronically high sexual arousal level in an already aggressive individual to increase the likelihood of further sexual aggression.

Chapter 5 showed that there was a general activation of the brain during sexual arousal but unfortunately it was not specific to the temporal lobe. Perhaps more powerful erotic stimuli will produce different results.

An erotic violence syndrome (EVS) was identified in Chapter 2. It was characterized by: (1) sexual arousal/climax to controlling, terrorizing, humiliating, injuring and/or destroying another person (sadism); (2) a history of rape and indecent assault; (3) feminine gender identity or gender ambivalence/indifference; (4) right temporal lobe brain abnormalities, both structural and functional; and in some cases (5) hormone abnormalities; (6) impotence or retarded ejaculation; and (7) some orgasmic crossdressing that occurred in non-EVS rapists as well.

The EVS cases tended to show less substance abuse and less of the wide ranging aggressive features seen by non-EVS rapists. If this finding is confirmed in a larger sample of cases, it suggests that the more dangerous rapists are harder to detect because they are similar to average men in the community. On the other hand the EVS presents clearer treatment goals because there may be a physically definable cause of the anomaly. The non-EVS rapist may be an oversexed antisocial person with a more limited prospect of treatment success.

PEDOPHILES

Pedophiles remain an enigma. We asked at the beginning of this volume why they took chances acting out sexually with children. The studies in Chapter 6 and Chapter 8 offered more reasons why they do *not* do it than positive explanations

for their behavior. They equate the child sexually in many ways with the adult; in body characteristics and desired responses. Moreover, pedophiles do not seem especially unassertive nor to have an aversion to the adult female. In fact, *the pedophile may be characterized by a failure to inhibit conventional albeit weaker sexual responses that the average man has toward children.* In other respects they are unremarkable.

Heterosexual, homosexual, and bisexual pedophiles were examined in Chapter 6. Altbough all groups showed some shyness they were not unassertive. In fact a minority were aggressive, particularly the heterosexual group. Some were interested in and expected adult sexual responses from children, that is, intercourse and oral genital outlets; suggesting that this group is not simply regressed or fixated at the "show and tell" exhibiting stage of childhood sexual development. Their satisfaction with adult females also indicates that their so called "inability to assert their masculinity" has been misconstrued. The child is serving some alternative needs, perhaps which the adult cannot provide.

Pedophilia is different from other sexual anomalies in two interesting ways. First, in some cases, the victim may be kin. A minor group of the incest offenders in Chapter 7 were pedophiles. The majority however appeared to be nonpedophiles. Second, one sees elderly sex offenders who predominantly violate children. Many other sexually anomalous men "burn out" as they age and lose their anomalous desires or, at least, keep them under control. Senile dementia did not appear to be a satisfactory explanation for the elderly sex offenders' behavior in Chapter 9. The reason for their pedophilia remains unknown. It is surprising that this interesting and incongruous elderly group has not been studied in greater depth.

HOMOSEXUALITY, TRANSVESTISM, AND TRANSSEXUALISM

The "effeminate" groups of sexual anomalies; homosexuals, transvestites and transsexuals, need to be reexamined. Homosexuals were found to be hormonally normal. Moreover they were masculine identified in general although some fewer were feminine identified. The trend to ambivalence/indifference of gender identity is noteworthy. Many homosexual men had above average intelligence and were aware of the incongruity of their social sex role and erotic preference. Some have described how the sex roles are "out there" separate from their self identities. Although heterosexuals can abstract sex roles from their individual identity, homosexuals are forced to do so because their erotic needs are incongruous with social conventions directed only at heterosexual relationships. It may be that gays are unable or unwilling to incorporate sex roles for reasons similar to those of other men with atypical sexual preferences. If gender is a social and arbitrary vehicle to express erotic needs, any gender dysphoria or

indifference may be secondary to the sexual anomaly. Homosexuals and perhaps sexually anomalous men in general do not desire the usual heterosexual outlet so typical gender patterns are not reinforced in their behavior. Rather, they are indifferent to them or only assimilate pieces of them. The presence of feminine gender identity in sadistic heterosexuals suggests that the association of non-violent homosexuality with femininity in general has been misleading.

An issue that needs clarification is the extent to which gender ambivalence or indifference reflects incoporation of both feminine *and* masculine gender identi-fication. In many cases our research participants "did not care" whether they played male or female roles. Was this because they greatly enjoyed and incorpo-rated both roles or because they identified with neither?

Transvestites who are presumably more feminine gender identified than the average heterosexual showed a surprising degree of involvement in the "mas-culine" courtship disorders of voyeurism, exhibiting, toucheurism, and even rape. So we come full cycle: some rapists crossdress and show femininity and some transvestites show aggressive sexual acting out.

REEXAMINING EROTIC PREFERENCE, GENDER IDENTITY, AND AGGRESSION

The studies in this volume have presented incongruous information. Aggressive sexual anomalies were associated with feminine gender identity or gender am-bivalence. Homosexual men were mainly masculine identified or ambivalent. Although femininity has been associated traditionally with passivity and nonag-gression, in our samples of men, the following hypthesis is suggested:

> *Feminine gender identity in "heterosexual" men may be associated with violence and sexual aggression.*

In some cases the violence may be directed inward, for example, as masochism shown by cases of transvestism and autoerotic asphyxia, noted in Chapter 12. It also may be directed outward as sadism and sexualized murder.

The results of Chapter 2 and those of Hoenig and Kenna (1979) suggest that an unusual brain condition may underlie many sex anomalies and gender distur-bances. A brain abnormality can be structural or functional. It may involve a gross lesion or a tumor that interferes with normal activity. These are unlikely in sexual and gender anomalies in general. However, brain damage may be subtle localized tissue atrophy, a biochemical imbalance, or a hypothetical "miswir-ing" of brain nerve connections. Consider the following information together:

1. Aggressive sexuality in the form of sadism and gender identity disturbance have been related to right temporal lobe brain abnormalities (Chapter 2).

2. Transsexualism, representing extreme gender dysphoria was associated with brain abnormalities, especially in the temporal lobes (Hoenig & Kenna, 1979).

3. Temporal lobe epilepsy has been associated with bizarre behavior but also in some cases with sexual anomalies and gender dysphoria (Blumer, 1970; Epstein, 1969; Kolarsky, Freund, Machek, & Polak, 1967).

This leads to the hypotheses that:

Sexually anomalous preferences may be associated with temporal lobe brain abnormalities, albeit in many cases, the abnormalities may be subtle.

The brain should be a major target for investigation of sexually anomalous behavior. There is an exciting new technology; EEG spectral analyses, CT scans, nuclear magnetic resonance (NMR) scans, and positron emission tomography (PET) scans that may provide fundamental insights into sexual behavior and its relation to structures and functions in the brain. There may be brain circuits that are crucial to the existence of "normal ertoic preference," that is, men are sexually aroused by adult females and desire sexual intercourse with them. If those circuits are disrupted by damage, miswiring, or biochemical imbalance, they may result in a sexual anomaly and perhaps other unusual behavior.

The temporal lobe and limbic system emerge as major foci for investigation. Pincus and Tucker (1978) have noted that the hippocampus, especially Ammon's horn, is particularly susceptible to reduced energy production caused by asphyxia, carbon monoxide poisoning, respiratory failure, and hypoglycemia. Thus, it is easily damaged, in part, by chance environmental events.

Stein, Rosen, and Butters (1974) and Finger, and Stein (1982) document exploratory studies aimed at understanding how, and if, the brain compensates for damage to its structures. Among the suggested mechanisms, is the sprouting of collateral afferent fibers that invade regions deprived of normal afferent flow because of damage elsewhere. Could this be the source of EVS fusion of aggression and sex? That is, could sex and aggression "centers" be miswired together as a result of damage to the temporal horn?

MacLean (1962) demonstrated that electrical stimulation of male monkeys' diencephalon produced erection but a mere millimeter away, stimulation produced anger, fear, and the showing of fangs. Although it has yet to be demonstrated that the mapping of monkeys' diencephalon brain cells is similar to humans', the potential for confusion of aggression and sexuality is apparent if cells must compensate for damaged ones nearby. One may hypothesize that since sex and aggression are frequently correlated in lower animals, and perhaps humans, an association of brain circuits eliciting aggression and sexual arousal is

to be expected. However, not everyone shows temporal horn abnormalities in the brain accompanied by preferential sexual arousal to sadistic stimuli. The nature of brain pathology in the temporal lobe and how it functions after recovering from the damage is unknown at present.

Possibly brain pathology or anomalies in the temporal area prevent incorporation of social roles in general.

> *Sexual anomalies may be linked to a general inability to incorporate social sex roles, including in some cases, social mores.*

Thus, some sexually anomalous men show not only gender dysphoria but an inability to be friends (some are loners or introverts), to hold down jobs, or maintain social mores (some are into crime, illicit drugs and alcohol or antisocial acts).

The other side of being unable to incorporate social and sex roles is that:

> *Sexually anomalous men in general tend to be egocentric.*

In the sexual context, at least, people are objects of erotic gratification. The ability of the exhibitionist, for example, to take on the role or feelings of others and to empathize with them is limited. He treats the female as a prop to his autoerotic act; she admires and he performs. The rapist does not care about the distress of his victim. As Barbaree, Marshall, and Lanthier (1979) pointed out, they enjoy themselves *in spite of* the females' discomfort. The fetishist and transvestite relate to things as if they were people. They are alternative props for an actor who needs no one else in his sexual acts. Some homosexuals can have five sex partners in one day perhaps because there are no social institutions to limit their behavior but maybe also because they see other men as little more than objects of erotic gratification.

Of greatest concern are sadistic murderers. One man interviewed for Chapter 2 had killed a woman and attempted to kill a second. In jail, it took over 5 hours to get clinical information because he described each offense in minute detail. He had previously spent similar lengths of time telling the police, tape recording, and telling his psychiatrist the same story. He derived great satisfaction from narrating the events. He even said he was having an erection in so doing. He laughed hysterically as he described killing her. When the examiner declined to hear about his second victim in the interests of finishing testing, he was insulted. He promptly finished the tests and refused even to say goodbye when he was returned to his cell. Other similar examples of extreme vanity or narcissism were evident in our sample and have been described by others. This phenomenon has had very little systematic investigation but it obviously merits closer attention. Such cases should serve as a warning to police and newspapers. These aggressive men thrive on publicity and attention. Too much attention may stimulate them to commit further offenses.

CONCLUSION

Many directions for research have been suggested by the studies in this book. Foremost, development of more and better measures of violence proneness are needed. The current state of aggression research is abysmal (Masters, 1981). Sex researchers should scrutinize every sexually anomalous man for violence. Criminal record and descriptions of offenses, preferably from the police, would add greatly to existing knowledge and assessments. The details of sexual acts need study. Violence is more common than we have been led to believe. It does not occur just in rapists. It does not appear to bear a particular relationship to voyeurism but it can occur in pedophiles and in men who manifest feminine gender identity in varying degrees. Investigators studying gender dysphoria ap-

TABLE 1
New Relationships of Erotic Preference, Gender Identity and
Aggression in Sexual Anomalies

Sex Anomaly	Erotic Preference		Gender Identity	Aggression
	Stimulus	Response		
Homosexual Androphiles	Adult Male	Mutual Pleasuring	Masculine undifferentiated	Average
Voyeurs	Mixed	Mixed	Mixed?	Some, but likely a chance relationship.
Pedophiles	Female Child	Adult Wide Range	Masculine?	Some, marked
—Heterosexual				
—Homosexual	Male Child	Adult Wide Range	Masculine?	Some
—Bisexual	Polymorphous	Polymorphous	Masculine?	Some, marked
Incest	Child/Adult	Adult Wide Range	Masculine?	Some, marked
Transsexual	Male+?	?	Ultra-feminine	Some, marked
Transvestite	Female/Self?	Masturbation crossdressed, courtship disorders +?	To a degree Feminine, ?	Some
Rapists, non-sadistic	Adult Female	Adult Wide Range	Masculine	Marked/Mixed
Sadistic Rapists—EVS	Adult Female	Controlling and terrorizing victim, injury	Feminine undifferentiated	Marked

parently have not routinely asked about violence either as a nonsexual interpersonal phenomenon or in the context of sadomasochistic acts. This oversight needs to be corrected to fully understand sexual anomalies.

Table 1 shows the groups outlined in the introduction. The information has been changed based on the studies in this book. The most noteworthy shift is in gender identity. Homosexuals are now masculine rather than feminine identified and a subgroup of rapists, the sadistic rapists, or EVS cases are feminine. Obviously replication studies in other settings are necessary before firm conclusions can be drawn. Results so discordant with expectations suggest that these groups be carefully reexamined. The measure of gender identity used, the FGI (Freund, Langevin, Satterberg, & Steiner, 1977) needs further development to sort out gender ambivalence from gender conviction. Both homosexual and sadistic groups can be considered ambivalent or indifferent to the gender axis of behavior. This raises doubts about the nature of treatment programs in which gender role behaviors are modified to "prevent later homosexuality or transsexualism." One has also to wonder how transvestites and transsexuals would score on the FGI scale using the revised method of Chapter 11. Further investigation of FGI, the brain, sex hormones, and erotic preference in a range of sexually anomalous men should be undertaken.

Many doors are closed by empirical research. This has been the major result of the studies in this book. Theories of anomalous sexuality have often been based on limited information. Our perception of unusual sexual behavior has been derived from a reflection on the needs of the average man. It often has been assumed that the pedophile, the homosexual, and so on, *really desire* to have intercourse with adult females but they cannot for psychological or other reasons. It has become increasingly clear that this model is ineffective. We must now examine what makes such men *qualitatively* different. The pedophile, the homosexual, and the rapist are not necessarily inadequate gynephiles. They are variants of human sexuality with their own unique features. Hopefully future research using this conceptualization will allow us to understand better their needs and problems so we can deal effectively with them clinically.

REFERENCES

Barbaree, H. E., Marshall, W. L., & Lanthier, R. D. Deviant sexual arousal in rapists. *Behavior Research & Therapy*, 1979, *17*, 215–222.

Blumer, D. Changes of sexual behavior related to temporal lobe disorders in man. *Journal of Sex Research*, 1970, *6*, 1173–1180.

Epstein, A. W. Fetishism: A comprehensive view. In J. Masserman (Ed.), *Dynamics of deviant sexuality*. New York: Grune & Stratton, 1969, 81–87.

Finger, S., & Stein, D. G. *Brain Damage and Recovery*, New York: Academic Press, 1982.

Freund, K., Langevin, R., Satterberg, J., & Steiner, B. Extension of the gender identity scale for males. *Archives of Sexual Behavior*, 1977, *6*, 507–519.

Hoenig, J., & Kenna, J. C. EEG abnormalities and transsexualism. *British Journal of Psychiatry,* 1979, *134,* 293–300.

Kolarsky, A., Freund, K., Machek, J., & Polak, O. Male sexual deviation: Association with early temporal lobe damage. *Archives of General Psychiatry,* 1967, *17,* 735–743.

MacLean, P. D. New findings relevant to the evolution of psychosexual functions of the brain. *Journal of Nervous & Mental Disease,* 1962, *135,* 289–301.

Masters, J. C. Developmental psychology. *Annual Review of Psychology,* 1981, *32,* 117–151.

Pincus, J. H., & Tucker, G. J. *Behavioral neurology.* New York: Oxford University Press, 1978.

Stein, D. G., Rosen, J. J., & Butters, N. (Eds.) *Plasticity and recovery of function in the central nervous system.* New York: Academic Press, 1974.

Appendix A
A New Version of the Clarke Sex History Questionnaire for Males

R. Langevin
L. Handy
D. Paitich
A. Russon
Clarke Institute of Psychiatry, Toronto

INTRODUCTION

In 1977 our research group published normative and validation information on a 225 item Sex History Questionnaire (hereafter old SHQ) for males that sampled a wide range of sexually anomalous behaviors as well as conventional heterosexual behaviors (Paitich, Langevin, Freeman, Mann, & Handy, 1977). Desire for, disgust for, and frequency of the behaviors were measured. The old SHQ is available in full in Langevin (1983). Although the old SHQ was sound psychometrically, some behaviors were not examined, and for some items the frequency of accompanying orgasm was not ascertained.

Paitich et al. reviewed existing sex history measures in 1977 and since that review, some new measures have been developed. (see Conte 1984 for a recent review). Bell, Weinberg, and Hammersmith, (1981) of the Kinsey Institute developed an extensive interview to study homosexual erotic preference. Their study was restricted to homosexuality and the 175 page interview requires training. Besides being very time consuming, it lacks general clinical application.

Derogatis (1978) reported the 260 item Derogatis Sexual Functioning Inventory (DSFI) that is primarily suited to studying sexual dysfunctions. Its scales are: Information, Experience, Drive, Attitudes, Symptoms, Gender Role, Fantasies, Body Image, and Satisfaction and two global indices: Sexual Functioning and Global Sexual Satisfaction. Only limited validation is available on the DSFI and it does not sample sexually anomalous behavior to any extent.[1]

287

Eysenck (1970) developed a Sexual Attitudes questionnaire containing 30 factors with eigenvalues greater than one. The factors were derived from 96 items subjected to principal components analysis and oblique promax rotation. Only 15 factors were used and Eysenck notes that even this may be too many. In fact, Whalley and McGuire (1978) reduced the 15 factors to nine measures: sexual satisfaction, heterosexual nervousness, sexual curiosity, tension, hostility, pruriency, sexual repression, heterosexual distaste, and sexual promiscuity. They have further validated the original questionnaire developed on normal men and women by using a sample of 135 alcoholics, sex offenders, and matched controls. Internal consistency and retest reliability were satisfactory for the measures. Although motivation, personality, sexual preferences, and behavior are mixed, the instrument may be valuable in understanding sexual behavior in general. The same may be said for the Mosher Forced Choice Guilt Inventory (Mosher, 1966; Mosher & Cross, 1971) which has sophisticated validation and includes a sex guilt scale.

Similarly Janda and O'Grady (1980) reported a 25 item Sex Anxiety Inventory with satisfactory psychometric properties but again it is restricted in understanding anomalous erotic preferences. Lo Piccolo and Steger (1974) developed a questionnaire to sample sexual dysfunction. Their Sexual Interaction Inventory assesses the respondent's perceptions of their own levels of sexual functioning and satisfaction. However, McCoy and D'Agostino (1977) found the reliability and validity of the instrument to be unsatisfactory.

Wilson and Lang (1981) developed a sexual fantasy questionnaire on a sample of 45 men and 45 women approached on the streets of London. The 40 item questionnaire was subjected to principal components analysis and oblique promax rotation. Four positively correlated factors emerged: exploration (group sex, promiscuity), intimacy (oral sex, passionate kissing), impersonality (sex with strangers, fetishism), and sadomasochism (whipping, being forced to have sex). The frequency of each set of behaviors was sufficiently high that one may wonder about the nature of the sample used. There was only a 30% return rate on the mailed in replies.

A MODEL FOR THE NEW SHQ

Langevin (1983) has described a model for studying sexual behavior that has been incorporated into the new SHQ. It involves both the concept of orgasmic preference and a stimulus-response matrix. In order to sort out behaviors and desires that are sexual curiosities from long lasting erotic preferences, the frequency of orgasm accompanying all behaviors should be ascertained. Those sexual behaviors that do not culminate in orgasm are often, but not always, less important in the individual's pattern of sexual behavior. Among the sexual

behaviors that do involve orgasm, some are preferred over others and it is these that are of greatest concern. In the 1977 SHQ report, about half of the cases were "multiple deviants" because they were not easily classified into the simpler anomalies. From our knowledge gained in using the old SHQ and employing the concept of orgasmic preference, the number of such cases has been substantially reduced.

Second, the pattern of all sexual behavior can be scrutinized in the stimulus response matrix. The stimulus is the object of erotic attraction, for example, adult females, physically immature boys, and so on, and the response is one's sexual behavior to the stimulus (e.g., intercourse or, exposing and masturbation,etc.). By using the matrix and comparing an individual's SHQ profile with the data of a large number of sexually anomalous men, we can see how prominent a particular sexual behavior is. Both the concept of orgasmic preference and the stimulus response matrix have been incorporated in the new SHQ. A more detailed discussion of the two concepts can be found in Langevin (1983).

A further important feature of sexual behavior was not directly sampled in the old SHQ, namely fantasies. In some cases, conscientious well socialized men with sex anomalies, desire to engage certain classes of stimulus people or to respond in certain ways but never or infrequently act out their impulses. For example, a married homosexual pedophile usually has sexual intercourse with his wife but desires most to have sex with a boy. He may only do the latter three or four times in his life. His sexual fantasy life may reveal a preoccupation with boys. Similarly some heterosexual pedophiles would like to have sexual intercourse with 8-to 10-year-old girls but the act is not physically possible so they settle for touching (cf. Forgione, 1976). In the new SHQ such fantasies were examined.

A number of findings have been reported on the old SHQ that indicate its value as a comprehensive instrument in examining sexually anomalous behavior. Many of the findings have been summarized in Langevin (1983) and elsewhere. For example:

1. Transsexual males who live as males were compared to those who live as females. The former showed a greater disgust than the latter for sexual interaction with men in spite of a desire for sex reassignment surgery (Langevin, Paitich, & Steiner, 1977). Both groups of trannsexuals used their penises frequently in sexual exchanges although they wanted them surgically removed.

2. Two studies on exhibitionists (Langevin, Paitich, Hucker, et al. 1979; Langevin, Paitich, Ramsey, et al., 1979) indicated that exhibitionists reacted most to physically mature females in spite of exposing to children and that they preferred more to be watched than to have intercourse, indicating a narcissistic preoccupation in their own sexuality. They were most likely to peep but did not engage especially in toucheurism, rape, or homosexual behavior. In therapy

outcome there were no differences in successful and unsuccessful candidates in terms of the frequency of exposing or the age of the victims nor in the incidence of erection and masturbation during the act of exposing.

3. In a study of rapists, aggressive nonsex offenders, nonviolent nonsex offenders, and nonviolent normal controls, the old SHQ showed that rapists had considerable sexual experience with physically mature women but they also had some sexual contact with adolescent females. An unexpected finding was the incidence of crossdressing in female clothes and with the new SHQ we know that many masturbate while so doing (see Chapter 1 and 2). These latter studies show the value of the new items added to the SHQ.

Some experimental results on the new SHQ have already been reported in this volume and elsewhere. The purpose of this report is to present normative data and validation results of the new SHQ. The reliability and validity measures used were similar to those of our 1977 report. The interested reader can examine the 1977 article for further statistical details.

In summary, our goals in developing the new SHQ were:

a. To have a broad spectrum instrument to sample sexually anomalous behaviors.
b. To sample orgasmic preference patterns.
c. To employ the Stimulus Response Matrix.
d. To sample behaviors missed in the old SHQ, including sexual dys-functions.
e. To sample sexual fantasies.
f. To improve research utility and statistical properties of scales, by using equal interval response categories.
g. To develop a simpler scoring method and computer program for the SHQ.
h. To use nonsex offender patient controls in the norms for a more practical control group in Forensic investigation.
i. To simplify the format of the questionnaire.

METHOD

Subjects

There were 219 men who came to the Forensic Service of the Clarke Institute either because of a sex offense or because they were troubled by their anomalous sexual behavior. A group of 50 nonsex offenders from the same service were also used. Charges ranged from theft to assault. The psychiatric and criminal history of the latter group was scrutinized as some validation that they had no sexual anomalies. Finally, a group of 22 community volunteers were paid for their

participation in answering questionnaires. They had no history of mental illness, crime, or sexual anomaly. In total there were 291 cases.

The subject groups were:

Erotic Preference/Offense	Number of Cases
Heterosexual Pedophilia	14
Homosexual Pedophilia	23
Exhibitionism	51
Androphilia (Homosexuality)	33
Incest	17
Rape	24
Miscellany	57
Community Controls	22
Offender Controls	50
Total	291

They were grouped on the basis of an erotic preference diagnosis (described in the introduction) for female children, male children, and so on. Incest and rape were offense categories rather than erotic preferences. These two groups contain some pedophiles and sadists but mostly sexually normal men. Their offense is of great concern to clinicians so they were included by offense. The miscellaneous group includes five subgroups that were too small alone for statistical analysis. It is noteworthy that only 20% were multiple anomalies compared to 50% for the old SHQ. Community and offender controls were sexually normal men but the latter offer a better comparison group to the sexually anomalous men. All patient groups in large part had criminal records and were referred to the same forensic service for a psychiatric assessment in reference to their charges.

There were group differences in age, education, marital status, and verbal IQ but not performance IQ (Table A.1). Statistical effects were weak and there was considerable overlap of the mean scores for all variables. Rapists and community controls were youngest, incest offenders and homosexual pedophiles oldest. Community controls and androphiles had the most education and incest offenders and rapists had least. These differences were reflected in VIQ scores. All incest offenders were married as expected while androphiles married least.

Materials and Procedure

All cases were administered the new SHQ and most had also the MMPI, Raven Standard Progressive Matrices, and a vocabulary test (Paitich, 1973). The latter two offered estimates of IQ and the MMPI, L, and K scales were measures of test taking attitude. Collectively they were used to examine the discriminant validity of the new SHQ items and scales from intelligence, naive lying, and social desirability response set.

TABLE A.1
Age, Education, Marital Status and IQ of Study Groups

| | Mean/% | | | | |
	Age ****	Education ***	% Univ./Comm. College ****	% Married Ever ****	VIQ **
Heterosexual pedophile	32	11	31	46	107
Homosexual Pedophile	36	10	29	27	108
Exhibitionist	28	11	25	55	105
Androphile	34	12	48	9	111
Incest	35	9	0	100	106
Rape	23	10	0	33	102
Miscellaneous	31	10	15	53	105
Community Control	24	12	94	36	112
Offender Control	29	10	14	46	102
Total	30	11	25	44	106

Note: **p < 01, ***p < 001, ****p < 0001.

The new SHQ consisted of 417 items that included the old SHQ items with minor changes. Questions on marital fidelity were dropped. Desire, disgust, and frequency items were sorted and answered separately. An additional 21 items asked whether orgasm accompanied the behaviors in question. There were 66 fantasy items. Finally, 67 items were included in an attempt to have *Ss* rank erotic preferences themselves.

The items have been arranged so that frequency, desire for, and disgust for each stimulus response category were answered separately. If the respondent had no sexual experience with such behaviors, he could skip to the next section. Thus administration time has been shortened.

The frequencies of behaviors have been changed to be equal intervals, thus:

(a) none or never, (b) only one, (c) 2–5
(d) 6–10, (e) 11–15, (f) 16–20
(g) 21–25, (h) 26–30, (i) 31–35, (j) 36 or more

One can collapse (b) and (c) and consider the eight intervals equal. The scales have also been dichotomized in the computer program as alternative (a) vs. (b) to (j). Finally, some behaviors that are infrequent have been included because our knowledge of them is very limited: sexual arousal by beating, hurting, humiliating, threatening, frightening, or embarrassing someone or having it done to you, seeing someone unconscious or unable to move or dead, incest with mother, father, daughter, or son, group sex, fire, and exposing to other males.

RESULTS

Discriminant Validity from Intelligence, Naive Lying, and Social Desirability

A test is useful if its items sample behaviors of interest, in this case, sexual history, and if it is not confounded by measures such as the setting from which the data was drawn or lying. Since prison-hospital samples such as ours often contain individuals who are less educated than the average person and who may want to hide their history, it is important to know that the questionnaire items do not correlate with education or intelligence nor with lying or responding in a way to make oneself look especially good or bad. It is still possible that respondents lied and we were unable to detect it. We attempted to avoid the problem by using only men who admitted their sexually anomalous behavior. This however is still a limitation of the SHQ and nonadmitters can provide invalid information, as noted in the introduction. The offenders may have lied only about their sexual behavior but not about other matters so the MMPI might not detect it.[2]

Of the 417 items, 67 were dropped immediately. They asked the patient to rank preferred behaviors. For whatever reasons they were confused by the task so the items were of no value. The number of significant correlations over .20, .30 and .40 between the remaining SHQ items and confounding discriminant variables are reported in Table A.2. From this many correlations, 17 are expected by chance at the p<.05 level and three at the p<.01 level. Results show that the numbers in most cases are close to expectation. Moreover, most correlations are

TABLE A.2
Number of Noteworthy Correlations of SHO *Items*
With Confounding Variables

	# *Correlations*			
	Over .20	*Over .30*	*Over .40*	*Total*
Age	7	0	0	7
Education	16	7	0	23
Advanced Education	10	2	0	12
Verbal IQ	21	5	1	27
Performance IQ	39	15	3	57
Marital Status	43	4	1	48
MMPI Lie	15	3	0	18
MMPI K	10	0	0	10

Note: Advanced education compares those men with some university or post high school education versus those without. Marital status compares single men versus those ever married. By chance 17 correlations are expected to be significant at p < 05, 3 at p < 01.

of low order, that is, less than .30 or sharing only 9% of their variance with the SHQ items.[3]

Age showed one positive correlation to frequency of intercourse with the same female (0.20), three to contact with females 12 or younger (0.22 to 0.28), one to masturbation fantasies of girls 16–20 (−0.24), to lack of disgust for such females (0.24), and one to disgust for anal intercourse (0.25).

Twenty five of the 35 correlations for education, including advanced education, related to homosexual outlets (three for actual contacts and the rest for desire, disgust, or fantasies). This reflects the fact that the androphiles in our sample tended to be brighter and perhaps are more intelligent as a rule (cf. Langevin, 1983; Weinrich, 1978). Seven Exhibiting Behavior items also related positively to education so that the more educated the male, the more likely he would masturbate while exposed and show the full pattern of exhibitionism. The remaining three items were fantasies of anal intercourse (0.21), humiliation by a female (−.21), and disgust of a female frightening you (0.27).

TABLE A.3
Reliabilities of New SHQ Scales

Items	Dichotomized	Full Scale	# Items
Heterosexual adult frequency	0.93	0.94	20
Heterosexual pedophilic frequency	0.96	0.93	23
Heterosexual hebephilic frequency	0.97	0.93	23
Androphilic frequency	0.98	0.97	13
Homosexual pedophilic frequency	0.94	0.92	13
Homosexual ephebephilic frequency	0.96	0.97	13
Crossdressing	0.86	0.96	12
Voyeurism	0.77	0.84	6
Obscene calls	0.82	0.81	2
Toucheurism and frottage	0.74	0.91	6
Rape	0.91	0.94	2
Sadism and masochism	0.91	0.95	13
Incest	−0.01	−0.02	4
Group sex	0.93	0.97	2
Fire	−0.01	−0.01	2
Exhibition frequency	0.90	0.88	5
Exhibitionistic behavior	0.87	0.88	11
Fantasies of Stimulus Persons	0.42	0.42	9
Desire for stimulus persons	0.42	0.43	9
Disgust for stimulus persons	0.81	0.81	9
Fantasies of sex responses to males	0.89	0.89	23
Fantasies of sex responses to females	0.92	0.92	27
Desire for sex responses to males	0.91	0.91	23
Disgust for sex responses to males	0.97	0.97	23
Desire for sex responses to females	0.91	0.91	27
Disgust for sex responses to females	0.92	0.92	27

Intelligence scores reflected the same pattern of results as education but with greater sensitivity. Homosexual items, including disgust for deviant acts such as sadomasochism involved 21 of the 27 VIQ correlations and 28 of the 57 PIQ correlations. Only four of the 27 VIQ and six of the 57 PIQ results involved actual behavior. Rather, desire, disgust, or fantasies were involved.

Marital status related in an obvious way to experience. Married men had more sexual experience with adult females than single men and they had fewer homosexual desires and fantasies.

The MMPI validity scales L (Lie) and K (highly correlated with social desirability response set) were unrelated to frequency of any behaviors except K correlated -0.20 with frottage. The remaining scores involved heterosexual desires and fantasies, predominantly normal ones.

In general, the items appear to have satisfactory discriminant validity from the undesirable sources of confounding variance, namely education, age, intelligence, lying, and social desirability, at least as measured by the MMPI. The same was true of the SHQ scales. Only three scales showed any correlation above .30. Experience with adult females correlated .33 with advanced education; MMPI Lie scores correlated $-.30$ with fantasies of sexual responses to females; and PIQ correlated .38 with desire for sexual responses to females. There were no correlations even above .20 for education or marital status, and 15 over 0.20 for the remaining measures in Table 12.1 of 192 possible significant correlations (10 expected by chance at $p < .05$). The scales may therefore be considered free of substantial bias by the confounding variables.

Reliability of SHQ Scales

The internal consistency of each SHQ scale was examined in two ways: using full scale scores and dichotomous scores.[4] Both methods produced comparable results in general and they will be discussed collectively. Most scales had satisfactory internal reliability (Table A.3) but "Incest" items and "Fire" items did not form scales. It has been maintained that incest tends to be carried on from one generation to the next but this was not supported in the present sample. In addition, too few men experienced sexual excitement to fire to be able to produce a scale. The incest and fire items will be retained however as useful *items* of information on the SHQ.

Fantasies of Stimulus Persons (adult female, male child, etc.) and desire for these persons did not form satisfactory scales although the corresponding response measures did. It seems that erotic preference for age-sex categories of persons is discrete and these *items* will be retained for their information value but they will not be used as scales. Fantasies of Sex Responses clustered conventional and sexually anomalous behaviors suggesting that a wide range of behaviors are fantasized by normal men or the scale reflects a general tendency to fantasize (versus not to fantasize). Wilson and Lang's (1981) results were similar

for their sexual fantasy questionnaire developed on community volunteers. They derived four factors using factor analysis with oblique rotation but they noted that a single factor underlaid the four. One implication of the finding is that fantasy of sex responses may not be especially useful in separating sexually anomalous and normal men. However, stimulus persons chosen for fantasies tend to be discrete.

Group Differences

After the initial screening, each of the 350 SHQ items left was examined for its discrimination of the various anomalous groups and controls.[5] Of the individual dichotomized items, 86 of the 350 were nonsignificant but 50 items were kept nonetheless because they involved rare behavior or fantasies of rare behavior such as sadomasochism. Some orgasmic items were nonsignificant such as crossdressing, frottage and this was due to the lack of appropriate cases in the sample to test the scales, that is, transvestites and transsexuals. Once again, the items were kept because, many items were similar to old SHQ scales which, containing appropriate groups, did discriminate as expected. Further samples may show significant results. The majority of items discriminated in the expected way or showed expected trends and were kept for the scale analysis.

Scale means and standard deviations (SD) for each group are presented in Table A.4. Each group will be discussed in turn.

Heterosexual Pedophiles sexually acted out most with immature females but they also showed average to above average experience with adult females. They had no experience with male minors, as expected, because of selection criteria. However, they had somewhat more experience with adult men than controls did but not more than average for the total sample. This group of pedophiles showed a lower incidence of exhibitionism than some of our previous samples. Those who did expose showed the pattern of Exhibiting Behavior characteristic of exhibitionists who engage adult female victims.

Homosexual Pedophiles showed the greatest frequency of sexually acting out with immature males. They were second only to androphiles in sexually acting out with adult males. Along with the androphiles, they had the least experience of any group in the sample with females of all ages. Like the heterosexual pedophiles, they showed a trend to exhibiting behavior characteristic of exhibitionists. As expected, their fantasies involved males more than other groups did.

Exhibitionists of course showed the highest scores of any group on Exhibiting Frequency and Exhibiting Behavior. They did not differ from controls on any other scale. Exhibitionists in some cases exposed to children, but they did not touch their victims. Their preference was for adult females. Surprisingly, voyeurism was not pronounced, although exhibitionists scored highest among the groups on this scale, and on toucheurism and frottage.

The *Incest* group showed only a greater incidence of sexually acting out with physically immature females. As noted in Chapter 7, they are a mixed group of pedophiles and sexually normal men. There were no other outstanding features.

TABLE A.4
Group Means and Standard Deviations for SHQ Scales

Items	P	Heterosexual Pedophiles Mean	SD	Homosexual Pedophiles Mean	SD	Exhibitionists Mean	SD
Heterosexual adult frequency	****	16.21[c]	3.76	10.22[ab]	5.75	15.18[c]	4.18
Heterosexual pedophilic frequency	****	5.71[ab]	6.03	1.56	3.50	2.41	5.21
Heterosexual hebephilic frequency	****	7.71[a]	7.13	1.00[b]	3.64	2.43[b]	5.91
Androphilic frequency	****	1.29[cd]	3.36	4.65[b]	4.90	1.33[cd]	2.81
Homosexual pedophilic frequency	****	0.00	0.00	4.74[a]	3.77	0.06	0.42
Homosexual ephebephilic frequency	****	0.00	0.00	3.30[a]	4.27	0.23	0.97
Crossdressing	*	0.36	0.84	0.09	0.29	1.02	1.77
Voyeurism	****	1.00[abc]	1.36	0.48[c]	1.04	1.63[ab]	1.75
Obscene calls	*	0.29	0.73	0.00	0.00	0.27	0.63
Toucheurism and frottage	****	0.36[ab]	0.74	0.04[b]	0.21	1.06[a]	1.35
Rape	***	0.14	0.53	0.00	0.00	0.10	0.41
Sadism & Masochism	****	0.21	0.80	0.61	2.13	0.43	1.46
Group Sex	****	0.64	0.93	0.52	0.85	0.31	0.68
Exhibition Frequency	****	0.79[bc]	1.67	0.04[c]	0.21	3.37[a]	1.45
Exhibitionistic Behaviour	****	6.57[bc]	8.35	3.60[c]	5.16	15.25[a]	5.66
Disgust for stimulus persons		13.57	4.54	14.56	2.41	13.69	4.78
Fantasies of sex responses to males	****	21.71[bc]	6.39	26.30[b]	3.14	22.67[bc]	6.30
Fantasies of sex responses to females	***	36.21[ab]	11.60	32.69[ab]	3.91	36.88[b]	8.95
Desire for sex responses to males	****	3.57	9.11	19.48[b]	13.39	6.82	11.92
Disgust for sex responses to males	****	4.93	13.31	28.13[a]	19.55	10.06	17.88
Desire for sex responses to females	****	35.57[bc]	10.90	26.30[b]	14.77	36.37[c]	11.45
Disgust for sex responses to females	****	40.21	12.21	36.17	20.06	38.69	12.26

(continued)

TABLE A.4 (Continued)

Items	Incest		Rape		Miscellaneous		Androphiles	
	Mean	SD	Mean	SD	Mean	SD	Mean	SD
Heterosexual adult frequency	16.21c	2.94	12.21bc	6.57	14.16c	4.93	8.24a	6.02
Heterosexual pedophilic frequency	7.35a	5.24	0.62	2.46	4.39b	6.87	0.00	0.00
Heterosexual hebephilic frequency	7.41a	7.56	3.37ab	6.34	3.67ab	6.77	0.06b	0.24
Androphilic frequency	0.82cd	2.35	0.67cd	2.28	2.75c	4.71	11.67a	2.76
Homosexual pedophilic frequency	0.00	0.00	0.00	0.00	1.19	3.07	0.27	1.15
Homosexual ephebephilic frequency	0.00	0.00	0.17	0.82	0.81	2.73	1.24	3.50
Crossdressing	0.47	0.72	1.50	2.87	1.47	2.66	1.48	2.66
Voyeurism	0.35c	0.61	1.33abc	1.76	1.82a	1.83	0.33c	0.85
Obscene calls	0.00	0.00	0.12	0.45	0.26	0.64	0.00	0.00
Toucheurism and frottage	0.00b	0.00	0.79ab	1.25	0.89ab	1.55	0.09b	0.38
Rape	0.00	0.00	0.46a	0.78	0.12	0.47	0.00	0.00
Sadism & Masochism	0.12	0.33	1.00	3.05	0.56	1.97	0.85	2.12
Group Sex	0.41	0.79	0.25	0.68	0.39	0.73	1.21a	0.93
Exhibition Frequency	0.00c	0.00	0.42c	1.06	1.16b	1.66	0.00c	0.00
Exhibitionistic Behaviour	1.35c	2.50	4.71bc	6.68	8.07b	8.32	0.94c	3.30
Disgust for stimulus persons	15.65	1.90	14.04	3.01	14.46	3.28	13.33	3.12
Fantasies of sex responses to males	23.41bc	1.28	23.71bc	2.51	24.17bc	5.89	30.85a	3.52
Fantasies of sex resp. to females	33.88ab	3.98	35.87ab	5.50	35.98ab	7.91	29.30a	4.15
Desire for sex responses to males	3.06	8.70	7.08	11.29	9.44	13.04	29.76a	6.43
Disgust for sex responses to males	3.94	11.73	12.08	18.51	15.14	19.42	36.85a	4.68
Desire for sex responses to females	34.35bc	3.79	34.79bc	9.02	34.10bc	11.77	10.09a	15.72
Disgust for sex resp. to females	45.18	6.98	40.37	10.43	39.16	13.16	14.58a	22.60

Items	Non-Sex Offenders		Community Volunteers		Total	
	Mean	SD	Mean	SD	Mean	SD
Heterosexual adult frequency	15.80[c]	3.71	15.14[c]	4.99	13.75	5.42
Heterosexual pedophilic frequency	0.48	1.92	0.09	0.43	2.25	4.87
Heterosexual hebephilic frequency	1.78[b]	5.01	0.00[b]	0.00	2.62	5.76
Androphilic frequency	0.38[d]	1.59	0.18[d]	0.85	2.71	4.67
Homosexual pedophilic frequency	0.24	1.56	0.00	0.00	0.69	2.26
Homosexual ephebephilic frequency	0.00	0.00	0.00	0.00	0.61	2.28
Crossdressing	0.48	1.31	0.77	1.11	0.95	2.00
Voyeurism	0.90[bc]	1.42	0.50[c]	0.74	1.09	1.55
Obscene calls	0.08	0.34	0.04	0.21	0.14	0.47
Toucheurism and frottage	0.54[ab]	1.07	0.41[ab]	0.73	0.58	1.15
Rape	0.04	0.28	0.04	0.21	0.10	0.40
Sadism & Masochism	0.20	0.57	0.00	0.00	0.46	1.69
Group Sex	0.44	0.81	0.27	0.70	0.48	0.81
Exhibition Frequency	0.04[c]	0.28	0.00[c]	0.00	0.90	1.62
Exhibitionistic Behaviour	3.40[c]	5.28	0.59[c]	2.13	6.06	7.63
Disgust for stimulus persons	13.24	4.83	14.73	1.98	14.01	3.75
Fantasies of sex responses to males	21.56[c]	6.62	23.23[bc]	1.11	24.11	5.74
Fantasies of sex responses to females	33.88[ab]	10.00	38.00[b]	5.26	34.69	7.96
Desire for sex responses to males	5.52	10.71	2.32	7.54	10.02	13.56
Disgust for sex responses to males	8.34	15.97	6.04	15.58	14.48	19.01
Desire for sex responses to females	33.24[bc]	10.83	38.82[c]	5.03	31.51	13.93
Disgust for sex responses to females	37.82	13.03	41.23	3.75	36.48	16.10

Note: *p < .05; ***p < .001; ****p < .0001. Means with the same superscript are not significantly different.

TABLE A.5
Intercorrelation of SHQ Scales

Items	1	2	3	4	5	6	7	8	9	10	11
Heterosexual adult frequency											
Heterosexual pedophilic frequency	11										
Heterosexual hebephilic frequency	18	47									
Androphilic frequency	−27	−04	−05								
Homosexual pedophilic frequency	−13	29	14	20							
Homosexual ephebephilic frequency	−07	09	10	37	54						
Crossdressing	−05	12	14	21	02	06					
Voyeurism	16	13	12	−04	04	−00	26				
Obscene calls	08	06	09	02	−00	03	21	36			
Toucheurism and frottage	05	15	21	02	02	09	44	42	46		
Rape	01	11	22	04	09	08	27	26	22	39	
Sadism and masochism	−16	14	13	28	21	26	22	22	22	28	39
Group sex	04	04	13	39	01	15	06	12	05	07	−01
Exhibition frequency	16	08	06	−11	−08	−03	19	35	24	38	01
Exhibitionistic behavior	12	08	05	−15	−01	−04	15	28	30	30	03
Disgust for stimulus persons	05	02	00	−07	−07	−14	−02	−06	04	−03	06
Fantasies of sex responses to males	−26	−07	−02	50	13	23	15	−04	−03	−00	01
Fantasies of sex responses to females	20	07	14	−17	−02	−07	07	23	18	20	14
Desire for sex responses to males	−38	−01	−08	64	23	33	15	−05	−06	01	00
Disgust for sex responses to males	−31	−03	−12	54	20	23	21	−02	−04	07	05
Desire for sex responses to females	37	10	15	−46	−06	−17	05	27	18	23	13
Disgust for sex responses to females	35	07	10	−42	−01	−15	−02	14	08	07	08

Items	12	13	14	15	16	17	18	19	20	21
Group sex	08									
Exhibition frequency	04	-06								
Exhibitionistic behavior	08	-10	79							
Disgust for stimulus persons	-04	-05	03	-00						
Fantasies of sex responses to males	20	22	-05	-12	21					
Fantasies of sex responses to females	-01	-10	25	25	47	27				
Desire for sex responses to males	24	24	-10	-03	-07	48	-11			
Disgust for sex responses to males	15	19	-07	00	01	35	-09	89		
Desire for sex responses to females	-11	-16	27	26	29	-18	59	-37	-25	
Disgust for sex responses to females	-15	-17	12	14	35	-16	42	-32	-22	87

301

TABLE A.6
Factor Analysis of SHQ Scales

Scale	Communality	Varimax Rotated Factor			
		Homosexual Versus Heterosexual	Courtship Disorders	Heterosexual Desire	Polymorphous Sexuality
Heterosexual adult frequency	23	−40	10	22	10
Heterosexual pedophilic frequency	20	−06	06	04	44
Heterosexual hebephilic frequency	28	−11	05	08	51
Androphilic frequency	62	74	−04	−23	12
Homosexual pedophilic frequency	21	25	−09	−02	36
Homosexual ephebephilic frequency	26	37	−05	−12	34
Crossdressing	24	21	34	−00	29
Voyeurism	34	−05	48	09	31
Obscene calls	26	−02	44	06	26
Toucheurism and frottage	52	04	57	04	43
Rape	26	05	18	07	47
Sadism and masochism	31	28	18	−11	44
Group sex	10	27	−01	−10	15
Exhibition frequency	67	−10	80	09	−11
Exhibitionistic behavior	62	−08	77	09	−11
Disgust for stimulus persons	31	06	−05	55	−07
Fantasies of sex responses to males	43	63	−05	18	02
Fantasies of sex responses to females	56	−00	23	71	08
Desire for sex responses to males	83	91	02	−09	−03
Disgust for sex responses to males	61	−77	06	−02	−04
Desire for sex responses to females	85	−38	23	79	14
Disgust for sex responses to females	66	−34	05	73	08
Unrotated Factor Eigenvalues		3.92	2.86	1.43	1.18
% Total Variance		18	13	6	5

Note: There may be slight discrepancies in communality versus sum of square factor loadings due to rounding.

Rapists were outstanding for higher incidences of rape, as expected, but also for voyeurism and crossdressing (cf. Chapter 1 and 2 for a discussion of these factors). Overall, they showed less sexual experience than the group of rapists reported in Chapter 1 did although it was comparable to the experience of community controls. There were no other outstanding features.

Androphiles showed less experience with adult females and more with adult males than controls, as expected. They also scored highest of all groups in experiencing group sex. Their erotic desires and fantasies reflected their behavior patterns.

Overall, group differences reflected previous research findings and the results suggest that the scales are useful clinically.

Scale Intercorrelations and Factor Analysis

The intercorrelation of the 22 scales are presented in Table A.5. They are low order correlations with 85% below .30 indicating that the scales are in general uncorrelated. In part, these low correlations may be due to the sample used or to the discrete criterion used to identify sexually anomalous groups. The factor analysis is presented in Table A.6. Four factors with eigenvalues greater than one emerged. All were weak factors as indicated from the correlation matrix suggesting that sexual behaviors tend to be discrete outlets. The factors were tentatively labelled: (1) homosexual versus heterosexual outlet; (2) courtship disorders (after Freund), (3) heterosexual desire; and (4) polymorphous sexuality. The first factor indicates that homosexual outlet, fantasy, and desire are polar opposites to heterosexual outlet, fantasy, and desire. The second clusters exhibitionism, voyeurism, and toucheurism, as indicated by Freund, Scher, and Hucker (1983) and discussed throughout the book. Rape did not load on this factor substantially but obscene calls did. Noteworthy is the weak but positive association of crossdressing with the cluster. The third factor is one representing heterosexual fantasy and desire and it is weak. The fourth residual factor explaining 5% of the total variance is a mixture of scales. It included heterosexual pedophilia and hebephilia, homosexual pedophilia and ephebephilia, voyeurism, toucheurism-frottage, rape, sadomasochism and to lesser degrees, crossdressing, and obscene calls.

DISCUSSION

The new SHQ is an improvement over the old SHQ but not as much as we had hoped. In part, this is due to the sample used which lacked pertinent cases, for example, transsexuals, sadomasochists, and so on. However, items on orgasmic erotic behavior have been useful. They offer a clear reference point for evaluating sexual anomalies that otherwise might be quite confusing (cf. Langevin,

1983 for a discussion of this problem). The group discriminations based on the scales are satisfactory and they should be valuable in future research efforts. However, items on ranking of erotic preferences were confusing and this task must still be done in a diagnostic interview. Fantasy items generally reflect desire items but little more. The fantasy and desire items have been left out of the version of the SHQ in Appendix B and they appear in Appendix C for the interested researcher. Experimental items on sexual dysfunction have been written into the SHQ but they should be treated with caution. Many men think they are sexually dysfunctional on questionnaires (e.g. premature ejaculators) but detailed examination in an interview shows this not to be the case.

In spite of its shortcomings, the SHQ remains the only comprehensive self-administered questionnaire that assesses sexual anomalies. It is reliable and has substantial discriminant validity. We have found it valuable as a clinical aid and in our research. The new 186 item version of the SHQ follows in Appendix B along with computer scoring.

REFERENCES

Bell, A. P., Weinberg, M. S., & Hammersmith, S. K. *Sexual preference: Its development in men and women.* Bloomington, IN: Indiana University Press, 1981.

Conte, H. R. Development and use of self-report techniques for assessing sexual functioning: a review and critique. *Archives of Sexual Behavior,* 1984, *12,* 555–576.

Derogatis, L. *The Derogatis sexual Functioning Inventory,* (DSFI). Leonard R. Derogatis, 1228 Wine SpringLane, Baltimore, MD., 21204, 1978.

Eysenck, H. J. Personality and attitudes to sex: A factorial study. *Personality,* 1970, *1,* 355–376.

Forgione, A. G. The use of mannequins in the behavioral assessment of child molesters: Two case reports. *Behavior Therapy,* 1976, *7,* 678–685.

Freund, K., Scher, H., & Hucker, S. The courtship disorders. *Archives of Sexual Behavior,* 1983, *12,* 369–379.

Janda, L. H., & O'Grady, K. E. Development of a sex anxiety inventory. *Journal of Consulting and Clinical Psychology,* 1980, *48,* 169–175.

Langevin, R. *Sexual strands: Understanding and treating sexual anomalies in men.* Hillsdale, NJ: Lawrence Erlbaum Associates, 1983.

Langevin, R., Paitich, D., & Steiner, B. W. The clinical profile of male transsexuals living as females versus those living as males. *Archives of Sexual Behavior,* 1977, *6,* 143–154.

Langevin, R., Paitich, D., Hucker, S., Newman, S., Ramsay, G., Pope, S., Geller, G., & Anderson, C. The effect of assertiveness training, provera and sex of therapist in the treatment of genital exhibitionism. *Journal of Behavior Therapy & Experimential Psychiatry,* 1979, *10,* 275–282.

Langevin, R., Paitich, D., Ramsay, G., Anderson, C., Kamrad, J., Pope, S., Geller, G., Pearl, L., & Newman, S. Experimental studies of the etiology of genital exhibitionism. *Archives of Sexual Behavior.* 1979, *8,* 307–331.

Lo Piccolo, J., & Steger, J. The sexual interaction inventory: A new instrument for assessment of sexual dysfunction. *Archives of Sexual Behavior,* 1974, *3,* 585–595.

McCoy, N. N., & D'Agostino, P. A. Factor analysis of the sexual interaction inventory. *Archives of Sexual Behavior,* 1977, *6,* 25–35.

Mosher, D. L. The development and multitrait-multimethod matrix analysis of three measures of three aspects of guilt. *Journal of Consulting Psychology,* 1966, *30,* 25–29.

Mosher, D. L., & Cross, H. J. Sex guilt and premarital sexual experiences of college students. *Journal of Consulting and Clinical Psychology*, 1971, *36*, 27–32.

Paitich, D. A comprehensive automated psychological examination and report. (CAPER). *Behavioral Science*, 1973, *18*, 131–136.

Paitich, D., Langevin, R., Freeman, R., Mann, K., & Handy, L. The Clarke SHQ: A clinical sex history questionnaire for males. *Archives of Sexual Behavior*, 1977, *6*, 421–436.

Weinrich, J. On a relationship between homosexuality and IQ tests: A review and some hypotheses. In R. Forleo & W. Pasin: (Eds.), *Medical sexology: The third international congress*. Littleton, MA: PSG Publishing Company, 1978.

Whalley, L. J., & McGuire, R. J. Measuring sexual attitudes. *Acta Psychiatrica Scandanavica*, 1978, *58*, 299–314.

Wilson, B. D., & Lang, R. J. Sex differences in sexual fantasy patterns. *Personality and Individual Differences*, 1981, *2*, 343–346.

ENDNOTES

Note 1. See Chapter 2 for some validation of this inventory.

Note 2. We wish to thank Dr. V. Quinsey for pointing this distinction out to us.

Note 3. A correlation of 0.16 is significant at $p < .05$ and $r = 0.23$ at $p < .01$ for a sample size over 100. Since significance level of the correlation is sample size dependent, an item's practical utility cannot be gauged by significance alone. In this study, 0.20 was used as a suggestive guideline for scrutiny of confounding factors and, more meaningfully, $r = 0.30$. Since many experimental effects explain in the order of 10% of the variance, $r = 0.30$ or 9% of the variance becomes a serious competing explanation of results. However, for the SHQ scales, inter-item correlations and scale reliabilities are of a much higher order so even $r = 0.30$ is a weak effect.

Note 4. SPSS program Reliability was used and Cronbach's Alpha computed. Scales were preselected because factor structure had been established for the old SHQ (Paitich et al., 1977) and analysis of this data set would be too costly. Dichotomous scores were "no experience" versus "*any* experience." Similar dichotomies were used for disgust, desire and fantasies.

Note 5. SPSS Oneway analysis was used on both raw scores and dichotomous data (no experience versus some, etc.). Inhomogeneity of variance was a major problem on the raw data and it will not be reported here. It is a feature inherent in sexual behavior. For example, the great majority of cases did not engage in homosexual pedophilic acts and score zero on the corresponding scales measuring such behavior. This creates skewed distributions of scores that are unavoidable. Even within a group such as the pedophiles, experience tends to be so varied that the same statistical problems emerged. The dichotomous scores in large part eleminated this problem but at the sacrifice of much information. In the computer printout raw scores are reported along with dichotomous Z-score results.

Appendix B
Sex History Questionnaires
Scoring Manual

Anne E. Russon
Clarke Institute of Psychiatry, Toronto

HAND SCORING OF THE CLARKE SHQ

The items for each scale are together to afford easy scoring. Simply give one point for each positive response in the scale. For example:

Response	Score
(a) none	0
(b) to (j)	1

Then add together the scores for the items in each scale to compute a total scale score. For example, the Heterosexual Adult Experience scale has 20 items. Thus, the minimum score for this scale is zero and the maximum is 20.

Results may then be compared with mean values in Table A.4 of Appendix A.

Scale	Items	Maximum Score
1. Hetersexual Adult Frequency	1–20	20
2. Heterosexual Pedophilic Frequency	21–43	23
3. Heterosexual Hebephilic Frequency	44–66	23
4. Androphilic Frequency	67–79	13
5. Homosexual Pedophilic Frequency	80–92	13
6. Homosexual Ephebephilic Frequency	93–105	13
7. Crossdressing	106–117	12

(continued)

Scale	Items	Maximum Score
8. Voyeurism	118–123	6
9. Obscene Calls	124–125	2
10. Toucheurism & Frottage	126–131	6
11. Sadism & Masochism	134–147	14
12. Group Sex	155–156	2
13. Exhibitionism Frequency	159–163	5
14. Exhibiting Behavior	164–174	11

COMPUTER SCORING OF THE CLARKE SHQ

Introduction

The program NEWSHQ is written to score raw sex history questionnaires, then to generate either or both of: a file containing scale scores calculated for each questionnaire submitted; and a printed report presenting each subject's response profile. The program was written in FORTRAN, to execute interactively on a DEC-2020 computer.

I. Input

1. The item alternatives 1 to 10 are entered for computer scoring as digits 1 through 9 respectively, with 10 represented as an A.
2. User may specify any format he chooses for entering the data for computer analysis. The existing format must be modified if user's is different from the standard provided (see subroutine Reader).
3. To print a separate page for each subject's report (on the DEC-20) the user must call his output file XXXXXX.DAT, where the 6 X's represent any name.
4. The interactive program does the rest.

II. Program Structure and Flow

The program contains the following subroutines:

1. Main Program. The main program merely controls the flow of operations, which are as follows:

a. Set run parameters as entered by the current user (subroutine PARAM).
b. Read each subject's raw sex history questionnaire (subroutine READER).
c. Check data for errors and recode some items (subroutine RECODE); reject item if key errors are found and proceed to next subject (go to [b]).

d. Scan selected items to determine occurrence of key behaviors (subroutine ITEMS).

e. Calculate scale scores (subroutine SCALES).

f. Calculate three Z-scores from the raw scale scores, based on three reference groups: the total reference group—deviants and controls; the appropriate deviant group; the heterosexual control group (Subroutine ZSCORE).

g. If requested, print a 2-page report for each subject presenting key behaviors (from subroutine ITEMS) and scale scores (from subroutine SCALES). (Subroutine PRINTS).

h. If requested, write subjects' scale scores to a data file for future use (subroutine WRITES).

2. Subroutine PARAM. This subroutine displays on the terminal screen a series of requests for information concerning the current run. The user must enter:

a. The name of the data file containing the raw questionnaires.

b. The name of the file to which printed reports should be written; leave blank if no reports are to be printed.

c. The name of the data file to which scale scores should be written, leave blank if no data file is required.

d. The character/number which represents missing data on the raw data file.

No checks have been programmed on these inputs; the program will abort if the file names submitted are inappropriate.

3. Subroutine READER. This subroutine reads individual subject's questionnaires from the raw data file named in subroutine PARAM. THIS SUBROUTINE MUST BE MODIFIED BY THE USER, *BEFORE* ATTEMPTING TO RUN THE PROGRAM, TO SPECIFY THE FORMAT OF THE DATA FILE.

The subroutine must read the following information into the following variables:

a. An identification number (up to 9 digits) for each subject in variable ID (1). This ID number is written on the printed report and the scored data file.

b. The subject's name (up to 30 characters) may be read into an array NAME (5 characters per array element). This is optional.

c. The date of testing into integer variable DATE (format DDMMYY); optional.

d. The 186 individual items from the sex history questionnaire should be read into array SHQRAW as digits 1 through 9. The last possible score, 10, is represented by "A". Thus a single digit field can be used to conserve space.

4. Subroutine RECODE. This subroutine performs range checks on questionnaire items to ensure that no critical response or data entry errors have occurred. A questionnaire is rejected if coding errors have occurred—appropriate error messages are printed identifying the subject and offending items.

Secondly, for error-free questionnaires, the subroutine recodes some questionnaire items, normally from category to frequency form.

5. Subroutine ITEMS. This subroutine scans key questionnaire items to determine maximum frequency of occurrence or the occurrence of specified sexual behaviors. The values so generated are printed on the first page of the report; they are not currently written to the scored data file.

6. Subroutine SCALES. This subroutine calculates scale scores on the 14 scales derived from the sex history questionnaire. These scale scores are written to the scored data file and printed on page 2 of the report.

7. Subroutine ZSCORE. This subroutine calculates three Z-scores for each of the 14 raw scales scores calculated in SCALES, each based on one of the three followup reference groups:

    a. The total group (deviants and heterosexual controls).
    b. The deviant group as determined by the anomaly being considered (ie. each scale has its own specifiec deviation group, unless this group was too small; in the latter case, one total sample was again used as a reference group).
    c. The heterosexual control group.

These comparison Z-scores are printed on page 2 of the report; they are not currently written to the scored data file.

8. Subroutine PRINTS. This subroutine generates a print-formatted report of each subject's profile. Page 1 of the report presents occurrences and frequencies of key behaviors (as per subroutine ITEMS). Page 2 of the report presents raw scale scores (per subroutine SCALES) and comparison Z–scores (per subroutine ZSCORE). Each two-page report is identified with the subject's name, ID number, and date of testing (as per subroutine READER). The report is written to the print file specified in subroutine PARAM. Once program NEWS-HQ has terminated, this file may be submitted to the printer if a hard copy is required or viewed on the display terminal.

9. Subroutine WRITES. This subroutine writes each subject's raw scale scores to the output data file specified in subroutine PARAM. Each subject's record contains: subject ID, name, and date of testing (as per subroutine READER), and the 14 raw scale scores (as per subroutine SCALES).

III. Program Utilization

1. Customize the Program:

Modify subroutine READER to reflect the stucture of the data set containing the raw questionnaires. (A sample subroutine has been included to demonstrate the required form).

2. Run the Customized Program:

In monitor mode, enter:

EXEC NEWSHQ.RUN (Return)

The program will be compiled and loaded, then display on the terminal screen requests for operator entry of run parameters (as per subroutine PARAM). One these values have been entered, the program proceeds to process all questionnaires in the specified raw data file. On termination, the requested output files (printed report and/or scaled data) may be further processed (viewed, printed, submitted to other programs for analysis etc.).

PROGRAM: NEWSHQ

PROGRAM TO SCORE REVISED NEW SEX HISTORY
QUESTIONNAIRE
PROVIDES SCORED INFORMATION IN DATA FORM OR IN
PRINTED PROFILE FORM

USER-MODIFIABLE PROGRAMMING
SUBROUTINE -PARAM- WHICH CONTROLS INPUT OF OPTION
SPECIFICATIONS (FILES, CALCULATIONS, ETC.)
SUBROUTINE -READER- WHICH SPECIFIES DATA INPUT (I.E.—
FORMATS, IDENTIFICATION INFORMATION).

****NOTE: THIS SUBROUTINE MUST BE MODIFIED****

AER   5/5/83

```
INTEGER ID(3),NAME(6),DATE,EOF,SHQRAW(186),ERR(10),DISPLA
DIMENSION SHQ(186),SCALE(14)
DIMENSION TOTALZ(14),DEVZ(14),HETCNZ(14)
DIMENSION PARTNR(6),SEXACT(21,2),RARE(7,2)
```

```
EQUIVALENCE (SHQRAW,SHQ)

DATA EOF/0/
DATE MISOUT/-99/
DATA IOUT/3/

*1. SET RUN PARAMETERS

    CALL PARAM(IOUT,MISSIN,MISOUT,DISPLA)

*2. READ EACH SUBJECT'S RAW SHQ QUESTIONNAIRE

    10 CALL READER(ID,NAME,DATE,SHQRAW,EOF,DISPLA)
       IF (EOF.EQ.1) GO TO 9999

*3. RECODE RAW DATA TO FULL SCALE

    CALL RECODE(ID,NAME,DATE,ERR,SHQRAW,SHQ,MISSIN,MISOUT)
    DO 20 I=1,10
    IF (ERR(I),GT.0) GO TO 10
20 CONTINUE

*4. KEY BEHAVIOUR SELECTION

    CALL ITEMS(SHQ,MISSIN,MISOUT,PARTNR,SEXACT,RARE)

*5. SCALE CALCULATIONS

    CALL SCALES(SHQ,SCALE)

*6. Z-SCORE CALCULATIONS

    CALL ZSCORE(SCALE,TOTALZ,DEVZ,HETCNZ)

*7. PRINT SCALED RESULTS FOR EACH SUBJECT

    IF (IOUT,EQ.1.OR.IOUT.EQ.3)
  1 CALL PRINTS(ID,NAME,DATE,PARTNR,SEXACT,RARE,SCALE,TOTALZ,DEVZ,
  2             HETCNZ)

*8. WRITE SCALE SCORES TO DATA FILE FOR EACH SUBJECT

    IF (IOUT.GE.2) CALL WRITES(SCALE,ID,NAME,DATE)

    GO TO 10

END OF FILE STOP

9999 STOP
     END
```

```
           SUBROUTINE: PARAM(IOUT,MISSIN,MISOUT,DISPLA)


SUBROUTINE TO ACCEPT SPECS FOR:
—IDENTIFICATION OF INPUT AND OUTPUT FILES
—WHAT KIND OF OUTPUT TO BE PROVIDED:
   —IOUT = 3 BOTH PRINT AND DATA FILES
        = 2 ONLY DATA FILE
        = 1 ONLY PRINT FILE
        = 0 NEITHER
—HOW MISSING INFORMATION IS CODED ON RAW DATA FILE
—WHETHER ID'S TO BE DISPLAYED ON SCREEN AS PROCESSED
```

```
      INTEGER MISSIN,MISOUT,DISPLA
      REAL*8 INFILE,PRFILE,DATFIL

101 FORMAT(///////////,'    SEX HISTORY SCORING PROGRAM    ')
101 FORMAT(/////,' ***** CHANGE FORMAT -100- IN READER FOR YOUR RAW DAT
    1A BEFORE CONTINUING *****',//,
    2'  INPUT DATA FILE NAME IS . . . .')
102 FORMAT(' OUTPUT PRINT FILE NAME IS (BLANK TO OMIT) . . . .')
103 FORMAT(' OUTPUT DATA FILE NAME IS (BLANK TO OMIT) . . . .')
104 FORMAT(A10)
107 FORMAT(' MISSING INFO IN INPUT DATA FILE IS CODED AS . . .')
108 FORMAT(A1)
109 FORMAT(' DISPLAY ID-S ON SCREEN AS PROCESSED (Y OR N) . . . .')

      TYPE 100

      TYPE 101
      ACCEPT 104,INFILE

      TYPE 102
      ACCEPT 104,PRFILE
      IF (PRFILE.EQ.'     ') IOUT=IOUT-1

      TYPE 103
      ACCEPT 104,DATFIL
      IF (DATFIL.EQ.'     ') IOUT=IOUT-2

      TYPE 107
      ACCEPT 108,MISSIN

      TYPE 109
      ACCEPT 108,DISPLA

      OPEN(UNIT=20,ACCESS='SEQIN',FILE=INFILE)
```

```
IF (PRFILE.NE.'      ') OPEN(UNIT=21,ACCESS='SEQOUT',FILE=PRFILE)
IF (DATFIL.NE.'      ') OPEN(UNIT=22,ACCESS='SEQOUT',FILE=DATFIL)

RETURN
END
```

```
SUBROUTINE: READER(ID,NAME,DATE,SHQRAW,EOF,DISPLA)


SUBROUTINE TO READ INPUT DATA FILE. MUST RETURN—
  —ARRAY ID WITH IDENTIFICATION INFO. ID(1) MUST
    CONTAIN UP TO 9 DIGIT INTEGER COMPLETE
    IDENTIFICATION NUMBER WHICH WILL BE WRITTEN IN
    FIRST 9 COLUMNS OF –DATFIL– INFORMATION FOR EACH
    SUBJECT
  —ARRAY NAME WITH SUBJECT NAME (UP TO 30
    CHARACTERS)
  —INTEGER DATE WITH DATE OF TESTING (FORMAT
    DDMMYY)
  —ARRAY SHQRAW WITH RAW ITEM RESPONSES
  —VARIABLE EOF=1 WHEN END OF FILE ENCOUNTERED ON
    INPUT

 *—THE FORMAT FOR THE RAW SHQ DATA FILE MUST BE
   CHANGED TO REFLECT THE ORGANIZATION OF THE
   USER'S FILE CHANGE FORMAT –100– BELOW
```

```
      INTEGER ID(3),NAME(6),DATE,EOF,SHQRAW(186),DISPLA

C 100 FORMAT(3I3,1X,70A1,4(/,10X,70A1))
```

```
      CHANGE THIS FORMAT TO REPRESENT YOUR DATA FILE

100 FORMAT(2I3,///////////////2(10X,70A1/),10X,46A1,///,10X)
```

```
110 FORMAT(' PROCESSING SUBJECT NO. ',I6)

      DO 10 I=1,6
      IF (I.LE.3) ID(I)=0
 10   NAME(I)='
      DATE=999999

      READ(20,100,END=9999) (ID(I),I=1,2),(SHQRAW(I),I=1,186)
C     WRITE(21,100) (ID(I),I=1,2),(SHQRAW(I),I=1,186)
      ID(1)=100*ID(1)+ID(2)
      IF (DISPLA.EQ.'Y') TYPE 110,ID(1)
      RETURN
```

```
*      SET END OF INPUT PARAMETER
9999   EOF= 1
       RETURN
       END
```

SUBROUTINE:
RECODE(ID,NAME,DATE,ERR,SHQRAW,SHQ,MISSIN,MISOUT)

SUBROUTINE TO RECODE RAW SHQ DATA INTO FREQUENCY FORM

```
       INTEGER SHQRAW(186),ALPHA(10)
       INTEGER ID(3),NAME(6),DATE,ERR(10),BADATA(2,20)
       DIMENSION SHQ(186)
       DIMENSION VALF(10),VALH(10)

       DATA VALF/1.5,5.0,17.5,45.0,135.0,285.0,547.0,912.0,1642.0,1825.0/
      1      ,VALH/0.0,1.0,3.5,8.0,13.0,18.0,23.0,28.0,33.0,36.0/
       DATA ALPHA/'1','2','3','4','5','6','7','8','9','A'/

200 FORMAT(1H1,'ID: ',I6,' NAME: ',6A5,' DATE: ',I6,//)
300 FORMAT(' REJECTED—FOLLOWING ITEMS CONTAIN OUT–OF–RANGE
       VALUES',/
      1    /,20I4,///)
400 FORMAT(' REJECTED—THE FOLLOWING KEY ITEMS MISSING OR
       INCORRECTLY
      2 CODED',//,20I4)

*  GENERAL ALPHA TO NUMERIC AND MISSING VALUE RECODE
       DO 5 I=1,10
     5 ERR(I)=0
       DO 20 I=1,186
       IF (SHQRAW(I).EQ.MISSIN) GO TO 15
       DO 10 J=1,10
       IF (SHQRAW(I).NE.ALPHA(J)) GO TO 10
       SHQRAW(I)=J
       GO TO 20
    10 CONTINUE
    15 SHQRAW(I)=MISOUT
    20 CONTINUE
C  400 FORMAT(5(10X,70I1,/))
C       WRITE(21,400) (SHQRAW(I),I=1,186)

*  FREQUENCY (10-POINT SCALES) & Y/N ITEM RECODES: MISSING=0, *
*  BAD=REJECT
       DO 30 I=1,163
       IF (I.EQ.9.OR.I.EQ.21.OR.I.EQ.44.OR.I.EQ.67.OR.I.EQ.80.OR.
      1    I.EQ.93) GO TO 25
       IF (SHQRAW(I),NE.MISOUT) GO TO 21
```

```
      SHQ(I)=0.
      GO TO 30
   21 IF (SHQRAW(I).GE.1.AND.SHQRAW(I).LE.10) GO TO 22
      SHQ(I)=MISOUT
      ERR(1)=ERR(1)+1
      BADATA(1,ERR(1))=I
      GO TO 30
   22 SHQ(I)=VALH(SHQRAW(I))
      GO TO 30
   25 IF (SHQRAW(I).EQ.1.OR.SHQRAW(I).EQ.2) GO TO 28
      ERR(2)=ERR(2)+1
      BADATA(2,ERR(2))=I
      GO TO 30
   28 SHQ(I)=SHQRAW(I)-1
   30 CONTINUE

*  FREQUENCY ITEM RECODES (5-POINT SCALE), MISSING=1, BAD DATA=REJECT
      DO 40 I=164,174
      IF (I.EQ.172) GO TO 40
      IF (SHQRAW(I).NE.MISOUT) GO TO 35
      SHQ(I)=1.
      GO TO 40
   35 IF (SHQRAW(I).GE.1.AND.SHQRAW(I).LE.5) GO TO 37
      SHQ(I)=MISOUT
      ERR(1)=ERR(1)+1
      BADATA(1,ERR(1))=I
      GO TO 40
   37 SHQ(I)=SHQRAW(I)
   40 CONTINUE

*  ITEM 172
      IF (SHQRAW(172).NE.MISOUT) GO TO 42
      SHQ(172)=VALF(10)
      GO TO 45
   42 IF (SHQRAW(172).GE.1.AND.SHQRAW(172).LE.10) GO TO 44
      SHQ(172)=MISOUT
      ERR(1)=ERR(1)+1
      BADATA(1,ERR(1))=172
      GO TO 45
   44 SHQ(172)=VALF(SHQRAW(172))
   45 CONTINUE

*  DUMP SUBJECT WITH MESSAGE IF OUT OF RANGE DATA OR MISSING KEY ITEMS
      IERR=0
      DO 60 I=1,10
      IF (ERR(I).EQ.0) GO TO 60
      IF (IERR.EQ.0) WRITE(21,200) ID(1),(NAME(J),J=1,6),DATE
      IERR=1
      GO TO (61,62) I
   61 WRITE(21,300) (BADATA(I,J),J=1,ERR(I))
      GO TO 60
```

```
 62 WRITE(21,400) (BADATA(I,J),J=1,ERR(I))
    GO TO 60
 60 CONTINUE

C  50 TYPE 100,(SHQ(I),I=1,10)
C     WRITE(21,100) (SHQ(I),I=1,200)
C 100 FORMAT(4X,10F7.2)
    RETURN
    END
```

SUBROUTINE:
ITEMS(SHQ,MISSIN,MISOUT,PARTNR,SEXACT,RARE)

SUBROUTINE TO SCAN INDIVIDUAL QUESTIONNAIRE ITEMS
FOR MAXIMUM FREQUENCY OF KEY BEHAVIOURS

```
    INTEGER MISSIN,MISOUT
    DIMENSION SHQ(186)
    DIMENSION PARTNR(6),SEXACT(21,2),RARE(7,2)

* MAXIMUM NUMBER OF PARTNERS OF EACH TYPE
    PARTNR(1)=AMAX1(SHQ( 8),SHQ(13),SHQ(15))
    PARTNR(2)=AMAX1(SHQ(52),SHQ(56),SHQ(58))
    PARTNR(3)=AMAX1(SHQ(29),SHQ(33),SHQ(35))
    PARTNR(4)=AMAX1(SHQ(71),SHQ(72))
    PARTNR(5)=AMAX1(SHQ(97),SHQ(98))
    PARTNR(6)=AMAX1(SHQ(84),SHQ(85))

* MAXIMUM FREQUENCY EACH TYPE OF SEXUAL ACTIVITY
*  HETEROSEXUAL BEHAVIOUR (IC,ANAL,FELLATIO,CUNNILINGUN)
    SEXACT(1,1)=AMAX1(SHQ(10),SHQ(11),SHQ(30),SHQ(31),SHQ(53),SHQ(54))
    SEXACT(2,1)=AMAX1(SHQ(18),SHQ(38),SHQ(61))
    SEXACT(3,1)=AMAX1(SHQ(14),SHQ(34),SHQ(57))
    SEXACT(4,1)=AMAX1(SHQ(12),SHQ(32),SHQ(55))
    DO 10 I=1,4
 10 SEXACT(I,2)=MISOUT

* CROSSDRESSING (FULL SCALE, INDIVIDUAL PIECES OF CLOTHING)
    SEXACT(5,1)=SHQ(106)+SHQ(107)+SHQ(108)+SHQ(109)+SHQ(110)+SHQ(111)
    SEXACT(5,2)=SHQ(112)+SHQ(113)+SHQ(114)+SHQ(115)+SHQ(116)+SHQ(117)
    DO 20 I=6,11
    SEXACT(I,1)=SHQ(100+I)
 20 SEXACT(I,2)=SHQ(106+I)

* VOYEURISM
    SEXACT(12,1)=MAX1(SHQ(118),SHQ(120),SHQ(122))
    SEXACT(12,2)=MAX1(SHQ(119),SHQ(121),SHQ(123))
```

```
* EXHIBITIONISM (FULL SCALE/EACH TYPE OF PERSON)
   SEXACT(13,1)=SHQ(159)+SHQ(160)+SHQ(161)+SHQ(162)+SHQ(163)
   SEXACT(14,1)=SHQ(160)
   SEXACT(15,1)=SHQ(161)
   SEXACT(16,1)=SHQ(162)+SHQ(163)
   DO 30 I=13,16
30 SEXACT(I,2)=MISOUT

* OBSCENE CALLS
   SEXACT(17,1)=SHQ(124)
   SEXACT(17,2)=SHQ(125)

* TOUCHEURISM AND FROTTEURISM
   SEXACT(18,1)=SHQ(126)+SHQ(128)
   SEXACT(18,2)=SHQ(127)+SHQ(129)

* SADISM AND MASOCHISM (FULL SCALE, SADISM, MASOCHISM SUBSCALES)

   SEXACT(20,1)=SHQ(134)+SHQ(138)+SHQ(142)+SHQ(146)
   SEXACT(20,2)=SHQ(135)+SHQ(139)+SHQ(143)+SHQ(147)
   SEXACT(21,1)=SHQ(136)+SHQ(140)+SHQ(144)
   SEXACT(21,2)=SHQ(137)+SHQ(141)+SHQ(145)
   SEXACT(19,1)=SEXACT(20,1)+SEXACT(21,1)
   SEXACT(19,2)=SEXACT(20,2)+SEXACT(21,2)

* MISCELLANEOUS RARE OR NON-STANDARDIZED BEHAVIOURS
* INCEST (MOTHER,DAUGHTER,FATHER,SON)
   DO 50 I=1,4
   RARE(I,1)=SHQ(150+I)
50 RARE(I,2)=MISOUT

* ANIMALS
   RARE(5,1)=SHQ(148)
   RARE(5,2)=MISOUT

* CORPSES
   RARE(6,1)=SHQ(149)
   RARE(6,2)=MISOUT

* FIRE
   RARE(7,1)=SHQ(157)
   RARE(7,2)=SHQ(158)

   RETURN
   END
```

SUBROUTINE: SCALES(SHQ,SCALE)

SUBROUTINE TO CALCULATE SCALE SCORES FROM SCORED RAW DATA

```
DIMENSIONS  SHQ(186),SCALE(14)

* CLEAR SCALES FOR NEXT SUBJECT
      DO 5 I=1,14
    5 SCALE(I)=0.0

* RECODE ALL ITEMS DICHOTOMOUSLY FOR SCALE CALCULATIONS  (Y=1, N=0)
      DO 6 I=1,163
      IF (SHQ(I).GT.0.) SHQ(I)=1.
      IF (SHQ(I).EQ.0.) SHQ(I)=0.
    6 CONTINUE

      DO 7 I=164,174
      IF (SHQ(I).EQ.1.) SHQ(I)=0.
      IF (SHQ(I).GT.1.) SHQ(I)=1.
    7 CONTINUE

      IF (SHQ(172).LT.1825.) SHQ(172)=1.
      IF (SHQ(172).EQ.1825.) SHQ(172)=0.

* SCALE 1.  HETEROSEXUAL ADULT FREQUENCY
      DO 10 I=1,20
   10 SCALE(1)=SCALE(1)+SHQ(I)

* SCALE 2.  HETEROSEXUAL PEDOPHILE FREQUENCY
      DO 20 I=21,43
   20 SCALE(2)=SCALE(2)+SHQ(I)

* SCALE 3.  HETEROSEXUAL HEBEPHILIA FREQUENCY
      DO 30 I=44,66
   30 SCALE(3)=SCALE(3)+SHQ(I)

* SCALE 4.  ANDRO FREQUENCY
      DO 40 I=67,79
   40 SCALE(4)=SCALE(4)+SHQ(I)

* SCALE 5.  HOMOSEXUAL PEDOPHILIA
      DO 50 I=80,92
   50 SCALE(5)=SCALE(5)+SHQ(I)

* SCALE 6.  HOMOSEXUAL EPHEBEPHILIA
      DO 60 I=93,105
   60 SCALE(6)=SCALE(6)+SHQ(I)

* SCALE 7.  CROSSDRESSING
      DO 70 I=106,117
   70 SCALE(7)=SCALE(7)+SHQ(I)

* SCALE 8.  VOYEURISM
      DO 80 I=118,123

   80 SCALE(8)=SCALE(8)+SHQ(I)
```

```
* SCALE 9.  OBSCENE CALLS
    SCALE (9)=SHQ(124)+SHQ(125)

* SCALE 10.  TOUCHEURISM & FROTTEURISM
    DO 100 I=126,131
100  SCALE(10)=SCALE(10)+SHQ(I)

* SCALE 11.  SADISM & MASOCHISM
    DO 110 I=134,147
110  SCALE(11)=SCALE(11)+SHQ(I)

* SCALE 12.  GROUP SEX
    SCALE(12)=SHQ(155)+SHQ(156)

* SCALE 13.  EXHIBITIONISM FREQUENCY
    DO 130 I=159,163
130  SCALE(13)=SCALE(13)+SHQ(I)

* SCALE 14.  EXHIBITING BEHAVIOUR
    DO 140 I=164,174
    IF (I.EQ.170) GO TO 140
    SCALE(14)=SCALE(14)+SHQ(I)
140  CONTINUE

    RETURN
    END
```

SUBROUTINE: ZSCORE(SCALE,TOTALZ,DEVZ,HETCNZ)

SUBROUTINE TO CALCULATE THREE Z-SCORES FROM RAW SCALE SCORES, BASES ON 3 REFERENCE SAMPLES:
  1. TOTAL GROUP (DEVIANTS + HETEROSEXUAL CONTROLS)
  2. DEVIANT GROUP (EACH SCALE HAS OWN SPECIFIC
                    DEVIATION REFERENCE GROUP, UNLESS
                    GROUP TOO SMALL—IN THIS CASE,
                    TOTAL GROUP USED)
  3. HETEROSEXUAL CONTROL GROUP
AER 21/6/82

```
DIMENSION  SCALE(14),TOTALZ(14),DEVZ(14),HETCNZ(14)
DIMENSION  TOTAL(14,2),DEV(14,2),HETCN(14,2)

DATA ((TOTAL(I,J),J=1,2),I=1,14)/
1         13.75,  5.42,
2          2.25,  4.87,
3          2.62,  5.76,
4          2.71,  4.67,
```

```
5            .69,   2.26,
6            .61,   2.28,
7            .95,   2.00,
8           1.09,   1.55,
9            .14,    .47,
*            .58,   1.15,
1            .46,   1.69,
2            .48,    .81,
3            .90,   1.62,
4           6.06,   7.63/
     DATA ((DEV(I,J),J=1,2),I=1,14)/
1            .00,    .00,
2           5.71,   6.03,
3           7.71,   7.13,
4          11.67,   2.76,
5           4.74,   3.77,
6           3.30,   4.27,
7            .00,    .00,
8            .00,    .00,
9            .00,    .00,
*            .00,    .00,
1            .00,    .00,
2            .00,    .00,
3           3.37,   1.45,
4          15.25,   5.66/
     DATA ((HETCN(I,J),J=1,2),I=1,14)/
1          15.80,   3.71,
2            .48,   1.92,
3           1.78,   5.01,
4            .38,   1.59,
5            .24,   1.56,
6            .00,    .00,
7            .48,   1.31,
8            .90,   1.42,
9            .08,    .34,
*            .54,   1.07,
1            .20,    .57,
2            .44,    .81,
3            .04,    .28,
4           3.40,   5.28/


     DO 10 I=1,14
     TOTALZ(I)=(SCALE(I)—TOTAL(I,1))/TOTAL(I,2)
     IF (DEV(I,1).NE.0.00) DEVZ(I)=(SCALE(I)—DEV(I,1))/DEV(I,2)
     IF (DEV(I,1).EQ.0.00) DEVZ(I)=TOTALZ(I)
     IF (HETCN(I,2).NE.0.00) HETCNZ(I)=(SCALE(I)—HETCN(I,1))/HETCN(I,2)
 10 CONTINUE

     RETURN
     END
```

```
                           SUBROUTINE:
     PRINTS(ID,NAME,DATE,PARTNR,SEXACT,RARE,SCALE,TOTALZ,
     1                  DEVZ,HETCNZ)


     SUBROUTINE TO PRINT SUBJECT'S SCALED SHQ
     QUESTIONNAIRE (N.B.   OUTPUT PRINTED ON UNIT 21)
```

```
      DIMENSION SCALE(14)
      DIMENSION TOTALZ(14),DEVZ(14),HETCNZ(14)
      INTEGER ID(3),NAME(6),DATE,PAGE
      INTEGER FIRST
      DIMENSION PARTNR(6),SEXACT(21,2),RARE(7,2)

      DATA FIRST/0/

100 FORMAT(1H1,///////////////,
     1'                        SEX HISTORY QUESTIONNAIRE ',//////,
     2/'      THIS SELF-ADMINISTERED QUESTIONNAIRE SHOULD NOT BE USED    '
     3/'      ALONE FOR DIAGNOSTIC OR THERAPEUTIC PURPOSES BUT AS AN AD-'
     4/'      JUNCT TO A SEXOLOGICAL INTERVIEW. ITS USE WAS ITENDED FOR'
     5/'      PROFESSIONALS TRAINED IN MENTAL HEALTH DISCIPLINES, AND IT'
     6/'      SHOULD NOT BE USED OTHERWISE. DETAILS ON THE QUESTIONNAIRE'
     7/'      DEVELOPMENT ARE AVAILABLE IN "EROTIC PREFERENCE, GENDER   '
     8/'      IDENTITY AND AGGRESSION", R. LANGEVIN (EDITOR), HILLSDALE,'
     9/'      N.J., ERLBAUM ASSOCIATES, 1983.')
200 FORMAT(1H1,/,79X,I1,/,24X,'SEX HISTORY QUESTIONNAIRE REPORT',///,
     1 '    NAME: ',6A5,' ID: ',I9,/,38X,' DATE OF TESTING: ',I6,//)
300   FORMAT(' SUBJECT HAS SEXUALLY INTERACTED WITH THE FOLLOWING
      CATEGO
     1 RIES OF PERSONS:',//,25X,'MAX # PARTNERS',//,
     2'    1. FEMALES-ADULT                               ',4X,F7.2,/,
     2'    2. FEMALES-PUBESCENT                           ',4X,F7.2,/,
     3'    3. FEMALES-CHILDREN                            ',4X,F7.2,/,
     4'    4. MALES   -ADULT                              ',4X,F7.2,/,
     5'    5. MALES   -PUBESCENT                          ',4X,F7.2,/,
     6'    6. MALES   -CHILDREN                           ',4X,F7.2,/)
400 FORMAT(' HAS ENGAGED IN THE FOLLOWING CATEGORIES OF SEXUAL ACTS:'
     1,//,39X,'   FREQUENCY      FREQUENCY',
     2 /,39X,'   OCCURRENCE     WITH ORGASM',//
     3'    1. HETEROSEXUAL INTERCOURSE        ',3X,F7.2,8X,'   N/A   ',/,
     4'    2. HETEROSEXUAL ANAL INTERCOURSE   ',3X,F7.2,8X,'   N/A   ',/,
     5'    3. HETEROSEXUAL FELLATIO           ',3X,F7.2,8X,'   N/A   ',/,
     6'    4. CUNNILINGUS                     ',3X,F7.2,8X,'   N/A   ',/,
     7'    5. CROSSDRESSING-OVERALL           ',3X,F7.2,8X,F7.2,/,
     8'    6.               -SKIRT OR DRESS   ',3X,F7.2,8X,F7.2,/,
     9'    7.               -UNDERGARMENTS    ',3X,F7.2,8X,F7.2,/,
     *'    8.               -STOCKINGS        ',3X,F7.2,8X,F7.2,/,
     1'    9.               -SHOES            ',3X,F7.2,8X,F7.2,/,
```

```
2'   10.                    -JEWELLERY              ',3X,F7.2,8X,F7.2,/,
3'   11.                    -WIG                    ',3X,F7.2,8X,F7.2,/,
4'   12. VOYEURISM                                  ',3X,F7.2,8X,'F7.2,/,
5'   13. EXHIBITIONISM-OVERALL                      ',3X,F7.2,8X,'    N/A    ',/,
6'   14.            -FEMALE CHILDREN                ',3X,F7.2,8X,'    N/A    ',/,
7'   15.            -PUBESCENT FEMALES              ',3X,F7.2,8X,'    N/A    ',/,
8'   16.            -ADULT FEMALES                  ',3X,F7.2,8X,'    N/A    ',/,
9'   17. OBSCENE CALLS                              ',3X,F7.2,8X,F7.2,/,
*'   18. TOUCHEURISM/FROTTEURISM                    ',3X,F7.2,8X,F7.2,/,
1'   19. SADISM & MASOCHISM-OVERALL                 ',3X,F7.2,8X,'    N/A    ',/,
2'   20.                    -SADISM                 ',3X,F7.2,8X,F7.2,/,
3'   21.                    -MASOCHISM              ',3X,F7.2,8X,F7.2,/)
500 FORMAT(' HAS ENGAGED IN THE FOLLOWING RARE/NONSTANDARDIZED
SEXUA
     1L BEHAVIOURS:',//,
     239X,' FREQUENCY      FREQUENCY',/,
     339X,' OCCURRENCE      WITH ORGASM',//,
4'    1. INCEST WITH MOTHER                         ',3X,F7.2,8X,'    N/A    ',/,
5'    2.        WITH DAUGHTER                       ',3X,F7.2,8X,'    N/A    ',/,
6'    3.        WITH FATHER                         ',3X,F7.2,8X,'    N/A    ',/,
7'    4.        WITH SON                            ',3X,F7.2,8X,'    N/A    ',/,
8'    5. SEXUAL CONTACT WITH ANIMALS                ',3X,F7.2,8X,'    N/A    ',/,
9'    6. SEXUAL CONTACT WITH CORPSES                ',3X,F7.2,8X,'    N/A    ',/,
*'    7. SEXUAL AROUSAL RE FIRE                     ',3X,F7.2,8X,F7.2)
600 FORMAT(///,27X,'RAW AND Z-TRANSFORMED SCALE SCORES',////,
     149X,'--------Z-SCORES---------',/,
     149X,'----- IN RELATION TO ------',//,
     137X,'   RAW   ','   TOTAL   ','  DEVIANT  ','  HET.CON.  '/' SCALE:',
     130X,'  SCORE  ','  SAMPLE  ','   SAMPLE   ','  SAMPLE',//,
1'    1. HETEROSEXUAL ADULT FREQUENCY               ',2X,4F10.2,/,
2'    2. HETEROSEXUAL PEDOPHILE FREQ.               ',2X,4F10.2,/,
3'    3. HETEROSEXUAL HEBEPHILIA FREQ.              ',1X,4F10.2,/,
4'    4. ANDROPHILE FREQUENCY                       ',2X,4F10.2,/,
5'    5. HOMOSEXUAL PEDOPHILIA                      ',2X,4F10.2,/,
6'    6. HOMOSEXUAL EPHEBEPHILIA                    ',2X,3F10.2,6X,'N/A',/,
7'    7. CROSSDRESSING                              ',2X,4F10.2,/,
8'    8. VOYEURISM                                  ',2X,4F10.2,/,
9'    9. OBSCENE CALLS                              ',2X,4F10.2,/,
*'   10. TOUCHEURISM & FROTTEURISM                  ',2X,4F10.2,/,
1'   11. SADISM & MASOCHISM                         ',2X,4F10.2,/,
2'   12. GROUP SEX                                  ',2X,4F10.2,/,
3'   13. EXHIBITION FREQUENCY                       ',2X,4F10.2,/,
4'   14. EXHIBITING BEHAVIOUR                       ',2X,4F10.2,/)

     IF (FIRST.EQ.0) WRITE(21,100)
     FIRST=1
     PAGE=1
     WRITE(21,200) PAGE,(NAME(I),I=1,6),ID(1),DATE
     WRITE(21,300) (PARTNR(I),I=1,6)
     WRITE(21,400) (SEXACT(I,1),I=1,4),((SEXACT(I,J),J=1,2),I=5,12),
    1              (SEXACT(I,1),I=13,16),((SEXACT(I,J),J=1,2),I=17,18),
    2              SEXACT(19,1),((SEXACT(I,J),J=1,2),I=20,21)
```

```
WRITE(21,500) (RARE(I,1),I=1,6),(RARE(7,J),J=1,2)
PAGE=2
WRITE(21,200) PAGE,(NAME(I),I=1,6),ID(1),DATE
WRITE(21,600) (SCALE(I),TOTALZ(I),DEVZ(I),HETCNZ(I),I=1,5),
1    SCALE(6),TOTALZ(6),DEVZ(6),
2    (SCALE(I),TOTALZ(I),DEVZ(I),HETCNZ(I),I=7,14)
RETURN
END
```

SUBROUTINE: WRITES(SCALE,ID,NAME,DATE)

SUBROUTINE TO WRITE SUBJECT'S SCALED QUESTIONNAIRE TO DATA FILE (N.B. OUTPUT WRITTEN TO UNIT 22)

SCALE SCORES ARE WRITTEN IN THE FOLLOWING ORDER:
1. HETEROSEXUAL ADULT FREQUENCY
2. HETEROSEXUAL PEDOPHILE FREQUENCY
3. HETEROSEXUAL HEBEPHILIA FREQUENCY
4. ANDROPHILE FREQUENCY
5. HOMOSEXUAL PEDOPHILIA
6. HOMOSEXUAL EPHEBEPHILIA
7. CROSSDRESSING
8. VOYEURISM
9. OBSCENE CALLS
10. TOUCHEURISM & FROTTEURISM
11. SADISM & MASOCHISM
12. GROUP SEX
13. EXHIBITION FREQUENCY
14. EXHIBITING BEHAVIOR

```
DIMENSION SCALE(14)
INTEGER ID(3),NAME(6),DATE

100 FORMAT(I9,1X,6A5,1X,I6/10X,10F7.2/10X,4F7.2)

WRITE(22,100) ID(1),(NAME(I),I=1,6),DATE,(SCALE(I),I=1,14)

RETURN
END
```

SAMPLE OF SHQ REPORT

This self-administered questionnaire should not be used alone for diagnostic or therapeutic purposes but as an adjunct to a sexological interview. Its use was intended for professionals trained in mental health disciplines, and it should not

be used otherwise. Details on the questionnaire development are available in "Erotic Preference, Gender Identity and Aggression", R. Langevin (Editor), Hillsdale, N.J., Erlbaum Associates, 1983.

SEX HISTORY QUESTIONNAIRE REPORT

Name: ID: 10713
                                                   Date of Testing: 999999

Subject has sexually interacted with the following categories of persons:

	Max # Partners
1. Females—adult	36.00
2. Females—pubescent	0.00
3. Females—children	0.00
4. Males—adult	1.00
5. Males—pubescent	0.00
6. Males—children	0.00

Has engaged in the following categories of sexual acts:

	Frequency Occurrence	Frequency With Orgasm
1. Heterosexual intercourse	36.00	N/A
2. Heterosexual anal intercourse	0.00	N/A
3. Heterosexual fellatio	36.00	N/A
4. Cunnilingus	36.00	N/A
5. Crossdressing—overall	72.00	72.00
6. —skirt or dress	18.00	18.00
7. —undergarments	18.00	18.00
8. —stockings	18.00	18.00
9. —shoes	18.00	18.00
10. —jewellery	0.00	0.00
11. —wig	0.00	0.00
12. Voyeurism	36.00	18.00
13. Exhibitionism—overall	0.00	N/A
14. —female children	0.00	N/A
15. —pubescent females	0.00	N/A
16. —adult females	0.00	N/A
17. Obscene calls	0.00	0.00
18. Toucheurism/frotteurism	0.00	0.00
19. Sadism & masochism—overall	1.00	N/A
20. —sadism	1.00	1.00
21. —masochism	0.00	0.00

(continued)

SEX HISTORY QUESTIONNAIRE REPORT

Has engaged in the following rare/nonstandardized sexual behaviors:

	Frequency Occurrence	Frequency With Orgasm
1. Incest with mother	0.00	N/A
2. with daughter	0.00	N/A
3. with father	0.00	N/A
4. with son	0.00	N/A
5. Sexual contact with animals	0.00	N/A
6. Sexual contact with corpses	0.00	N/A
7. Sexual arousal re: fire	0.00	0.00

SEX HISTORY QUESTIONNAIRE REPORT

Name: ID: 10713
                                               Date of Testing: 999999

Raw and Z–Transformed Scale Scores

| | | | Z–Scores in Relation to | |
Scale:	Raw Score	Total Sample	Deviant Sample	Het.Con. Sample
1. Heterosexual adult frequency	19.00	0.97	0.97	0.86
2. Heterosexual pedophile freq.	0.00	−0.46	−0.95	−0.25
3. Heterosexual hebephilia freq.	0.00	−0.45	−1.08	−0.36
4. Androphile frequency	10.00	1.56	−0.61	6.05
5. Homosexual pedophilia	0.00	−0.31	−1.26	−0.15
6. Homosexual ephebephilia	0.00	−0.27	−0.77	N/A
7. Crossdressing	8.00	3.53	3.53	5.74
8. Voyeurism	2.00	0.59	0.59	0.77
9. Obscene calls	0.00	−0.30	−0.30	−0.24
10. Toucheurism & Frotteurism	2.00	1.23	1.23	1.36
11. Sadism & Masochism	2.00	0.91	0.91	3.16
12. Group Sex	2.00	1.88	1.88	1.93
13. Exhibition frequency	0.00	−0.56	−2.32	−0.14
14. Exhibiting behavior	1.00	−0.66	−2.52	−0.45

SEX HISTORY ANSWER SHEET

Column headers (left and right blocks):
none or never (a), only one (b), 2–5 (c), 6–10 (d), 11–15 (e), 16–20 (f), 21–25 (g), 26–30 (h), 31–35 (i), 36 or more (j)

(11)
1. a b c d e f g h i j
2. a b c d e f g h i j
3. a b c d e f g h i j
4. a b c d e f g h i j
5. a b c d e f g h i j

6. a b c d e f g h i j
7. a b c d e f g h i j
8. a b c d e f g h i j
9. a b c d e f g h i j
10. a b c d e f g h i j

11. a b c d e f g h i j
12. a b c d e f g h i j
13. a b c d e f g h i j
14. a b c d e f g h i j
15. a b c d e f g h i j

16. a b c d e f g h i j
17. a b c d e f g h i j
18. a b c d e f g h i j
19. a b c d e f g h i j
20. a b c d e f g h i j

21. a b c d e f g h i j
22. a b c d e f g h i j
23. a b c d e f g h i j
24. a b c d e f g h i j
25. a b c d e f g h i j

26. a b c d e f g h i j
27. a b c d e f g h i j
28. a b c d e f g h i j
29. a b c d e f g h i j
30. a b c d e f g h i j

31. a b c d e f g h i j
32. a b c d e f g h i j
33. a b c d e f g h i j
34. a b c d e f g h i j
35. a b c d e f g h i j

1 2 3 4 5 6 7 8 9 A

36. a b c d e f g h i j
37. a b c d e f g h i j
38. a b c d e f g h i j
39. a b c d e f g h i j
40. a b c d e f g h i j

41. a b c d e f g h i j
42. a b c d e f g h i j
43. a b c d e f g h i j
(54) 44. a b c d e f g h i j
45. a b c d e f g h i j

46. a b c d e f g h i j
47. a b c d e f g h i j
48. a b c d e f g h i j
49. a b c d e f g h i j
50. a b c d e f g h i j

51. a b c d e f g h i j
52. a b c d e f g h i j
53. a b c d e f g h i j
54. a b c d e f g h i j
55. a b c d e f g h i j

56. a b c d e f g h i j
57. a b c d e f g h i j
58. a b c d e f g h i j
59. a b c d e f g h i j
60. a b c d e f g h i j

61. a b c d e f g h i j
62. a b c d e f g h i j
63. a b c d e f g h i j
64. a b c d e f g h i j
65. a b c d e f g h i j

66. a b c d e f g h i j
(77) 67. a b c d e f g h i j
68. a b c d e f g h i j
69. a b c d e f g h i j
70. a b c d e f g h i j

1 2 3 4 5 6 7 8 9 A

(continued)

327

SEX HISTORY ANSWER SHEET (*Continued*)

Column headers (both columns): none or never / only one / 2–5 / 6–10 / 11–15 / 16–20 / 21–25 / 26–30 / 31–35 / 36 or more

Left column

(11)
71. a b c d e f g h i j
72. a b c d e f g h i j
73. a b c d e f g h i j
74. a b c d e f g h i j
75. a b c d e f g h i j

76. a b c d e f g h i j
77. a b c d e f g h i j
78. a b c d e f g h i j
79. a b c d e f g h i j
(20) 80. a b c d e f g h i j

81. a b c d e f g h i j
82. a b c d e f g h i j
83. a b c d e f g h i j
84. a b c d e f g h i j
85. a b c d e f g h i j

86. a b c d e f g h i j
87. a b c d e f g h i j
88. a b c d e f g h i j
89. a b c d e f g h i j
90. a b c d e f g h i j

91. a b c d e f g h i j
92. a b c d e f g h i j
(33) 93. a b c d e f g h i j
94. a b c d e f g h i j
95. a b c d e f g h i j

96. a b c d e f g h i j
97. a b c d e f g h i j
98. a b c d e f g h i j
99. a b c d e f g h i j
100. a b c d e f g h i j

101. a b c d e f g h i j
102. a b c d e f g h i j
103. a b c d e f g h i j
104. a b c d e f g h i j
105. a b c d e f g h i j

1 2 3 4 5 6 7 8 9 A

Right column

(46)
106. a b c d e f g h i j
107. a b c d e f g h i j
108. a b c d e f g h i j
109. a b c d e f g h i j
110. a b c d e f g h i j

111. a b c d e f g h i j
112. a b c d e f g h i j
113. a b c d e f g h i j
114. a b c d e f g h i j
115. a b c d e f g h i j

116. a b c d e f g h i j
117. a b c d e f g h i j
118. a b c d e f g h i j
119. a b c d e f g h i j
120. a b c d e f g h i j

121. a b c d e f g h i j
122. a b c d e f g h i j
123. a b c d e f g h i j
124. a b c d e f g h i j
125. a b c d e f g h i j

126. a b c d e f g h i j
127. a b c d e f g h i j
128. a b c d e f g h i j
129. a b c d e f g h i j
130. a b c d e f g h i j

131. a b c d e f g h i j
132. a b c d e f g h i j
133. a b c d e f g h i j
134. a b c d e f g h i j
135. a b c d e f g h i j

136. a b c d e f g h i j
137. a b c d e f g h i j
138. a b c d e f g h i j
139. a b c d e f g h i j
140. a b c d e f g h i j

1 2 3 4 5 6 7 8 9 A

(*continued*)

		none or never	only one	2–5	6–10	11–15	16–20	21–25	26–30	31–35	36 or more
(11)	141.	a	b	c	d	e	f	g	h	i	j
	142.	a	b	c	d	e	f	g	h	i	j
	143.	a	b	c	d	e	f	g	h	i	j
	144.	a	b	c	d	e	f	g	h	i	j
	145.	a	b	c	d	e	f	g	h	i	j
	146.	a	b	c	d	e	f	g	h	i	j
	147.	a	b	c	d	e	f	g	h	i	j
	148.	a	b	c	d	e	f	g	h	i	j
	149.	a	b	c	d	e	f	g	h	i	j
	150.	a	b	c	d	e	f	g	h	i	j
	151.	a	b	c	d	e	f	g	h	i	j
	152.	a	b	c	d	e	f	g	h	i	j
	153.	a	b	c	d	e	f	g	h	i	j
	154.	a	b	c	d	e	f	g	h	i	j
	155.	a	b	c	d	e	f	g	h	i	j
	156.	a	b	c	d	e	f	g	h	i	j
	157.	a	b	c	d	e	f	g	h	i	j
	158.	a	b	c	d	e	f	g	h	i	j
	159.	a	b	c	d	e	f	g	h	i	j
	160.	a	b	c	d	e	f	g	h	i	j
	161.	a	b	c	d	e	f	g	h	i	j
	162.	a	b	c	d	e	f	g	h	i	j
	163.	a	b	c	d	e	f	g	h	i	j
	164.	a	b	c	d	e	f	g	h	i	j
	165.	a	b	c	d	e	f	g	h	i	j
	166.	a	b	c	d	e	f	g	h	i	j
	167.	a	b	c	d	e	f	g	h	i	j
	168.	a	b	c	d	e	f	g	h	i	j
	169.	a	b	c	d	e	f	g	h	i	j
	170.	a	b	c	d	e	f	g	h	i	j
	171.	a	b	c	d	e	f	g	h	i	j
	172.	a	b	c	d	e	f	g	h	i	j
	173.	a	b	c	d	e	f	g	h	i	j
	174.	a	b	c	d	e	f	g	h	i	j
(45)	175.	a	b	c	d	e	f	g	h	i	j
		1	2	3	4	5	6	7	8	9	

	none or never	only one	2–5	6–10	11–15	16–20	21–25	26–30	31–35	36 or more
176.	a	b	c	d	e	f	g	h	i	j
177.	a	b	c	d	e	f	g	h	i	j
178.	a	b	c	d	e	f	g	h	i	j
179.	a	b	c	d	e	f	g	h	i	j
180.	a	b	c	d	e	f	g	h	i	j
181.	a	b	c	d	e	f	g	h	i	j
182.	a	b	c	d	e	f	g	h	i	j
183.	a	b	c	d	e	f	g	h	i	j
184.	a	b	c	d	e	f	g	h	i	j
185.	a	b	c	d	e	f	g	h	i	j
186.	a	b	c	d	e	f	g	h	i	j

329

CLARKE SEXUAL HISTORY QUESTIONNAIRE—MALE

We realize that sex may be very private for you but it is an important part of a person's life and we hope that you will help us understand this aspect as well as the other personal matters that we are dealing with.

Some of the questions may not seem to apply to you. Each person's experience is different. Read the questions carefully and answer them as well as you can.

DO NOT ANSWER ON THIS BOOKLET
USE SEPARATE ANSWER SHEET

Revised November, 1982

CLARKE SEXUAL HISTORY QUESTIONNAIRE—MALE

Instruction:

The following questionnaire asks about your sexual experience. Some of the questions asked may not apply to you. When they do not concern your experience, be sure to carefully mark that the question does not apply to you by marking "none" or "never" for those questions. You are not required to answer all sections so read instructions carefully.

Indicate how often you have done the stated act or how many partners you have had as follows:

    a. None or never
    b. Only one
    c. 2–5
    d. 6–10
    e. 11–15
    f. 16–20
    g. 21–25
    h. 26–30
    i. 31–35
    j. 36 or more

For example, #1—"About how many girls or women have you gone out with on dates since the age of 16?"—If you have never dated a girl or woman, mark (a) beside #1 on the answer sheet; if you have dated only one, mark (b) beside #1

on the answer sheet; if you had dated 2 to 5 girls or women, mark (c) and so on. For your convenience, you will find these numbers reproduced *above* the letters on the answer sheet.

The following items refer to sexual experience with females 16 or older.

1. About how many girls or women have you gone out with on dates since the age of 16?

2. How many girls or women have you kissed on the lips since the age of 16?

3. How many girls or women have you touched on the breasts since the age of 16?

4. How many girls or women have you touched on the naked breasts since the age of 16?

5. With how many girls or women have you kissed or put your mouth on their breasts since you were 16 years of age?

6. Since the age of 16, how many girls or women 16 and older have you touched between the legs with your hands?

7. Since the age of 16, how many girls or women 16 and older have done this to you?

8. What is the total number of girls or women that you have had intercourse with from the age of 16 up to now?

9. Have you had any form of sexual contact with girls or women 16 or older since you were 16?

   Answer (a) no (b) yes on the answer sheet. If your answer is "no", skip to Section B on page 2. Otherwise continue with #10.

10. How many girls or women have you had intercourse with once and no more?

11. What is the most often that you have had intercourse with the same girl or woman since you were 16?

12. How many *TIMES* have you kissed or put your mouth between the legs of a girl or woman, since the age of 16?

13. With how many different girls or women 16 and older have you done this?

14. How many *TIMES* have girls or women done this to you, since the age of 16?

15. How many different girls or women have done this to you?

16. How many times have you put your finger into the rear end (rectum) of a girl or woman since the age of 16?

17. How many times have girls or women done this to you?

18. How many times have you put your penis into the rear end (rectum) of a girl or woman since the age of 16?

19. How many times have you touched the rear end of a girl or woman with your mouth since the age of 16?

20. How many times have girls or women done this to you?

SECTION B

The following items refer to sexual experience with girls 12 and younger (those who have not reached puberty, that is, physical maturity).

21. Have you had any form of sexual contact or sexual touching with girls 12 or younger since you were 16?

    Answer (a) no (b) yes on the answer sheet. If you answer is ''no'', skip to Section C on page 3.

22. About how many girls 12 and younger have you gone out with on dates since you were 16?

23. How many girls 12 and younger have you kissed on the lips since you were 16?

24. How many girls 12 and younger have you touched on the breasts since you were 16?

25. How many girls 12 and younger have you touched on the naked breasts since you were 16?

26. With how many girls 12 and younger have you kissed or put your mouth on their breasts since you were 16 years of age?

27. Since the age of 16, how many girls 12 and younger have you touched between the legs with your hands?

28. Since the age of 16, how many girls 2 and younger have done this to you?

29. What is the total number of girls 12 and younger that you have had intercourse with from the age of 16 up to now?

30. How many girls 12 and younger have you had intercourse with once and no more since you were 16?

31. Since you were 16, what is the most often that you have had intercourse with the same girl 12 or younger?

32. How many *TIMES* have you kissed or put your mouth between the legs of a girl who was 12 and younger since the age of 16?

33. With how many different girls 12 and younger have you done this since you were 16?

34. How many *TIMES* have girls 12 and younger done this to you since the age of 16?

35. How many different girls 12 and younger have done this to you since you were 16?

36. How many times have you put your finger into the rear end (rectum) of a girl 12 and younger since the age of 16?

37. How many times have girls 12 and younger done this to you since you were 16?

38. How many times have you put your penis into the rear end (rectum) of a girl 12 and younger since the age of 16?

39. How many times have you touched the rear end of a girl 12 or younger with your mouth since the age of 16?

40. How many times have girls 12 and younger done this to you since you were 16?

41. What is the total number of times that you have touched girls 12 and younger in a sexual way since the age of 16?

42. How many girls 12 and younger have you rubbed against with your penis since the age of 16?

43. What is the most often that you have had sexual contact with the same girl 12 and younger, since you were 16?

SECTION C

The following items refer to sexual experiences with girls 13 to 15 years of age (those who are pubertal or in the process of physical maturity).

44. Have you had any form of sexual contact or sexual touching with girls 13–15 years of age since you were 21?

    Answer (a) no (b) yes on the answer sheet. If your answer is ''no'', or if you are not yet 21, skip to Section D on page 4. If your answer is ''yes'', continue with #45.

45. About how many girls 13 to 15 have you gone out with on dates since the age of 21?

46. How many girls 13 to 15 have you kissed on the lips since the age of 21?

47. How many girls 13 to 15 have you touched on the breasts since the age of 21?

48. How many girls 13 to 15 have you touched on the naked breasts since the age of 21?

49. With how many girls 13 to 15 have you kissed or put your mouth on their breasts since the age of 21?

50. Since the age of 21, how many girls 13 to 15 have you touched between the legs with your hands?

51. Since the age of 21, how many girls 13 to 15 have done this to you?

52. What is the total number of girls 13 to 15 that you have had intercourse with from the age of 21 up to now?

53. How many girls 13 to 15 have you had intercourse with once and no more since you were 21?

54. What is the most often that you have had intercourse with the *same* girl 13 to 15 since you were 21?

55. How many *TIMES* have you kissed or put your mouth between the legs of a girl 13 to 15 since the age of 21?

56. With how many different girls 13 to 15 have you done this since you were age 21?

57. How many *TIMES* have girls 13 to 15 done this to you since the age of 21?

58. How many different girls 13 to 15 have done this to you since you were 21?

59. How many times have you put your finger into the rear end (rectum) of a girl 13 to 15 since the age of 21?

60. How many times have girls 13 to 15 done this to you since you were 21?

61. How many times have you put your penis into the rear end (rectum) of a girl 13 to 15 since the age of 21?

62. How many times have you touched the rear end of a girl 13 to 15 with your mouth since the age of 21?

63. How many times have girls 13 to 15 done this to you since you were 21?

64. What is the total number of times that you have touched girls 13 to 15 years in a sexual way since the ae of 21?

65. Since the age of 21, how many girls 13 to 15 have you rubbed against with your penis?

66. What is the most often that you have had sexual contact with the same girl 13 to 15 years since you were 21?

SECTION D

The following items refer to male sexual partners age 16 and older.

67. Have you had any form of sexual contact or sexual touching with boys or men 16 years of age or older since you were 16?

Answer (a) no (b) yes on the answer sheet. If you answer is "no", skip to Section E on page 7. If your answer is "yes", continue with #68.

68. How many males 16 or older have you kissed on the lips since the age of 16?

69. Since the age of 16, how many boys or men 16 or older have handled your private parts?

70. Have you ever handled the private parts of a male 16 or older with your hands since the age of 16? How many boys or men?

71. Since you were 16, have you ever kissed or put your mouth on the private parts of a boy or man who was 16 or older? How many boys or men?

72. Has a male 16 or older ever done this to you since you were 16? How many boys or men?

73. Since you were 16, have you ever put your finger into the rear end (rectum) of a boy or man who was 16 or older? How many boys or men?

74. Has a male 16 or older ever done this to you since you were 16? How many boys or men?

75. Since you were 16, have you ever put your penis into the rear end (rectum) of a boy or man who was 16 or older? How many boys or men?

76. Has a male 16 or older ever done this to you since you were 16? How many boys or men?

77. With how many males 16 or older have you had sexual contact once and no more since you were 16?

78. Since you were 16, what is the most often that sexual contact has taken place between you and the same boy or man who was 16 or older?

79. How many males 16 and older have you had sexual contact with 5 times or more since you were 16?

SECTION E

The following items refer to male sexual partners 12 and younger (those who have not reached puberty that is, physical maturity)

80. Have you had any form of sexual contact or sexual touching with boys 12 or younger since you were 16 years of age?

    Answer (a) no (b) yes on the answer sheet. If your answer is "no", skip to Section F on page 6. If your answer is "yes", continue with #81.

81. How many boys 12 and younger have you kissed on the lips since the age of 16?

82. Since the age of 16, how many boys 12 and younger have handled your private parts?

83. Have you ever handled the private parts of a boy 12 or younger with your hands since the age of 16? How many boys?

84. Have you ever kissed or put your mouth on the private parts of a boy 12 or younger since you were 16? How many boys?

85. Has a boy 12 or younger ever done this to you since you were 16? How many boys?

86. Have you ever put your finger into the rear end (rectum) of a boy 12 or younger since the age of 16? How many boys?

87. Has a boy 12 or younger ever done this to you since you were 16? How many boys?

88. Have you ever put your penis into the rear end (rectum) of a boy 12 or younger since the age of 16? How many boys?

89. Has a boy 12 or younger ever done this to you? How many boys?

90. With how many boys 12 and younger have you had sexual contact once and no more since you were 16?

91. What is the most often that sexual contact has taken place between you and the same boy 12 or younger since you were 16?

92. How many boys 12 and younger have you had sexual contact with 5 times or more since you were 16?

SECTION F

The following items refer to male sexual partners 13–15, those undergoing puberty, that is, changing from child to a physically mature person.

93. Have you had any form of sexual contact or sexual touching with boys 13–15 years of age since you were 21?

    Answer (a) no (b) yes on the answer sheet. If your answer is ''no'', skip to Section G on page 7. If your answer is ''yes'', continue with # 94.

94. How many boys 13 to 15 have you kissed on the lips since the age of 21?

95. Since the age of 21, how many boys 13 to 15 have handled your private parts?

96. Have you ever handled the private parts of a boy 13 to 15 with your hands since you were 21? How many boys?

97. Have you ever kissed or put your mouth on the private parts of a boy 13 to 15 since you were 21? How many boys?

98. Has a boy 13 to 15 ever done this to you since you were 21? How many boys?

99. Have you ever put your finger into the rear end (rectum) of a boy 13 to 15 since the age of 21? How many boys?

100. Has a boy 13 to 15 ever done this to you since you were 21? How many boys?

101. Have you ever put your penis into the rear end (rectum) of a boy 13 to 15 since the age of 21? How many boys?

102. Has a boy 13 to 15 ever done this to you? How many boys?

103. With how many boys 13 to 15 have you had sexual contact once and no more since you were 21?

104. What is the most often that sexual contact has taken place between you and the same boy 13 to 15 since you were 21?

105. How many boys 13 to 15 have you had sexual contact with 5 times or more?

SECTION G

Answer all questions.

Have you ever worn articles of women's clothing or tried them on, since the age of 16?

106. Skirt or dress?   How many times?

107. Undergarments?   How many times?

108. Stockings?   How many times?

109. Shoes?   How many times?

110. Jewelry?   How many times?

111. Wig?   How many times?

Have you ever masturbated or had climax (some people call this "coming", orgasm or ejaculating semen) in other ways while wearing articles of women's clothing?

112. Skirt or dress?   How many times?

113. Undergarments?   How many times?

114. Stockings?   How many times?

115. Shoes?   How many times?

116. Jewelry?   How many times?

117. Wig?   How many times?

118. Since you were 16, have you ever secretly and intentionally tried to see a man and a woman having sexual relations by looking in windows or by other means (not counting movies and sex shows)? How many times?

119. If your answer to #118 is 1 or more times, did you masturbate or have a climax in other ways while watching a man and woman having sex relations? How many times?

120. Since you were 16, have you ever seen a man and a woman having sexual relations with the couple knowing you were watching? How many times?

121. If your answer to #120 is 1 or more times, did you masturbate or have a climax in other ways while watching a man and woman having sex relations? How many times?

122. Since you were 16, have you ever secretly and intentionally tried to see women undressing by looking in windows or by other means? (not counting movies and sex shows) How many times?

123. If your answer to #122 is 1 or more times, did you masturbate or have a climax in other ways while watching women undressing in windows, etc. How many times?

124. Have you ever telephoned a girl or woman *who did not know you* in order to have a sexual conversation or talk dirty to her? How many times?

125. If your answer to #124 is 1 or more times, did you masturbate or have a climax in other ways while talking on the telephone to the girl or woman who did not know you? How many times?

126. Since you were 16, have you ever intentionally rubbed up against girls or women *who did not know you* in a sexual way in a crowd? How many times?

127. If your answer to #126 is 1 or more times, did you masturbate or have a climax in other ways while rubbing up against the girls or women you did not know? How many times?

128. Since you were 16, have you ever intentionally touched girls or women *who did not know you* in a sexual way, in a crowd, with your hands? How many times?

129. If your answer to #128 is 1 or more times, did you masturbate or have a climax in other ways while touching the girls or women? How many times?

130. Since you were 16, have you ever touched girls or women *who did not know you* in a sexual way, against their will, in a lonely place? How many times?

131. If your answer to #130 is 1 or more times, did you masturbate or have a climax in other ways while touching the girls or women in lonely places? How many times?

132. Have you ever tried to have sexual intercourse with a female *who did not know you* against her will? How many times?

133. If your answer to #132 is 1 or more times, did you ejaculate during intercourse or have a climax in other ways at these times? How many times?

134. Have you ever been sexually aroused by physically hurting or humiliating or embarrassing someone? How many times?

135. If your answer to #134 is 1 or more times, did you have a climax in doing this? How many times?

136. Have you ever been sexually aroused by someone hurting you physically, humiliating you or embarrassing you? How many times?

137. Have you ever had a climax while being physically hurt, humiliated or embarrassed by someone? How many times?

138. Have you ever been sexually aroused by threatening or frightening someone? How many times?

139. Have you ever had a climax while threatening or frightening someone? How many times?

140. Have you ever been sexually aroused by someone threatening or frightening you? How many times?

141. Have you ever had a climax while someone threatened or frightened you? How many times?

142. Have you ever been sexually aroused by beating someone? How many times?

143. Have you ever had a climax while beating someone? How many times?

144. Have you ever been sexually aroused by someone beating you? How many times?

145. Have you ever had a climax while someone beat you? How many times?

146. Have you ever been sexually aroused by seeing someone unconscious or unable to move? How many times?

147. Have you ever masturbated or had a climax by other means by seeing someone unconscious or unable to move? How many times?

148. Have you ever had sexual contact with an animal?

149. Have you ever had sexual contact with a dead person? How many times?

150. Have you ever masturbated with your penis out of your pants, in some place such as a car, alleyway or park, thinking that nobody could see you? How many times?

151. Have you ever had sexual contact with your mother? How many times?

152. Have you ever had sexual contact with your daughter? How many times?

153. Have you ever had sexual contact with your father? How many times?

154. Have you ever had sexual contact with your son? How many times?

155. Have you ever taken part in group sex? How many times?

156. Have you ever had a climax during group sex? How many times?

157. Have you ever been sexually excited by the thought of fire? How many times?

158. Have you ever had a climax while thinking about fire? How many times?

Have you ever exposed your penis on purpose to a girl who did not know you, in a more or less public place such as a street, a park, or a field, an alleyway, a car, in a show, or through a window?

159. How many times altogether?

160. How many times to girls 12 or younger?

161. How many times to girls 13 to 15 years?

162. How many times to girls 16 to 20 years?

163. How many times to women 21 or older?

SECTION H

Answer the following questions only if your answer to #159 is 1 or more., Otherwise, skip to Section I on page 11.

164. How often have you had an erection (enlarged penis) when you exposed yourself in a more or less public place to a girl who did not know you?
    a. never   b. sometimes   c. often   d. almost always   e. always

165. How often have you masturbated while exposing yourself in this way?
    a. never   b. sometimes   c. often   d. almost always   e. always

166. How often has the indecent exposure happened suddenly?
    a. never   b. sometimes   c. often   d. almost always   e. always

167. Do you feel that you are in a fog mentally or that things are unreal when you expose yourself?
    a. never   b. sometimes   c. often   d. almost always   e. always

168. When you expose yourself to females publicly do you hope tht they will get enjoyment out of seeing your penis?
    a. never   b. sometimes   c. often   d. almost always   e. always

169. Do you hope that they will be impressed by the size of your penis?
    a. never   b. sometimes   c. often   d. almost always   e. always

170. Have you ever tried to have sexual relations with the peson that saw you?
    a. yes   b. no

171. Have you ever felt an urge to do this?
    a. yes   b. no

172. When is the last time you exposed your penis in public?
    a. 1 or 2 days ago   b. 3–7 days ago   c. 2 or 3 weeks ago   d. 1 or 2 months ago   e. 3–6 months ago   f. 7–12 months ago   g. 1–2 years ago   h. 2–3 years ago   i. 4–5 years ago   j. over 5 years ago.

173. If a girl or woman who saw you wanted to go some place to have sexual relations with you what would you do?
    a. run away   b. walk away   c. go with her.

174. Have you ever used vulgar language on the person who saw you? How many times?

SECTION I

171. Has a sex partner ever complained that they were not satisfied after having sex with you?
a. no   b. yes

176. How many partners complained?
a. none   b. a few   c. quiet a few   d. almost all   e. all

177. What is the most often a partner has complained?
a. never   b. sometimes   c. often   d. almost always   e. always

178. How often have you come (climaxed, ejaculated) before penetrating your female partner?
a. never   b. sometimes   c. often   d. almost always   e. always

179. How often have you come (climaxed, ejaculated) before your sex partner was satisfied?
a. never   b. sometimes   c. often   d. almost always   e. always

180. How often have you been unable to come (climax, ejaculate) after penetrating your sex partner?
a. never   b. sometimes   c. often   d. almost always   e. always

181. How often have you been unable to get an erection with a sex partner?
a. never   b. sometimes   c. often   d. almost always   e. always

182. Are you *unable* to become sexually aroused by *any* means (masturbation, male or female sex partner, etc.)?
a. no   b. yes

183. In the past six months, have you had erections under *any* circumstances (including the time when you wake up in the morning)?
a. never   b. sometimes   c. often   d. almost always   e. always

184. Do you lose your erection during sex with a partner?
a. never   b. sometimes   c. often   d. almost always   e. always

185. In the past 6 months have you been unable to come (climax, ejaculate) by any means?
a. no   b. yes

186. Have you lost all desire for sex in the past month?
a. no   b. yes

Appendix C
Supplementary SHQ Scales

Ron Langevin,
Lorraine Handy,
Daniel Paitich,
Anne E. Russon
Clarke Institute of Psychiatry, Toronto

SECTION J

The following section concerns the fantasies or things you imagine when you *think sexually* and/or when you *masturbate*.

What type of person do you think of during your fantasies? Check as many as appropriate.

1. Boys 12 or younger.	a. no b. yes
2. Boys 13–15.	a. no b. yes
3. Boys or men 16–20 (excluding yourself).	a. no b. yes
4. Men 21 or older (excluding yourself).	a. no b. yes
5. Only yourself.	a. no b. yes
6. Girls 12 or younger.	a. no b. yes
7. Girls 13–15.	a. no b. yes
8. Girls or women 16–20.	a. no b. yes
9. Women 21 or older.	a. no b. yes

SECTION K

Which of the following kinds of sexual contact or touching have you *desired* since you were 16, even though you may *not* have had any such contact?

10. Boys 12 or younger.
    a. no desire   b. some desire   c. moderate desire   d. strong desire
    e. very strong desire

11. Boys 13–15.
    a. no desire   b. some desire   c. moderate desire   d. strong desire
    e. very strong desire

12. Boys or men 16–20 (excluding yourself).
    a. no desire   b. some desire   c. moderate desire   d. strong desire
    e. very strong desire

13. Men 21 or older (excluding yourself).
    a. no desire   b. some desire   c. moderate desire   d. strong desire
    e. very strong desire

14. Only yourself.
    a. no desire   b. some desire   c. moderate desire   d. strong desire
    e. very strong desire

15. Girls 12 or younger.
    a. no desire   b. some desire   c. moderate desire   d. strong desire
    e. very strong desire

16. Girls 13–15.
    a. no desire   b. some desire   c. moderate desire   d. strong desire
    e. very strong desire

17. Girls or women 16–20.
    a. no desire   b. some desire   c. moderate desire   d. strong desire
    e. very strong desire

18. Women 21 or older.
    a. no desire   b. some desire   c. moderate desire   d. strong desire
    e. very strong desire

SECTION L

If you had the following kinds of sexual contact or touching, which ones would you find *disgusting* even though you may *not* have had such contact.

19. Boys 12 or younger.
    a. no disgust   b. some disgust   c. moderate disgust   d. strong disgust
    e. very strong disgust

20. Boys 13–15.
    a. no disgust   b. some disgust   c. moderate disgust   d. strong disgust
    e. very strong disgust

21. Boys or men 16–20 (excluding yourself).
    a. no disgust   b. some disgust   c. moderate disgust   d. strong disgust
    e. very strong disgust

22. Men 21 or older (excluding yourself).
   a. no disgust   b. some disgust   c. moderate disgust   d. strong disgust
   e. very strong disgust

23. Only yourself.
   a. no disgust   b. some disgust   c. moderate disgust   d. strong disgust
   e. very strong disgust

24. Girls 12 or younger.
   a. no disgust   b. some disgust   c. moderate disgust   d. strong disgust
   e. very strong disgust

25. Girls 13–15.
   a. no disgust   b. some disgust   c. moderate disgust   d. strong disgust
   e. very strong disgust

26. Girls or women 16–20.
   a. no disgust   b. some disgust   c. moderate disgust   d. strong disgust
   e. very strong disgust

27. Women 21 or older.
   a. no disgust   b. some disgust   c. moderate disgust   d. strong disgust
   e. very strong disgust

SECTION M

How often do you imagine that the following things are going on in your sexual fantasies? Answer only if you ever have *any* sexual fantasies of men or boys.

28. Kissing a male partner on the lips.
   a. never   b. sometimes   c. often   d. almost always   e. always

29. Touching another's penis.
   a. never   b. sometimes   c. often   d. almost always   e. always

30. Male partner touching your penis.
   a. never   b. sometimes   c. often   d. almost always   e. always

31. Putting your mouth on another's penis.
   a. never   b. sometimes   c. often   d. almost always   e. always

32. A male partner putting his mouth on your penis.
   a. never   b. sometimes   c. often   d. almost always   e. always

33. Placing your penis in male partner's rear end (anal intercourse).
   a. never   b. sometimes   c. often   d. almost always   e. always

34. Exposing to a boy or man from a distance (no physical contact).
   a. never   b. sometimes   c. often   d. almost always   e. always

35. Being watched by a boy or man.
    a. never   b. sometimes   c. often   d. almost always   e. always

36. Penis being admired by a boy or man.
    a. never   b. sometimes   c. often   d. almost always   e. always

37. Forcing a boy or man to have sexual contact.
    a. never   b. sometimes   c. often   d. almost always   e. always

38. Beating a male partner.
    a. never   b. sometimes   c. often   d. almost always   e. always

39. A male partner beating you.
    a. never   b. sometimes   c. often   d. almost always   e. always

40. Dressing as a woman and a male partner having intercourse with you.
    a. never   b. sometimes   c. often   d. almost always   e. always

41. Saying obscene things to a boy or man.
    a. never   b. sometimes   c. often   d. almost always   e. always

42. Touching a boy or man *who does not know you* in a crowd in a sexual way.
    a. never   b. sometimes   c. often   d. almost always   e. always

43. Sexually touching a boy or man *who does not know you* in a lonely place.
    a. never   b. sometimes   c. often   d. almost always   e. always

44. Threatening or frightening a boy or man.
    a. never   b. sometimes   c. often   d. almost always   e. always

45. A boy or man threatening or frightening you.
    a. never   b. sometimes   c. often   d. almost always   e. always

46. Humiliating or embarrassing a boy or man.
    a. never   b. sometimes   c. often   d. almost always   e. always

47. A boy or man humiliating or embarrassing you.
    a. never   b. sometimes   c. often   d. almost always   e. always

48. Seeing a boy or man unconscious or unable to move.
    a. never   b. sometimes   c. often   d. almost always   e. always

49. Being in pain with a man or boy.
    a. never   b. sometimes   c. often   d. almost always   e. always

50. Seeing a boy or man in pain.
    a. never   b. sometimes   c. often   d. almost always   e. always

SECTION N

How often do you imagine that the following things are happening in your sexual fantasies? Answer only if you ever have *any* sexual fantasies of women or girls.

51. Kissing a female partner on the lips.
    a. never   b. sometimes   c. often   d. almost always   e. always

52. Female partner touching your penis.
    a. never   b. sometimes   c. often   d. almost always   e. always

53. Touching her vagina (between the legs).
    a. never   b. sometimes   c. often   d. almost always   e. always

54. Touching her breasts.
    a. never   b. sometimes   c. often   d. almost always   e. always

55. Vaginal intercourse.
    a. never   b. sometimes   c. often   d. almost always   e. always

56. A girl or a woman putting her mouth on your penis.
    a. never   b. sometimes   c. often   d. almost always   e. always

57. Placing your penis in female partner's rear end (anal intercourse).
    a. never   b. sometimes   c. often   d. almost always   e. always

58. Cunnilingus (putting your mouth on female partner's vagina).
    a. never   b. sometimes   c. often   d. almost always   e. always

59. Exposing to a girl or woman from a distance (no physical contact).
    a. never   b. sometimes   c. often   d. almost always   e. always

60. Being watched by a girl or woman.
    a. never   b. sometimes   c. often   d. almost always   e. always

61. Penis being admired by a girl or woman.
    a. never   b. sometimes   c. often   d. almost always   e. always

62. Forcing a girl or woman to have intercourse.
    a. never   b. sometimes   c. often   d. almost always   e. always

63. Beating a female partner.
    a. never   b. sometimes   c. often   d. almost always   e. always

64. A female partner beating you.
    a. never   b. sometimes   c. often   d. almost always   e. always

65. Imagining that you are a woman having intercourse with a man.
    a. never   b. sometimes   c. often   d. almost always   e. always

66. Secretly watching a woman undress.
    a. never   b. sometimes   c. often   d. almost always   e. always

67. Secretly watching a man and woman have intercourse.
    a. never   b. sometimes   c. often   d. almost always   e. always

68. Saying obscene things to a girl or woman.
    a. never   b. sometimes   c. often   d. almost always   e. always

69. Touching a girl or woman *who does not know you* in a crowd in a sexual way.
    a. never   b. sometimes   c. often   d. almost always   e. always

70. Sexually touching a girl or woman *who does not know you* in a lonely place.
    a. never   b. sometimes   c. often   d. almost always   e. always

71. Threatening or frightening a girl or woman.
    a. never   b. sometimes   c. often   d. almost always   e. always

72. A girl or woman threatening or frightening you.
    a. never   b. sometimes   c. often   d. almost always   e. always

73. Humiliating or embarrassing a girl or woman.
    a. never   b. sometimes   c. often   d. almost always   e. always

74. A girl or woman humiliating or embarrassing you.
    a. never   b. sometimes   c. often   d. almost always   e. always

75. Seeing a girl or woman unconscious or unable to move.
    a. never   b. sometimes   c. often   d. almost always   e. always

76. Being in pain with a girl or woman.
    a. never   b. sometimes   c. often   d. almost always   e. always

77. Seeing a girl or woman in pain.
    a. never   b. sometimes   c. often   d. almost always   e. always

SECTION O

If you have *not* had any desire for sexual contact with men or boys, skip to Section Q. If you have some interest in sexual contact with males, answer all the following questions:

Which of the following have you *desired* as a sexual outlet, even though you may *not* have had any such experience?

78. Kissing a male partner on the lips.
    a. no desire   b. some desire   c. moderate desire   d. strong desire
    e. very strong desire

79. Touching another's penis.
    a. no desire   b. some desire   c. moderate desire   d. strong desire
    e. very strong desire

80. Male partner touching your penis.
    a. no desire   b. some desire   c. moderate desire   d. strong desire
    e. very strong desire

81. Putting your mouth on another's penis.
    a. no desire   b. some desire   c. moderate desire   d. strong desire
    e. very strong desire

82. A male partner putting his mouth on your penis.
    a. no desire   b. some desire   c. moderate desire   d. strong desire
    e. very strong desire

83. Placing your penis in male partner's rear end (anal intercourse).
    a. no desire   b. some desire   c. moderate desire   d. strong desire
    e. very strong desire

84. Exposing to a boy or man from a distance (no physical contact).
    a. no desire   b. some desire   c. moderate desire   d. strong desire
    e. very strong desire

85. Being watched by a boy or man.
    a. no desire   b. some desire   c. moderate desire   d. strong desire
    e. very strong desire

86. Penis being admired by a boy or man.
    a. no desire   b. some desire   c. moderate desire   d. strong desire
    e. very strong desire

87. Forcing a boy or man to have sexual contact.
    a. no desire   b. some desire   c. moderate desire   d. strong desire
    e. very strong desire

88. Beating a male partner.
    a. no desire   b. some desire   c. moderate desire   d. strong desire
    e. very strong desire

89. A male partner beating you.
    a. no desire   b. some desire   c. moderate desire   d. strong desire
    e. very strong desire

90. Dressing as a woman and a male partner having intercourse with you.
    a. no desire   b. some desire   c. moderate desire   d. strong desire
    e. very strong desire

91. Saying obscene things to a boy or man.
    a. no desire   b. some desire   c. moderate desire   d. strong desire
    e. very strong desire

92. Touching a boy or man *who does not know you* in a crowd in a sexual way.
    a. no desire   b. some desire   c. moderate desire   d. strong desire
    e. very strong desire

93. Sexually touching a boy or man *who does not know you* in a lonely place.
    a. no desire   b. some desire   c. moderate desire   d. strong desire
    e. very strong desire

94. Threatening or frightening a boy or man.
    a. no desire   b. some desire   c. moderate desire   d. strong desire
    e. very strong desire

95. A boy or man threatening or frightening you.
    a. no desire   b. some desire   c. moderate desire   d. strong desire
    e. very strong desire

96. Humiliating or embarrassing a boy or man.
    a. no desire   b. some desire   c. moderate desire   d. strong desire
    e. very strong desire

97. A boy or man humiliating or embarrassing you.
    a. no desire   b. some desire   c. moderate desire   d. strong desire
    e. very strong desire

98. Seeing a boy or man unconscious or unable to move.
    a. no desire   b. some desire   c. moderate desire   d. strong desire
    e. very strong desire

99. Being in pain with a boy or man.
    a. no desire   b. some desire   c. moderate desire   d. strong desire
    e. very strong desire

100. Seeing a boy or man in pain.
    a. no desire   b. some desire   c. moderate desire   d. strong desire
    e. very strong desire

SECTION P

Which of the following would you find *disgusting* even though you may not have done it? Answer only if you have had sexual desire for men or boys.

101. Kissing a male partner on the lips.
    a. no disgust   b. some disgust   c. moderate disgust   d. strong disgust
    e. very strong disgust

102. Touching another's penis.
    a. no disgust   b. some disgust   c. moderate disgust   d. strong disgust
    e. very strong disgust

103. Male partner touching your penis.
    a. no disgust   b. some disgust   c. moderate disgust   d. strong disgust
    e. very strong disgust

104. Putting your mouth on another's penis.
    a. no disgust   b. some disgust   c. moderate disgust   d. strong disgust
    e. very strong disgust

105. A male partner putting his mouth on your penis.
    a. no disgust   b. some disgust   c. moderate disgust   d. strong disgust
    e. very strong disgust

APPENDIX C 351

106. Placing your penis in male partner's rear end (anal intercourse).
    a. no disgust   b. some disgust   c. moderate disgust   d. strong disgust
    e. very strong disgust

107. Exposing to a boy or man from a distance (no physical contact).
    a. no disgust   b. some disgust   c. moderate disgust   d. strong disgust
    e. very strong disgust

108. Being watched by a boy or man.
    a. no disgust   b. some disgust   c. moderate disgust   d. strong disgust
    e. very strong disgust

109. Penis being admired by a boy or man.
    a. no disgust   b. some disgust   c. moderate disgust   d. strong disgust
    e. very strong disgust

110. Forcing a boy or man to have sexual contact.
    a. no disgust   b. some disgust   c. moderate disgust   d. strong disgust
    e. very strong disgust

111. Beating a male partner.
    a. no disgust   b. some disgust   c. moderate disgust   d. strong disgust
    e. very strong disgust

112. A male partner beating you.
    a. no disgust   b. some disgust   c. moderate disgust   d. strong disgust
    e. very strong disgust

113. Dressing as a woman and a male partner having intercourse with you.
    a. no disgust   b. some disgust   c. moderate disgust   d. strong disgust
    e. very strong disgust

114. Saying obscene things to a boy or man.
    a. no disgust   b. some disgust   c. moderate disgust   d. strong disgust
    e. very strong disgust

115. Touching a boy or man *who does not know you* in a crowd in a sexual way.
    a. no disgust   b. some disgust   c. moderate disgust   d. strong disgust
    e. very strong disgust

116. Sexually touching a boy or man *who does not know you* in a lonely place.
    a. no disgust   b. some disgust   c. moderate disgust   d. strong disgust
    e. very strong disgust

117. Threatening or frightening a boy or man.
    a. no disgust   b. some disgust   c. moderate disgust   d. strong disgust
    e. very strong disgust

118. A boy or man threatening or frightening you.
    a. no disgust   b. some disgust   c. moderate disgust   d. strong disgust
    e. very strong disgust

119. Humiliating or embarrassing a boy or man.
  a. no disgust   b. some disgust   c. moderate disgust   d. strong disgust
  e. very strong disgust

120. A boy or man humiliating or embarrassing you.
  a. no disgust   b. some disgust   c. moderate disgust   d. strong disgust
  e. very strong disgust

121. Seeing a boy or man unconscious or unable to move.
  a. no disgust   b. some disgust   c. moderate disgust   d. strong disgust
  e. very strong disgust

122. Being in pain with a boy or man.
  a. no disgust   b. some disgust   c. moderate disgust   d. strong disgust
  e. very strong disgust

123. Seeing a boy or man in pain.
  a. no disgust   b. some disgust   c. moderate disgust   d. strong disgust
  e. very strong disgust

SECTION Q

If you have *not* had any sexual desire for women or girls, you are finished the questionnaire. Otherwise, answer all the following questions.

Which of the following have you desired as a sexual outlet, even though you may not have had any such experience?

124. Kissing a female partner on the lips.
  a. no desire   b. some desire   c. moderate desire   d. strong desire
  e. very strong desire

125. Female partner touching your penis.
  a. no desire   b. some desire   c. moderate desire   d. strong desire
  e. very strong desire

126. Touching her vagina (between the legs).
  a. no desire   b. some desire   c. moderate desire   d. strong desire
  e. very strong desire

127. Touching her breasts.
  a. no desire   b. some desire   c. moderate desire   d. strong desire
  e. very strong desire

128. Vaginal intercourse.
  a. no desire   b. some desire   c. moderate desire   d. strong desire
  e. very strong desire

129. A girl or a woman putting her mouth on your penis.
  a. no desire   b. some desire   c. moderate desire   d. strong desire
  e. very strong desire

130. Placing your penis in female partner's rear end (anal intercourse).
    a. no desire   b. some desire   c. moderate desire   d. strong desire
    e. very strong desire

131. Cunnilingus (putting your mouth on female partner's vagina.
    a. no desire   b. some desire   c. moderate desire   d. strong desire
    e. very strong desire

132. Exposing to a girl or woman from a distance (no physical contact).
    a. no desire   b. some desire   c. moderate desire   d. strong desire
    e. very strong desire

133. Being watched by a girl or woman.
    a. no desire   b. some desire   c. moderate desire   d. strong desire
    e. very strong desire

134. Penis being admired by a girl or woman.
    a. no desire   b. some desire   c. moderate desire   d. strong desire
    e. very strong desire

135. Forcing a girl or woman to have intercourse.
    a. no desire   b. some desire   c. moderate desire   d. strong desire
    e. very strong desire

136. Beating a female partner.
    a. no desire   b. some desire   c. moderate desire   d. strong desire
    e. very strong desire

137. A female partner beating you.
    a. no desire   b. some desire   c. moderate desire   d. strong desire
    e. very strong desire

138. Imagining that you are a woman having intercourse with a man.
    a. no desire   b. some desire   c. moderate desire   d. strong desire
    e. very strong desire

139. Secretly watching a woman undress.
    a. no desire   b. some desire   c. moderate desire   d. strong desire
    e. very strong desire

140. Secretly watching a man and woman have intercourse.
    a. no desire   b. some desire   c. moderate desire   d. strong desire
    e. very strong desire

141. Saying obscene things to a girl or woman.
    a. no desire   b. some desire   c. moderate desire   d. strong desire
    e. very strong desire

142. Touching a girl or woman *who does not know you* in a crowd in a sexual way.
    a. no desire   b. some desire   c. moderate desire   d. strong desire
    e. very strong desire

143. Sexually touching a girl or woman *who does not know you* in a lonely place.
     a. no desire   b. some desire   c. moderate desire   d. strong desire
     e. very strong desire

144. Threatening or frightening a girl or woman.
     a. no desire   b. some desire   c. moderate desire   d. strong desire
     e. very strong desire

145. A girl or woman threatening or frightening you.
     a. no desire   b. some desire   c. moderate desire   d. strong desire
     e. very strong desire

146. Humiliating or embarrassing a girl or woman.
     a. no desire   b. some desire   c. moderate desire   d. strong desire
     e. very strong desire

147. A girl or woman humiliating or embarrassing you.
     a. no desire   b. some desire   c. moderate desire   d. strong desire
     e. very strong desire

148. Seeing a girl or woman unconscious or unable to move.
     a. no desire   b. some desire   c. moderate desire   d. strong desire
     e. very strong desire

149. Being in pain with a girl or woman.
     a. no desire   b. some desire   c. moderate desire   d. strong desire
     e. very strong desire

150. Seeing a girl or woman in pain.
     a. no desire   b. some desire   c. moderate desire   d. strong desire
     e. very strong desire

SECTION R

Which of the following would you find *disgusting*, even though you may not have done it? Answer only if you have had sexual desire for women or girls.

151. Kissing a female partner on the lips.
     a. no disgust   b. some disgust   c. moderate disgust   d. strong disgust
     e. very strong disgust

152. Female partner touching your penis.
     a. no disgust   b. some disgust   c. moderate disgust   d. strong disgust
     e. very strong disgust

153. Touching her vagina (between the legs).
     a. no disgust   b. some disgust   c. moderate disgust   d. strong disgust
     e. very strong disgust

154. Touching her breasts.
    a. no disgust   b. some disgust   c. moderate disgust   d. strong disgust
    e. very strong disgust

155. Vaginal intercourse.
    a. no disgust   b. some disgust   c. moderate disgust   d. strong disgust
    e. very strong disgust

156. A girl or a woman putting her mouth on your penis.
    a. no disgust   b. some disgust   c. moderate disgust   d. strong disgust
    e. very strong disgust

157. Placing your penis in female partner's rear end (anal intercourse).
    a. no disgust   b. some disgust   c. moderate disgust   d. strong disgust
    e. very strong disgust

158. Cunnilingus (putting your mouth on female partner's vagina).
    a. no disgust   b. some disgust   c. moderate disgust   d. strong disgust
    e. very strong disgust

159. Exposing to a girl or woman from a distance (no physical contact).
    a. no disgust   b. some disgust   c. moderate disgust   d. strong disgust
    e. very strong disgust

160. Being watched by a girl or woman.
    a. no disgust   b. some disgust   c. moderate disgust   d. strong disgust
    e. very strong disgust

161. Penis being admired by a girl or woman.
    a. no disgust   b. some disgust   c. moderate disgust   d. strong disgust
    e. very strong disgust

162. Forcing a girl or woman to have intercourse.
    a. no disgust   b. some disgust   c. moderate disgust   d. strong disgust
    e. very strong disgust

163. Beating a female partner.
    a. no disgust   b. some disgust   c. moderate disgust   d. strong disgust
    e. very strong disgust

164. A female partner beating you.
    a. no disgust   b. some disgust   c. moderate disgust   d. strong disgust
    e. very strong disgust

165. Imagining that you are a woman having intercourse with a man.
    a. no disgust   b. some disgust   c. moderate disgust   d. strong disgust
    e. very strong disgust

166. Secretly watching a woman undress.
    a. no disgust   b. some disgust   c. moderate disgust   d. strong disgust
    e. very strong disgust

167. Secretly watching a man and woman have intercourse.
    a. no disgust   b. some disgust   c. moderate disgust   d. strong disgust
    e. very strong disgust

168. Saying obscene things to a girl or woman.
    a. no disgust   b. some disgust   c. moderate disgust   d. strong disgust
    e. very strong disgust

169. Touching a girl or woman *who does not know you* in a crowd in a sexual way.
    a. no disgust   b. some disgust   c. moderate disgust   d. strong disgust
    e. very strong disgust

170. Sexually touching a girl or woman *who does not know you* in a lonely place.
    a. no disgust   b. some disgust   c. moderate disgust   d. strong disgust
    e. very strong disgust

171. Threatening or frightening a girl or woman.
    a. no disgust   b. some disgust   c. moderate disgust   d. strong disgust
    e. very strong disgust

172. A girl or woman threatening or frightening you.
    a. no disgust   b. some disgust   c. moderate disgust   d. strong disgust
    e. very strong disgust

173. Humiliating or embarrassing a girl or woman.
    a. no disgust   b. some disgust   c. moderate disgust   d. strong disgust
    e. very strong disgust

174. A girl or woman humiliating or embarrassing you.
    a. no disgust   b. some disgust   c. moderate disgust   d. strong disgust
    e. very strong disgust

175. Seeing a girl or woman unconscious or unable to move.
    a. no disgust   b. some disgust   c. moderate disgust   d. strong disgust
    e. very strong disgust

176. Being in pain with a girl or woman.
    a. no disgust   b. some disgust   c. moderate disgust   d. strong disgust
    e. very strong disgust

177. Seeing a girl or woman in pain.
    a. no disgust   b. some disgust   c. moderate disgust   d. strong disgust
    e. very strong disgust

Appendix D
Supplement to Chapter 11

Jerald Bain,
Ron Langevin
University of Toronto

R. Michael Sanders
Malcolm Grove Hospital, Maryland

Table D.1 shows the intercorrelations of FGI and femininity scales. The FGI scores have high intercorrelations and show little bias from IQ, naive lying, or social desirability. They all show a weak positive relationship to MMPI F that may reflect carelessness but also confusion or emotional disturbance associated with increased femininity in men.

The Mf scale showed a moderate correlation with FGI scores (0.40–0.50 range) but less with BEM scores. The overlap of gender identity and gender role is not as large as one might expect.

Factor analysis in Table D.2 shows the FGI measures cluster with MMPI-Mf, separate from BEM, IQ and test taking, indicating FGI scores are useful measures related to femininity.

The BEM Scales tended to be factorially complex. The Bem SRI has attracted considerable interest and criticism in recent years (see Bem, 1981; Collins, Waters, & Waters, 1979; Spence & Helmrich 1981; Yonge, 1978; for example). The idea of androgyny or a balance of masculine and feminine traits is an interesting one and reflects the older Freudian notion that we are all inherently "bisexual" both in erotic orientation and gender (cf. Stoller, 1972). However, it mixes gender identity, sex roles, and gender roles, much as earlier theorists did. As shown in Table D.1 and Table D.2, androgyny tends to be an entity unto itself with some weak relation to the FGI scale and MMPI Mf. Moreover, other work suggests that its psychometric properties leave room for considerable improvement (see Sines & Russell, 1978; Waters, Waters, & Pincus, 1977, for example).

TABLE D.1

Intercorrelations of GI and Mf Measures, Test Taking Attitudes and IQ for the Total Sample

	1	2	3	4	5	6	7	8	9	10	11	12	13	14
1. FGI—Standard														
2. —Intensity	65													
3. —Duration	68	87												
4. GI—Revised	99	64	68											
5. —Intensity	85	57	64	86										
6. —Duration	87	57	62	88	92									
7. MMPI—Mf	51	44	41	51	39	41								
8. BEM—Femininity	24	12	10	24	23	19	26							
9. —Masculinity	-30	-20	-30	-33	-39	-38	-22	01						
10. —Androgyny	32	19	23	35	44	36	31	59	-65					
11. —Soc. Des.	11	-01	-04	08	05	04	-10	04	08	-12				
12. Full IQ	01	-01	-02	02	-08	-09	16	04	17	-13	11			
13. MMPI—Lie	07	01	-02	06	02	-01	-11	-03	11	-03	19	-06		
14. —F	30	22	32	32	30	33	23	-13	-19	01	-26	03	-13	
15. —K	-08	-19	-22	-10	-11	-14	-20	01	31	-12	32	04	48	43

Note: N = 100.

358

TABLE D.2
Varimax Rotated Factor Matrix of Gender Identity, Femininity and
Validity Measures

	Communality	Factor 1	Factor 2	Factor 3	Factor 4
FGI—Standard	.92	.94	.15	.07	−.05
—Intensity	.56	.74	.01	−.10	.05
—Duration	.65	.79	.00	−.15	.01
GI—Revised	.93	.94	.17	.05	−.06
—Intensity	.84	.88	.20	.05	−.18
—Duration	.83	.88	.14	.00	−.16
MMPI—Mf	.41	.47	.33	.22	.17
Bem—Femininity	.47	.09	.65	.03	.19
—Masculinity	.48	−.28	−.28	.19	.53
—Androgyny	.98	.21	.88	−.06	−.39
—Social Des.	.25	.08	.04	.44	.22
Full IQ	.28	.01	.08	.02	.52
MMPI/Lie	.26	.04	−.08	.49	−.10
MMPI/F	.32	.36	−.11	−.42	−.08
MMPI/K	.78	−.14	−.05	.87	.09
Eigenvalue		5.69	1.98	1.56	1.36
Percent Total Variance		38	13	10	9

REFERENCES

Bem, S. L. The BSRI and gender schema theory: A reply to Spence and Helmreich. *Psychological Review*, 1981, *88*, 369–371.

Collins, M., Waters, C. W., & Waters, L. K. Factor analysis of sex-typed items from the Bem sex-role inventory: A replication. *Psychological Reports*, 1979, *44*, 517–518.

Sines, J. O., & Russell, M. A. The BSRI, M, F, and androgyny scores are bipolar. *Journal of Clinical Psychology*, 1978, *34*, 53–56.

Spence, J. T., & Helmreich, R. L. Androgyny versus gender schema: A comment on Bem's gender schema theory. *Psychological Review*, 1981, *88*, 365–368.

Stoller, R. J. The "bedrock" of masculinity and femininity: Bisexuality. *Archives of General Psychiatry*, 1972, *26*, 207–212.

Waters, C. W., Waters, L. K., & Pincus, S. Factor analysis of masculine and feminine sex-typed items from the Bem sex-role inventory. *Psychological Reports*, 1977, *40*, 567–570.

Yonge, G. D. The Bem sex-role inventory: Use with caution if at all. *Psychological Reports*, 1978, *43*, 1245–1246.

Author Index

Subject Index